SHOOTING FROM THE HIP

Changing tunes in Jazz

John Fordham

KYLE CATHIE LIMITED

This compilation first published in 1996
by Kyle Cathie Limited
20 Vauxhall Bridge Road
London
SW1V 2SA

Cover design by Neil Sayer
Cover photograph of Sonny Rollins by Val Wilmer, taken at the Berlin
Jazz Festival in 1966
Design by Jayne Jenkinson

ISBN 1 85626 181 6

A Cataloguing in Publication record for this book is available from the
British Library

Typeset by SX Composing DTP

Printed in Great Britain by WBC Book Manufacturers Ltd

SHOOTING FROM THE HIP

John Fordham is a jazz critic, writer and broadcaster who has been writing about jazz for more than 20 years, initially for the London listings magazine, *Time Out*, and then for a variety of papers including *Melody Maker*, *Sounds*, *Zig-Zag*, *Wire* and *Q*. Since 1978 he has been a regular jazz correspondent for *The Guardian*, and, more recently, for *The Listener*. His biography of Ronnie Scott, *Let's Join Hands and Contact the Living*, was published in 1986 to enthusiastic reviews; it was published in paperback in 1995 under the title *Jazz Man* by Kyle Cathie Limited. An illustrated jazz history, *The Sound of Jazz*, was published in 1989 and an extensive illustrated survey *Jazz* (Dorling Kindersley) in 1993. In 1991 John Fordham wrote the bestselling jazz reference guide *Jazz on CD*, first published by Kyle Cathie Limited in 1991 and now in its third edition. John Fordham has acted as a jazz adviser for the Arts Council of Great Britain, and the Greater London Arts Council, and was also editor of *Time Out* from 1978 to 1981, and co-editor of *City Limits* from 1981 to 1986.

FOR MY MOTHER
WHO MADE IT UP AS SHE WENT ALONG

Contents

FOREWORD

This is a book about a long love affair, still going on after three decades of entrancement and occasional disenchantment, promises kept and re-written, revelations, mystifications, separations, reconciliations. The other party in this affair is jazz, a tempestuous and sometimes vexing music that is nevertheless only as volatile as any art in process rather than in museums (though its evolution from the one to the other is now accelerating) and which has irrevocably quickened the pulse of twentieth-century life. Since I first encountered it as a teenager, I have never been able to stay out of its spell for long. Perhaps, as the century approaches its end, we are that much closer to confirming the observation of the American composer Carla Bley: 'This music has stood the test of time, and it will turn out to be the great music of the age'.

This book isn't, I hope, masquerading as an adequate lens through which to track the passage of such a dazzling comet, still less predict its course, but perhaps it catches some scattered light. It is a collection of pieces about music and musicians driven by jazz, or at least under its influence, written for a variety of publications, beginning in 1970 and ending in the summer of 1995. The process began when Tony Elliott, proprietor of *Time Out* and a student friend, called me to ask if I could review jazz records for the magazine he had just launched on a wing and a prayer. Maybe I was the only person he knew who could spell Thelonious Monk, but his query came close enough to my reading *New Yorker* writer Whitney Balliett's *Sound of Surprise* collection to strike while vanity's iron was hot. The first gropings around this unfamiliar landscape were in an attempt to locate the newly-emerged British saxophonist John Surman's second album, and the piece opens this collection.

I hope that at least a little of the magic that jazz has worked on me will emerge in these pages – either in, or between, the lines. If it doesn't, then further explanation here is too late anyway. One thought always does return to mind, however, about the sound that hooked me all those years ago. It was beautifully put to me in 1989 by Charlie 'Bird' Parker's widow Chan, remarking that she didn't like tunes to wind up where it seemed as if they ought to wind up: 'I wanted something not to resolve to the tonic, you know, and that was Bird'. I don't think I'd had the words for what happened to me when I first heard jazz until then.

There are a few pragmatic points to sketch in, not as alibis, because these pieces have to stand on their own feet or not, but as circumstantial detail. For one, jazz journalism and analysis in Britain has usually been a part-time pursuit; national newspapers and magazines have rarely hired staff jazz writers as they might hire specialists in other arts, so freelancing has obliged the species to keep one ear on the music and the other on the proximity of the wolf to the door. Another is that daily newspaper reporting, in particular, lives with daily newspaper realities – notably pressures of space and topicality. Both these things influence judgements, though not invariably for the worse.

Three tight paragraphs would thus be the rule of thumb for coverage of most jazz performances. And daily arts reporting is *news*, not recollection in tranquillity, which isn't necessarily a bad thing and sometimes gives the process a distinct tingle. Many of these pieces (particularly during the 1980s) had to be written and called through immediately after the show was over, and sometimes while it was still going on. Alfresco work-stations abounded – a corner of a crowded bar, maybe a payphone with a fellow-caller pursuing what sounded like the critical stages of a vitupera-tive divorce in the next booth.

There would rarely be more than half-an-hour for writing a live review, and the result would then have to squeeze into whatever space was left on an otherwise finished arts page – a process that might see another paragraph or so disappear on the editor's desk. If the gig was too late for the last editions, it would have to be written and filed from wher-ever life took you next morning, maybe hoping an office colleague wouldn't barge in to propose an urgent meeting or crack a nervous breakdown over your head until you'd got to the last line. As Hunter S. Thompson has often observed, the logistics of the reporter's work fre-quently loom as large as the assignment. One late-night telephone copy-taker (a long-suffering breed, with every excuse for rebellion) once interrupted my fantasies about a particularly avant-garde performance to enquire: 'don't you hate this fucking shit?' The resulting debate down the wires went on way past the deadline. It was the kind of disruptive intervention that jazz musicians themselves would appreciate.

Although these pieces are propped between the convenient bookends of decades, and I have also added overviews which might provide a little perspective for newcomers to these events, this is no exhaustive account of the state of jazz in Britain since 1970. Some big events were missed, covered by others, or spiked. Work that has taken me away from jazz has been more pressing at some periods than others, and also leaves holes.

Regrets? I've had a few, and a lot of them are in cold print. But though I have sometimes used the original rather than the published version when it was available, shortened some pieces to keep the book to manageable lengths, and added a word or two of clarification where the passage of time and fashion made the original statement impenetrable, I have otherwise tried to resist the blandishments of hindsight and leave these thoughts as they were published.

Among the multitudes to whom I owe a variety of debts, I must risk the blushes of some by naming names: Ron Atkins, Nigel Fountain, Penny Valentine, Val Wilmer and Richard Williams for their insights and friendship; a succession of broadminded and supportive editors including Tim Radford, Patrick Ensor, Roger Alton, Ian Mayes, Claire Armitstead, John Mulholland and Alan Rusbridger at *The Guardian*, Richard Cook and Graham Lock in their days at *The Wire*, John Aizlewood at *Q*, Alan Lewis at *Sounds*, James Saynor at the late-lamented *Listener*, John Goudie at the BBC, and Tony Elliott at *Time Out* for opening the door in the first place when I would never have thought of knocking. Musicians too numerous to mention have helped shape my thoughts and enriched my life, among those of many others. I am profoundly grateful to all the publications involved, particularly *The Guardian*, for permission to reproduce these articles. And, of course, there are the people who had to witness the contortions and exultations of this process whilst trying to balance the probabilities of their own nervous breakdowns against mine: Kyle, Catherine and Emma at Kyle Cathie Ltd, my agent Andrew Nurnberg and lastly, and most of all, the family – love and thanks, as ever, to Ros, Fred and Leo.

John Fordham
London, January 1996

1970s

'In the myopic late '60s' wrote the New York *Village Voice*'s astute critic Gary Giddins, 'it was fashionable to say that jazz was dead; the observation is made whenever jazz is mutating.'

In music industry terms, jazz had been edged steadily out into the commercial cold for a decade or more, since the rise of rock and roll in the mid 1950s. As the 1970s opened, it was so marginalised that some record companies and promoters thought it unwise to mention the j-word even in marketing material that was quite clearly better described by its use than by any other term.

How had this come about? Jazz certainly wasn't dead as a form of creative music-making – gifted players, young and old, were still energetically making it. But it had lost its public, symbolic role. 'The Cool School', that restrained and careful but popular chamber-jazz which had seemed such a symbol of youthful intellectual independence fifteen years earlier, had been swept aside by rock's first wave, just as comprehensively as the mostly glib and cosy postwar pop mainstream of ex-big band singers and close-harmony groups had been. Rock represented a much more direct and confrontational form of rebelliousness than the most bohemian and impassive hipster-jazz could inspire, one that dealt directly in the currency of white youth with songs about pony-tails, school romance, cars, jeans, love-hating mom and dad.

Rock and jazz were of course close relatives in the same African-American family – Louis Jordan's popular 1940s 'jump music', a progenitor of rock, had been a mixture of jazz, blues and boogie-woogie. But from its simple, three-chord, do-it-yourself origins in the early years of the century, jazz had evolved into a highly sophisticated and multi-faceted art-form, and in that development lay its eventual disappearance from the charts. By the 1960s, jazz displayed at one end the dedicated primitives, the Dixieland revivalists in baggy jumpers who replicated the street-band sounds of early jazz, and who in the 1950s inspired a merger with country music that in Britain briefly became the influential Fifties 'skiffle boom'. At the other end were the beboppers – awesomely professional guardians of a complex, logical and sophisticated music that represented the modern jazz equivalent of the baroque era of classical music, an elite corps in shades and Italian suits.

Without being able to compete with the raw charisma of rock and roll for a new audience, however, some younger jazz musicians at the start of the 1960s were reacting to the more hermetic qualities of bop without simply trying to bolt on elements that might work at the box office. Miles Davis, a former trumpet partner of bop saxophonist Charlie Parker but an architect of 'cool' music as well, with a poignant, haunting sound and extraordinary subtlety of timing, worked with the emerging saxophone giant John Coltrane on the *Kind of Blue* session of 1960, a set of meditative, moody music and restrained passion that began to open up jazz form towards the creative use of cycles of scales (like Indian music) rather than European harmony. Coltrane continued these developments throughout the Sixties, evolving a hymnal, incantatory style (and an astonishing technique which enabled him to suggest several saxophones playing at once) that even gave him a rare jazz commercial hit with a young generation preoccupied with spirituality in the devotional improvisation 'A Love Supreme'.

In orchestral jazz, composer-arrangers George Russell and Charles Mingus were similarly splicing a looser approach to improvisation, abstract impressionism, blues, soul, and traditional big-band bravura. But perhaps the biggest single inspiration to the free-jazz musicians was the revolutionary Texan alto saxophonist Ornette Coleman. When he was on the threshold of celebrity (notoriety, to some) in the late 1950s, Coleman was quoted as saying: 'I think one day that music will be a lot freer. The creation of music is just as natural as the air we breathe.' Coleman had come up in the blues and honky-tonk joints, a rhythm-and-blues saxophonist reflecting jump music and the black churches. His cause was taken up by the prominent white classical composer/conductors Gunther Schuller and Leonard Bernstein, and though his adventurous music was branded anti-jazz (or even anti-music) by some, he gradually emerged as an artist whose music reflected many of the most fundamental energies of jazz – spontaneity, a uniquely personal sound, the direct appeal of the blues.

'Free-jazz' also had a symbolic significance, among African-American intellectuals particularly, that went beyond musical evolution alone. It arose alongside the most acute crisis in race relations in the United States (concurrently with the Vietnam War, in which black soldiers were seen by many as shouldering the brunt of the cost), and several works of free jazz bore titles associated with the civil rights struggle. But the music has a symbolic significance elsewhere in the world too.

Free jazz, and Ornette Coleman particularly, inspired a transformation of attitude and technique among many jazz musicians – and one that, among other things, had an incalculable effect on the capacity of jazz to cross frontiers. When jazz seemed as indissolubly American as chewing gum or Humphrey Bogart's accent, its disciples around the world found it hard to escape the anxiety that they could never really sound the same. But the loosening of its formal structures, a new emphasis on reflex, intuition, 'naturalness', seemed to offer a green light to performers in London, or East Berlin, or Oslo, or Archangel to merge the sounds of jazz with the sounds unique to their own homelands. Some of these changes led to a localised rootsiness, like the Plymouth saxophonist John Surman's evolving blend of Coltranesque improvisation and English folk-song, or Norwegian Jan Garbarek's gradual introduction of North European folk-traditions into a similar primary inspiration based on Coltrane. Some versions – in Europe particularly – grew closer to the contemporary classical notions of John Cage, Karlheinz Stockhausen, Iannis Xenakis and Luciano Berio. In America and in Europe, some adventurous musicians formed self-help collectives to present concerts, publicise their work, even record and distribute their own discs.

But for much of the Western world's youth from the 1960s through the 1970s, these changes might have been happening on another planet. Dixieland jazz, though it had enjoyed a brief boom at the beginning of the decade, had quickly come to seem a quaint hobby for buffs, and modern jazz, free music and bop were widely perceived as too private and cerebral to provide anthems for a generation on a consensual roll. The American Dave Brubeck group had had chart successes with catchy rhythmic variations on bop as the decade turned but, a few years later, the collective consciousness of a generation drawn together by an independence born of affluence, an expanding student population, more relaxed sexual codes, experiments with drugs, and a drive to express social and political issues (generation conflicts, injustice, equality, a voice for youth, the Vietnam

War) made popular music a very different phenomenon from the one that it had been only a few years previously.

This situation continued throughout the 1960s. Some jazz musicians tried to combat the rootsy appeal of rock and Motown soul by emphasising the more direct elements of the jazz traditions. 'Hard bop', a powerful modern style of the period, was a variation on bebop which frequently pushed its most preacherly aspects to the front – repetitive, incantatory melody lines, raw, bluesy soloing, themes close to soul music. But hard bop discs of the 1950s also reflected the feel of live jazz for the first time, in the documentation of long and complex solos, made possible by the invention of the microgroove 'long-playing' record.

Crossovers between this idiom and Latin dance or soul styles produced a few hits for jazz musicians in this otherwise inhospitable era – 'Watermelon Man' for pianist Herbie Hancock, 'The Sidewinder' for trumpeter Lee Morgan, for instance – but the exceptions were few. Cool jazz surfaced in the most successful Sixties crossover of all, the 'bossa-nova' boom that brought together the gossamer saxophone sound of Stan Getz and the samba-derived compositions of the Brazilian Antonio Carlos Jobim. The charismatic blues and soul musician Ray Charles, however, sustained a vibrant compromise between gospel, soul and old-fashioned big-band jazz throughout the period.

'Fusion' or 'crossover' music, forms of jazz that blended the most accessible versions of the idiom with the materials of rock, soul, rhythm-and-blues and funk, was about the only version of jazz to make money during the 1970s, a decade when box office and record shop takings for jazz sharply declined. Columbia executives suggested to Miles Davis that his brilliant band of the mid-Sixties (a virtuoso collaboration between the trumpeter and other gifted improvisers touching on both bop and free jazz that finally came to be properly appreciated by Wynton Marsalis's generation fully fifteen years later) was all well and good, but Jimi Hendrix was shifting a lot more product.

Technology was also offering new materials. The Moog synthesiser, invented in the late Fifties, was making it possible for a keyboard to imitate the sound of other instruments – or for a trumpet to sound like a guitar, an option Miles Davis adopted during the Seventies. Rhythmic concepts were being drawn from soul sources like Motown and Stax.

'Jazz' started to disappear in the music press, as a word with only old associations. But the sound of jazz was often still audible under the surface, if
you listened beneath the backbeat. Rhythm-and-blues orchestras such as
Blood Sweat and Tears employed jazz virtuosi like trumpeter Randy
Brecker and saxophonist Joe Henderson. A new generation of guitarists
(Pat Metheny, John Scofield, Larry Coryell) emerged, who were creatively
blending the intricacies of bebop linear construction with textures drawn
from the rock guitarists Jimi Hendrix and Eric Clapton. In Britain the connection between the rhythm-and-blues and modern jazz scene was so
close that Cream, one of the country's most successful 'progressive rock'
bands of the era, featured two jazz musicians (drummer Ginger Baker and
bassist Jack Bruce) alongside Clapton, and Newcastle guitarist John
McLaughlin was as often in blues bands as jazz groups before his departure for the States and the Miles Davis group in 1970.

Later in the decade, various former partners of Miles Davis spread a
variety of fusion messages into the wider world. His former saxophonist
Wayne Shorter and keyboardist Joe Zawinul formed an innovative instrumental fusion group called Weather Report, pianist Chick Corea explored
a lyrical Latin American dance music with 'Return To Forever', drummer
Tony Williams (a key musician in pulling funk's taut groove and jazz's
sexy playfulness together) played in the savage, rugged electric band
Lifetime with Jack Bruce and guitarist McLaughlin. McLaughlin himself
enjoyed some of the biggest successes of fusion's first wave with his
Mahavishnu Orchestra, a mix of rock, jazz and Indian music.

This was the background against which jazz continued to develop from
1970 onwards. In Britain, although there was still a small but steady audience (mostly in the pubs) for reruns of more traditional forms of jazz,
younger players were moving steadily towards either the free-improvised
music of Ornette Coleman and John Coltrane, (sometimes with European
academic music graftings and borrowings), or towards jazz-rock, with the
numerical and commercial emphasis massively in favour of the latter.
During the decade, attempts to focus on what seemed to remain as
immutable characteristics of jazz were made all the harder by the addition
to the turmoil of the deaths of its indisputed leaders.

Louis Armstrong, the intuitive trumpet genius on whose irrepressible
energies so much of the idiom's early development had rested, died in

New York in July 1971. Duke Ellington, having attained the status of one of the century's great composers in any idiom, and having evolved an extraordinary osmotic technique of semi-collective composition with his improvisers, followed in 1974. And, as if overwhelmed by the exposure that such departing legends bequeathed, Miles Davis unexpectedly quit the business in 1975, ostensibly on grounds of ill-health and creative burn-out. He left a deafening silence that lasted until 1981.

But there were hints that if jazz had by this time been obliged to travel under an assumed name to be listened to, its fundamental qualities of freshness, feline rhythmic fluidity, openness to the unexpected, and fre-quently a quirky lyricism derived from the musicians' fondness for turning familiar songs on their heads, would still get noticed. Another ex-Miles Davis pianist, Keith Jarrett, became one of the best-known jazz musicians in the world during the 1970s – and not for electric music, but for a solo style on a conventional piano that joined Chopinesque romantic delicacy, country-rock intonation and driving grooves. Jarrett's 1974 *Köln Concert* record became the best-selling solo piano record of any idiom, of all time, and its profits set up the influential German independent record label ECM, which has steadily documented the American and European avant-garde from that day to this. Guitarist Pat Metheny also joined bop concepts, country-rock, pop-song structures with his successful groups during the decade.

Some jazz musicians approached the 1970s as a period in which they would have to lead double lives, or even triple lives. The fine pianist Herbie Hancock, who had proved his instinct for the mechanics of pop hits a decade before with 'Watermelon Man', pursued a brilliant career as an acoustic piano improviser, had a massive funk hit with 'I Thought It Was You' in the late Seventies, yet began the decade with a subtle and delicate electro-acoustic group called Mwandishi which influenced the sounds of many small bands years later. The guitarist George Benson, whose main-stream soul-pop career was made with his 1976 hit album *Breezin'*, restricted his jazz life to unleashing his spectacular improvising skills on unscheduled drop-ins at small New York jazz clubs.

And, in 1975, an event largely unheralded in Europe at the time helped trigger what came to be known as the 'jazz renaissance' of the 1980s and 1990s. The veteran saxophonist Dexter Gordon, who had taken up residence in Copenhagen as a refuge from a generally uninviting American jazz world, made a triumphant return to New York's Village Vanguard club with a repertoire of the kind of forcefully mesmerising hard bop that had apparently disappeared off the map for ever and a mixture of Gordon's engagingly louche charisma, shrewd PR, and a substantial slice of music lovers who had maybe heard one too many disco records did the rest. Gordon's return became a symbol of the next turn of the jazz wheel.

First Shots – John Surman
Time Out, April 1970

Considering that John Surman's collaborations with Mike Westbrook began nearly ten years ago, it's perhaps a little odd that it took the public so long to prick up its ears – though slow progress to recognition is nothing new in jazz. Now he takes *Melody Maker*'s awards for overall top baritone player, as well as displacing Tubby Hayes as top British musician. Whether or not you give any weight to these things, his influence is everywhere in British experimental jazz – but *How Many Clouds Can You See* is a showcase for his own talents.

Though the opening of 'Galata Bridge' is gentle enough, Surman rapidly elbows his way into the subdued doodling of his rhythm section with a series of broad, ponderous sweeps, before erupting into an increasingly furious combat with the baritone in which the instrument seems to be grudgingly but inevitably surrendering the uncharted territory of its upper register like a boxer being forced into a corner.

Surman forsakes his overkill technique for the beautiful and whimsical opening of 'Event' and for 'How Many Clouds Can You See' – combining baritone and soprano on the latter, a delicate, autumnal piece, the soprano imparting its characteristic sad, yearning tone. These are the rarer moments of the session, relief from the sensation of having just struggled the wrong way up an escalator in the rush hour.

Much of Surman's huge range on the baritone comes across, but glimpsed in snatches – like his booming, zigzagging conclusion to 'Event' with drummer Tony Oxley loosing off a tantalisingly brief fusillade of rimshots at the height of his progress. It is a precious episode. Surman being the unique and consistently surprising musician that he is, it is likely that such moments will become increasingly frequent.

Nucleus
Time Out, May 1970

Nucleus has been formed by trumpeter Ian Carr, late of the Rendell-Carr quintet, and pianist Karl Jenkins. Its music is crisp, sharp, integrated, and it has a perpetual quality of surprise. The band begins without preamble, they make no announcements, they play non-stop for an hour and then cease abruptly as if the fuses had blown. The only generally unambiguous sensation about their appearance on stage is their enthusiasm.

A powerful influence in the band is Chris Spedding the guitarist, crouching over the instrument and weaving slightly with the pace of the music like a spidery tree in a breeze. Predominantly rock-influenced, he makes the guitar bark clusters of chords like a nervy delivery of sharp commands as if hustling the others to order. His job is more gently complemented by Karl Jenkins on electric piano, producing a fragile, shimmering, bell-like sound. Jenkins, apart from being a prolific writer, occasionally solos on oboe, as he did with Graham Collier, and though he generally starts out tremulous and off-key, like a stranger forced into introducing himself when the party's already in full swing, the instrument slides into the hammering pace surprisingly well. The edge on its tone is more brittle than the soprano sax. Ian Carr's technique is unobtrusive and depends on understatement. All this unlikely collection of instruments combines to provide some telling moments, particularly in the brooding, malignant 'Torrid Zone', through which the repeated pattern of the guitar and bass throbs like an unformed threat.

The band's first LP, *Elastic Rock* is due for release shortly, and it's excellent. Most of the omnivorous tendencies of the guitar are dispelled by better balance, the horns have more room to move and the compositions, outwardly simple but compelling, come over with an impressive clarity. It is a fusion of elegant, stylish melody, driving rhythms and imaginative soloing.

'It's a lot more lively than I thought it was,' Carr remarks with growing enthusiasm as he listens. He needn't have been surprised. What the band captures at its best is really one of the elements that jazz started out with – the magnetism of a successful interplay between musicians that flares out occasionally like sparks off a stone. Carr insists, 'I wanted musicians that burned' – a personal viewpoint about the future of jazz which is widely shared; that for some years it has had the choice of trotting in the wake of Western art music, or of going back to the roots. Carr wants his music to be physical rather than cerebral.

The LP will be the best representation of what they have achieved so far, since their live performances still tend towards raggedness, partly through the continual shuffling of the line-up. In Wood Green several weeks ago their music was fiery and aggressive, though stand-in tenor player Art Themen (whose talent is as considerable as it is under-rated) seemed badgered by the series of crescendos that the growing link between Spedding and Jack Bruce encouraged from drummer John Marshall. Bruce was sitting in on bass for the evening and ended up dominating the second half of the gig. At the Marquee a few Fridays later it was all a bit more listless, though Tony Levin replaced John Marshall with remarkable dynamism.

Somebody complained bitterly that you couldn't call it jazz. You could call it fish and chips for all the difference it makes, but whether it's played on saxophones, electric guitars or E flat vacuum cleaners if it's unpredictable, varied, exciting and improvised then there's no reason why it shouldn't be called jazz. These, in one form or another, have been its qualities for half a century and jazz will only cease to be jazz when it loses them, and not merely because this jazz doesn't sound the same to somebody who stopped at King Oliver or Charlie Parker. Nucleus have something new and fresh. Listen to the record. Nobody on it wastes a second.

SOME ECHOES, SOME SHADOWS
Time Out, March 1971

A decade or so ago, Michael Gibbs abandoned a science degree in Rhodesia for a course in arrangement and composition at Boston's Berklee College of Music, so irresistibly pulled by the sounds of jazz in the late Fifties and posthumous exposure to Charlie Parker's music, as to completely alter the direction of his life. Then he made contact with the work of Gil Evans whose early collaborations with Miles Davis (*Miles Ahead, Sketches of Spain, Porgy and Bess*) led the critic Max Harrison to write: 'These scores represent the full expression of Evans' powers. In elaboration and richness of resources they surpass anything previously attempted in big band jazz and constitute the only wholly original departure in that field outside of Ellington's work.'

Choosing his words with care, as if he regards them as second-class members of the family of sounds, Michael Gibbs acknowledges the same thing. 'The most important figure for me was Gil Evans – a lot of his work with Miles Davis came out about that time. Herb Pomeroy, who was the principal teacher at Berklee, believed in Ellington above all, but I was less interested in his orchestration than the general looseness he seemed to achieve with the band.' Gibbs found flexibility through an open mind and Gary Burton, the vibraharpist, who has played his tunes throughout the Sixties, made him increasingly amenable to contemporary pop music through the persistent country-rock flavour of his playing. In 1968, after six years in this country, the BBC invited a concert from Gibbs, and the tunes he had written for Burton were the basis of it. Now after a handful of shows, an LP and a variety of freelance gigs as a trombonist, he plays the Queen Elizabeth Hall on 30 March and another record follows. The first record, simply entitled *Michael Gibbs*, ran the breadth of musical sensations, at least as far as jazz bands have taken them, and is still a reliable guide to what remain the early days of a growing musical force.

Like Gil Evans, whose presence is still strong in him, Mike Gibbs's music never fails to impart a grasp of mood and space. The soloists move through it like figures in a landscape, and on the first LP Ken Wheeler, Alan Skidmore, John Surman and Chris Pyne were the principal silhouettes against Gibbs's rich backgrounds.

It is a collection of precious moments. Tinkling percussion shocked by

sonorous trombone sounds introduce 'Nowhere' – then a strident dissonance ending with a fury of shrieking, whistling trumpets, launching John
Marshall into a restless, to and fro motion over the drums punctuated by
irritable snaps from the cymbals before the orchestra closes in with a chilling fusillade of brass. 'On the Third Day', one of the strongest of the tunes,
and a perfect vehicle for soloists, opens with a succession of cumulative
comments from the instruments, all strung over a lazy, almost diffident
rock beat.

Under Gibbs's direction, rock rhythms are invested with gentle swing.
Chris Pyne brings a selective and leisurely approach to his trombone passages, while the other instruments worry at him with repeated phrases
like admonitions. Surman's baritone, following him with a typically
brusque opening statement, voices every aspect of his firm, imperious
technique in a few choruses. Big band jazz, from whose instrumentation
and approach it is undeniably derived, has rarely thought such diversions
worthwhile, preferring a more declamatory, tub-thumping delivery.
Michael Gibbs has joined the succeeding generations of Ellington and
Evans in gently insisting on travelling his own road.

The principal trumpet soloist on this disc, and at the coming concert, is
Kenny Wheeler – a man who redefines the word 'jazz' every time he
unpacks the trumpet, not as a dead definition but as a unique kind of personal statement. For myself, Wheeler's ability to turn the basis of his solo
into a melody or a composition as compelling, or more so, than the one he
starts out with (notably on the second part of Mike's piece 'Some Echoes
. . . Some Shadows') just about encapsulates it. His style is indefinable,
with a classic, sculpted grace that seems far from the origins of jazz and the
mutations it has been through. But despite its slightly bloodless approach,
it is a quintessence of personality conveyed in sound. Emotion filters
through Wheeler's trumpet, half-smiles rather than euphoria. The band
shares something of this bridled quality, but the warmth is always there
just the same. Henry Lowther, another trumpeter of superb technique
without bravura, may take Wheeler's place sometimes, or support him.

Listening to a tape of the brooding, spacious 'Canticle', written for the
concert in Canterbury Cathedral last year, and featured on the coming LP,
it occurred to me that there was so much vibrant energy here already that
there sometimes seemed no need for a rhythm section at all. It's another
suggestion of the depth of Gibbs's resources.

'The more I think about it, the more I realise I don't really listen to jazz
all that much,' Gibbs says. 'If I want to listen to something, its more likely
to be Debussy or Messiaen or Crosby Stills and Nash or The Band. But jazz
is what I've come from, or come through, all my roots are in it.' He says
this cautiously, as if all his statements are fresh discoveries. Jazz still
means much to him, not as a convenient term for cordoning off a musical
area, but as a set of impressions as elusive as mannerisms, impressions
that lie in rhythms and silences, inflexions of tone and time. 'I thought I

knew what it was when I heard Charles Mingus at Ronnie's recently. But I couldn't define it now.' While his work is distinctive enough not to belong in the main stream of jazz writing, *Melody Maker's* jazz poll has given him top rank in the composers' section, and work outside the band already includes a projected LP with Cleo Laine.

We talked fitfully about styles and tastes . . , me hunting for labels to get my bearings. But Michael Gibbs seemed as infectiously contented with his tape of the French composer Messiaen as with the Gil Evans that preceded it and the Gary Burton that followed. After staring at the floor for so long that I expected it to fall apart and confess, he wound the matter up.

'You shouldn't be so concerned about the quality of an emotion as the fact that the emotion is there at all. Whatever feeling music evokes, the important thing is that it is being evoked. That applies to rock as much as anything else.'

And it applies to the Michael Gibbs Band and the beautiful and surprising sounds that grow out of it, as tinged with a gentle warmth, as coloured with alternations of openness and reticence as he is himself. Like the man said, it's a sound that glows. Go to the Queen Elizabeth Hall and watch it happen.

INFINITY

Time Out, June 1971

Jazz, that ecstatic, impulsive and occasionally quintessential fount of sounds, has a different refinement of pleasure for every one of its subtleties of form. One is surprise, which can spring from familiar or unfamiliar contexts. Another is the pleasure of the predictable format and the freshness that can still thrive within it. These three releases, part of a first batch for Polydor's new 'Black Lion' label under the direction of Alan Bates, contain between them most of the rewards of jazz music, as far as records can.

In a backwater of jazz taste Sun Ra is one of the only leaders of a large group to have unflinchingly encountered the demands of advancing instrumental techniques in terms of compositional and orchestral methods. Not all his adventures are encompassed by *Pictures of Infinity* (a 1968 recording of a New York concert), but it has a fine mixture. 'Saturn', outwardly a straight and rolling big band piece, begins with the horns conversing garrulously, and sounding as if the eventual theme is being tossed about for consideration. After they straighten it out, John Gilmore, a hard-toned, demanding tenorist (and a recently acknowledged influence on Coltrane) plays a powerful series of statements. Two gentler episodes, 'Song of the Sparer' and 'Spontaneous Simplicity', have some beautiful textures too, trombones crossed with flutes, harsh harmonies laced with the thread of Sun Ra's piano. A kind of lyricism is always there, even in the looser moments – like the swirling, imperious alto passage on 'Somewhere There'. There's an underlying innocence around that is quite uncanny.

Customers in the front row for a gig by Dexter Gordon ought to be issued with ear muffs – even on record his sound is enormous. So many tenorists in their prime now were weaned on Gordon (now 48) and Lester Young, and that dry, spare tone is as effective as ever. He takes most things here at a restrained lope, as if trying to hold the notes back – except for the Sonny Rollins blues 'Sonnymoon for Two' which defies repetition and the respiratory system. Dexter holds out for twenty-eight choruses himself and sounds as if he could double it.

Ben Webster's record on the other hand has a misty laziness about it and odd moments of the kind of diffident coasting that Webster always used to fall into even in younger days. But the notes still well up and glide away as if mesmerised and there are even bits of his engaging grumbling when he's not quite sure of what he wants to do next. The ballads, as usual, are cycles of lovely sound vanishing into puffs of air. Now that his Ronnie Scott appearances show Ben sits down to play and is more languid than ever, there'll be many who will start to wave him goodbye. But as long as he lives and plays he will always be a mobile lecture on the constants underpinning the furore of jazz, as a man who never lost a unique personality. His supremacy will never be threatened by fashion, any more than Sun Ra's will, given time. Jazz is a way of talking – it's only the changing languages that throw people.

MILES
Time Out, November 1971

Miles Davis was last seen here at a rock festival on the Isle of Wight. Davis's trumpet style, though processed by a succession of rebellions within himself, remains much as it was: inscrutable, restive, squeezed-off and cut short as if regretting rash assertions. Like Ornette Coleman, he began his apprenticeship in the era of bebop, but by twenty-two, exasperated by the technical fireworks going on around him, got together a band of his own in which the overall sound carried as much weight as the soloing, and which was boosted by the use of unfamiliar jazz instruments such as tubas and French horns.

Since those early 'Birth of the Cool' recordings for Capitol (with the Canadian composer/arranger Gil Evans), a barefoot entrance on pile carpet to what had gone before), Miles seems to have shuttled back and forth between small groups with powerful soloists and larger ensembles.

During the late Fifties, while he maintained a travelling band that included saxophonist John Coltrane and drummer Philly Joe Jones, there were ambitious orchestral collaborations with Evans for the second time around, which resulted in some highly evocative one-act dramas on *Porgy and Bess* and *Sketches of Spain*. Miles was the only soloist against some of the richest backdrops since Ellington. A little later, trying to nourish the freedom of group-improvising, Davis embarked on a recording session in March 1959 to produce a soft, hypnotic series of ruminations that was the classic *Kind of Blue*. Coltrane exhibited his early mournful tone, yet to embark on those odysseys through which he discovered sounds within the tenor that could chill your blood. *Kind of Blue* heralded a break with conventional chord patterns and a shift into an area that spread out the harmonic roots of a tune – a carrier of shadowy tensions, the record went into the history books.

Miles's subsequent associations with Herbie Hancock (piano), Wayne Shorter (saxes), Ron Carter (bass) and a schoolboy drummer called Tony Williams, began to stretch his trumpet playing harder than ever. The title track of a 1967 release, *Sorcerer* (CBS), without adopting Coleman's tireless, sweeping lyricism or Coltrane's shattering assaults, had a lighter, more collaborative sense of the enjoyment they shared.

Then in 1968, when jazz audiences were still uneasy after almost a decade of wayward harmonies and broken rhythms in free music, *Miles in the Sky* was released and bluntly presented a transformed Tony Williams, stonily ticking off a dragging rock-time with curt chordal assertions from Hancock in the background, now on Fender electric piano. Miles Davis, after twenty years, was half out of his shell, his trumpet approaching shrillness at times, cutting across the regularity of the beat, the urgency of his tone and the odd mispitching and bending of notes giving the band a vitality that its imitators, who emerged with indecent haste like pack-wolves, could never catch. By the time they got there he'd gone anyway, and back came *eminence grise* Miles Davis, controlling events from the shadows. He now had a new world of recording studio toys to play with. Phasing several simultaneous layers of sound over each other, Miles's favourite mood came back in the ethereal, hypnotic drift of 'In a Silent Way' and 'Bitches Brew' – and the sound was so firmly contemporary, shot through with the odd rocking bass riff, that it sold in quantities unusual even for albums with his name on the sleeve.

The musicians, now less free to move, changed several times within this period, Miles's current discipline appearing to shorten the already brief life of a band. Dave Holland, his British bassist, complained of claustrophobia and departed with pianist Chick Corea. Their own free-music band, Circle, flared briefly. Wayne Shorter, having switched to soprano sax, also left and worked intermittently with Joe Zawinul, Miroslav Vitous and other ex-Davis session players. Miles however, still commands the respect of those who leave him.

Some believe him to be following contemporary sounds rather than leading them for the first time in his life, but at least his return to the world of sound available only through recording is no surprise – he's been going back to it on and off for years. Recently, perhaps with one eye on his sales, he's regarded recording as a different order of event from performing on a stage. But with an unerring sense of timing and a wealth of experience, Miles Davis will go on getting it right.

ORNETTE
Time Out, November 1971

Innovators always seem to nourish themselves somehow, however hostile the environment. Ornette Coleman, now forty-one, acknowledged the difficulties early on. Session musicians he worked with in the Fifties thought he didn't understand chords and couldn't stay in tune. His early spells as a tenorist in blues bands were shortlived. Despite that it was the recommendation of musicians that got him his first recordings with Contemporary Records in Los Angeles in the spring of 1958 – and in the years that followed, as an alto player, then as a trumpeter and violinist, he sidestepped a jazz world obsessed with playing standards, and forced the concepts of improvisation into totally unfamiliar shapes.

Within a year at Contemporary, Ornette Coleman had made two albums, (*Something Else* and *Tomorrow Is the Question*) and caught, with both of them, the dilemmas of jazz at the time. Though Ornette swung like Charlie Parker, he had simplified things to the extent that those balanced, pebbly chordal runs of the previous era now came out as a slurred, rougher, more candid style, and the unnecessarily florid presence of a pianist gave a peculiarly anachronistic twist to the sessions. Coleman hadn't found his place yet. But already he was suggesting what were to be his most important qualities, since his style had been maturing a long time before he ever got near a recording studio. The mobility of his ideas – a leisurely passage suddenly interrupted by a swerve into a furious, dodging run, almost impenetrably intricate phrasing mixed with moments of an innocent simplicity, made him the most articulate and interesting horn player of his day, as Parker had been before him. 'He can express on his horn what he hears,' said Don Cherry. Less restricted by what was judged harmonically admissible, Ornette was discovering unheard-of sounds.

In a series of sessions for Atlantic between the autumn of 1959 and March 1961, Coleman got the group he really needed – trumpeter Donald Cherry, six years his junior and one of the few front-line partners who could live with him, Billy Higgins or Ed Blackwell on drums, and a series of bassists of whom one was capable of investing notes with what seemed an everlasting corona of resonances – Charlie Haden became a regular partner. A new Atlantic release, *The Art of the Improvisors* has reissued some of the unused cuts from that period and Ornette, relaxed and happy, sounds as he did on *This Is Our Music* and *The Shape of Jazz to Come* – volatile, unpredictable enough to keep his phrasing hypnotic from first to last, Cherry reflecting the same alternations of complexity and openness, and Ed Blackwell's drums as crisp as footsteps on frost.

After this time of intense activity, Ornette Coleman did not visit a studio for some years. There are two Blue Note albums of a concert in Stockholm during the 1965/6 European tour that captured much of the earlier fire. Charles Moffett on drums at least leaves Ornette to go his own way, David Izenzon (though his bass playing is a bit well-groomed for Coleman's blunt manners) is a delight. It is a fine set because his partners are continually trying to clear the music's path.

As does Haden again, the bassist for Coleman's return to the studio on *The Empty Foxhole* (Blue Note) in a trio with his son Denardo, just ten years old. Imports of Blue Note albums have been about the only means of hearing Coleman since the mid-Sixties (except for *Town Hall Concert* on Fontana and *Ornette at 12* on Impulse) and the two most recent, *New York Is Now* and *Love Call* put him in a studio with the old Coltrane rhythm team of Jimmy Garrison and Elvin Jones. The pair's familiarity with each other permits them to go their own way and it isn't always Ornette's.

But this Friday night's concert, probably with Haden, Blackwell and tenorist Dewey Redman, should prove he's lost little. Now slightly distanced from the turning tide of jazz, Ornette Coleman can play to a British audience that, in 1971, ought to be better equipped to receive him.

MONK

Time Out, November 1971

Thelonious Monk, Art Blakey and Dizzy Gillespie are three of the surviving men who helped stage a concerted guerrilla action on the state of jazz in the Forties. Monk, now fifty-four, is still unwittingly eccentric and obstinately introverted enough to make hippies look like choristers, but plays the piano with a quirky charm that resembles a perfectly comprehensible pidgin English. As a composer he's a neglected master, and 'Round Midnight' and 'Blue Monk' are two tunes that everybody knows, even if they think they don't. 'Monk has the most complete harmonic ear in jazz,' said Ornette Coleman once.

Blakey, the drummer, ties together some loose ends. Accompanying Monk on his best work in the Fifties and one of the few to understand him, he was also Wayne Shorter's last employer before Miles Davis. Gillespie, the man who somehow got the trumpet to talk like a racing commentator, and altoist Sonny Stitt (the most powerful living tribute to Charlie Parker), are also in the team, with trombonist Kai Winding, and bass player Al McKibbon. It is a group likely to enjoy itself as much as the audience will, and fittingly signs off a weekend of music that's sufficiently varied to be an improvement on the previous autumn shows that used to be called 'Jazz Expo'.

There are omissions, inevitably. Don Cherry, for instance, is now in Europe and beginning to explore directions that need an airing here. In many ways, the events of next week are likely to provoke more nostalgia than shock. But since we don't get much of either on the drifting music scene that the media seem sincerely to believe is alive and well, November's semi-spectacular is an indispensible weekend on the town.

INTERVIEWS OF OUR TIME

Time Out, December 1971

'Lenny Bruce was a Jewish comedian who worked the New York café circuit in the pre-folk club era – a tragic hero as it turned out. His vision seemed manic but was at root totally sane . . .'

Well, the sleevenote adds weight to the tribute. Lenny Bruce is far funnier than this collection (*Interviews of Our Time*, United Artists) makes him out, a reissue of bits and pieces from 1958. But if the jokes are blunt, the presence that gave his act a peculiar intimacy remains there even on record. His voices are instinctively perfect, irony deftly tripping languid footsteps trying hard to tread fears into the necks of people like him. His life was a flashpoint for the bewilderment with which generations face each other.

A junked-up jazzman and a cheerfully unhip Jewish bandleader, both having their own delusions of the self-evident:

'. . . that's the most important thing, man, to swing with your axe, you know like? So, like, really, if you wanna do the thing, baby, like, you dig?'

'Wad de hellya talkin about?'

'. . . I don' wanna bug you, man, but can I get a little bread out front?'

'Ya hungry? Ya vanta sandvich?'

'. . . I don' wanna cop out on myself there, but I got a monkey on my back . . .'

'Oh, that's all right, ve like animals around here . . .'

Turn the other side into monsters and you can get your side out on the streets. Leave the enemy as just victims of circumstance and immediately there's a sharp realism that quickly finds its way out as laughter. Lenny Bruce saw but didn't choose. Both sides looked ridiculous to him. He sensed that there was enough of the just and the unjust in all of us to make the Final Discovery of Truth an achievement that no honest guy could announce with a straight face.

MAHAVISHNU
Time Out, January 1972

A record has appeared from America called *The Inner Mounting Flame*. It is only the third session as leader for the British guitarist John McLaughlin (who can list as his previous employers Georgie Fame, Graham Bond, Tony Williams and Miles Davis), but the initial sales in the States suggest that at least 20,000 people knew enough about him to buy the album within the first three weeks of its release. Leading a five-piece band alongside two Americans, an Irishman and a Czech. McLaughlin has called it the Mahavishnu Orchestra.

McLaughlin, who has been through the most unspiritual decade of jamming his nights away in smoke-fogged cellars, is now a man of God. If you're fighting a temptation to be cynical in remembering the number of musicians who've recently gone the same way, this is as he is now.

'Maybe it was in my stars. Capricorn is supposed to be ambitious, I'd always wanted to be good. Not knowing why or how, just that it was something I wanted to accomplish. And you work and you go through all kinds of frustrations because your consciousness is so limited and puny and your body's even impure as well. And out of all that, you try to be an artist – it's a complete joke. But you have to have faith. Faith in yourself first, then you can start to have faith in God. It was a process of evolution for me. I got interested in the mystic and the occult, then I went to America and ultimately I became a disciple, which was a great blessing. The greatest blessing of my entire life. Of my entire *lives*.'

At the time John McLaughlin was first picking up the instrument, nearly twenty years ago, the guitar was in a transitional position. Charlie Christian, the first great improvising master of the electric guitar, was dead in his middle twenties by 1942. Barney Kessel, Jimmy Raney, Tal Farlow all followed him but rarely broke down the tonal weaknesses of amplification then. Jim Hall, in the cautious whisper of many white jazz players, found a style of his own – sparse and muffled, as if someone was squeezing a sponge over the strings after every note. And Wes Montgomery arrived too, perhaps the most relaxed and spontaneous improviser since Christian – but a man who eventually surrendered to the sort of music to get himself into record collections alongside Andy

Williams. It seemed as if only through rock or through schmaltz could inventive guitar players ever reach more than a minority audience.

McLaughlin must have heard all this, but listened harder to blues players, and then to Django Reinhardt. Coming to London from the jazz clubs of Northumberland, already seven years a guitarist, he joined organists Georgie Fame, and then Graham Bond – who was playing host to Jack Bruce, Ginger Baker and saxophonist Dick Heckstall-Smith. Though his musical surroundings were increasingly infused with rhythm and blues, other sounds attracted McLaughlin – the later work of tenorist John Coltrane for one, combining impossible technical command with an increasingly disciplined grasp of discovering and sustaining emotional peaks. McLaughlin, who was now well accustomed to hard melody lines going down an uncluttered road from inception to climax, heard affinities – he was looking for an accessible form that was at the time demanding and exciting to play. In 1969, not long before he finally left for the States, he directed his first solo album (*Extrapolation* – Polydor) with John Surman on reeds, bassist Brian Odges and drummer Tony Oxley.

'That was quite an experience for me, never having made a record of my own before. You learn a lot – about what you really want. It was the way I felt at that period. I didn't really cut loose at all, but it didn't seem to matter. I was so concerned with the music, making sure that was right and getting that suite movement from one piece to another, I got so involved with the form.'

That form was fairly conventional, but loose enough to act as an encouragement to the players who responded by turning it into a brilliant set. In some ways it exhibited a more exciting solo approach than McLaughlin chooses now, tension through implication rather than saturation. Not long out of rock and roll bands, there was much bustling chord playing, acting as a superb accompaniment to Surman's volcanic horn style and gravelly tone. After that, things changed rapidly, and drummer Tony Williams, (now 'good enough to leave Miles') asked him to go to the States as part of a new band, Lifetime. It lasted two years, but both John McLaughlin and Jack Bruce still have memories of almost frightening penetration through the music they made with Williams and Larry Young. Of Williams, whose approach to playing and being is ostensibly so different from his own, McLaughlin remains circumspect:

'He just stimulated detachment. You can't tell people how to be. You have to accept them first and then be what you are. So we were both coming from different places, you could say, but at the same time we met and produced music together. And sometimes it was incredible music. Sometimes'.

Now an American citizen and having moved from practising yoga to becoming a spiritual disciple of Sri Chinmoy, who he met in Connecticut, McLaughlin made two albums for the Douglas label, both of which eventually turned up here as imports. The first, *Devotion*, was a furious shout-up in the company of rock drummer Buddy Miles. The second was a totally unforeseen event and clearly a very personal declaration of new resolves by John McLaughlin. *My Goal's Beyond* had a side of minor key ruminations for acoustic guitar, violin, sitar, tamboura, soprano sax, bass and assorted percussion, and a side for acoustic guitar alone, playing jazz standards and originals. Of all the things it might have been, it wasn't put together with an eye on the sales charts.

'It was just something I'd wanted to do. It's like a painter wants to paint a picture, but he doesn't know *why* really. I knew beforehand it would work – the soprano and the violin together. I had a little static from the record company, which probably wanted more of Buddy Miles. But we got round that.

'The goal is perfection. Which is your true nature, which is my true nature. Becoming what we really are. It's only in ignorance that we think we're separate from each other. "I", "me", "mine", "ego". All misery comes from ego. Music is a manifestation of the spirit. Clothing the spirit with sound.'

McLaughlin's search for an improvising band that was rhythmically powerful, expert and musically resourceful, finally found its feet as the Mahavishnu Orchestra and a first album for Columbia – *The Inner Mounting Flame*. The violinist remained (Jerry Goodman from Flock) and a superb drummer, Billy Cobham. Rick Laird joined on electric bass and a pianist, Jan Hammer, introduced by courtesy of the Czech bassist and Hammer's compatriot, Miroslav Vitous.

'We all feel it's complete now. Because of the feeling that exists between each member. Sensitivity, empathy, lack of ego, I must say, lack of ego in that band. If I get the instruments that I love and the people are right, the the sound's taken care of. The sound of this band was inevitable.'

But despite all the energy, this isn't really a blowing session. The ensemble playing relies heavily on simple patterns turning up in unexpected places, each instrument with a theme of its own, and all butted up against each other. McLaughlin maintains solos at full stretch.

'Free jazz is, frankly, a dead end street to me. No way out. Because it doesn't have the delight of rhythm. Rhythm is delight. It's the universal dance. There are very few European new jazz musicians who play rhythm. Han Bennink is one of them. He's one of the most incredible drummers in Europe, and in the world too. And I hope he reads that because I love him. He's incredible, as a man and a musician.

'So America has been encouraging in every way for me. More dynamic, more opportunity. Europeans have been obsessed with what has happened in the States, and now lack their own inner direction. In improvisation you can manifest utter and complete liberation. To be free and to be master of yourself. I just want to let the music be rather than get in its way. And I find the Eastern concept more conducive to that than the West. Spontaneous music belongs to the heart. Spontaneous expression, and Eastern music is just that. Love, joy, delight, happiness, sadness, yearning, longing, all these things that we all feel. In the Western world you might have a concert where you're going to play Beethoven's "Moonlight Sonata" on October 21st, 1973 and you do it whatever. But the Indian musician goes there, and he feels the presence of the audience first, and he feels his own condition too, and he doesn't know what he's going to do. He doesn't know what he's going to sing, what he's going to play. But from his intuition, which is developed and cultivated, he knows what's right for him and right for them, and he plays it. I'm nowhere near that, but I'm going to get deeper into classical Indian music, and I'm going to become a student at the Wesleyan University in Connecticut where they have several Indian masters teaching. And I'm not going to stop doing what I'm doing but at the same time I'm going to get more deeply involved in the Indian classical tradition which is entirely spiritual and devotional.'

McLaughlin's compositions and his choice of musicians have always been as important as his own playing, and never more so than on this album. 'Peace Two' from *My Goal's Beyond* was typical of that too – the instruments and the melody together turned it into something beyond its parts. If it suggested a clean sky after dawn it was the keening soprano sax and the violin singing together that induced that picture as directly as the notes themselves. McLaughlin writes song and plays songs, though he's never used a vocalist. Expanding that will probably occupy the rest of his life.

'The wonderful thing about music is that it embraces everybody inside of it. Musicians should realise the responsibility that they have. People love music, people cannot live without music, musicians will always be in demand. If a musician becomes more spiritual and his music takes on a deeper aspect, a deeper quality, then people are going to be affected in that way. Musicians don't realise the power that's in their hands, which is frittered away.'

SMALL WORLD
Time Out, February 1972

'Nobody wants this music,' said the American composer Carla Bley, without bitterness. Ronnie Scott takes the stand in his club most nights and berates empty tables. 'You should have been here last week. The bouncers were throwing them *in*.' Dick Letchford, one half of the paid administration of London's struggling Jazz Centre Society, leans on a crumbling window-ledge on the ground floor of a battered docklands warehouse and runs through names. 'Look at John Stevens, one of the best drummers around. Or Stan Tracey – years of work and study and dedication. Music for them is a way of expression. And if the money comes from it, that's an incidental bonus. Of course, it never does come.'

'I think rock and roll is jazz,' said Carla Bley. 'And jazz is classical music. And classical music has become rock and roll. They've all gone round one turn on the clock. I heard a tape of Jack Bruce's that was jazz, and the most beautiful jazz – it was directly traceable to the earliest jazz roots and yet it was totally rock and roll. I think that what we're doing is not jazz and hasn't been for a long time.'

'Call it non-profit music,' she ended up.

It's not that there's nobody left to listen. When the redoubtable promoter Harold Davison used to run a week's international festival in the autumn of every year, these Jazz Expo concerts drew audiences from all over the country and filled huge mausoleums like the Hammersmith Odeon. Last November, Ornette Coleman, Miles Davis and the Dizzy Gillespie group with Thelonious Monk played three consecutive nights in London and it happened again. Maybe the basic group of enthusiasts remains the same, but only the superstars can bring them all out of hiding at once. Meanwhile Britain's Jazz Centre Society has just four hundred members, who will occasionally receive its laboriously typed bulletins and mostly sit at home listening to Charlie Parker.

Much of this, though it appears to be a reaction to the fact that money in the music business is now firmly diverted elsewhere, is nevertheless not a new story. Its origins go back as far as the early Fifties when Ronnie Scott had a hand in the founding of the Club Eleven, the city's first home for modernists. London was emerging from the war, modern jazz had already burst into flames across the Atlantic and Ronnie Scott, a teenage saxophone star from the East End ('I spent most of my early years playing Jewish youth clubs') was about to make a trip to New York that would put an ambition in his head. 'The first thing we did was to take a cab to 52nd Street which was full of jazz clubs in those days. And the first one we went to was the Three Deuces, I think. There was a certain atmosphere and sound about it that left an impression on me. I suppose I thought it would be nice if a place like that could exist in London.'

It was October 1959 before Scott found his home, in Soho's Gerrard Street, and in competition with clubs like the Flamingo and Studio 51. His was the first jazz club in the country to be run by a practising musician and survive. The businessmen behind the others moved on when fashions changed. During the next six years, musicians of the calibre of Zoot Sims, Stan Getz, Dexter Gordon, Sonny Rollins, Wes Montgomery and Roland Kirk came and went through the club, alongside local players who grew in confidence with the challenge of working with the best in the business.

'The mystique and aura that surrounded American musicians was broken down after this,' recalled Ronnie Scott. 'People realised that when these musicians were in a club for two or three weeks, playing night after night, they would have their good nights and their bad nights, and that British guys could play with them and were impressive in their own right. And I think the standard of the local guys improved as a result of realising that these people were human after all.'

In December 1965 came the move to Frith Street, where the club is now. But the first Gerrard Street club stayed open briefly, until the lease ran out. Dick Letchford remembers 'the Old Place' as a birthplace. 'Hundreds of talented local musicians would turn up there and play for peanuts. And then suddenly it wasn't possible. We realised that something would have to replace it.' Scott acknowledges that the moment of his expansion meant a shift of policy.

'The Old Place was important, and we tried to keep it open as long as we could. But the club here could never remain a purist jazz club for a number of reasons. The overheads are enormous for a start. It's very important for our existence that the number of people coming through the door is always reasonable. Not having enormous capital behind us, if we have a bad month it's going to take another couple of months to get out of trouble. And of course, the novelty of seeing American players has worn off now. I might bring in someone who's a fantastic player like Hank Mobley or Johnny Griffin and be lucky to get out paying the rent at the end of the engagement. We've created a rod for our own backs in that way, I suppose.'

By now, Scott's club, apart from being internationally renowned, was unique in London as a jazz club that was also a plush, waitress-service night spot. 'I wanted a place that I could enjoy being in. If you spend seventy per cent of your life in a place, as I do, it's got to be halfway agreeable.' Having burned his boats, Scott now had to make ends meet; that meant that only international attractions would keep the place alive. British players, despite having developed the confidence they had long missed, were clearly going to have a harder time. The most adventurous ones on the avant-garde, unless deftly paired with a guest of comparable aims, like Ornette Coleman, would almost certainly put the frighteners on the average audience at Frith Street. But once a month now, the club is let to the experimental Musicians' Cooperative on a Sunday night and unsuspecting visitors, anticipating 'Sophisticated Lady', find themselves face to face with the daunting prospect of Tony Oxley scraping sheet metal with a cello bow or Evan Parker playing a keyless, timeless, breathless tenor solo for as long as the fancy takes him. 'You get some odd reactions,' I said. 'I can imagine,' mused Scott.

One London avant-garde player treated this setting for the monthly Co-op concerts as a joke. 'The Cooperative in *Ronnie Scott*'s Club? That's like staging a demo inside a police station.' Howard Riley, one of the country's leading contemporary pianists, thought the opposite. 'I'd never put Ronnie's down. They've had their battles and they've survived. We've just got to do the same.'

With changes in style, enthusiasts for this music have altered too. They no longer fit the beret-shades-and-beer stereotypes. Dick Letchford is young, very funny and very energetic, a part-time bass player and one-time rep for CBS, a builder's labourer and occasional car dealer. He resists the languid elitism of armchair jazz fans who never venture further than Dobell's record shop in the pursuit of their music. After the Jazz Centre's demise at Hampstead's Country Club, where the overheads were running them into the ground and the place was often empty, he and his wife Julia are now organising the conversion of part of a disused warehouse near Tower Bridge, which has been leased to them as a gift. This time the Jazz Centre isn't going to be just for performance alone, but a place that might serve for tuition, rehearsal and information about the music. First and foremost they want it to be a social centre that people might be glad to visit for its own sake.

'I dig the enthusiasm of the people who like this music, all the people who've come down here at weekends to get covered in shit and paint – people giving up their spare time to come down here and get dirty, get cold, stumble about in the dark, because they want to see this happen. Environment is what we're about now. Trying to get people to come down here so they can say, "I'm a jazz fan and I don't mind fucking admitting it."'

The closure of Gerrard Street sparked it off. With virtually no other clubs ready to risk presenting experimental players, it looked as if young musicians would have to stick to playing bebop or stay at home. The Jazz Centre Society was born out of a desperation to find new outlets. 'Everything we do has a policy behind it. Because we're an organised body with a constitution and stuff, we can approach the Arts Council and ask for bread for concerts – and the JCS puts on concerts that no one else will. Once we say to them that we know we're going to lose such and such bread on a concert and they accept that they'll provide the rest, then the music is suddenly no longer operating on a commercial level. There was a vicious circle that we had to break out of. I might have this idea in my head for something I'm going to play – I've got to put it over to someone, but I can't because I've never performed it before anywhere so the guy who's going to put me on is worried he'll lose money, he's heard I'm going to drive all these people out of his place. So I don't get a gig. Now we say, come in and do it. If the people listen, that's fine, and if they don't, they don't. But we'll try to safeguard the financial side of it. Some people even think we're the establishment already. After three and a half years! But we don't discriminate over what sort of music we present. If anyone thinks we do, then it's only because of the sort of misunderstanding that happens when you're finding your feet. But we are what we say we are. A non-profit making charity.'

Dick Letchford is not the only one wrestling with jazz arithmetic. Graham Goode is a final-year student at Kentish Town's Northern Polytechnic, actively involved in the running battle between the Poly's union and the administration. He tries to keep his club open for weekly concerts but finds that most of his audience comes from outside the student body. 'Students will complain about paying 30 pence to hear jazz. Tomorrow night there'll be a rock band on and they'll happily fork out a quid.' He leaves this year and the club will probably go with him. John Clare is in a similar situation, a postgraduate at Bedford College who spends most of his days doing social work with teenagers in Paddington. He has run Saturday nights at Bedford for four years with a union grant of £15.

'I think even the Chess Club gets more than us. It doesn't even pay for the year's phone calls,' Clare says. Some of the clubs, though presenting modern music, tailor it carefully to the audience they already have – like the Phoenix in Cavendish Square, Finchley's comfortable Torrington, or the Bull's Head in Barnes, seat of an assured and fluent brand of home-grown bebop.

Oxford Street's 100 Club has long been viewed as a fortress of tradition-alism, but on Mondays it is run by the Mike Westbrook band's manager John Jack. A man of Ronnie Scott's generation, the sort who only appears to come alive after dark, living above Collet's in Charing Cross Road in a tiny flat swamped with records and magazines, he always seems to sug-gest that his roots are deep in a period when people had no doubt what the word jazz meant.

'Rigid working conditions in this country are no help to any music. You've either got the publican screaming at you to stop, or the college jan-itor rattling his padlocks and setting his dog on you, but wherever you go, there's this terrible compulsion to get it over with and piss off as quickly as possible. So Ronnie's fills a social necessity for a lot of us. Over the years he's somehow managed to hang on. I'm sure there are plenty of people like myself who are basically club-orientated to that whole pattern of life which exists generally throughout the continent, but hardly at all here.

'For the public, jazz has gone down and something else has come up. With all the publicity directed towards one area of the music, there are suddenly enormous commercial pressures exerted on kids to conform. Of course money is still being invested in it by people who don't know what they're doing – so they're pouring money into rock which most of them will lose, but it is generating something which didn't exist before. Now rock spins off into the dress business, the book business, anything that can usefully be dragged in to take money off people. But the best of jazz music, presented in an unbiased situation, can hold its own against anything else. It doesn't need any excuses. You don't expect that it's going to dominate but there's a place in the entertainment world that it can fill. Entertainment doesn't preclude it from being art. All art should be entertaining. But if you take it out of the market place completely and prop it up with subsi-dies, then at once you rarefy it and narrow your audience.'

But if the music must stand on its own feet, what happens to the players who are still working to create a new vocabulary for their music and the nucleus of an audience for it? Do they starve or give up?

A year after the move to Frith Street in 1966, Ronnie Scott remarked to the writer and photographer Valerie Wilmer: 'I'm not sure that guys like Archie Shepp and Albert Ayler would mean very much economically at the moment. They may well do so in the future.' They didn't of course. Ayler ended tragically in the East River and Shepp lives on to see his identity as a serious black artist sidelined by the products of white-dominated record companies. Round about the same time, American critic Dan Morgenstern wrote, 'More than the poet, the painter or even the actor, the jazz musician is at the mercy of those who grant him the opportunity to be heard.'

Jazz musicians have always fallen between two lifestyles. Having brought some of the most powerful Western music of the twentieth century out of dance halls and whorehouses, having coaxed the sweeping freedoms of improvisation out of a few rudiments of ballads and blues, and having expanded the technical scope of nearly every instrument they touched, up to and beyond that of straight music, these men and women found and are still finding that a lot of people in the business hadn't really listened.

But if changes must come, what kind of changes will they be? Times *have* changed. Jazz as a useful descriptive term will die, except as a name for what is already history. Never before has it crossbred its influences so much or so successfully. Carla Bley was right about Jack Bruce. John McLaughlin leads what is probably one of the best and most unusual rock and roll bands in the world. Rock musicians increasingly improvise.

The established view maintains dominance by splitting the world into fragments. Being a 'jazz fan' is a fragment, acceptance of being an under-dog or part of an elite. Being a 'serious artist' is a fragment too. So go out and listen to *everything*. Accepted on their own terms, the new forms will flower. Look for what's really happening. The rest's easy.

LIVE EVIL
Time Out, March 1972

Miles Davis's last appearance in London was enigmatic. Half an hour late, he moves gracefully on stage, trumpet under his arm, mutes in a canvas bag, sidestepping a cluster of cables and roadies – almost before he's unpacked, the rhythm section is off like dogs emerging from the traps. Gary Bartz, Keith Jarrett, Miles downstage, Leon Chancler and three per-cussionists up the other end facing each other like contestants on a panel game. Much of *Live Evil* (CBS) reflects that music – a collection of assorted odds and ends from the past couple of years, the album includes his illus-trious temporary sideman John McLaughlin and the old rhythm partnership of Dave Holland and Jack DeJohnette.

It's easy to say that Miles's present choice of raw materials is predictable and even clumsy (high speed rock-time mostly without Tony Williams's brand of explosive variations, soloists riding doggedly over the rhythm to produce spindly frameworks of empty runs and irritable squeals of the kind of effortless vacancy that suggests they might rather be doing something else, like playing billiards or running for President), but he still has presence and he's unmistakable. Playing open horn, his tone is probably less sour than his early days, sometimes beautifully disjointed into a mixture of chilling shrieks and wild, rubbery runs that never land in the obvious place, if they land at all. 'Sivad' is one track that's just rescued by him, and by Keith Jarrett tirelessly composing memorable lines in his solos. The rest of it is so languid that it was just threatening to nod off altogether when CBS got there first with the scissors.

Newcomer Jarrett dominates these cuts, demonstrating his class with a jaunty finesse that borders on the arrogant – with the foresight of a medium and the reactions of an athlete, he spins on the rhythm, stalks across it with endless flurries, fills holes with dark chords. His second solo on 'What I Say' (after contributions from Bartz and McLaughlin of the kind of blunt frankness that suggest they had something to get straight, delivered it and split) almost manages, in its rich, chiming harmonies, to invest the wild-eyed fervour of the surroundings with a touch of pale charm.

The other double album is a Blue Note reissue of two Davis records that appeared in the mid-Fifties on the same label – it includes more than one take of some of the tunes, and the alternation of Kenny Clarke and Art Blakey on drums elicits startling shifts of mood (Clarke was on the first 1952 album, Blakey arrived a year later). Six of the tracks were for a fine quartet of Miles, Blakey, Horace Silver and Percy Heath. Fairly unambitious in his melodic scope, unsettled by anyone hurrying him, on a knife edge with his pitch, Miles gradually turned his limitations into the kind of bruised dignity that produced his subsequent classics. Here, his lyricism comes through a sound as natural as breathing, his attack is so reined and retarded as to occasionally make the rhythm sound as if it's trying to catch the last bus. Kenny Clarke's reserve by contrast with Blakey's continual elbowing of the rhythm, gunfire rimshots and blurred, drenching snare drum rolls, sounds positively polite.

These aren't Miles's most important recordings of the period (the strife-torn sessions with Thelonious Monk shortly afterwards are overpowering by comparison), but they represent a renaissance for Davis, beginning to find his feet after a hard time in life. If overall sound is all you need, like buying a car for the colour of the paint, then *Live Evil* has got the hip trademark on it, though *Miles in the Sky*, one of the earliest in this style, still gets my vote for the restrained mastery of 'Stuff'. The Blue Note sessions, however, are a must for anyone who walked out of the Festival Hall, and a good few that didn't.

WHERE FORTUNE SMILES
Time Out, May 1972

This group came together for a session in the States recently, composed of men who have come to it from widely divergent backgrounds and who will leave for equally divergent directions. John McLaughlin, often a shadowy figure on his recordings with Miles Davis, and a slightly cautious one on his nevertheless magnificent debut *Extrapolation*, seems to have bottled up every unexplored musical statement he ever considered and uncorked it all. Surman has also used the record as a safety valve and burns up his solo space with breathless energy. His soprano passage on the opener 'Glancing Backwards', which is worth a turn for the theme alone, refuses to touch the ground – when he does settle, for a few yearning low notes, they seem to prod him into taking off again to assault the upper reaches of the horn. Karl Berger has taken the sugary quality out of the vibes.

McLaughlin's abrasive sound, and his jerky, angular lines bypass lyricism with an ecstatic accumulation of notes spiralling upward to burst like a flare. His chordal technique, chiming and clanging, is the backbone of this LP. It's background like this, and the physical control of bassist Dave Holland that puts what are basically traditional elements of time and statements of melody and theme in a class by themselves. These five have explored where jazz has been and remade it as enthusiastically as if they had forged the chain of development themselves. Fortunately it appears to stretch to a distance beyond measure.

CARLA
Time Out, June 1972

Last January the American composer Carla Bley and her trumpeter husband Michael Mantler were in London to talk about the triple album *Escalator over the Hill*, produced by the New York Jazz Composers' Orchestra Association (JCOA), a self-help organisation set up to promote and distribute the work of the East Coast's most creative jazz performers.

They mentioned almost in passing that they needed to sell 30,000 copies of a triple-record to pay back the money they'd borrowed to make it. With no advertising. With no franchise on a chain of stores, or an option on television time. With just the two of them, and two hours of music with John McLaughlin, Jack Bruce, Linda Ronstadt, Paul Jones, Viva, Don Cherry and Roswell Rudd and the rest of an illustrious cast. Five years of work and a fortune in borrowed money – but within their scheme are the seeds of a sort of freedom. The laws of supply and demand in art never worked out as smoothly as they did for other commodities. It repeatedly and inconveniently struggled into areas that were not yet part of public knowledge – and therefore could not be *demanded*.

Carla Bley was first married to the Canadian pianist Paul Bley. The past five years have involved her in threading together the poetry of Paul Haines into a dislocated jigsaw of a libretto that became the opera *Escalator over the Hill* – the latest and longest of the Jazz Composers' Orchestra Association's works for jazz orchestra and soloists. By bringing in a rough approximation to a story, and extensively using vocalists, a new dimension entered not only their music, but the contemporary view of improvisation as drawn from jazz roots.

Carla Bley, whose voice is sufficiently alive with enthusiasm or indignation to be music in itself, seems a musical spirit composed by somebody of unusual talents. She once described the origins of the opera in a kind of affectionate written autobiography of the past five years.

'In the beginning, around 1967, Paul Haines, a friend for life, who had written pieces for the back covers of many albums I had been involved with, sent me a set of lyrics that fitted mysteriously into a piece of music I was writing . . . we decided to write an opera together, or rather, apart, since he was then living in New Mexico and about to move to India. . .

'Over the next three years we worked on it. Paul would send a batch of lyrics and I would put them on the piano and stare at them for hours. Sooner or later certain lines would seem to have a melody to them. Then it would be just a matter of working at it, with the form and rhythm of the lyric leading the way. Sometimes I would have to skip around, omit things, etc., as the musical viewpoint developed, but more often whole blocks of words would end up exactly in their original order, with music to them. The full meaning of the words would not occur to me until I had worked with them for months, sometimes years. I began to feel as if I was not writing music so much as reading poetry, with the resulting music as the painstaking and complicated by-product of revelation. When I was stuck, Paul would send me another batch and in it somewhere would be the solution. Through this process (I can only speak of my end of the work, God knows how Paul managed to write the words in the first place) we eventually accumulated about twelve major pieces of music and I started thinking about *Escalator over the Hill* – (the long-decided title) as a whole, and who we should get to perform it.'

Escalator happens in 'Cecil Clarke's Old Hotel', and in its rooms lost voices go through the motions of living. The characters are realised by forms of music, so the changes are there to be felt and heard rather than deduced. Country singer Linda Ronstadt plays Ginger, wearily occupying another stranger's room. Boredom has made strangers of lovers, and excitement a memory. Jack Bruce leads a rock band and Don Cherry an Eastern band as signposts to the places where emotions might be rediscovered. Both of them play superbly, and Jack has Mahavishnu John McLaughlin to back him up.

Carla Bley is constantly aware of the effect of her high-profile performers.

'I didn't know Jack Bruce was so famous as he is over here. I used him as a musician and as a singer with a voice that didn't have a category, which was something I was looking for. Linda Ronstadt was used because Paul Motian [the drummer] knew her and thought that she might be interested and it turned out that her manager knew us and thought it might be good for her to do it. So that was another accident really. . .

Jack Bruce was rich too, but it didn't get in the way of a performance more powerful and coherent than most of his recent work since the demise of Cream. Carla says wonderingly:

'Jack sang the material better than anyone in the world and he was our Caruso – we couldn't have wanted anything else. Mike was as impressed as I was afterwards, and wrote two pieces for Jack with words by Samuel Beckett. But he can't get a record date. So those beautiful pieces lie there. But what is Mike to do? He can't do it on JCOA because he's had his turn and we've got twenty more people to record before we get back to him.'

Is there a debilitating effect to commercialisation? Or was Jack Bruce right when he said good music would always make it?

'I don't think that the truly great player would ever be discovered that way. The truly great player has to spend five years waiting to get discovered and then five years wondering if it's worthwhile to be discovered and trying out alternative ways of life, and then the next five years realising that he's got to be discovered in a nefarious manner, doing that, and then five years making a living, finally, getting some kind of a document out about his creative life if he has any creativity left by that time – then he spends the rest of his life being asked to do things that he no longer has any desire to do, and so he imitates himself until he dies. It's so sad, it's more than that, it's almost inconceivable that this pattern repeats itself and no one complains and points it out.'

And yet of course people do complain and point it out but know at the same time that the answers are not as accessible as the problem seems to be. The freedom to mature, independently of every other pressure, is something that's bought, and people can't afford it.

Some eight years ago the JCOA was originally the Jazz Composers' Guild of New York. Mike Mantler recalls that 'the personalities involved and the way it was done didn't work out and it failed'. Much of the initial attendance to the problems of finance and distribution and company law should have been all done within the first two years rather than the first four or five . . . 'we should be at a much further point than we are'. The fact that the second attempt at holding out against the market has been conspicuously more successful is attributable, Carla Bley believes, to a changed climate.

'I suppose we'll get thrown back on the floor again soon. But then five years later we'll rise again, it just makes sense to me. This happens to be a period of growth and expanding which will be followed by . . . the opposite . . . and as long as you understand it, you won't be disappointed.'

'The jazz people particularly, have come from very tough environments and couldn't help but want a lot of money and for civilisation to make it up to them and their race. So I've never been able to accuse any of those people of doing the wrong thing, they couldn't help it, but now I think that what that scene offers is no longer attractive to anyone. Mass adulation and all of that.'

There was some help with *Escalator* – the distribution system now involves no money and all the co-operative record companies in Europe (Incus, Futura, ECM, ICP, etc.) are handling the album in exchange for distribution of their material in the States. But a challenge of this size would never have entered Carla's head in the early days.

'I started to change around about the time of *Genuine Tong Funeral* in the Sixties which was the first time I'd moved into longer forms. That was another record date I wasn't able to get for myself – nobody who heard the tapes liked it so I put that music away for a year and finally decided that the only way I could do it was with Gary Burton, the vibes player. But it was Mike who started changes off in me . . . we find out that things don't have to be that way and the next step is to change them and if you have any success you get very excited and try to change everything.'

There is an expression that if you don't get what you want it may be simply that you don't want it enough. Carla Bley and Mike Mantler, like the growing community of independent creative musicians around the world, have decided to want something badly enough to handle the resistance to its unfamiliarity. Jack Bruce sings at the beginning of 'Rawalpindi Blues', 'You've got to give up what you don't want, to get what you do.'

AFRO-ROCKER
Time Out, July 1972

At five o'clock in the morning outside a motel somewhere in Germany, a distant voice is stubbornly arguing with a silent opponent while the dawn shakes the sleep out of its eyes. Incredulous birds thronging the trees thereabouts are looking down at a powerfully built black man who's doggedly insisting that they're all singing hopelessly out of tune with him.

For Dudu Pukwana, who has been found at a similar hour of the morning singing along with a leaky bathroom tap and reflecting incredulously on the tap's musical imagination, such episodes aren't exceptional. What they don't show is that Pukwana, alto saxophonist with Chris McGregor's Brotherhood of Breath and a South African who has spent the last seven years in Britain, has one of the most commanding voices, both in his music and his feelings about it, to be found in this country. And no amount of absorption into the ways of this detached and diffident place will alter the

African in him.

Conversation with him is like attending a performance. He responds to events, not just in his head, but in restless movements, exploding into a shout of laughter. Dudu Pukwana would have trouble with the cool style. Lucid and relaxed as he is off the bandstand, his energy triggers him bewilderingly into directions that leave you breathless. Describe to someone who's never seen it what he does on stage and it will come out sounding like showmanship – all that stamping and shouting, leaning back defiantly with the saxophone, then cutting the time and the volume by half and bending, twisting away from the audience as if about to start a private conversation with the horn. The disarming part comes with realising how totally unselfconscious it all is.

As the night goes on Dudu becomes less and less separate from the band. What the others are doing becomes a part of his music and his theirs. He takes his music apart and rebuilds it bit by bit in sympathy with the audience, the band, even the room he's in.

'You can't play without time,' Dudu says. 'Time is there, it's natural, like day and night. There is a drum inside you, while it keeps on pumping you keep on living and that's time too. The music is what you are and what you've been. It's a story that's going on all the time. You can't be out of it. When I play it's like listening to a conversation – and it has to do with rhythm, with what you can *feel*. We grew up with it all around us in South Africa – and although there is melody there too, the melody develops out of it. So I'm not sorry that pop music is as it is in Western Europe now – because it has a beat that a child can feel, it's a way of looking at life, of letting yourself loose.

'We started with street music and developed it – like you don't worry about the rhythm no more, it's there and you know it's there. After that you can start to express yourself naturally. So with Chris's small group or with Brotherhood or whatever, the band, there's no real difference. Just more voices – with a rhythm that becomes a part of those voices. So that if we should get in a different drummer, he gets to the point where he can say, Jesus Christ, I'd better be *there*, because we know where we're pushing, so he's ready too. We *know* each other now. There's a circle been formed and we keep dropping right into it.'

Peter Sinclair, another South African who now manages the band, marvels at the pitch of Dudu's energy. 'Chris (McGregor) put it right once. He said that when an African picks up an instrument and starts playing, it automatically comes out as jazz.' That suggests a view of jazz as broad as Pukwana's own playing experience, from 'Afro-rock' through folk music and up to Ornette Coleman and beyond. The release of personality through improvisation is something that the flood of third-rate packaged sounds has virtually drowned in the Western world. If you or I sing a tune, it's always somebody else's tune.

'I see it all the time at home. There'll be guys working in the street, man, and you might find them singing. They'll work out a rhythm with a pick and a shovel. You can stand there and enjoy watching them. Even in the mines, man, you'll see how they take it out with music. Music is a social thing, not something you only get in concert halls. That's how it is at home. Only afterwards do you start wondering – what the *hell* are these people happy about?'

Dudu Pukwana met Brotherhood's leader Chris McGregor in Cape Town. After a jazz festival in Johannesburg they formed a bebop group and called it the Blue Notes. In 1964 McGregor and several others including Mongezi Feza (trumpet), Louis Moholo (drums) and Johnny Dyani (bass) left South Africa and made a living with a small group in England. Brotherhood of Breath is the second big band. 'The previous one,' says Sinclair, 'only did about six performances and then went out of business. What was too much for people then is maybe not so hard now. Interest in music is more open. Brotherhood is a jazz group but it has visual excitement too.' Dudu is part of that excitement. And his respect for McGregor and his music is never concealed.

'Chris is very open. It's under his direction but everybody's communicating with him. He comes out more when he's working with other people. Take Duke Ellington for instance – there's so much that Duke wants to put down, but he can't because he only has the piano, so the horns contribute to this voice of his and *add* to it too. So we can do things that Chris accepts, which we know is still within his direction. It's a conversation. It goes way back. And it's all music, that's all you need call it. If it's good, man, it shouldn't worry *nobody*.'

The Brotherhood's first album, released a few months back, features Pukwana on a ballad called 'Davashe's Dream' that reveals the strength of Ellington's influence on McGregor. Dudu lurks amidst rich textures from the trombones before bursting out like a flare over the rest of the band. His gentler side, the deepest part of him, is there in that quivering tone in the low register. He puts all his faith in himself rather than his technique, so playing the first thing that comes into his head and believing it to be right normally works out fine. But an audience is almost essential, so that he can feel that his music is going back where it came from, like all folk music ultimately does. He's an ordinary man with talent, not a talented man with training. The difference keeps him alive to everything.

'We don't let audiences conduct. We lead them, we talk with *them*. That knocked me out about our tour in Germany – with old men and little children in the audiences, giving us a standing ovation. I looked at it and I thought, WHAT? When did I last see this? And we opened after a pop group, a real down-to-earth pop group. That I couldn't believe. It reminded me of home. That's how it was then – when everybody wants to show you, I can hear it, I can *hear* it, man! It happened even here sometimes. But audiences still hold themselves back. They ask themselves, is it *right*, should I show people what I feel. You look at a kid, you see how he can open up naturally. People want to do it, for them it's a chance of release. They're told, don't talk so loud, don't get yourself noticed.

'Look at our festivals at home – you'll have a *kwela* thing going here, a jazz group there. And there's the audience all around it, the same audience. If you're going to split up the people then they will grow up believing in those differences. And it depends on the promoters because that's how *they* see it. What can the people do? You are starting a war with the people. So for some, jazz is nonsense – just as others think that rock is nonsense. But look at the scene now – with people like Miles Davis. If it were true that one kind of sound is bullshit and the other isn't, how the hell does one guy manage to play the other's music in *his own way*?'

When he fronts Brotherhood's reeds on the South Bank on Wednesday, Dudu Pukwana may reflect on how far he's come on a journey that began in the music festivals of Africa and crossed most of the jazz clubs of Europe. If the Queen Elizabeth Hall is full (and judging by the sales of that first LP it seems reasonable) then he's quite likely to find an audience that will willingly join him on his irrepressible voyage through McGregor's magnificently whimsical ideas about music. Dudu's style is largely unclassifiable, which is just as he would want. Though the likelihood of finding Johnny Hodges and Archie Shepp side by side might give you a glimpse of a little of what's there. It gives his playing, an emotional scope all the way from wistful sentimentality through the threatening restlessness of the blues and into a swooping display of rage that you cower away from. 'What saved us,' he says, 'is that we didn't get to hear too many American players.' Because of that unfashionable mixing of the old and the new (which Chris McGregor shares) it's unlikely that Dudu Pukwana will be imitated too often. To duplicate one Pukwana, you'd need half a dozen performers. Having quite unintentionally developed around himself a totally personal legend of extraordinary exploits, and not all of them musical ones, he's probably discouraged imitation for good. For someone who respects the individuality of other players as much as he works to preserve his own, that too is just as he would want.

VIENNA BOY
Time Out, August 1972

One day, three years or so ago, a letter arrived from a pianist I'd known as a student, and parts of it said something to the effect of 'go and listen to a new Miles record called *In a Silent Way*. Put yourself in a warm room in an armchair with the cans over your ears and you'll float away into another world.'

John McLaughlin, who had been Graham Bond's guitar player, had moved to the States by that time and was on the session. Another Englishman, Dave Holland, a bassist who had worked with the most uncompromising adventurers in London and silenced everyone with his technique, was there too. And the remains of an earlier Davis group, with Wayne Shorter on saxophones, Herbie Hancock on keyboards, Tony Williams on drums, playing better than at any time in his young life.

Sound textures suggested the moods for improvisers now, rather than the time or the tune – and the electric piano, which could release thunder-claps or raindrops, became indispensable. Tony Williams played rock-time mesmerically, except when he splintered it into lightning rolls across the drums. The title composition 'In a Silent Way' occupied the entire second side, introduced gently by McLaughlin's guitar over rip-pling keyboards. And it was written by a forty-year old pianist from Vienna of all places, called Josef Zawinul.

Zawinul had a strange background to get into such illustrious company. Because he had perfect pitch, they invited him to join the Vienna Boys' Choir, but he changed his mind, went to the Vienna Conservatory, spent a brief spell in Czechoslovakia, went back home and by 1952 had got far enough removed from the exam room to be playing night club gigs as a house pianist. Friedrich Gulda, the concert pianist, introduced him to jazz. Zawinul said later, 'I had to get to the United States if I was to grow as a musician. I had to have contact with the music as a living force.' He arrived in the States in January 1959 and though he had a scholarship to the Berklee School of Music he went on the road instead, with Maynard Ferguson (Wayne Shorter was in the band at the same time) then Dinah Washington and from 1961 onwards, a long stint with the Cannonball Adderley group. The wheel has come full circle. Adderley's group, which Zawinul left five years ago, is now playing a watered-down version of early electric Miles. And so is nearly everyone else.

In 1966, people used to draw attention to the fact that Joe Zawinul was one of the few Europeans to have made a firm contribution to the music in its own home. They wouldn't say it now. Not only does Weather Report, one of the most resourceful of the electric jazz bands, have Zawinul play-ing shoulder to shoulder with the magnificent Wayne Shorter, but they're all ceaselessly propelled by a bass player who has tone and dexterity in superhuman quantities. His name's Miroslav Vitous and he's a Czech. Can white men sing the blues?

HAN

Time Out, August 1972

Somebody who has certainly never allowed his style to be cramped by the

occasionally Spartan disciplines of 'free' improvisation is the remarkable
Dutch percussionist Han Bennink, who makes one of his rare London
appearances at Ronnie Scott's on Sunday. Bennink's extraordinary technique and energy have impressed many musicians a lot better known than
he is. Though his playing is indescribable, if you could imagine the combined assault of a charging bull, a couple of hedgefuls of chirping crickets,
a dozen assorted tinsmiths, carpenters and blacksmiths working overtime,
doors slamming in empty buildings, people having a row in the flat
upstairs (intermittently heaving crockery and loose change at each other)
with 'Match of the Day' playing in the background, it might give you an
idea. The ubiquitous guitarist Derek Bailey, a long time partner, will do his
best to keep up.

TOPOGRAPHY

Time Out, October 1972

When Incus Records, an independent co-operative organisation, established itself two years ago, it was already clear that the big companies
weren't going to be sweating over the competition. The orders a label like
this can expect to handle number hundreds rather than thousands, and the
only point of voluntarily embarking on the kind of stormy sea that Incus
is currently bobbing about on, is that it answers overdue needs. Without
it, and its parallel in Holland (ICP – the Instant Composers' Pool) the
discography of Evan Parker – a twenty-eight-year-old saxophone player
of ferocious capabilities – would be a strong contender for the world's
shortest book.

Parker, who in his more hirsute days would have driven Jerry Garcia
schizoid had they ever come face to face, has grown steadily as a player
since the mid-Sixties when he was a fairly constant participant in the
Spontaneous Music Ensemble. The duo that he frequently formed with the
drummer John Stevens in those days, has reappeared as a playing situation he clearly feels at home in – his partner now is Paul Lytton, a man who
often appears to be relentlessly unseating him by apparently going off at
alarming tangents but whose independence Parker values as a stimulant.

The din, if you're unprepared, can verge on the traumatic, but the
strangeness is not an accident. For some, it is a necessary adjunct to a real
relaxation of outlook, not only toward music, but toward everything else.
The politicising of music doesn't end with writing lyrics about Vietnam
from a poolside in Beverley Hills. Commercial music's sameness is its politics, its predictability is its politics. When R. D. Laing prefaced *The Politics
of Experience* with the warning 'few books today are forgivable', he might
have said the same for records too.

'I don't think you can apply universal laws,' Evan Parker says, ' so this is nothing new that we demand of an audience. This condition has always existed with music that is genuinely of its time. If the music's innovatory, then you need new ways of listening to it, and they must be ways that the music itself suggests. It seems clear that what most people want from music, if they want anything directly from the music itself, is reassurance, that music is what they think it is. This is the function that the musician is supposed to fulfil but presumably at the expense of his own integrity.

'I know when that reassurance is taking place for me, and I know that it's something that feels good. But I know that it doesn't feel anywhere near as good as hearing something that I've *never* heard before that also sounds good. And I don't accept, given that you understand roughly the elements that the musicians are working with that you need hear a thing a thousand times before you can begin to understand what it means musically, I think that meaning is there from the first moment. It's got nothing to do with analysis or technique, those are only ways of dissecting music after the event. And music was never about those things.

'Paul Bley said somewhere a long time ago that you get the sound you hear. And I've found that to be increasingly true for me, from my own experience. Before Stockhausen wrote the so-called intuitive pieces which are just instructions about emptying the mind and not making any sounds until you hear the sounds that should be made, all those activities were things that that Little Theatre Club group of musicians in London were already into for at least a year before those pieces came. But because the culture machine works for the composer and works for the academies of music, then this whole stream of ours lacks that kind of cultural acceptance. Everything else is a fringe, avant-garde, lunatic, spend-a-small-percentage, token kind of activity. That's dangerous, very dangerous I think. It just means that you have to make a total capitulation to the system in order to take advantage of the means of communication that it offers. I have the feeling, for example, that Derek Bailey is one of the best guitar players in the world and he should be better known by anyone who's interested in the development of the guitar. Probably in his case it's such a force that it can't be avoided'.

Bailey uses no dazzling runs. No rhythm-and-blues. No elegant chord patterns. He frequently gets sounds from behind the bridge of the guitar and his progress begins to resemble a trail of shards and splinters, none of the effortless artistry that passes for good entertainment.

'So who do they all like, John McLaughlin or somebody?' Parker enquires. 'To me it's just hot licks, that style of playing. And when you know that the consciousness of the guys involved goes beyond it, you can't help but feel that what they're doing is playing down to people, and that's hard. But most people would probably find that a fantastic idea, that John McLaughlin might be playing down to them, because they've been hyped into believing that it's an incredible move *up* for them, that if they can dig that then they must be really into something.

'Nowadays the policies of the major record companies seem to originate in the accounts department. So they will define what a successful record is and how it behaves or what constitutes an acceptable sales graph for a record which will involve quantities plotted against time, and if a particular record doesn't meet that definition then it's deleted very quickly. The system of no returns makes it more difficult for a shopkeeper to take a chance on something that he feels to be on the fringes of his customers' tastes, because he knows that if he orders it, he's lumbered with it. So the record companies are moving closer toward a standardisation of taste. After all, people can only choose from what's made available to them, so the effective choices are in fact made by middle-men, in music as much as in anything else'.

Partly in his originality but mainly in his vigour as a saxophonist, Evan Parker is himself a powerful argument against the view that this music is still the private domain of the black American.

'The trouble with making the claim that there's a certain sort of music that only black people can play, is that there's no logical reason if that's true, why white people should be able to hear it and understand it either. And somebody like Leroi Jones would probably say, "You're right, you can't fucking hear it because you've had 2,000 years of a culture that won't let you hear it." I'd accept that from Leroi Jones, but not from some of the whites who've tried to say it. Of course, behind all that there's the reality that the whole creative force that sustained the jazz business edifice came from the black community in the States and not much of the money found its way back there. The changes in the political and social awareness of the Sixties have begun to modify that. Miles decided to become a rock star. Sonny Rollins stopped making records, so did Cecil Taylor. Don Cherry lives in Europe. Milford Graves and Sun Ra have their own record companies . . . and their work seems to me to be the most significant.'

Some of the avant-garde is boring, much of it is refreshing, a little of it is piercingly beautiful. It will probably never become the kind of public knowledge that carried much weight in the world, but Evan Parker's attempt to put his talents to the most honest possible use (pursuing his own intuitions rather than the ghosts of other people's) is fortunately typical of the work of one of the most daring and resilient musical movements in Europe.

THE MARCH HARE OF FRITH STREET

Zigzag, October 1973

Stan Tracey, a forty-six-year-old pianist, vibraharpist and composer, whose prickly distinctiveness has been matched only by his reluctance to present a public face any other way but on the bandstand, reaches his thirtieth year as a professional musician with a celebratory concert at the Queen Elizabeth Hall on 19 November. Journalists have always lavished praise on him, and he's won and kept the respect of musicians on both sides of the Atlantic since the late Fifties, but praise comes cheap. Three years ago it was only the prospect of winter mornings that kept him from slinging the business and taking up a new vocation as a postman.

Stan Tracey was a working musician long before the cultural weather changed and jazz, while never a licence to print money, was at least a tolerable life in the late Fifties. The Modern Jazz Quartet and Dave Brubeck used to bulge out concert halls in those days. The Marquee Club and the Flamingo used to present jazz most nights of the week, black polo necks and CND badges were everywhere. Then two revolutions happened. The Beatles proved that haunting and unforgettable music could come out of the pop machine from guys without much in the way of technique. And in America, the home of all that was supposed to be fresh in jazz, the opposite was taking place. It was getting more complicated and abstract every day, less and less capable of being whistled, still less danced to or even nodded at.

By this time Stan Tracey was a familiar figure at Ronnie Scott's Club as the house pianist in the challenging role of accompanist to a flood of American visitors. His career up till then had jolted along the hit-and-miss lines of most of the pros who'd grown up in the dance bands of the Forties; their life was in 'the business' of erratic dealings with palais bands and variety shows, hollow contracts and agents disappearing down the fire escape with the cash. No Arts Council, no independent record labels, not many music diplomas either. Like Ronnie Scott, Tracey had done his stint with the fearsome Ted Heath Orchestra, and since entering the profession as an accordion player with ENSA during the war had taken to the road with the Gang Show, Bob Monkhouse, Cab Calloway on a British trip, and various of Scott's own bands. It was an apprenticeship that never said much about Art (c.f. Lenny Bruce's classic 'Shorty Pederstein's Interview': 'What do you think about Art?' – 'I think Art blows the most, man.') Even now, Tracey rarely mentions it. When he's playing a gig he's 'working'. All this from a man whose 1965 recording of 'Under Milk Wood' is probably the most stunning forty minutes of improvisation and indelibly original composition ever Made In England.

Because the nearest landmark to Tracey's two-fisted style is the correspondingly wayward Thelonious Monk, Tracey has frequently been passed off as an imitator. But like most apparent eccentricities, the style came naturally. Jazz piano in those days was mostly an attempt to transpose Charlie Parker's saxophone playing wholesale; frequently it resembled a typing pool on speed. 'I'd listened to Monk, sure,' Stan Tracey says of his first steps toward a trademark, 'and of all the people around at that time, I happened to agree with his approach to music, but I didn't very deliberately figure out that I was going to get this bit together just like Monk, or that bit together. I could appreciate what was involved in all the rest of bebop piano playing but it seemed so limited – once you'd got to the way of doing it you knew what was coming, there was nothing to grab you by the balls or goose you, there was very little opportunity to bring into use the things that the piano can do better than anything else.'

Getting on with playing for his living, Tracey hadn't given much thought to the problem of whether or not a white Londoner had much chance of finding himself in the family album of jazz celebrities. 'Most of the relationships between British jazz and American jazz I found out from the critics, that's where I get most of my information. They were playing jazz and we were playing jazz and that was the way it was. The first time I went to the States with a British band (I'd been several times before on the boats and copped people like Parker and Gillespie and Bud Powell in Birdland in New York) was in 1957 with Ronnie Scott; we went in exchange for Dave Brubeck. And just to make everything cosy they bunged us into a rock'n'roll show with Chuck Berry and Fats Domino and a lot of other people. The audience was ninety-nine and a half per cent black because the show was, and we used to play two tunes at the beginning of the gig in these huge stadiums while people were still wandering about looking for their seats; so in the middle of all this these six little white faces would come on, blow a couple of choruses each and off. The audience was as astonished by it all as we were to be there. We got £25 a week but you had to pay your own hotel and find your own food. And then they had the nerve to get us to sign a form when we left stating that we'd earned the *equivalent* bread to the Dave Brubeck Quartet. You can imagine how likely it was that he would have been earning £25 a week in 1957.

'Ted Heath's tours were a different story because at least the bread was more realistic and they loved that band to death in America; it was all middle-class white audiences who don't know much about anything but they know what they like and they liked Ted Heath. God knows why, the music was terrible.'

But it was Heath's rhythm section that cut *Showcase*, Tracey's first album as a leader, with Ronnie Verrell and John Hawksworth. Tracey, playing in a less implacable version of his later style, performed a dozen standards on it. But though he has always had his own special way with standards, he clearly wasn't happy with jazz's affair with Tin Pan Alley. Tracey won't listen to *Showcase* now, or face the chubby innocent descending the Royal Court Theatre's steps on the sleeve, but while his playing on that record occasionally propelled itself into dead ends, the promise of it soon came good.

A year later he made an album with drummer Phil Seamen and bassist Kenny Napper called *Little Klunk* and his wife Jackie Tracey, working for

Decca at the time, went about setting up the outlets for her husband that he wasn't likely to hustle up under his own steam.

In March 1960, Stan Tracey began the job that lifted the blinkers from his experience as a musician, accelerated his most creative years as a writer and a player, saw him hooked on junk and sparked off, matured and destroyed, a relationship with Scottish tenorist Bobby Wellins that took their music into the world league. When Ronnie Scott set up shop in Gerrard Street the long and pointless feud between the British and American Musicians' Unions had ended and the giants of the music were suddenly within arm's length. Don Byas, Zoot Sims and Al Cohn, Lucky Thompson and Dexter Gordon were among the early visitors, reflecting Scott's personal allegiances to the tenor saxophone. During the same period, the New Departures Quartet was formed in London to improvise with the poetry of Michael Horowitz and Pete Brown. Bobby Wellins was appearing with drummer Tony Crombie's band at the Flamingo Club when Tracey met him ('it was instant rapport') and New Departures was completed by Laurie Morgan and a young bassist who had already worked with Tony Kinsey and Tubby Hayes and was soon to get his face and his playing better known with Dudley Moore – Jeff Clyne.

Tracey says of Wellins: 'The thing we had together I've never experienced before or since. I couldn't wait to play, I still feel that way about playing, but with Bobby there was that thing that whatever I did or whatever he did, I knew that we'd both more or less think it at the same time. He had a unique way of playing anything, and his sound was so beautiful. We had a repertoire to start from, but every night it would be a different story. It was a joy to hear how he would do it.'

After *Klunk*, recording became a fond memory again, though critic Victor Schonfield, a man with an ear for originality that's apparently immune to the prevailing wind direction, arranged for the New Departures group to record in 1961. A transatlantic album, *The New Departures Quartet* later emerged, with a thoroughly un-American blues by Wellins called 'McTaggart', a shuffling up-tempo contribution by Tracey called 'Afro-Charlie' (that was later to find its way into the big band book), a wry medley of sentimental ballads and Wellins's superb 'Culloden Moor' – an early and tentative free-time performance. After *Klunk* it was a slightly indecisive set. Wellins, however, appears capable of endless variations and seems at times to impel every chorus with a fresh idea, alternating force with grace, splintering barely exhaled puffs of air with mournful, swooping wails that echo more of the Highlands than Harlem. Occasionally resembling a less dandified version of Stan Getz, it was the tremble in the voice of Wellins's music that lowered a veil of wistful resignation so sharply contrasted with Tracey's pungent declamations.

Between them they personified a defiance and a kind of fragile pessimism that was unique. 'Culloden Moor' opens on a stormy landscape, Tracey's piano a deep and foreboding murmur over rumbling drums.

Wellins's tenor, stating the theme, is statuesque. It was an achievement that was to be repeated four years later with more or less the same band, on an album of eight tunes inspired by Dylan Thomas's *Under Milk Wood*, a play Tracey knew like the back of his hand. The album emerged without a slack moment, headed readers' polls, ran critics dry of superlatives and included Bobby Wellins's best recorded performance in a solemn and lustrous expansion of 'Starless and Bible Black'.

But in the intervening years things were going wrong, though the evidence wasn't to be plain for a while yet. Ronnie Scott's galaxy of stars were wearing the novelty off transatlantic visitors, rhythm-and-blues was elbowing the jazzmen out of the clubs or signing them up, and the shadow of hard drugs hovering over the jazz world settled on Wellins and Tracey. Tracey, in a rare bout of unhesitating lucidity, recalls the period from the seminal New Departures forward:

'I was well screwed up myself at that time, but I still hung on to the music and to Jackie and the kids. It was pitiful, we used to meet, both out of our minds and wondering, has he got shit, has he got shit, and I said, Bobby we've got to do something about this, the music's where it's at, we've got to get straight, and he'd say, yeah, you're right, we've got to give it up. In the end we just drifted apart.

'I don't know why musicians get into it so much, there are all sorts of reasons. When I was at Ronnie's you'd have a smoke, and I was drinking at that time too, and you could get blues easily, and speed very cheaply, and it was part of the excitement of the scene at that time because at Ronnie's Old Place then it was so beautiful to be playing with all those guys who were coming over and it went on, month after month, year after year, it was like eternal Christmas playing with those people. And then suddenly you find you're getting a bit tired keeping up with somebody like Roland Kirk at three in the morning, so you start taking a few blues and a smoke and a drink, and that feels good and then somebody tells you about cocaine and you go on and play and you feel *great* and you come off and it's party time all the time; and the way I got on horse was one night the guy who used to sell me cocaine hadn't got any but he had got heroin and I had that and went on and played and it felt good and gave me a completely different kind of feeling about the music, a real steamroller feeling. After a bit you find yourself waking up in the morning and nodding off to kip in the middle of the afternoon so you have a snort of horse and suddenly you find you're not tired any more.

'And then you find out a bit later that you've got a habit. And you think, I'd better knock this off, it's getting a big strong, and you go without and you find you've got terrible diarrhoea, goose pimples, a terrible taste in your mouth all the time, the smell of food makes you puke, and if you want to eat and be like everyone else and stay normal you've got to have some horse – just to stay normal. You don't get a buzz any more. It was available and it was cheap, and I think that a lot of the guys who got ruined at that time, got there in pretty much the same way I did. That was all before the pop scene, and now the pop scene has taken over cocaine and it's become terribly expensive. Where they're going to come off better than we did is that while cocaine will put you in a mood to try anything, horse isn't as freely available as it was when I was into all that. If it was, I think you'd have a lot of junkie pop musicians.'

If junk was affecting Tracey physically – normally a robust-looking man, his cheekbones were by now stretching his flesh and his eyeballs had receded into a shadowy blur – his appetite for work was apparently unlimited. In between deals with the pushers who searched him out at the club, and his occupation of the bandstand, he was scribbling snatches of melodies on scraps of paper, an idea that might have come between him and Rollins or Kirk, a way of harmonising an old tune in a new mood, plans for suites and orchestras and arrangements. On the first bus out to Streatham at four in the morning he'd rescue all the fragments, get home and work as many more hours as it took to get the suggestions of the night turned into scores and shapes. The momentum of six nights a week on the go turned him into an apparently unquenchable source of original music.

'Of course it was an incredible time for me, but not simply because I was playing with those guys, it wasn't stars in the eyes over American musicians. After the first three or four people I accompanied, I soon got that bit straight in my mind. I knew then that they were just like everyone else, they were either a prick, or they were all right, you could either talk to them, play with them, be with them, and it was pleasant or it was unpleasant. People like anybody else. Lucky Thompson was very strongly anti-white, and when it came to playing he wanted a machine behind him and he didn't want you to mess with him. Guys like Lucky and Don Byas, if they played something that suggested an idea to you and you followed it up you'd get the old elbow in the ribs through what they played, the message would come across in the music, don't fool about, you do that, *I'll* do this.

'But people like Roland Kirk and Rollins and Charlie Mariano, you'd make a little statement that embellished or embroidered something they'd done, and you'd feel them taking it up, and considering it, and developing it . . . So I suppose it was during that period that I learned most of what I've got together now. Playing with so many people who had their music really together. In so many varying styles and approaches, I was learning all the time. I was developing what I was into, plus being able to play every night, and I now realise what a luxury *that* was. I couldn't wait to get to work and pick up where I was the night before, and all the time I was looking for new sounds, a new way of doing this and that, and stockpiling it all in my mind. I was learning about time and about how to swing, and you get a bit of that from each player.'

From *Milk Wood* in 1965 and for the next seven years, Stan Tracey at least had the ear of record producer Dennis Preston; an odd enough liaison in itself, since Preston's principal output was along the folksy-wallpaper lines of Wout Steenhuis and Roger Whittaker. Eventually Preston suggested that he write a straight work for piano and string quartet, the soloist to be the American classical pianist Tom McIntosh and improvising to be firmly locked out of the studio. Tracey was worried by a music world that he knew little about, and by a fee of £100 which was supposed to encourage him to risk his neck. 'Preston explained,' recalled Tracey, 'that "we're not doing this for ourselves" – all this from a bloke who's got a record company and a palatial home and bread that he's never going to use if he lives to be a hundred and fifty – and he's saying, "This isn't for us, it's for my son, and your son . . ." and I said, "Screw him, what about *me*?" I mean, honestly, what a load of cobblers. And they're telling me, jazz is finished, it's out, it's all over. So at that point the composer laid down his pen.'

Despite Preston's change of heart on inspecting the sales figures, he'd made possible a peculiar mixture of recordings that took in the rest of Tracey's studio work with Wellins (*With Love from Jazz*, 1968), two excellent big band albums (*Alice in Jazzland*, 1966, and *Seven Ages of Man*, 1971), a set of Ellington arrangements for the Duke's seventieth birthday in conjunction with Joe Harriott, Tony Coe, Don Rendell and Ian Carr, and his only all-round misfire on record, *The Latin American Caper*.

Stan Tracey abandoned the orchestral side of his work three years ago with an album he arranged for Ben Webster (*Webster's Dictionary*). Bobby Wellins vanished to Bognor and never came back, though the Jazz Centre Society once mounted a benefit concert to help him get his horn out of hock, and the Parkerish alto player Pete King took his place in the quartet. By the time that *Free n' One* was made, things were moving fast. Miles Davis was easing into rock'n'roll, electronics were obsessing musicians everywhere, everyone who could disappeared into session work. *Free n' One* and *Perspectives* – Tracey's last album with Preston, including Brian Spring and Dave Green, but missing King – were agreeable studio jams that were breaking down the leader's long and exhaustive apprenticeship on 'playing the tunes'.

The record business, aware of a few vestiges of moral obligation but hoping to be relieved of an unpleasant scene by the jazzmen getting fed up and departing of their own accord, was now trying discreetly to shift the music's foot from its doorway, or at least persuade it to change its shoes. Tracey, after a struggle to get himself free of drugs and a confused and exhausted departure from Ronnie Scott's after eight long years, was ready to take the hint.

'They said jazz was finished and I couldn't argue, because you only have to pull out my record sales and there's no more to be said. So I thought, sod this for a game, what's it all been for anyway? And I was all set to become a postman then, and it was only getting up on winter mornings that put me off. But the idea of just toddling about, with nobody bothering me and a joint in one hand and a sack of letters in the other, I thought that would be a gas. All told, at that time I was feeling totally obsolete.'

It was only finding some of Wellins's sad fire in the playing of ex-Westbrook altoist Mike Osborne that kept Tracey off the streets and brought him into contact with a completely different music world, populated with the younger men for whom Coltrane and Shepp and Cecil Taylor were contemporaries and fierce inspirations. It was a long way from Ted Heath and 'Hawaiian War Chant' but, trying to recover his health in his mid-forties, Stan Tracey was forcing himself to start all over again. 'When you're playing one sort of music for a long time you don't realise that you're building up a confidence in playing that music, using past experience for the situations that occur, and when I started playing this new music, I realised that I had none of that to fall back on. I went through a lot of doubt, I felt completely naked. Now that I've been playing it for a while, there's a new sort of confidence building up. I've become a bit more aware of a lot of things I didn't know before, and the politics of the music industry is one. Having come to all that so late in life, I find I can't handle it, it really brings me down. When it comes to jazz, a business that more or less turns you into a second-class citizen anyway, there's just so much to do.

'I don't think about survival. There wouldn't have been much point, in this business. Even the fact that I have a family never makes me think maybe I should do this or do that. I see so many people who are worried sick about money, but haven't got any more of it than I have. Your mind has to be free if you're going to do anything with it. Worrying about security just holds you back and drags you down. You can't think for it. If you're in the Sahara and you break your leg, there's not much point in rubbing it with a pound note.'

On 19 November, Stan Tracey recollects it all in more tranquillity than he could have called up a few years ago. Miles Davis is at the Rainbow Theatre the same night, and Tracey doesn't expect that nowadays they'll be stealing audiences from each other. With two sidemen from the early days, Lennie Bush and Tony Crombie, plus part-time tenorist and orthopaedic surgeon Art Themen – who'd worked all around the jazz scene and in Jack Bruce's short-lived band with Chris Spedding and Dick Heckstall-Smith – Tracey opens the concert with music from *Under Milk Wood* and the early quartet's work. After a session for the orchestra playing music from the two big-band albums, he gets himself up to date with a set for solo piano, which he can still bring off more convincingly than anyone in the country, and duets from time to time with saxophonist Mike Osborne. There's a final glimpse of the free music of the new quartet – Open Circle with John Stevens and Trevor Watts from the Spontaneous Music Ensemble, and ex-Pentangle bassist Danny Thompson. That's more than anything a cut-down version of a superb band called Splinters that probably performed no more than half a dozen gigs and included Ken Wheeler on trumpet, Tubby Hayes on tenor and Phil Seamen on drums as well as Stevens. The deaths of Hayes and Seamen in the last year rubbed the point about the London club life of the Sixties cruelly home. Stan

Tracey hopes that a new beginning is going to lead somewhere worth going to. His recording career is only of interest to the independent labels now, the big companies being run, as Evan Parker has remarked, 'by the accounts department' and looking to jazz only for a new Mahavishnu. Tracey won't ever be able to give them that. But as long as he plays music, listening to it won't be the hopes of getting your mind blown, but like a conversation with an old friend.

SONNY

Time Out, August 1974

The sometime painter, Brooklyn cab driver and Missing Person, Sonny Rollins, unpacks his saxophone in London next week, after an absence that feels like more years than it is. Rollins, who combines the build of a barn door with the volume of a fog-horn, is forty-four now. Such changes as he has made to his playing have invariably been at his own rather phlegmatic pace, so that the hurricane of 'new wave' musicians of pretty mixed virtues that swept through the back half of the Sixties has slightly eclipsed his prominence. Stardom not being something he'd ever strained himself to reach in the first place, it slipped further away with several long and voluntary layoffs from music which prevented him from retaining a working band, and knocked holes in his career.

In the Fifties, with a lot of Charlie Parker's methods on his mind, Rollins was one of the forerunners of a style that later became known as hard-bop – something that sprang up partly as an antidote to the slightly soggy, colourless, 'cool school' of the same time. Musicians like Rollins and Clifford Brown kept the virtuosity of the bebop of the Forties, extended the solo space, and hung most of the improvising on a loose, porous, chordal framework. The result was frequently a hard, sinewy, perversely graceful music, despite Rollins's regular departures at a tangent to the chords, disappearing into a husky, ponderous growl, like an ungainly animal with an itch it can't reach.

It was once written of him that an evening in his company would be far more likely to encompass religion, philosophy, and unconventional health-care than music, because Rollins feels that the music doesn't come without some resolution of all the rest. Accordingly, in 1959, after a string of glittering performances, he went into hibernation for two years. Not long after his return, he went to Japan on a tour, studied with a Zen teacher and developed a lasting interest in yoga. When his recording contract with Impulse lapsed in 1966, he didn't bother to secure himself another, and now seems to have so little interest in recording that only two new albums under his name have surfaced since.

Rollins appears to be engaged in an endless struggle to express himself without mannerism, and yet his raw materials by today's standards are almost archaic. Nine years ago he said he was 'as good now technically as I'm going to get, so the thing to do is to work on myself so I can play me'. Rollins and a saxophone have always looked and sounded inseparable. He has the most personal, idiosyncratic, genial, and instantly recognisable way with shape and tone of anyone in the short but august history of black American music. Self-discipline and a sense of order have never let him parody himself or slip into repetition, nor have they let him get rich.

For some, he lacks the tension and restlessness of Coltrane in his prime, and he never really abandoned rhythm and the frequently flimsy tunes that improvisers used as pegs to hang a style to. He didn't have Trane's hollow, dolorous, occasionally morbid tone, or his blistering intensity. But his sense of humour and the speed of thought that enabled him to build up a spontaneous passage with as much internal strength as if he'd written it out, probably compressed a wider and more colourful slice of life into the narrow and rickety syntax of jazz. Much of his gift is for implication, suggesting notes that he doesn't actually play, glancing off others as if they were liable to scald him, and running through a series of tone changes capable of making the tenor sound like anything from a clarinet to a baritone.

Sonny Rollins's music won't date because the unquenchable vigour and enthusiasm in his nature is always well ahead of his style. If the fire hasn't damped down, and it seems inconceivable, Ronnie Scott's Club is the place to be a fortnight from Monday.

DOLLAR BRAND

Time Out, September 1974

In these early days of Ellington's absence*, everyone suddenly looks dwarfed by his shadow and the recollections that it takes his departure to rekindle. One of his less vaunted achievements was discovering the South African pianist Dollar Brand, a man not all that far from the Duke's own musical notions yet just as much an experimentalist as if he hit the piano strings with crowbars. Lately Brand has blossomed into one of the most humane and heartening keyboard players currently to be heard. On two new albums, both recorded in Germany, he features his own compositions, *Afrikan Space Program* being an extended orchestral piece largely written around an old and memorable tune of his called 'Tintayana' and mostly a long and slightly ragged blow for the soloists; and *Afrikan Sketchbook*, an unbroken solo improvisation. The wild, rolling, hymn-like sound of his songs has been reinforced nowadays with a thick and brood-

ing intensity and this thunderous blend gives *Sketchbook* as precious a balance of simplicity, poetry and warmth as you might hope for: qualities that
contemporary art is sometimes miserly with.

*Duke Ellington had died in New York in May.

BACK ON LINE
Time Out, 1976

Lee Konitz, the wisecracking Chicago altoist now in his fiftieth year, has
thankfully got down to brass tacks again after a fallow period for the rather
frosty West Coast 'cool school'. It is an acquired taste, but the Danish
Steeplechase label has lately been doing what America has neglected to do
and presents Konitz both solo and in partnership with pianist Hal Galper.
The first (*Lone'lee*, Steeplechase) reveals a great deal of the saxophonist's
allegiance to keyboard guru Lennie Tristano in its mesmeric web-spinning
of long melodic lines from simple chords, though at times it shows Konitz
at his bleakest. With Galper – an inventive pianist with more than the current allegiances to Corea, Jarrett and Tyner – Konitz drops much of his
listlessness though his sound is as brittle and yearning as ever. When he
erupts into a triumphant rising coda to the pianist's closing flourish on
Solar, it is as of he'd suddenly wrestled out of a tight coat on a hot day.

Back in the much more toothy and winsome world of nightclub jazz,
there is Zoot Sims (*Motoring Alone*, Sonet). Sims is a tenorist possessed of
a sleek and glossy style, as lazy and measured as a cat stretching, and one
of the trademarks of his long partnership with Al Cohn is a swooping
counterpoint through which the two tenors seem to glide in an infectious,
highfalutin' waltz, Certainly as sharp and breezy an example of this rather
urbane kind of jazz as its fans could wish.

A much more breathless and brow-mopping style is presented by
Buddy Tate and friends on *Kansas City Joys* (Sonet), a more or less routine
celebration of that town's heated Basie-esque swing style, full of beanbag
cymbal rhythms, slamming rimshots, hoarse and bossy tenors hustling
like fairground barkers. Out of it sprang bebop, which is probably more
frequently recorded even now than any other innovation in jazz. *The Bop
Session*, though cut in 1975 with Dizzy Gillespie, Max Roach, Percy Heath,
Hank Jones, John Lewis and Sonny Stitt, actually doesn't do much more
than remind you of better days, but a scalding European session recorded
last March by Charlie Parker's 1946 partner Red Rodney (*Yard's Pad*,
Sonet) shows Rodney to be one of the few originals still willing to risk outrageous cliffhanging in his playing and the result has a great deal more
bounce and tension than you get from the rather casually masterful Dizzy

Gillespie these days. On 'Red Rod' the trumpeter hurtles into a solo as if passing across the stage on the way to catch a plane, and in between eruptions he sidles along in the middle register as if skulking in doorways. Brassmen are much in evidence in the Sonet releases, and Art Farmer and Howard McGhee also get their chances, Farmer in particular managing to create a music that, like Rodney's, belongs naturally to both Then and Now, though of a much more spacious and introspective kind.

BLACK SAINTS

Sounds, June 1976

To judge by Charles Mingus's autobiography (*Beneath the Underdog* – Penguin) the 55-year-old bassist and composer from Watts, Los Angeles has been angry, extravagant, hung-over, and capable of immense tenderness and vulnerability about every aspect of his work and his life.

Mingus strikes many people as being the closest contender to the late Duke Ellington for the jazz composers' crown; and Ellington's inspiration is to be heard not just in the warmth and urgency of the orchestration, but in use of music that tells a story, grows out of the idiosyncrasies of the players in the band, and draws almost exclusively on the jazz tradition alone.

In the Fifties and Sixties Charles Mingus's music also got itself a reputation for being way-out – though in fact Mingus had never gone in for free-jazz in a big way or strayed far from blues and gospel music in his compositions. From those days to this, Mingus's music has kept turning up the same intriguing trick – conjuring the richest of orchestral textures from a handful of instruments (economies and his own pugnacity have prevented him from running large orchestras for long). On top of all that, he's one of the finest virtuoso double-bass players in all jazz. It's a gift that has frequently made his soloists sound even better than they are.

Now that the American Broadcasting Company are farming out their excellent Impulse label at last, records like Mingus's *Black Saint and Sinner Lady* no longer have to be on the import list – it's included on the latest batch of Impulse albums now marketed by Anchor Records.

Since it was made in 1963 *Black Saint* has regularly been mentioned in despatches as Charles Mingus's crowning achievement, and it certainly has more cohesiveness than anything else he's written. Side One mostly acts as a kind of prolonged overture, so it's the second side where the band really starts to steam. Charlie Mariano on alto and Mingus on piano get most of the soloing – the saxophonist skating gently in and out of pumping rifts from what sounds like a colossal brass section but actually only numbers two trumpets, one trombone and a tuba.

The resemblances to Ellington also stem from Quentin Jackson's presence on trombone – Jackson replaced Tricky Sam Nanton in Ellington's own band and duplicated a good deal of his plunger mute style, the sort of thing that sounds like an indignant sea-lion.

A good deal of the variety and power to surprise that jazz had in the early Sixties was made possible by a cherishing of space and silence (free music, not being hamstrung by galloping drummers, is recovering a lot of it) and the whole cooling-out approach was exemplified by a record like Miles Davis's *Kind Of Blue*.

All of this is much in favour on Oliver Nelson's *Blues and the Abstract Truth* (Impulse). Nelson cut this album in 1961 before hitching his fortunes to the Jimmy Smith circus, an ailment from which he never recovered. Nelson's best-known tune 'Stolen Moments' opens the record, and still purrs irresistibly fourteen years later.

In the band are Eric Dolphy, Freddie Hubbard and Bill Evans, with Roy Haynes on drums. Hubbard, hardly out of short pants at the time, is masterly – full of bright ideas and perfect timing, faultless at the fastest tempo. Dolphy's creaking and restive sound on alto rubs up against Nelson's arrangements, and Evans dabs fastidiously at the keyboard as if trying not to leave his prints on it.

STILL BLOWING

Sounds, November 1976

Roland Kirk, who wound up a fortnight's season at Ronnie Scott's last week, seems fated to remain a highwire act in jazz. A stunning technique gave him the freedom to play pretty much anything he wanted, including three reed instruments simultaneously, and sometimes even different tunes on two of them.

But all this was never just flash. A born entertainer rather than a stone-faced master saxophonist, Kirk's performances were whirling displays of half-audible monologues on any subject that entered his head, a combination of scat-singing and flute playing, headlong tenor solos with his cheeks and neck muscles pumping like bellows, invitations to the rest of the band blown on hooters, whistles, duck-calls or any of the other paraphemalia he took to the stage with. He radiated energy, and he swept his audience with him.

This time though, things are different. Ron Burton, Kirk's sensitive and stylish accompanist has gone from the piano, though he's ably replaced by the young Hilton Ruiz – a musician in the manner of McCoy Tyner. But the Vibration Society has slowed down to suit the changed world of its leader, and Michael Hill, a silky but occasionally erratic singer, is added to take some of the strain. Because ironically, after decades of audience astonishment about his ability to play three instruments at once, Roland Kirk has now been hit by a stroke that has left him one-handed – so now they ask 'How the hell do you play an instrument at all?' There are notes on the horn that a one-handed man ought not to be able to make, but make them he still does. Kirk now plays a flute curved like a hockey stick so that the keys are vertical. Electronics might ease him over some of the obstacles, but Kirk hates their use in jazz. The foundation of his music – he calls it 'black classical music' – is still intact; and searching now for what has suddenly become just out of reach after being on top of it for so long, has given Kirk's formerly dazzling music a tension it has rarely had. The Vibration Society wasn't flying like the old days, but I'll think I'll remember this gig.

VARIABILITY

The Sunday Times, April 1977

Hell hath no fury like a jazz audience that thinks it's at the wrong show, so last week's Camden Festival series of concerts at the Shaw Theatre got off to a turbulent start on Monday when a local free-jazz group (Keith Tippett's Ark) and a flashy American big band (Clark Terry's) found themselves on the same premises. Pairing the London Sinfonietta with the Syd Lawrence Orchestra could hardly have caused more aggravation.

This was unfortunate for Tippett and his musicians, who had not only played pretty well in a sombre and restless kind of way, but had contrived to build their hour-long set into some sort of cohesive whole. Terry's band, despite the leader's fleet and glistening flugelhorn style, had slipped into the groove of the barnstorming big-band by adopting a cocky, elbowing manner that was both relentless and routine at once. Unlike Count Basie's Orchestra for instance, it stuck to the letter rather than the spirit of jazz – which made the reaction to Keith Tippett's ragged but ambitious performance something of a paradox.

As happens in all jazz festivals, there were some chilly and closeted affairs for brilliant technicians as well – like Tuesday's quartet led by the 50-year-old bop guitarist Jimmy Raney and his son Doug. Notes cascaded from the stage like ping-pong balls, and the contrapuntal passages between the two guitarists occasionally resembled a pair of cattle auctioneers sharing a microphone. Chris McGregor's Blue Notes, an African band that combines home-grown *kwela* music with post-Ornette Coleman jazz brought the gig to the boil with a blistering and truculent set that had exactly the combination of infectious confidence and open-handed spontaneity that is so elusive and essential in jazz.

It was briefly caught by the enormous London Jazz Composers' Orchestra (Thursday) – a mixture of jazz and modern conservatoire methods that frequently rumbles away like somebody moving sideboards in an upstairs room, but occasionally uses its harsh, atonal scores to bludgeon the soloists into sounding quite unlike themselves.

Despite the presence of a popular John Dankworth ensemble that was really a fairly bland and camouflaged jazz-rock group with strings, Friday's concert was already stolen by an irresistible performance of 'Under Milk Wood' from the redoubtable Stan Tracey's quartet. Though one of the pianist's earlier enterprises, this suite is probably being played better now than it's ever been. The variety of the Jazz Centre Society's Camden programme certainly reminded the packed houses that jazz continues to be a term more handy than definitive.

NAMYSLOWSKI

The Guardian, March 1978

Just about the most over-cooked chestnut on the menu of current jazz controversies is the one about whether rock music has had anything useful to offer to jazz. On the second of the Camden Jazz Week's concerts, shared by the Polish saxophonist Zbigniew Namyslowski and the nine-piece band led by Elton Dean, both sides of the argument were there if you were looking for them, but the outcome was still deuce.

Namyslowski's group opened the concert and mostly played an orderly, deliberate kind of jazz-rock. Namyslowski's style is so varied as to border on a dispassionate case-history of recent jazz saxophone if it weren't for a distinctive tone that at times makes the alto sound as gruff as the tenor, and gives his playing a sweep from the raw to the demure that takes in Jimmy Guiffre, Dexter Gordon, blues saxophonists, occasionally even Ornette Coleman. He wound up with a very fast, gipsy-like tune in which the rhythm section soon skidded to a halt and left him to whirl on alone through a stretch of quick-silver bebop alto playing that revealed how deep and instinctive his grasp of that idiom is, even though he keeps it well in the background of his playing these days.

After Namyslowski's thoughtful, rather expository performance, Elton Dean's Ninesense arrived for the second half like a collection of gate-crashers, but revealed – not least because of the presence of the pianist Keith Tippett and the explosive drummer Louis Moholo – that it's still one of this country's most spirited, raucous and spontaneous bands. Tippett's contribution is often to perform spontaneously what an orchestration would be obliged to furnish in a band more straitlaced than this.

BREUKER
The Guardian, March 1978

Eric Morecambe's contention that *Hamlet* was all right but a bit short of laughs would have rung a bell with the avant-garde of Dutch improvising musicians – that rather sombre combination of Sixties American jazz and European conservatoire music that has influenced many young players on this side of the Atlantic has generally bypassed the Dutch, who go to work with their tongues firmly planted in their cheeks. The contrast was neatly encapsulated by last night's performance by the Tony Oxley quartet opposite the 11-piece Kollektief led by the Dutch reed player Willem Breuker.

Oxley's group played the first half, featuring the leader on amplified percussion and violin, Barry Guy on bass, Phil Wachsmann on violin and Larry Stabbins on saxophones. Oxley's kit enables him to play both conventional drums (at which he has few rivals in Europe) and the kind of electronic effects that can sound like anything from windows breaking to somebody trying to tune a radio. But his group's performance was by and large a scorching and rather brutal affair.

Breuker's band was formed seven years ago, and the ensemble has always been as much involved in music theatre as it has been in pure improvisation, Breuker having written compositions for productions of works by Brecht and Peter Handke. His music on this occasion turned out to be a mixture of vaudeville routines, dance rhythms, circus music and cod-casbah ditties for which one of the band optimistically addressed the soprano sax to a snake-basket.

Breuker's band isn't going to change the course of European music in quite the way that Oxley's group sounded as if it had promised itself to attempt (the Kollektief in fact spends most of its time dusting off history), but everybody sounded as if they were having the time of their lives.

WILLPOWER
The Guardian, July 1978

Bracknell, that fearsome agglomeration of roundabouts, no-entry signs, parking lots and windswept precincts, could be considered something of an armpit of a town at the best of times but on a grey and drizzing July day, the circumstances conspired to make enthusiasm for the town's fourth jazz festival a triumph of the will. The arrival of the great American saxophonist Ornette Coleman was the light at the end of the tunnel on the festival's first day, the groundwork being done by several excellent British bands. As it happened, Coleman was more than challenged by the musicians who preceded him – like Elton Dean's Ninesense, a collection of contemporary players whose infectious and open-hearted themes made the bridges between free-playing and composition so apparently natural that its excursions into atonality never rattled the crowd.

The rain was cascading off the tent roof by the time Ornette Coleman's Prime Time band took to the stage. After a bit of preliminary feinting and weaving, his sextet (two guitars, two drummers, bass and Coleman on alto, violin and trumpet) launched into a thunderous rock-pulse in which the drummers – Ronald Shannon Jackson and the leader's son Denardo – set up a furore of cross-rhythms and the guitars maintained a curious, clattering accompaniment that came to resemble a kind of coded version of the accents in Coleman's own horn playing. In this respect, Coleman has once again pulled off a coup by creating a rock band that only barely plays like one.

But despite the audacity and swing of Jackson in particular, the group – which played like one big rhythm section throughout – eventually acquired an obstinate, bludgeoning sound, Coleman seemed cramped for musical space and was often inaudible, and there was little enough of the kind of collective variety that the leader has presumably opted for in taking a direction so discouraging to his own genius for improvisation.

ROMANCE

The Guardian, August 1978

Of all the precocious American saxophone stars to have flourished in the back-to-the roots movement inspired by the directness and raw eloquence of men like Albert Ayler, one of the youngest and brightest is tenorist David Murray – a man already possessed of the rare knack of making himself recognisable from his first few notes. Murray is the perfect riposte to the view still occasionally swatted around that the avant-garde's cavalier attitude to form would turn its adherents into musical illiterates with no roots. A formidable free-player, who generates the most ferocious heat, Murray also has at his fingertips the sensuous touch of all the romantics of the tenor.

Though his eerie, quavering tone is very reminiscent of Ayler, Murray has absorbed recent innovations in saxophone technique to the point where his high-register playing is as firm, piercing and controlled as a trumpeter. His second British appearance within a month featured him with his own band, which delivered two hours of subtle but muscular music. Much of it was conventional swing, much of it of consummate skill (particularly the drumming of Clifford Jarvis), and much of it extremely beautiful. The only catch was that some of the expressiveness that Murray can reveal unaccompanied was swamped by the energy of his quintet, and he probably played just a shade too long. But the band – working with a mixture of collective improvisation, orthodox soloing and a repertoire of taut and strivingly amiable tunes – was almost arrogantly on top of its demanding and audacious methods. Jarvis was apparently making his first appearance in this company but his loose-flowing style, unperturbed by the fastest tempos, was an effortless and assured as if Murray's music had been his life's work.

Fiesta

The Guardian, May 1979

Ronnie Scott, the downbeat, wisecracking saxophonist and nightclub proprietor, celebrated twenty invaluable years in the risky business of presenting an uncommercial music in commercial surroundings with a South Bank concert featuring his own quartet, Art Blakey's Jazz Messengers and a big band led by the swing drummer Buddy Rich.

Curiously, out of these three, it has been Scott's own band that has shown the most evidence of gradual change, moving from a hard and expansive swing to something close to contemplativeness recently. His opening set for this gig was pensive to the point of diffidence.

Blakey, who followed Scott in the first half, had no such inclination to hide his light and the group delivered the usual jubilant and fiesta-like performance. The Jazz Messengers have always thrown all their energies into a routine of climax and relaxation, every chorus of the skeletal tunes in the repertoire being embroidered first with Blakey padding contentedly in the soloist's wake, then inserting a string of seething rolls like gravel being tipped on to glass, finally drenching the whole affair in a furore of noise from which the business is recycled again. It works like a charm.

Buddy Rich's orchestra provides very little of the spontaneous feel you get from musicians such as saxophonist Dave Schnitter and pianist James Williams in Blakey's group. Consequently, Rich's concerts are almost always a disappointment to anyone who isn't sold on streamlined swing bands and drum spectaculars. Nevertheless, the drummer's elegant way of starting his tunes off is so relaxed that the openings could go on all night and say goodbye to the pumping riffs and crackling brass. In all this swagger and flash, the remarkable Mr Rich performs with about as much superfluous movement as if he were sorting mail.

EXOTICA

The Guardian, September 1979

For a musician of fairly exotic interest, the reed player Yusef Lateef has picked some pretty run-of-the-mill circumstances to work in, if his records are anything to go by. Yet Lateef's own playing, full of rare inflections, has never blended comfortably with the effusive clack and rattle of jazz-rock.

As he is currently proving at Ronnie Scott's, he is a fascinating improviser, with a thin, brittle and slightly querulous tone to his soprano playing and a mobility, richness of reference and fondness for the blues on the tenor that rather resembles a latter-day Archie Shepp. Lateef's enthusiasm for the phraseology of Middle Eastern music as well as jazz (an influence that came to him along with his adoption of the Muslim faith in the late Forties) has led him to play an eerie, displaced kind of mutant bebop and and techniques inherited from Charlie Parker and the obligations of getting his tongue around the ethnic reed instruments he favours, have nourished each other just about equally.

Lateef is in London until the end of next week, in the company of a pianist (Caleb Moss), a bass guitarist (Don Pate) and a drummer (Marty Barker). At first he seemed content merely to rattle the audience with the occasional raunchy blues licks and a few special effects in the form of ghostly whispers delivered on the wooden flute. But by his second set on Monday night, it soon became apparent that both Lateef's own personal strengths (the languid development of the theme, the lazy sway of his timekeeping, the fascination of his sound, which is like somebody speaking a familiar language in an unfamiliar accent) and the sparkiness of the rhythm section were making subtle transformations to some thoroughly travel weary materials.

PRIVATE LIFE

The Guardian, November 1979

The atmosphere of jazz-funk is established by the dance-pulse, the instrumentation and increasingly by the studio facilities. If an improvising player subverts the idiom too much, it is a fast route to unemployment; if the player cohabits with it too much, the personality is apt to melt in the glow.

The latter is a development that – in their recorded work at least – has struck two very great saxophone players indeed: Wayne Shorter (late of the wonderful Miles Davis bands of the middle Sixties and a current member of the jazz-rock band Weather Report) and Jackie McLean, the boppish alto saxophonist who recently visited this country to considerable acclaim during the Camden Jazz Week.

McLean's trip to London, with one of the most technically accomplished bands he could possibly have assembled (including the gifted Spanish pianist Tete Montoliu and percussionist Billy Higgins, one of the most musical drummers to be heard) brought an almost audible sigh of relief from those of his fans who had heard *Monuments* (RCA). McLean as good as declared in a recent *Downbeat* interview that people shouldn't attach much importance to it. The album rustles with angelic choirs, laconic monologues on absent friends, and such an overwhelming sensation of stagey Good Times that McLean's own playing – tumbling and agile as it is – is only fitfully discernible.

Weather Report, which has consistently demonstrated itself to be – on record at least – the most exciting and original band to have been thrown up by the whole jazz-rock movement, has released a double album (*8.30*, CBS) of fave raves from recent concert tours. As a result the band's customarily other-worldly quality is slightly undermined by a background noise that sounds like a football crowd, and a good many self-conscious special effects – thunderclaps, noises like police sirens, hovering UFOs, hysterical synthesisers. There are also some longueurs such as the laboriously-developing 'Scarlet Woman', once a startling composition. It must be difficult, when a band gets this big, not to treat the audience's reactions to familiar signals in a rather dispassionate, Pavlovian manner.

Nevertheless, the old charm still lingers. The band's strengths have always been a collective sound that bursts with vitality, some inspired writing, and an appetite for variation that is rare in the idiom, and enough of it is left to save *8.30* from the appeal of simple reminiscence. Wayne Shorter's saxophone has long had little more than a walk-on part with this band, but on pianist Joe Zawinul's ballad 'A Remark You Made', his sound is so fragile and melancholic as to seem to be rolling towards you over a darkening sea.

Zawinul, who makes electronic instrumentation on sound about as musical as it ever can, gets chords to sound like humming tops gradually slowing down. 'In a Silent Way', which was the title tune of one of Miles Davis's earliest and most haunting rock records, finds Zawinul's souped-up keyboards booming like an orchestra. Shorter's thin, keening soprano curls wraith-like around it.

The *Jan Garbarek Group* (ECM) is a quintet featuring the excellent Norwegian saxophonist: a man who, in an age when keyboard players like Zawinul are doing their best to sound like saxophonists, seems to have very little trouble sounding like an electronic keyboard with just a regular saxophone. Garbarek is unquestionably unique. None of his devices are tiresome, few are borrowed; and his sound – frosty, and faintly malevolent – is hypnotic and seductive in an unnerving rabbit-and-snake kind of way.

In the company of the delicately intelligent guitarist Bill Connors, the resourceful British pianist John Taylor and the German bassist Eberhard

Weber, Garbarek's characteristic edge manages to overcome the frequently languid air of ECM sessions, though he is inclined to open one too many tunes by sidling quietly past the rhythm section's rather sepulchral introductions like a latecomer entering a church unnoticed.

Also on ECM is *Arcade* (ECM), a quartet session led by a young guitarist of real nerve and maturity, John Abercrombie. Abercrombie's previous albums have naturally gained much of their punch from the presence of Dave Holland and Jack DeJohnette on bass and drums, a benefit now withdrawn. But in pianist Richie Beirach, who attractively resembles mid-Sixties Herbie Hancock, the guitarist has a partner to match his melodic ingenuity. Only the sudden disinclination to swing causes a twinge of disappointment.

DIALECTS
The Guardian, October 1979

The ability to think in a tongue other than the one you were raised with is apt to emerge long after mere fluency with the vocabulary. This is an inhibition especially liable to afflict classically trained players who take to jazz, and a concert at the Riverside Studios illustrated it.

The idioms of the gig were virtually all down-the-line modern jazz, blues, Latin funk à la Chick Corea, old chestnuts like 'Autumn Leaves', 'Green Dolphin Street' and 'Round Midnight', Coltraneish modal pieces like John Surman's 'Winter Song'. But this repertoire, which would have been at home in any cocktails-and-pretzels establishment on the planet, was being delivered by the odd combination of a sleek and shiny New York piano trio (Jay Bianchi's), a young British classical flautist (David Heath) and an even younger British classical violinist (the Royal Philharmonic Orchestra's Nigel Kennedy).

Bianchi was erudite, meticulous, elegant and restrained, close in melodic approach to Chick Corea, but more fond of the frills, arpeggios and block-chord playing of the swing pianists. Heath was adroit and lyrical, disposed to bugging the flute so that it sounded like a keyboard instrument, his sound more engaging than his improvisation.

Kennedy, a shy, puckish individual, who comported himself as if he were standing in the wings rather than the spotlight, had his limitations in this territory too, but they were the kind of limitations that made your ears prick up. The music he played was so detached from the mannerisms of jazz, so cavalier about the straitjacket of chordal improvisation and indifferent to the romanticism of the violin as to almost surmount the discomfort with uptempo swing that led him to repeat the same string of crescendos time after time.

1980s

T hough many suspected its sincerity as an unaccustomed embrace, international appreciation of jazz expanded fast in the Eighties. More jazz records were bought, older listeners who had put their jazz collections in the attic brought them down again, and younger listeners sought role models in a stream of talented, technically astonishing newcomers emerging from a strengthened jazz college system. This new enthusiasm not only put neon-lit names to new faces, but rejuvenated the careers of veteran players such as Dexter Gordon, Art Blakey, Horace Silver and Johnny Griffin.

This renewal happened against the background of a rapidly evolving international music community. The Eighties was the decade of 'world music', in which faster communications further shrank the globe, growing understanding between Western and non-Western cultures accelerated the sharing of musical languages, and traditional frontiers between 'high' and 'popular' art relaxed. For the first time, jazz became a truly international language without the old pecking order of nations that could and couldn't swing. Russian jazz musicians toured the States; American jazz musicians collaborated with Europeans; Australians, Japanese, South Africans and Bulgarians were increasingly at ease with vocabularies coined in Harlem and Kansas City, and even more enthusiastically invented new ones of their own. Scandinavian saxophonist Jan Garbarek mixed Coltrane's haunting tenor sound with North European folk music including elements such as the cattle-calls of Norway. Ever more technically skilled newcomers treated Parker's and Coltrane's innovations as valuable preparation, a starting point rather than an ultimate destination.

The heartbeat of the comeback was bebop. Dismissed by many as anti-jazz or even anti-music in the early Forties, it became the gracefully swinging idiom that most casual listeners identified as the sound of jazz. The world of 52nd Street clubs and the spreading bohemianism of 'modern jazz' in the postwar era was far enough in the past to be reinvented in semi-fictional late-Eighties feature films such as Clint Eastwood's *Bird!* (devoted to Charlie Parker) and Bertrand Tavernier's *Round Midnight*.

Portraying the central figure (modelled on Lester Young), this movie turned saxophone star Dexter Gordon into more of a celebrity as an actor than he had been as a player.

New interest in the era that spawned bop brought back some of its most powerful, experienced practitioners, proving that in the years when their styles were supposed to be dead they had been making fine music. Among the most powerful was Joe Henderson, one of the few saxophonists with an approach similar to Sonny Rollins. Trumpeter Woody Shaw was an older bop-oriented master, who had worked in Paris with one of the idiom's founders, drummer Kenny Clarke. Like fellow trumpeter Freddie Hubbard, who swung back from mostly routine fusion to some inspired straight-ahead playing, Shaw had a brilliant technique, warm tone and an improviser's imagination that could project way beyond the next four bars. Something of Shaw's desire to extend the regular bounds of bop was long a feature of the group led by tenorist George Adams and pianist Don Pullen, prolific ex-Mingus sidemen, who ran a band from 1979 to 1989 with the rhythmic propulsion of another Mingus legend, drummer Dannie Richmond, driving it on. The Adams-Pullen group unfailingly delivered thrilling blends of free music, blues, bop, and down-the-line swing, which were only silenced by Richmond's death.

After years of adding his own delicate flourishes to others' records, saxophonist Mike Brecker waited until he was thirty-eight to make a superb debut album in 1987, which tellingly mixed bop and bursts of Coltraneish fire, and featured a spectacular band including guitarist Pat Metheny. For all his lyrical soft-fusion reputation, Metheny was one of the great bop improvisers of his generation, occasionally demonstrated in a powerhouse straight-jazz trio with drummer Roy Haynes and bassist Dave Holland. McCoy Tyner, a consistently strong, committed performer since his days with Coltrane, was also fervently active, occasionally with a hard-swinging and imaginative big band.

Other pianists – Joanne Brackeen, Steve Kuhn, Geri Allen and Keith Jarrett – hit independent routes. Allen emerged as a virtuoso performer, mingling the rich keyboard voicing of Bill Evans with a steely, rational resolve and occasional Monk-like truculence. Jarrett continued to be one of the era's most remarkable phenomena. Since the running success of his 1975 *Koln Concert*, Jarrett had continued to attract big audiences for an intense acoustic music. He spent the period in astonishing productivity with solo piano recitals and small-group shows with his Standards Trio.

But it was not just older listeners and a new cognoscenti who supported the revival. Teenage dancers and young DJs in cities around the world discovered the hard-bop records of the Fifties and Sixties, and a nightclub scene sprang up that depended heavily on classic jazz records – even very rare ones on 1970s labels such as Black Jazz, Strata East and Flying Dutchman. They mixed standards with funk, rap and Latin grooves. Teenagers learned that Art Blakey could not only put a beat under a band that sent the music into orbit, but was still alive and hurtling on with it in the 1980s. Blakey had always been a sorcerer, with an ever-changing roster of gifted apprentices and his ardent, bluesy bands were still packed with rising young stars. From 1980, his Jazz Messengers included trumpeter Wynton Marsalis and his saxophonist brother Branford.

Wynton Marsalis spearheaded a movement that came to be bracketed as neo-classical, and a search for his musical roots obsessed him through the 1980s. A brilliant technician, at home in classical music and jazz, he spent the decade working back from bop-oriented jazz and the influence of Miles Davis's acoustic bands to a sound recalling the ensemble voicings of early New Orleans, with the group approach of Charles Mingus. He also began to develop his ensemble writing.

If Marsalis was investigating virtually all jazz, regardless of the era, to find a voice, others made their journeys to sources more limited in focus. The mainstream style, which in the Fifties meant musicians who played like cut-down Basie swing bands, embraced couplings of swing and other idioms. Saxophonist Scott Hamilton and trumpeters Ruby Braff and Warren Vache were lyrical and rhythmically effortless exponents. Some younger players, who were also inspired by the past but who spliced styles together in a less scholarly way, formed highly entertaining, theatrical outfits. One of the most irrepressible was the Louisiana-based Dirty Dozen Brass Band, a fresh and exuberant young eight-piece that delivered Cajun music, funk and bop in unpredictable proportions.

Apart from young American virtuosi, such as the measured, mature, trumpet prodigy Roy Hargrove, the Blakey-like Harper Brothers, and the hauntingly Miles Davis-like Wallace Roney, vigorous neo-bop

developments took place outside the States. Britain produced an evocative, technically remarkable saxophonist in Courtney Pine – whose work
drew together Coltrane, African pop music, and reggae from his West
Indian parents' homeland – and the quirkily melodic saxophonist Andy
Sheppard. There was also London pianist Julian Joseph, an inspired interpreter of a relaxed, Herbie Hancockish style. Pine and Sheppard worked
in home-grown big bands too, reflecting creative blends of the looseness
of Charles Mingus's ensemble, elements of free jazz, and local references
of their own.

Meanwhile fusion, the triumphant instrumental music of the Seventies
had not gone away. Sometimes criticised for rigidities of structure that
cramped improvisation, and for sacrificing the loose, surging rhythms of
jazz to a hard, inexorable backbeat, fusion and acoustic jazz techniques
increasingly began to meet on equal terms.

The big news at the beginning of the 1980s was that Miles Davis was
returning after a five-year layoff due to ill-health and creative exhaustion.
Davis sounded hesitant, and his music was ostensibly oriented towards
winning airplay on black radio stations. But though his power to stun an
audience with a single note had diminished, Cyndi Lauper's 'Time After
Time' on the 1984 album *You're Under Arrest* demonstrated that Davis had
recovered much of his old lyricism. On the same record, the guitarist John
Scofield combined bop-like melodies with a funky beat and bass lines in a
promise of a revitalised jazz. Scofield became one of the most interesting
guitarist/composers of the era.

Weather Report, the longest-lasting and frequently most musical of
fusion bands, broke up in 1985, though it released its influential saxophonist Wayne Shorter to recover his muscular way of playing and
composing with his own bands. Pianist Chick Corea began to divide his
time between an acoustic and an electric band, and soul-sax star David
Sanborn made the jazzy album *Another Hand* in the Eighties as a startling
personal departure from his more pop-oriented style.

All these musicians seem to have been consolidating music of the
Seventies. Despite the fact that his health was failing, Miles Davis kept
looking forward. His posthumously completed last record, *Doo-Bop*,
reflected the dance rhythms of hip hop and insistent, emphatic accents
of rap. Though some of it was self-congratulatory, Davis's solos were as

jazz-like as anything he had recorded in twenty-five years and suggested one way that contemporary jazz might go.

Young musicians, like members of New York's M-Base collective, also searched for meeting points between the jazz tradition and new black American dance music. Saxophonist Steve Coleman, a devastating bop player as likely to quote James Brown as Charlie Parker when asked about his influences, formed the Five Elements band and developed a music in which shifting rhythmic patterns drawn from funk seemed to replace older notions of melody. Gary Thomas and Greg Osby, two other M-Base saxophonists, explored similar ground, Osby occasionally finding inspiration among the young hip-hop and dance-jazz musicians developing their own sound in London. Cassandra Wilson, an agile, fierce-toned singer influenced by New York street sounds, funk and Betty Carter, was a major international talent spawned by the M-Base ethos in the Eighties. And Betty Carter, the doyenne of jazz vocalists after the death of Sarah Vaughan and the decline in health of Ella Fitzgerald, continued to tour the world with a spine-chillingly dramatic, personal show that recalled Billie Holiday.

Not all Eighties developments were what most listeners might describe as jazz, yet the sound and approach towards spontaneous music-making were sufficiently identifiable as a jazz line for the term to fit. All over the world, the free-improvised music that was generated in the Sixties and early Seventies had released jazz-oriented musicians in many cultures to find their own voices. In Europe, a highly sophisticated free scene developed, players from different countries working together in ever-changing bands. Pianist Cecil Taylor, one of the geniuses of the American avant-garde, worked fruitfully in Europe with local players. In New York, the composer John Zorn developed music impossible to categorise but significantly motivated by the Euro free scene. Zorn depended on improvisers, and his listening habits put Japanese pop next to Bobby McFerrin, next to reggae, next to hard-core punk. It became obvious from the Eighties on that younger musicians were increasingly listening to music in the same flexible way.

From Jazz, *by John Fordham (Dorling Kindersley, 1993)*

1980-83

At the beginning of the 1980s, some courses in the jazz firmament continued to be charted in time-honoured ways (big-time American touring packages would traverse Europe's concert halls every summer, bringing the music's veteran Great and Good, like Count Basie and Ella Fitzgerald, and tireless travelling bands like hard-bopper Art Blakey's would appear at Ronnie Scott's), and some were being investigated for the first time. The Blakey band's appearance on London's Camden Jazz Week in 1981 occasioned passing mention of a startling new trumpeter in the Messengers' ranks – Wynton Marsalis.

At the more abstract end, public arts funding for jazz and improvised musics had increased throughout Europe, often from departments of the arts bureaux also dealing with contemporary classical work. This led to a general increase in activity – and interactivity – on the European free-music scene, with more festivals, more recordings, and more pooling of ideas between performers of different nations. British avant-garde musicians, particularly, reported that only by constant travel throughout Europe could they sustain a living. But they also remarked on the stimulating effect of such loose cross-cultural exchange.

Miles Davis came back. This was certainly the biggest news on the world jazz stage at the beginning of the Eighties. Having locked himself in his house for much of the latter part of the previous decade, sustaining contact with the world (to judge by his autobiography) only via a trusted inner sanctum of musicians, cocaine-couriers and a rather more catholic assortment of sexual partners, he returned to public performance at 1981's Kool Jazz Festival, and appeared in Britain the following year. He looked frail, played sparingly, and his group pursued funk routines that couldn't be compared to the rhythmic dynamism of his pre-1970s bands, but he was there, and his horn still sounded unique.

A few months later in that same summer of 1982, the virtuoso trumpeter Wynton Marsalis, then just twenty years old, led his own band on an international tour for the first time. When he played in Britain, in a style devoted to the Miles Davis group sound of fifteen years previously, but displaying trumpet playing of an astonishing maturity and eloquence, he started a ball rolling that still rolls now. Young musicians everywhere saw in him an inspiration. He not only sounded completely, devastatingly, in command of himself and his instrument, he looked as if he was in command of his aspirations and his destination in the profession. 'Respect' was a word that gained a gathering resonance in black street-speak during the period of Eighties' recessionary economics in which respect of all kinds became increasingly hard to win. For young jazz musicians, black or white, Wynton Marsalis looked and sounded like a young man who had it covered.

Marsalis got it right in all respects (showing dazzling skill in both jazz and classical music) except distinctive creativity. But if the wind wasn't blowing their way yet, other gifted musicians pursued their own paths. The drummer Jack DeJohnette formed one of the great offbeat fusion bands with Special Edition. The singer Betty Carter sidestepped commercial difficulties by starting her own record label, and put herself back in contention with appearances in the musical Don't Call Me Man. And early warnings of a much tougher, wilder form of fusion yet to come emerged in the form of drummer Ronald Shannon Jackson's Decoding Society.

DOLLAR BRAND
The Guardian, March 1980

When Dollar Brand, the quiet, dignified pianist from Cape Town, plays a solo concert, there's definitely magic in the air. His music draws on the orchestral pianists such as Thelonious Monk and Duke Ellington, and has a universal appeal that is very rare for postwar jazz players. Sailing on Brand's wide and winding river are all the reveries, passions, reminiscences and frustrations of South African life.

On Friday, at a concert for the African National Congress, Brand – who has now formally adopted his Muslim name of Abdullah Ibrahim – coaxed out the same old irresistible spell. His music is a mixture of thunderous, percussive hammering of the bass chords which makes the piano resemble a vast string section all pursuing a crescendo, and piquant, understated melodies, most of which resemble hymns. Late in the performance, after a series of rippling meditations, urgent drumlike admonitions and quietly persuasive songs, he played a medley of Monk tunes at which his music took on the crisper, more formal quality of orthodox jazz improvisation.

It was, as ever, an occasion at which you felt that Brand had bared his soul as unreservedly as a musician can. The only intrusion into the dignity of the proceedings came from the MC for the night, who not only made a string of spectacularly impenetrable announcements in the anguished falsetto of a man who suspects that his trousers are on fire, but was three times defeated in the attempt to find his way back through the curtain. It was a performance worthy of *The Muppet Show* and was – deservedly – just as affectionately received.

ALWAYS YEAR ZERO

The Guardian, April 1980

Derek Bailey, the wry and lugubrious ex-session guitarist from Sheffield (Gracie Fields and Kathy Kirby, to name an incongruous few, had the benefit of his services in the days before he elected to shun the commercial music business for keeps) was talking once about that cycle of nascent imagination, maturity and decay which the avant-garde seems to pass through almost in the batting of an eyelid. Any improvising band will be all right, he opined, until the day when it Discovers Its Music. At this point everybody within earshot – the press, the punters, the promoters, the musicians themselves – will get embroiled in the obsessive chemistry of coagulating the band's new found 'identity'. Bailey hoped for a music that would keep on exterminating such creations before they could swallow their parents.

But what he preoccupied himself with resisting has, of course, already happened to the first wave of British avant-garde jazz to abandon the strictures of orthodox form. The music that was produced by that early constellation of pioneers which included Evan Parker, Tony Oxley, Howard Riley and Barry Guy has now established its vocabulary and is concentrating on investigating how many new combinations of dialect and conversational gambits it can have with it. Such refinements are frequently chortled at by fans of the notion of permanent revolution (and any innocent music-lover who had never heard of such things would be staggered at the idea that the early work could ever have come to be described as conservative) but the fact remains that the original members of the London Musicians' Cooperative of 1970 produced, and still produce, some of the most exciting improvised music of recent times.

An early instance is the reissue of the London Jazz Composers' Orchestra's *Ode* (Incus Records, 6/7), recovered in honour of its recent appearance on the Camden Jazz Week. The band's music is broadly based on a lattice-work of graphic scores, and its predominant quality has always tended to be a thunderous and malevolent tramping around of the trombones and deeper reeds, through which the gentler instruments bob and tumble like small craft in a typhoon.

Breaking up into a succession of improvisations between smaller groups of players, the session enables you to rediscover all the extraordinary instrumental departures that were making their first headlong flights at the time: Paul Rutherford's eel-like melodic lines on the trombone, Evan Parker's guttural tenor harangues, Tony Oxley's sense of drama and surprise on percussion. All these virtuosi may have acquired the elegance of maturity over the eight years since this recording was made, but the rough edges only enhance its eerie compulsiveness. Guy's band was seen as something of a Frankenstein's monster at the time, but hearing this set again is a delightful surprise.

Something rather less varied from much the same territory is *Circadian Rhythms* (Incus, 33), a set of three extracts from a thirteen-hour concert that was performed at Camden Town's London Musicians' Collective in the summer of 1978. The event was a compromise on saxophonist Evan Parker's original intention to play around the clock, and the whole event smacked disconcertingly of that contemplative, organic, woolly-hat happening so beloved of refugees from the middle Sixties. The general dynamic of long improvised concerts for large groups of musicians playing small-scale instruments (percussion, home-made instruments, found objects) is a great deal of caution and musical pussyfooting around, from time to time illuminated by flares of brief passion, but the effect is rather as if someone were tiptoeing around a house in the dark, occasionally bumping into crates of milkbottles, empty dustbins and dolorous ghosts dragging chains. However, but for moments of inspired juxtaposition such as the long, ponderous alpine-horn noise accompanied by the strikers of twangy, nervous-sounding piano wire devices, the all-round effect is desultory.

The drawing of mainstream saxophonist and clarinettist Tony Coe (you hear his sultry tenor on the *Pink Panther* theme) into the orbit of Derek Bailey's Company was almost as significant an inclusion as the Americans Anthony Braxton, Steve Lacy and Leo Smith in ensuring that the band could never be the kind of musical collective that could repress or deny its cultural past in jazz. *Time* (Incus, 34) celebrates Coe's shy, fawn-like lyricism and reveals Bailey's startling sensitivity to partnerships, for all his frequently avowed enthusiasm for musical dogfights. Behind his famous crabwise swing and glimmering harmonics there is a participatory quality that almost resembles a counterpoint. To such permanent revolutionists, such things are revisionism indeed.

FIESTA

The Guardian, April 1980

Like a sermon, a drama, a stand-up comedy routine and a history lecture all at once, the Art Ensemble of Chicago never lets you rest. Regarded by some as the contemporary jazz group that embodies and projects the essence of the music as no other can, the Art Ensemble has firmly set foot in this country now, following a hair-raising performance at the Roundhouse last year with something only marginally less spirited at the considerably less spirited Queen Elizabeth Hall.

A quintet comprising Joseph Jarman and Roscoe Mitchell on reeds, Lester Bowie on trumpet, Malachi Favors on bass and Don Moye on drums, the Art Ensemble once again rubbed in the point that it is very definitely an improvising band preoccupied with performance rather than rumination.

Apart from the makeup and the eccentric couture, their music is so atmospheric and dense that it invokes an incessant slide show of powerful images (forests seething with life, village fiestas, traffic jams, arguments, stampedes) and the musical framework on which it is all festooned features references from every era of jazz.

The band's art is to avoid the most crippling pitfalls of the music (self-congratulatory performance of surefire rabble-rousers) by subverting conventional devices at every turn. Even regular bop-time, which Moye plays with a demonic relish, is continually shot through by fusillades of hoots, bleats, whistles, klaxons and reverberating gongs. As if to draw the audience gently into their web, the band played a short opening set that predominantly featured bleary Mingus-like tunes: the second half was hung around a long, scorching up-tempo group improvisation, but featured a magical alto solo from Mitchell that wreathed like smoke in a breeze, but within which flames tantalisingly flickered.

THE VANGUARD'S RETURN

The Guardian, June 1980

In the alternately bumpy and ardent relationship between improvised music and its audience there are unexpected contingencies and there are strategies so perfect that they would make the knees of Pavlov's descendants twitch with glee. For all that jazz is frequently described as adventurous, difficult or iconoclastic, the purest impulses of its vanguard practitioners never to play anything remotely easy on the ear always founder on the practicalities of audience appeal, the desire to celebrate or manipulate the culture from which the music has come, and straightforward business sense. The effect on an audience when a hardline avant-garde improvising band slips into that delicious sway of orthodox jazz time is rather as if it were briefly glimpsing land after being lost in a storm.

The Art Ensemble of Chicago, the most celebrated and entertaining improvising band out of the black jazz tradition currently doing the rounds, has been demonstrating the knack increasingly lately; and the recent London concerts of both the Ensemble and the Ornette Coleman-style Old and New Dreams band have illuminated the very unsurprising idea that there is an audience music in even the most apparently radical departures, and there is a buffs' music. The latter continually feeds the former but can never become too much like it without losing its iconoclastic impetus. At the present stage of its development the Art Ensemble navigates between the two strands with an almost careless confidence.

The group's most recent album, *Full Force* (ECM, 1167), reveals it at its most irresistible. A quintet of multi-instrumentalists, it specialises in springing blinding eruptions of idiomatic playing out of a kind of primeval soup of tinkles, bells, chimes, marimbas ringing like music boxes, and the baleful padding of soft, slack-sounding drums.

The themes that emerge from all this racketing around may resemble Latin American music, or reggae, or regular bebop, and the most riveting example of the latter on the current album is the tribute to the late Charles Mingus called 'Charlie M', in which, after an appropriately lazy, red-eyed introduction, bottom-heavy with a crafty presentation of Mingus's trombone section by means of the bass saxophone, Lester Bowie flicks affectionately through the jazz trumpet scrapbook with a string of slurs, inquisitive-sounding trills, and open conversational phrasing. Bowie, though his comprehension of the modern jazz trumpet is voluminous, still favours the bluesy, vocalised tone of the earliest players.

ECM have also been fortunate enough to be the proprietors of what will probably turn out to be the other indispensable record of 1980 – the Old and New Dreams band's second album (ECM, 1154) which in some respects is a close contender for the Reassuring Avant-Garde category, if only because the idiom in which it plays is still regarded as unaccountably weird in some quarters twenty years after these men helped invent it. Performing a mixture of marching music, ethnic beachcombing of all kinds, bright, tumbling tunes and a compulsively out-of-synch counterpoint, the band has a precision about it that makes every note take on a hard, diamond-like glitter.

BRACKNELL 1980
The Guardian, July 1980

Although black America tends to be treated as the top-line attraction at the Bracknell Jazz Festival, the event remains peculiarly parochial. Shapeless blokes in baggy Levis wheel beer barrels about, people in tents watch Wimbledon on portable TVs, earnest balding individuals in gold-rimmed specs clutch sleeping babies and read scholarly magazine articles with titles like 'How Cells Become Animals', as if to trying to figure out how they got into this situation in the first place.

Saturday's performance even wound up with a collection of local kids pogo-dancing to the George Coleman band, a rugged A-team of hard-cop players who look like New York cab drivers and who were comfortably old enough to be their fathers. It was one of the most euphorically weird occurrences I have ever seen at a gig.

In a billing for all comers, it was ensured that jazz-rock, the European avant-garde, and bop, would each get a fair crack of the whip, and by and large the audience was amicably inclined towards all of it. During the afternoon, the Pat Metheny Band won its customary tumultuous reception with a mixture of soft-rock, jazzy ballads and sharp technique. Metheny, a young Missouri guitarist with a sound like the country specialist Chet Atkins but possessing a truly sophisticated grasp of chordal improvising, played some tasteful quiet pieces but cut loose on a boppish version of 'All the Things You Are' and concocted tune after tune of his own from the harmony.

Harmony was, of course, nowhere within earshot when the London Jazz Composers' Orchestra took to the stage in the evening, and the omission caused a degree of fractious behaviour from a member of the audience who only withdrew his objections when sworn at by neighbouring punters and approached by drummer John Stevens, waving sticks.

The orchestra performed a stark and skeletal arrangement that brought virtuoso performances from all the sections in turn; though members of the band had already played some of the most urgent, wiry and robust sounding music of the day in smaller combinations around the recital rooms.

The George Coleman band closed the show with a repertoire of tight arrangements, peppery solos, and beautiful drumming that ran like a Rolls-Royce for an hour. Coleman, Frank Strozier on reeds, and Harold Mabern on piano, all demonstrated that bop can still burst with ideas for musicians with a love of it, and Billy Higgins supported it all in his customarily caressing, effortless fashion at the drums. The Bracknell skinheads, leaping gleefully in unison in front of the stage, undoubtedly got the message.

Ghost

The Guardian, July 1980

The best Bill Evans group for years is presently at work at Ronnie Scott's, which is an unexpected delight for his long-time devotees as well as being a necessary reminder that freshness in music doesn't invariably spring from playing in ways that nobody has thought of before. Over recent years, Evans has seemed like a tired man. Hunched over the piano, playing hushed, reluctant harmonies with a touch occasionally bordering on the effete, his natural introversion was leading him virtually to evaporate before an audience's eyes and ears.

All this has changed. The musical originality that had identified Evans as one of the great jazz pianists in the mid-Fifties has re-acquainted itself with the quiet assertiveness of his earlier work, with the result that on his present trip he looks and sounds nothing short of buoyant.*

Unquestionably one of the most harmonically sophisticated pianists around, Evans's development of familiar themes is such a profusion of eddies and swirls that the tune itself dissolves into a ghostly, wraith-like semi-presence. He further refines all this rich intelligence with a firm control of dynamics and an inclination to shaft through the most lush and languorous passages, with sudden crisp needling phrases, often flavoured with blues. Keith Jarrett, who has learned a lot from Evans, has a little of the older man's purposeful, craftsmanlike air.

Evans is accompanied on this trip by Mark Johnson on bass and Joe La Barbara on drums. Both perform with sympathy and unshowy virtuosity, La Barbara's arms wheel lazily as if scattering seeds, and he works up a controlled head of steam on up-tempo tunes like 'Suicide is Painless'.

*It was almost Evans's last hurrah. He died on September 15, aged fifty-one.

Storm

The Guardian, October 1980

Everything about the German saxophonist Peter Brotzmann is over the top. He looks like a cross between a teddy boy and an Edwardian village blacksmith, plays virtually every reed instrument he can lay his hands on at the full pitch of his lungs and is possibly the loudest saxophone player alive. But though his performances represent a crude and blustering form of free-jazz, they can also be remarkably exhilarating, like being caught in violent weather. The storm washed over the 100 Club on Monday night.

Brotzmann was accompanied by two men whose long experience

together has welded them into a virtually indivisible organism. South Africans Harry Miller and Louis Moholo on bass and drums are not only capable of providing all the eddies and cross-currents that batter and pull at Brotzmann's headlong flight but they function as a musical unit in their own right that you could happily listen to all night.

Miller, a strong and passionate player, eschews orthodox melodic accompaniment in favour of an unbroken barrage of drumlike chord playing, feverish pizzicato work, dolorous bowing and a range of slurs, thumps, twangs and thunderclaps that completely transform the art of timekeeping. Mostly the band went in for loud and raucous free episodes, but would occasionally lapse into a straight jazz pulse (in which Miller and Moholo unpack their entire arsenal) or even march-time. Brotzmann subverted the latter by alternating playful tootles with hyena-like cackles, as if two dislocated personalities were at work within him.

Brotzmann's method is sheer hyperbole, and a long way from the virtuoso technique of Evan Parker, who was also on the bill. Parker's playing has moved markedly closer to tonality of late, even to the extent of occasionally resembling the rather whimsical air of Steve Lacy: but though technically breathtaking there is a seething creativity within its implacable style that is rare in free jazz. Parker is unquestionably a master.

Unlike Poles

The Guardian, November 1980

ECM Records, the German label pioneered by the perfectionist Manfred Eicher, has been the recipient of a good deal of unfriendly comment of the profound-on-the-surface variety, but the fact is that it has brought about some remarkable conjunctions of unlikely players which has enhanced the most spontaneous qualities of jazz.

Among the liveliest of the new ECM releases is *In Europe*, a recording of a concert in Switzerland by Jack DeJohnette's New Directions band. This version of the group features DeJohnette on drums, John Abercrombie on guitar, Lester Bowie (of the Art Ensemble of Chicago) on trumpet and Eddie Gomez on bass.

DeJohnette, a fiery, muscular performer whose drive gives every tune an eager and expectant air, has worked extensively with Abercrombie in the guitarist's own band and between them they have comprehensively demonstrated the attraction of unlike poles.

Where DeJohnette is sweeping and imperious, Abercrombie is reserved, terse, deliberate, like a rock-generation Jim Hall. The band plays a loose, unhurried swing almost throughout, which repeatedly falls into quiet, suspended passages in which Bowie's whistling valve effects, sly whines and delightful squeals occasionally spiral off unexpectedly into the silences.

Fast passages, such as the opening of 'Multo Spilagie', find Bowie delivering crouched, skidding runs like a late-Sixties Miles Davis, with Abercrombie playing furry, muttered chords rather reminiscent of George Benson's occasional playing with the Davis band. A vital, spiky session, and a genuine interplay.

DeJohnette is also present on *80/81*, a double-album of pieces by a group led by the young guitarist Pat Metheny, who came to the fore with the Gary Burton band. In spite of the presence of the great bassist Charlie Haden, tenorist Dewey Redman, and a surprisingly buoyant Mike Brecker (also on tenor) Metheny has brought the silky touch he usually deploys in high-class funk bands to a much more open and improvisatory setting and the result doesn't really ignite. But Metheny's sound, a ringing resonant tone like a zither with loose strings, is unfailingly attractive. Compared to Abercrombie's brittle, nervy quality, though, he's just a little too clean-cut for the company's he in.

One of the most dolorous and god-forsaken sounds on the planet is that of the Norwegian saxophonist Jan Garbarek, the Ingmar Bergman of the European jazz scene. Garbarek's horn sounds like a snake charmer's flute played down a fjord, and the generally chilly effect is compounded on *Aftenland* by the ghostly presence of a pipe organist. Mostly the two of them while away the hours on slow, wraith-like themes that occasionally border on the tantalising, such as the soft evaporating murmur of 'Enigma', which perpetually teeters like a candle flame in a draught. But on the whole you're left with the bewildering impression that you could have come in anywhere.

On the other hand, Colours, the band led by the German bassist Eberhard Weber, has made one of its more absorbing albums in a session dubbed *Little Movements*. Generally much given to that soporific spreading-ripples music which perhaps unfairly became ECM's early trademark, Weber's band has on this occasion come up with a session that has thematic echoes from all over the jazz and rock marriages of the past decade, including Mothers of Invention circa *Peaches en Regalia*, the Michael Gibbs band (Terry Rileyish piano riffs), very little heavy funk, the odd free passage that sounds like somebody turning a radio tuner, and some undramatically imaginative playing from pianist Rainer Brunginhaus (a disciple of Keith Jarrett) and saxophonist Charlie Mariano who really does sound like a snake charmer. Faintly mournful good vibes.

Faintly sugary good vibes are to be heard on the latest Gary Burton/ Chick Corea collaboration, in which the vibraharpist and the pianist duet for four sides on a concert performance from Zurich in 1979. Both men being supreme at the art of pretty tunes, their embroidery of their material sweeps smugly on through Corea's own Latin-tinged pieces, a boppish tribute to Bud Powell, solos in which they wring their instruments dry, and some of the lazily swaying tunes that bassist Steve Swallow has written for Burton.

FATHER TIME

The Guardian, March 1981

Nature being what it is, the day ought presumably to come when Art Blakey's revolving eyeballs, chainsaw chuckle and affectionately domineering percussion will no longer be a feature of occasions such as the Camden Jazz Week, but the veteran drummer and bandleader has probably struck a private deal with Father Time on the strength of all that they have in common.

Blakey played the Roundhouse with a sextet version of his Jazz Messengers, a group that he has led in various forms since 1948. Their music still sounds like several people running for a train, a wild dishevelled quality it has had since the early days. Like all great drummers, Blakey's art is to make whatever is going on in his band sound as good as it can possibly sound. But he is not merely sensitive to the work of soloists, suiting his contribution to theirs.

Blakey goes further than this, performing an extraordinary therapy of encouragement, remonstrance, suggestion and interrogation, eventually taking the whole thing by the scruff of the neck – an activity he goes in for with just about everybody. Even though you might have heard it a hundred times before, Blakey's melodrama of the stealthy pulse, the gathering storm on the ride cymbal, the bumpy left-hand work seems to set an almost malevolent presence breathing down the soloist's neck.

The band played the standard blend of hard bop and blues, and the Mingus-like Charles Fambrough on bass, Bobby Watson's impassioned alto playing and newcomer Wynton Marsalis's crackling trumpet work kept the show irresistibly rolling.

Matters were rather less decisive in the band led by the Oklahoma singer Joe Lee Wilson, whose unquestionably arresting vocal style was forever being enveloped in the curiously aimless character of much of his repertoire, a shakiness that seemed to discourage his musicians, after a brisk start, from attacking the material. Only Bobby Few, an imaginative free pianist making a guest appearance, threatened to wrench the performance out of its determinedly bewildered mood.

SWEETS AND LOCKJAW

The Guardian, March 1981

That winking, chuckling, corner-of-the-mouth jazz played by the dwindling veterans of the swing bands of the Forties is getting the full breezy treatment at Ronnie Scott's in the form of Harry 'Sweets' Edison's trumpet and Eddie 'Lockjaw' Davis's tenor.

Both men, who wear cavernous grey suits and make barn doors look like cat-flaps, go about their business with an affectionate relish, and the enterprise is being suitable hustled along by an excellent local band featuring Eddie Thompson on piano, Len Skeat on bass, and Jim Hall on drums. Hall in particular is a brisk performer, who lifted, soothed and shepherded the front men as if he had been working with them for years.

The repertoire inevitably consists of the evergreens. Edison plays 'Mean to Me' with the mute on, gradually dropping the volume until he's soloing over the bass alone, letting the melody disappear into puffs of air – a manoeuvre that reduced the punters to complete and unaccustomed silence.

Davis was more subdued, but the attractively slurring phrasing, thumping chorus playing and skidding runs that are his trademark still jostled through the proceedings. The composition of the band is perfectly suited to making this kind of music buzz and hop. The chorus of 'Bye Bye Blackbird' sounded for all the world as if it were being played by a line up of car-horns.

BELLS AND SIGHS

The Guardian, March 1981

Gil Evans's wonderful concert at the Royal Festival Hall in 1978 has already been celebrated on one album (RCA, PL 25209) but the evidence of the most recent selection from that night's music is that RCA missed the boat. The huge, jostling, electric presence of the band, its looseness and responsiveness, the cool, organised strength of Susan Evans on drums, the way Masabumi Kikuchi's keyboards and the mini moog would snake between the more forthright proclamations of the acoustic instruments – is all simmering away on Mole Jazz's *The Rest of Gil Evans – Live at the Royal Festival Hall* (Mole, 3).

Evans' palette of sound effects embroiders a sense of space and shape as broad as Duke Ellington's, and since the early Seventies he has kept his music moving by incorporating funk into the rhythm section and extensively drawing on the songs of Jimi Hendrix as staples of the repertoire.

Four pieces from the South Bank concert are included on this album, among them the opener, Thelonious Monk's 'Rhythm-a-ning'. Two are high spots of the performance, being the wide-screen swing of 'Up from the Skies' (just a simple repeated motif that wheels its way through a series of accumulating textural shifts from the keyboards) and the almost painfully protracted 'Variation on the Misery', which, like so many Evans slow pieces, lifts gradually through a mist of chiming bells and half-finished piano figures, drifting like sighs until Marvin Peterson's trumpet solo – which starts as dolorous as the theme, slips into a desperate, manic cackle, and then falls back into an evaporating murmur engulfed by the pianos.

Osmosis Records (6001) has released some Albert Ayler sessions from 1964 with Don Cherry on cornet, Gary Peacock on bass, and Sunny Murray on drums. They date from the band's European trip which followed Ayler's famous New York recordings for ESP, with Cherry augmenting the regular trio.

Ayler's characteristic bluesiness (sobbing vibrato, the ethereal feel created by incessant sliding away from a tonal centre, the abrupt, cannoning honks) flood out on 'Spirits', which is also the track that most revealingly touches on the optimism and warmth within Ayler's disconcerting fire. And in 'No Name', he sustains a quivering passion that is as effective as the emotional high points of any form of music, jazz or otherwise.

More down-to-earth these days is Archie Shepp, who is to be heard on two new albums, *Attica Blues* (Blue Marge, 1001, French import), and a duet with the drummer Max Roach in *The Long March* (Hat Hut, 13). The big band record is a mixture of soul singing, blues clichés, a lot of well-oiled jazz orchestra standbys, through which good solos from Shepp and Marion Brown fitfully gleam.

Much more interesting is Shepp's duo with Roach, a drummer who could undoubtedly offer respiration to the dead. The record reiterates how much fluidity and melodic grace has entered Shepp's playing over the years (the early inspiration of Coleman Hawkins is ever more prominent) and his tenor solos develop through long, sensuous flows of sound, flecked with glitters of melodic ingenuity. He is to black saxophone playing what Warne Marsh is to the white West Coast school – immense lyrical sophistication and ingenuity with conventional materials.

Roach is also to be heard on the same label in another duo context, *One in Two, Two in One* (Hat Hut, 6), working with the reed player, Anthony Braxton. This set was recorded at the Willisau Jazz Festival in 1979, on the day after Roach's exchange with Shepp. Through Braxton is sometimes inclined to a rather rarefied air, Roach's remorseless thunder keeps rumbling around him, which leads him to play with an almost apprehensive urgency.

Roach is amazing. As Braxton slides into a passage of swooping yelps, Roach, having maintained a bumpy, clattering attack, takes to slapping the hi-hat, then climbs into an immense blitzkreig behind Braxton's squeaky sopranino. Then he turns to a tinkling of finger cymbals through which the reed player's sea-monster bass clarinet insinuatingly slithers. A score of such moments make the record an object lesson in fresh improvisation.

CONFUSION
The Guardian, May 1981

'Fusion' is a word of the moment, but in the whole of that initially volatile and eventually incisive phase which began in the Sixties and down-turned in the middle Seventies, the really interesting 'fusion' was the one going on between the musicians' own inclinations and elements such as these: the pressures of the market, the state of the recording business, the prospects for patronage, the ramifications of dope culture, the involvement of the broadcasting networks – the status of artists in societies which in little more than a decade were turning from a brief flurry of liberal elevation to a sour austerity. Musicians have had to adapt to survive, and they live in the world, so what they play is by no means the result of pure and holy inspiration.

The great jazz players who are still of an age and inclination to be flexible have included Miles Davis and Ornette Coleman, and reflections on their weathering of the prevailing climate are occasioned by CBS's release of an interesting set of Davis out-takes and the recent announcement of a visit by the Ornette Coleman band to this country in June.

Although it is clear why some of these tracks didn't make it in the first place, Davis's record (*Directions*, CBS, 88514) is a sharp reminder of the kind of stampede there would be if the enigmatic and visionary trumpeter decided to break his current silence. Davis, it seems, made the most fruitful use of the musical changes that fortune thrust upon him, but who can tell what he'd do now?

Apart from the availability of previously unreleased material, *Directions* telescopes the trumpeter's development between 1960 and 1970 in a way that is, for once, an enhancement of virtues. Beginning with an excursion with the Gil Evans Orchestra from the *Sketches of Spain* session, the album follows the remarkable suppleness of the modal-music band that produced *Sorcerer*, through the restrained early electric sound of 1967 and the boiling atmosphere that swept in around the period of *Bitches Brew*, when Davis started using enlarged rhythm sections texturally.

Through it all, the magnitude of Davis's illumination never flickered, but swathed the music in ever-changing hues. His ability to imply movement by his own periods of stillness, the sensuality of his sound and unexpected bouts of anger, and the evolution of his vocabulary to suit fast rock through lazy bent notes and sharp monosyllables that hang behind the beat – all of it is to be heard on *Directions*, though the themes themselves aren't memorable.

Live in East Berlin (Leo Records, 102) is a session recorded in East Berlin in April 1979 featuring the Russian trio of Vyacheslav Ganelin (piano), Vladimir Tarasov (drums) and Vladimir Chekasin (alto). It is a startling insight into a culture that many assume possesses no adventurous jazz at all, since the trio puts together music of typhoon-like energy.

Leo Records also presents singer/pianist Amina Claudine Myers in a tribute to Bessie Smith (Leo, 103). Myers is in the company of percussionist Jimmy Lovelace and bassist Cecil McBee. The great beauty of her playing is that she manages to keep the simple euphoria of gospel music so fresh that you imagine it to be a well-recorded version of something that could have been taped forty years ago. Since most musicians turn out celebrations of the past that sound like Hollywood remakes, this is some achievement.

SOCIAL INSECURITY
The Guardian, June 1981

Harold Pinter was once asked on television why it was that he wrote plays for characters who conversed in such inexplicably eccentric ways. Pinter gave every impression of being genuinely perplexed. It was, he gently hinted with all humility, the way the world sounded to him.

Ornette Coleman, the great Texan saxophonist and composer who turned the course of jazz inside out in the late Fifties, has been subjected to much the same line of enquiry over the years, and has patiently delivered much the same answer. In 1967 the British critic Victor Schonfield wrote of Coleman: 'Ornette's music confirms the identity of jazz and demonstrates the continued life and potency of the jazz tradition. His lovely tone is essentially the sound of jazz, like those of Johnny Dodds, Bubber Miley, Lester Young, and Charlie Parker.'

Fourteen years later, Schonfield's assessment has lost none of its impact. Coleman's work on the saxophone retains extraordinary freshness. Though possessed of a boundless natural facility for composition and for playing anything he can hear, his music has never hardened into mannerism, and in that respect his playing has retained an almost childlike quality. He is at once the most sophisticated of players and the most innocent.

Through the years Coleman's playing has been faithful to three principles. One is that 'playing in tune' is not the simple practice that it is taken to be; Coleman's idea of 'playing in tune' has much to do with the motives and responses of the performers and little to do with traditional musical intonation. The second is the abiding principle of collective playing, a method that goes back to New Orleans jazz. The third is the central role of melody, on which all Coleman's improvising is based.

Coleman was born in Fort Worth, Texas ('I was twenty-two years old before I had a conversation with a white person') and took up the alto saxophone in 1944, later switching to the tenor to get work with the rhythm and blues bands. A self-taught musician, he absorbed musical theory at a prodigious rate and to this day continues to regard the world's music as the book from which those with the inclination can read a multitude of songs yet to be uttered.

He had a rough time with the commercial bands early in his career because his pitching was so idiosyncratic, but his playing in the latter part of the Fifties (which led to his first recordings for Contemporary Records in Los Angeles) has since been widely acknowledged as yielding some of the most passionate and vigorous music yet to have emerged in jazz. As he said to Nat Hentoff in 1958, 'You can always reach into the human sound of a voice on your horn if you're actually hearing and trying to express the warmth of a human voice.'

Coleman's current European tour sees him with his electric band that features two guitars, two basses and two drummers, but his longer-range plan is to produce a symphony for 160 musicians of all persuasions. His hardest task always is to dislodge the habits of a lifetime.

'A style gives you social security,' says Coleman, 'but it doesn't keep you creative. The combinations in instrumental music are really endless. Its only when you want to succeed in a pattern style' (his oblique and ruminative conversation is full of such telescopings of ideas) 'that you become limited. In Western societies, everything has to have a design, like architecture. Music fits into the same social pattern – it doesn't tell you how exciting things could be by letting you find out all the different things that sound effects could do to you.'

In the Seventies, Coleman could have profitably settled on that delightful mixture of quirky tunes, brisk swing and bleary contrapuntal playing which characterised his work of the previous decade. Instead he went in search of new ideas. He visited Nigeria and Morocco, played with the legendary Master Musicians of Joujouka, came across some Madagascan music 'where fifty guys were playing from just breathing in their nose, and it was as intense as any symphony I've ever heard.

'And when I heard the musicians in Morocco, sounding like individuals, but still sounding like *one*, I became convinced that the sound and the emotional motive had to be stronger than the pattern. When I went to Nigeria I said I wanted to hear their best talking drummer. I hired him for a few days, found out that rhythm acts like the oxygen for sound. When you get a real pure, good rhythm, *everything* starts happening.'

ELITE ANARCHY
The Guardian, July 1981

Though Company's membership comes from many walks of musical life – lapsed or practising classical players, jazz and pop players, artists beyond category – it increasingly represents an attitude towards free improvisation in which the creators' ability to listen, imagine and respond (long a feature of the best of jazz and many ethnic musics) is a hallmark of the most memorable performances. This is not the truism it seems. Large-group improvisation, a crude, simplistic and rather bleak form of collaboration is falling increasingly out of favour, as is the false 'demo-cracy' of the unskilled performer.

Company continues to be an elite, and one that works best in sub-groups of four or five. The reed player Lindsay Cooper, who took a turn with the New York avantist Charles Morrow on Saturday night, ran into the contradictions of the endless-permutations theory. Most attempts to assemble longer lines were broken down by interjections from Morrow (who sings like a rabbi and plays a variety of objects such as cowbells and jew's-harps).

Two performances that made up for this rather exasperating affair came late from a quartet that featured a trumpeter, Kondo Toshinori, David Toop (bass guitar, water flutes), a percussionist, Jamie Muir, and a dancer, Min Tanaka.Toshinori, an irrepressibly lively player, delivered a good deal of straight jazz mixed with blurted, exclamatory sounds.

Tanaka's usual performance costume makes it unmistakably clear that the only place he has body hair is on his eyelids. Removing the tracksuit that made him resemble an extra from *The Seventh Seal*, he joined the quar-tet that closed the show featuring trombone, saxophone, guitar and bass. It was one of the most collaborative and considered of Company perfor-mances, though dominated by Steve Lacy's cool intelligence on the soprano and Maarten van Regteren's bass, and wound itself up on a hushed, tiptoeing exchange of light, glassy sounds, cadences of sighs, and barely audible whistles from the sax. The audience broke into sponta-neous applause.

PARABOLAS

The Guardian, July 1981

The atmosphere summoned by a Carla Bley band is uncharacteristically picturesque for contemporary jazz, which tends to be a practical, technical and materialistic business that regards mood music as rather vulgar. In this respect, Ms Bley's work has more in common with the parodic Dutch style of composers like Willem Breuker than with anyone from the American tradition.

Nobody knows quite why she inclines to this marriage of down-at-heel Twenties hauteur with the unmannerly directness of contemporary jazz. Yet the force of modern improvisation is often thrown into startling relief by it, and in gradually accelerating the more elemental side of the music as if it were an escapologist breaking free, Carla Bley creates the effect of a kind of slow-motion musical metamorphosis going on as you listen.

Social Studies (Watt Records, No. 11) is the latest recording by Ms Bley's current band, which begins as a suite of bleary and deadpan tangos into which Mike Mantler's Don Cherry-like trumpet and Steve Swallow's electric bass gradually insinuate themselves. Carla Bley's music always suggests a sensuous quality of fluidity and movement within harmonies, and in her Ellington-like composition 'Copyright Royalties', the paths of the chords – highlighted in the embroidery of the trombone and piano – cross and recross in slow, graceful parabolas.

ECM has released another album by the guitarist Pat Metheny and pianist Lyle Mays, this time with the assistance of the percussionist Nana Vasconcelos and entitled *As Falls Wichita, So Falls Wichita Falls* (ECM, 1190). The title piece and first side is purely a piece of atmosphere and tone colour, full of cocktail-shaker percussion, yielding tom-tom sounds, sepulchral organ chords, swooping electronics and few interjections from a voice solemnly intoning numbers, sounding disconcertingly like ex-President Jimmy Carter. Through it all ghostly conversations, that sound as if they're taking place in subway tunnels, wander in and out.

The second side consists of four tunes in that chattery manner which Mays and Metheny have cultivated with each other, where everything sounds like a folksy Keith Jarrett composition. Some of this has a leaning towards the fey. But it's a subtle, patient and seductive record.

The out-and-out jazzy album of the month has to be the new Jack DeJohnette record *Tin Can Alley* (ECM, 1189), a must for fans of the big blow. By comparison with Metheny's set, this sounds like a lot of boulders rolling downhill, and DeJohnette, one of the most exciting straight-time drummers in the business, is joined here by Chico Freeman on tenor, John Purcell on baritone and Peter Warren on bass. DeJohnette manages to make his kit sound as if it has about five times more sound-producing implements than it does, partly through a remarkably resourceful range of cymbal accents. The opener and title track has a pugnacious, Mingus-like feel to it, but the leader demonstrates his depth of musical understanding in the slow piece 'Pastel Rhapsody'. As spinners of captivating lyricism, Freeman on tenor and DeJohnette on piano turn out to be neck and neck.

EFFERVESCENCE

The Guardian, July 1981

Appearing at Ronnie Scott's until the weekend is Betty Carter, the effervescent and diminutive jazz singer whose tantalising manner with a lyric and a rhythm manages to turn familiar songs inside out. That she does this so successfully without ever taking on the mannered deliberation common to the art is a powerful tribute to her ability to make a song sound as unformed and idiosyncratic as a conversation in a bar. It is also an indication of the talent of her trio – which pursues her eccentric progress of abrupt accelerations and slamming halts, time changes, exclamations and interrogations with an affectionate relish.

Confidence rules the show. When a singer elects to perform the second tune on a Monday night in something close to a whisper, to the accompaniment of the bass alone, you know that something unusual is abroad. Much of Better Carter's work is done to minimal accompaniment and fairly *sotto voce* because her pitching, which spins notes in the air and tries to fool you as to where they're going to end up, demands room to breathe – though 'Old Times', normally handled as ballad, is taken at a scalding tempo in which the words jostle and ricochet.

In creating a personality that delivers such fragmented versions of what were once smoothly flowing lyrics as if they were personal confidences (a process bolstered by sketching the lines of the melody with her hands and the arch of her back) Ms Carter captures almost effortlessly the jazz singer's greatest prize, and does it with a voice as slight but as expressive as a flute. Only in scat singing, a dubious device in which people try to sound like instruments and end up resembling the Swedish Chef in *The Muppet Show*, does she overplay and break the spell. Pianist Khalid Moss, bassist Curtis Lundy and drummer Louis Nash play with great élan.

TRANSITION
The Guardian, May 1981

On Monday night, when the whole town was mopping its brow, two high-class American bands were loping through their repertoires as if they were heading into a cool breeze. The saxophonist Arthur Blythe, hailed as a young master, brought a quartet to the 100 Club that played an attractive distillation of jumpy Eric Dolphy-like tunes, quavering ballads and fast blues and which successfully featured the peculiar line-up of tuba (playing the bass parts), guitar, alto and drums.

Meanwhile, at Ronnie Scott's, the legendary pianist McCoy Tyner was opening a two-week session in his customary slam-bang fashion. Tyner's attack, which leaves you feeling as if you've just been massaged by a yeti, veers towards the relentless but the musicianship of his band is always in a class of its own. But where the pianist's work has hardened in recent years, increasingly coming to resemble a streamlined reconstruction of those passionate journeys that Tyner had travelled on with

John Coltrane, Blythe's work has remained conspicuously in transition.

A forty-one-year-old West Coast altoist whose style blends the work of Coltrane, Dolphy and Albert Ayler, and whose physiognomy resembles the young Mingus, Blythe gives an impression both of coherence and unpredictability in his playing as if all the music that has influenced him is still ebbing and flowing in his mind. He is an emotional, forthright player, steeped in the jazz tradition (a graceful version of 'Misty' is included in his repertoire), whose appeal lies in the comprehensiveness with which he has gathered up the revolutionary movements of the past twenty years, and moulded them into a mature style.

What took his performance from the level of consummate craftsman-ship to real pleasure was his empathy with the remarkable drummer Bobby Battle, and with the clangy dishevelled guitar-playing of Calvin Bell. Bell's work, in fact, resembled a sophisticated version of James 'Blood' Ulmer's.

JAZZING IT DOWN
The Guardian, September 1981

One of the most convincing arguments for the virtues of music that doesn't rattle your eardrums is currently being displayed on a tour of the British Isles by the legendary American jazz musicians Red Norvo and Tal Farlow. They are taking their highly concentrated distillation of elegant euphoria around twenty-odd venues and achieving the kind of reverential silences for their quiet, conversational style of improvising that makes a church service sound boisterous.

Norvo, a portly, affable and humorous man of seventy-three, is a pioneer of the use of the vibraharp in jazz and his partner, Farlow, a sixty-nine-year-old from Carolina, is one of the most influential improvising guitar players to have followed in the wake of Charlie Christian during the war years. Between them, they have pulled off a rare piece of musical sleight-of-hand. By establishing such an atmosphere of serene, unhurried conversation, the two musicians seem to suspend in the listener all per-ception of competing motion, except the pendulum-like sensation of what is passing between them. The result is that their music-box world of glis-tening harmonies, sly quotes, fleet runs and the gently rippling pools of sound that spread from Norvo's vibes has been hypnotising audiences now since the group's reformation at New York's Michael's Pub in June.

All this is a surprising success in a world of headbanging amplification. It is also a surprise if your taste is for blunter, tougher forms of jazz; such ingredients in the hands of a band like the Modern Jazz Quartet, for instance, led more often than not to a rather becalmed self-absorption in which the celebrated stature of the players somehow became the creation instead of the means. To their credit, Norvo and Farlow have remained consummately musical.

Norvo formed his trio in 1949, on the pragmatic assumption that the sextet he ran was too big to get work in the California of the late Forties; Charles Mingus was one of the group's early bassists, and the three enjoyed a fruitful (and relatively storm-free) relationship for several years. Norvo had begun in a marimba band in 1925, and described the vibes offhandedly as simply 'a glockenspiel with a motor'.

His playing style is warm and personable, yet unvarnished, and full of incidental pleasures. Not the least of them is his bell-like accompaniment of other people's solos (the mallets padding stealthily over the keys while Norvo watches the audience amiably, his hands crossing and recrossing with the most minimal of movements, like someone dealing cards to himself) which serve to produce a delightful buoyancy, even in the band's rather less urgent moments.

The group's repertoire is virtually all tunes that are as old as Broadway and beyond. Songs from musicals, jazz classics, fast, flashy show pieces like Fats Waller's 'Jitterbug Waltz' and 'Fascinating Rhythm', the latter running at a breathless tailchasing gallop in which the guitar and the vibes take the unison theme neck and neck. And all still played at such a hush that the clink of a glass sounds like a shattering window.

'They all said it couldn't be done,' says Norvo of the softness of their approach, 'but that softness has made it possible for us to get the blend we have. It's difficult for us to catch that sound – even on records. The best records we ever made were in Chicago when I asked the engineer to leave the mixer alone. He said, "OK. I've only been doing this four weeks." That was perfect.'

Farlow, a tall, softly spoken man with hands that one feels could comfortably strangle a buffalo, takes up the mysterious secret of 'the blend', particularly on the long passages in which the bass drops out and leaves the guitar and vibes to thread an unbroken stream of counterpoint across the abyss of suspended rhythm. 'It may seem like we're just playing alongside each other, but we're listening all the time. Sometimes I'll get right in his range and see what he does, sometimes I'll go under it or over it.' Norvo says, 'Your musicianship makes you aware that there's got to be motion at all times. It's like throwing a football, you're not supposed to drop it. And the idea is to take it the way he gives it to you. That's important. Then you do something of your own with it and pass it to the next guy.' Through all of this, the role of the bass is crucial and Norvo has a characteristic shorthand for expressing the quality he wants. He remarks, 'He's got to have a "point on the note". That's the only way I can describe it. Mingus had it and the bassist we use in the States, Steve Novosel, has it.' Farlow adds helpfully: 'We have to hear the attack. If you play without drums that's very important.'

The beauty of their music is that the audience can hear the attack too, every nuance of it. The night I heard them in the Pizza Express I sat next to a professor of neurophysiology from Chicago who opined: 'Jazz is one of the highest levels of motor activity that human beings can exhibit.' I think he must have meant something like 'far out'.

GOOD OLD BOYS

The Guardian, October 1981

When you consider that the combined age of the Savoy Sultans probably runs into millions, the verve with which they pitch into the dance band music of the Thirties makes you feel faintly nervous for them. Led by their drummer Panama Francis, a stocky, genial young man in his sixties, the band is playing a season at Ronnie Scott's and getting the sort of reception for its energetic blend of elegant ensemble playing, lyrical soloing, sly dynamics and gentle hamming that would probably have been counted as ecstatic even in the heyday of the Savoy Ballroom.

The Sultans came back to popularity a few years ago with a successful record and some festival appearances which demonstrated that they were nobody's idea of a museum piece. They have taken the ballroom classics of their early days – the highly rhythmic, riff-laden style of Count Basie and Chick Webb – and brought them back to life with a mixture of leisurely orchestral expertise and highly imaginative improvisation.

In the line-up are George Kelly on tenor, Eugene Ghee on alto, and the trumpeters Irvine Stokes and Francis Williams. Kelly, an emotional, hard-toned and melodically ingenious player in the mould of Coleman Hawkins, delivered a solo on 'Girl Talk' that swept out of the background with imperious conviction. Francis's drumming kept the band breezily on course, his style characteristically fixated on the snare, the loose, slapping cymbal sound, and a regular bass-drum accent. His crisp and springy solo on Chick Webb's 'Clap Hands, Here Comes Charlie' had a punchy brevity that others would do well to emulate.

COLOSSUS

The Guardian, November 1981

For anyone who ever witnessed any of the stunning club performances that saxophonist Sonny Rollins played in London during the Sixties, or compulsively collected every scrap of his recorded work, this extraordinary jazz musician inspires an affection that is one of the warmest pleasures that music can offer.

Rollins, an improviser capable of generating the most rhapsodic flights of fancy from the thinnest of materials is a big, amiable man in his fifties who looks like a retired heavyweight. He has worried his old admirers in recent years by flirtations with disco and soul music that made approaching last night's concert at the Theatre Royal, Drury Lane, a matter for some trepidation, but all worries were unnecessary. Supported by a young and fiery band, Rollins played a majestic show.

In some ways Rollins has certainly changed. His tone is sweeter than formerly (it used to be uncompromisingly bleak) and he's less inclined to follow all his stubborn, mysterious fancies to a conclusion. But he is still quoting from every tune under the sun, still inclined to play elaborate, snakey codas and endlessly postponed finales, still punctuating his improvisations with stuttering, grumbling sounds and bleary honks.

His fondness for dance rhythms came over in his beloved 'Don't Stop the Carnival'. His improvising genius, blown from the horn as effortlessly as bubbles, emerged in a rich, luxurious version of 'I'll Be Seeing You'. It was like a supercharged version of a Coleman Hawkins swing solo. Rollins's band did him proud too, but his drummer Tommy Campbell did him proudest. Campbell's exploits before the interval, built around a counterpoint of tapping noises, abrupt and brutal bumps and echoing tom-tom sounds, all pitched over an incessant, ominous bass drum rumbling, made something fresh out of the unpromising territory of the long drum solo.

GUNSLINGERS
The Guardian, March 1982

On successive nights, the Art Ensemble of Chicago and the grizzled tenorists Dexter Gordon and Johnny Griffin have demonstrated all the virtues of jazz that resist explanation. Proving once again that it can play the socks off any black American idiom whatsoever, the Art Ensemble ran through a slowly developing ritual on Friday. Gordon and Griffin did something much straighter – that gunslinging two-tenor badinage that has been popular since the Forties – and though, much of the time, they failed to hit the dead-eye omnipotence that characterises the style, the result was an unexpectedly passionate and moving performance.

Gordon, a shambling giant of a man in his late fifties, one of the most influential of all tenorists, has lately shifted from his celebrated tumbling, barrel-toned bop forays, tirelessly laced with quotes, yodelling warbles, and thunderous honks, and adopted a languorous and half-steam approach that recalls both Lester Young and the early and quirkier playing of Sonny

Rollins. Griffin's lightning-fast technique seemed all the more manic and cliffhanging by contrast, and in Kirk Lightsey the band has a pianist – whose attack resembles Griffin's own – capable of stealing a show from anybody.

MJQ
The Guardian, April 1982

The Modern Jazz Quartet was laid-back long before anybody thought of the expression – and they stayed that way after it went out of currency. Eventually, after thirty years, their tinkling, metronomic, glassily-perfect music came to a halt, as if they were clockwork musicians whose spring had finally wound down.

But this year they are back – pianist John Lewis a little portly, drummer Connie Kay in spectacles, but unquestionably fondly remembered. The upshot of their broken retirement, though, has been more nostalgic than invigorating, whilst the silvery embroidery of their work has frozen.

Much of the early part of their concert – in the cavernous Dominion Theatre, echoing with empty seats – was given over to some rather colourless new material. The seductive elegance of the band's work remained in evidence in the quietly pushing piano backing of Lewis, and in the characteristic dynamic balance of the group. Percy Heath's purring base motors stealthily ahead of the drums, which are hushed to the volume of footsteps on gravel.

Their tendency to coyness was apparent in 'Hornpipe for the Queen' – and to resembling a high-class Palm Court outfit in 'That Slavic Smile' though the interplay between Milt Jackson's shapely phrasing and Kay's clipped rimshots rescued it. Jackson, a supreme vibes player still, soloed unaccompanied on 'Nature Boy', drenching the theme with arpeggios, and the whole affair developed some blood in its cheeks on the Caribbean-sounding 'Wailin' Walking Stomp'.

It's nice to see them back and in their long and musical career they undoubtedly turned a lot of people on to jazz. But at this stage in their come-back the pleasure has more to do with the past then the present.

LOCKJAW
The Guardian, April 1982

There's something eerie about the way Eddie Lockjaw Davis fixes the audience with a hard, unblinking stare while he's making saxophone lines spin like planes in an aerobatics display. Though maybe it's just that he's matter of factly informing you that he could really do all this with one hand behind his back if he felt the urge, or even in the middle of snatching forty winks.

Davis has now refined a witty, humane and vigorous swing style – his way of playing closely resembles a Brooklynite telling you a long and involved joke and getting mad at you in the middle – into a collection of finely tuned mannerisms that nowadays tend only to shift into overdrive in the company of a friendly rival like Johnny Griffin or Art Farmer.

Nevertheless, this was Davis's opening night, into which he launched himself without so much as a sound check, and he was greatly assisted in getting his bearings by the presence of the Brian Dee trio (Dee on piano, Len Skeat on bass, Martin Drew on drums) which played with the kind of intelligence which is, unfortunately, not always to be heard among piano accompanists at The Canteen.

Dee's bluff, urbane appearance makes you expect a chord player as efficient as a tape loop: in fact he has a clipped, inquisitive way of phrasing and a crispness that is occasionally reminiscent of a more genial Bill Evans, a quality that particularly emerged in his unaccompanied passage on 'Secret Love'.

Davis rolled out his repertoire of squirted, admonishing squeals, caressing mid-register canoodlings and dramatic headlong, scything charges. However, he also added an elegant fluttering sound in longer runs which made the notes seem possessed of tiny paper wings on 'Just One of Those Things', introduced by cascading arpeggio from Dee. Davis reveals in his performance how much his effectiveness depends on sharp contrasts between his wild and cantankerous side and the deceptive reassurance of that wide and warbling vibrato. All the old tricks never quite served to disguise the routine nature of the assignment for Davis. But at his age, one can only feel that he's entitled to it.

HYBRIDS

The Guardian, July 1982

Under clouds that were frequently *basso profundo* and on ground like a rice field, the eighth Bracknell Jazz Festival, that most British of multi-cultural celebrations, rumbled through its second day. In most respects it was as good a day's music as has been heard at Bracknell or anywhere else for a long time, and next week's Capital Jazz Festival will have to go some way to top it.

On Saturday afternoon the festival's commission was performed by a group led by the Scottish tenorist Bobby Wellins, a man whose future in music was despaired of a few years back, and who is now performing with much of his old punch. The piece, which sounded like a distillation of old Dave Brubeck riffs, was negotiated by Wellins with his characteristic mixture of nervous, scrambling phrases and sudden piercing cries. The percussion, which had a rather studied, pompous air about it, was curiously distracting, as if Wellins was trying to start a speech against the contributions of an over-zealous toastmaster.

If the older members of the throng were wondering why the haircuts of some of the punters made them look as if they were on the run from an aviary, the loud, youthful and theatrical rock band, Rip, Rig and Panic then arrived to provide the explanation. Rip Rig are one of the conduits through which the jazz developments of the past twenty years are getting through to an audience that wasn't born when Coltrane died and – like all jazz-pop hybrids – they've been lovingly tended by many people whose secret wish is that free-improvised music would go away.

Mostly performing at frantic tempos, the band sometimes recalls Brotherhood of Breath, early Seventies Miles Davis, Bow Wow Wow and a string of other borrowings and gatherings. As a tribute, they played a roaring version of a Dollar Brand theme, pumped up adrenalin by the gallon, and played an encore.

By comparison with the rest of the day's music it was ragged, unfinished, and maybe oversold its goods, but it represented a popular development of jazz that at least wasn't sanctimonious about technique, was confident about free-playing and unbowed by its ancestry. The crowd was keen and some were entranced – older jazz players will have cause to be grateful for Rip Rig's ambassadorial role. A small girl astride her father's shoulders drummed ecstatically on his head.

Bands led by John Stevens and Trevor Watts brought other kinds of idiosyncrasies to the affair – Stevens leading an excellent bebop band that included altoist Peter King, Watts performing with the curious line-up (percussion and bass, violins, reeds, piano) that appeared at Camden earlier this year. The band's work, which heavily features repeated riffs and fast, splashy drumming, was bludgeoning then, but is much tighter and more colourful now, and it was deservedly a bit hit.

Abdullah Ibrahim (formerly Dollar Brand), the South African pianist who preceded Watts, brought the marquee to its feet with a set of spectacular warmth and depth, performed in the company of saxophonist Carlos Ward. Ibrahim is one of the greatest exponents of the art of releasing devastating effects from simple material. Entire orchestras seem hidden in his chords, space and silence set you straining for the slightest murmur of sound, drum-like tattoos release tumultuous organ-like reverberations.

The night wound up with the Lester Bowie band, playing 'From the Root to the Source', a raucous and feverish celebration of gospel and blues performed by the trumpeter's quintet and three singers, Fontella Bass,

Martha Bass and David Beaston. It was the sort of thing you used to get in festivals years ago.

Beaston, a man with the voice of a contralto and the physique of a Mack truck, kept teasing the crowd with tantalising pauses on his way to stratospheric notes; Bowie played with his customary impishness and bluster and drummer Phillip Wilson, one of the world's best, played with consummate taste.

THE ONLY BLUES I KNOW

The Guardian, September 1982

A jazz performance can be many things, and maybe only for a certain kind of ascetic enthusiast is it ever at its best when swinging out over the edge of a long drop. This is not an aspect of the music that has featured overmuch in the promotions of Norman Granz, who has brought Ella Fitzgerald, the Count Basie Orchestra, Oscar Peterson and Joe Pass to the South Bank for almost a week of performances, but the omission has compensations.

Granz has been shuttling this kind of wide-screen music around the world since the Fifties, and for all the fact that package-tour jazz often lacks spontaneity, he has possessed a liberality, enthusiasm and energy that has probably helped to create more jazz fans than it has exasperated. A particular heroine in Granz's epic is the perennially popular Ella Fitzgerald, whose voice is one of the most playful, invigorating and beautiful things in all music.

The early part of Saturday's show was taken up by longish sets from Basie's band and from the Oscar Peterson group with guitarist Joe Pass in tow. Basie, now seventy-eight, arrives on stage on wheels, but his gnomic, mischievous features and tiptoeing piano style haven't lost any of their charm in sixty years at the business. Most of what the band did, as usual, sounded like a long and very sophisticated drum solo, mingled with the kind of snakey, between-solo fillers that sounded like the purring of a hundred cats. Some of the work of the younger players had a knowing, music-school air about it, though, not entirely dispelled by the wittily lugubrious reflections of Sonny Cohn on trumpet and Eric Dixon on tenor.

Oscar Peterson's knowingness, on the other hand, is something altogether more imperious. Peterson is the unfortunate victim of one of the most spectacular piano techniques in jazz. All his performances feature the same mix of flooding arpeggios, cascading introductions and codas, ragtime and barrelhouse pastiches, and solos at impossible tempos, which all retain an eerily impassive quality nonetheless.

Ella Fitzgerald rightly dominated a long night, swooping and soaring through a repertoire that included 'Blue Moon', 'I Get a Kick Out of You,' 'In a Mellotone' and eventually a roaring 'St Louis Blues' ('the only blues I know'). If anything, the years have improved her ability to penetrate and transform songs, which was often masked by sheer vocal charisma (she has always been more of a straightforward popular singer than, say, Billie Holiday, who *couldn't* approach songs by the front door) and in 'God Bless the Child' she caressed the powerful lyrics as if trying to protect them from the elements.

WILL O' THE WISP

The Guardian, October 1982

The atmosphere at the Odeon, Hammersmith, had a rare tingle for the first of Miles Davis's three return concerts in London. Six years out of circulation, he could have come on stage and read out his laundry list and his frail, stooping figure in the spotlights would have been satisfaction enough.

As it turned out, he was a lot more generous, though it is clear that playing marathons is not yet uppermost in his mind. Performing with a quintet that featured guitarist Mike Stern, bassist Marcus Miller and saxophonist Bill Evans, with Mino Cinelu on percussion and Al Foster on drums, Davis – wearing a white cap, still sporting his old pensive playing stance, and occasionally smiling at his partners – slipped his sensuous voice into a predominantly funky rhythm that put you in mind of his bands at the time of *Bitches Brew*. But he abandoned the trumpet electronics and now plays the instrument straight. As if compressing the essence of everything he has played into the purest and leanest form, he releases sparks and bubbles of sound suggesting that his famous fondness for distillation is more marked than ever.

Nostalgia, though, may have touched even Davis's remote and elusive spirit. In the first half he played a medley of themes from *Porgy and Bess*, though the violence of Stern's attentions sometimes blew away the curling wisps of his thoughts.

COOL

The Guardian, November 1982

Jimmy Giuffre is one of the stalwarts of 'cool' jazz. Best known for quiet small-group excursions, notably with musicians of the class of Jim Hall and Steve Swallow, Giuffre is one of the few practitioners of the clarinet in modern jazz, and he also plays the alto, the flute, and occasionally the bass flute – the latter an outlandish instrument that looks as if it were made from a car exhaust and occasionally sounds like one.

Giuffre has been a serious student and teacher of jazz for years and a gentle revolutionary in his way – predating Ornette Coleman in some of the innovations of phrasing and structure but doing it in a subdued, rather nonchalant manner that naturally attracted less attention.

This spare and sidelong style requires accompanists of some restraint, which was not altogether evident from pianist Geoff Castle and bassist Ron Mathewson at the Pizza Express on Wednesday. Both are technically excellent players but delivered their contributions at times with such bull-ishness that they seemed to be separated from the American by a screen. The effect was particularly conspicuous on a hesitant, porcelain-like blues that Giuffre played at mid-tempo from the clarinet and which turned into a gallumphing charge as Castle's synthesiser solos got warmed up.

Giuffre then played 'Yardbird Suite' at a brisk trot, the clarinet at such a tempo beginning to sound edgy and soprano-like, and the improvisations a mixture of poise and indecision, like someone trying to run along a high-wire. A slow, atmospheric piece called 'Moonlight' brought on the bass flute, which delivered the rather colourless theme in a muffled gurgle to the accompaniment of portentous drum rolls and reverberating bass notes. Though everything fell much more happily into place in a crisp and racy version of Giuffre's most famous tune, 'The Train and the River', the combination of players is not ideal, and is probably keeping the leader's delicate ingenuity from finding its feet. Giuffre is currently at the Pizza Express, and things may tighten up.

SAINT

The Guardian, November 1982

If the designers of the Barbican Hall ever had hopes that their stage would be a fit place for mortals to be elevated into heroes, the reception for Keith Jarrett's only London concert this year was the realisation of all of them. Jarrett – who, it had been announced earlier, was hampered by a back injury – played four encores and looked as if he could have kept on coming back all night.

It was an accolade he deserved, since this was a vigorous and full-blooded display by the pianist who has restlessly touted the cause of acoustic music, developed a unique and popular style of solo improvisation, and founded on a mixture of gospel, straight music, songs and the legacy of musicians like Bill Evans a reputation that will last a very long time.

Jarrett's recent records – and he issues so many that only his most devoted fans would ever find a way of distinguishing between them – reveal a sentimentality and fondness for mannerism that confirms him as one of the great consolidators of jazz styles rather than an innovator. So the verve of his show this week, particularly in the second half, came as a welcome relief.

His favourite devices are rolling, gospelling bass figures over which the right hand swerves and wreathes, harp-like slow pieces, baroque semi-classical interludes and – on this occasion – such a trance-like flight into soul music that you felt he was about to ascend to the tasteful stripped pine roof of the hall.

STEAM

The Guardian, January 1983

The squat, grizzled veteran drummer Art Blakey – a man whose pleasure in his work is as evident now as it undoubtedly was four decades ago – is playing at Ronnie Scott's with as good a band as any in recent years and a spectacular head of steam even by his own standards.

Blakey's principles are simple. The arrangements never stray far from the tight and laconic style that has been the Jazz Messengers' trademark over the years – unsentimental tunes underpinned by pungent, bunched-up chords. And by his own Svengali-like presence at the drumkit, Blakey drives the rest of the band as if he were piloting a sports car – getting them to cruise quietly by dropping his volume to the rustle of the hi-hat, accelerating them with a beckoning cymbal beat, hurling them into extravagances with explosive flares of sound.

Blakey's groups are always workmanlike and often downright exhilarating and this one was particularly enlivened by the presence of the young altoist, Donald Harrison, a performer who mostly abandoned melodic intricacies for wild, tumultuous, off-the-register squeals and fierce, bluesy simplicity. In Harrison, the maestro had a sideman of much the same uncomplicated energies as himself, a congruity born out by the tour de force of the opening set, a barnstorming version of the gospelly blues, 'Moanin'.

The supporting act was something else. Two lightly-attired and heavily misguided blondes, who shall be nameless, worked their way through a terrible cabaret repertoire of sexual innuendo, slag-offs of trade unions, and general seediness. As a senior citizen, poor Blakey deserved more respect than to be asked to keep such company.

Stan

The Guardian, February 1983

This was one of the great jazz performances. Ironically, the band that perpetrated it at the 100 Club had been filmed in action for Channel Four only days previously, in a competent but restrained mood. So as often happens with the genie-like spirit of improvisation, the magic came, worked miracles and evaporated for ever into the smoke.

The occasion was a performance by a British band, the Stan Tracey Sextet, currently about to embark on a tour here which, on this evidence, no self-respecting music lover should miss. The line-up was Tracey Snr on piano, Tracey Jnr on drums, with Roy Babbington on bass and Tone Coe, Don Weller and Art Themen (looking increasingly like a young S. J. Perelman) on saxophones.

Tracey, who lately chooses to be more explicit about his bop allegiances (particularly the work of Thelonious Monk), went to town on all that in his second set. The band played a delicious mid-tempo version of the classic Miles Davis tune, 'All Blue' (the horns riffing off-hand comments on the choruses coming out of the bass solo that sounded for all the world like the Mingus band at work) that featured a typically butting-and-swerving solo from Don Weller. Weller played brilliantly throughout – when he bends his knees like a weightlifter in a solo, you always know he feels relaxed.

Tour de force of the night was a sublimely freewheeling version of Monk's 'Bemsha Swing', by which time the horn players were not hearing their contributions as individual comet-like spurts into space but as a series of interlocking orbits whirling around each other.

It culminated in some effortless and ingenious contrapuntal playing between Coe (intense, sophisticated), Themen (spikey, stuttery and rugged) and Weller (his solos increasingly turning into great switchback rides of sound) in which the whole band purred like a Rolls.

An act that could have graced any club in the world – but, knowing the form, almost certainly won't. Catch it if you can.

Gil

The Guardian, March 1983

Few things have made as profound an impact on jazz as the music of Gil Evans. Not only for itself – Evans has always been able to write blurred, vocal-sounding, deceptively casual compositions as if they were instrumental solos – but also because he has managed with success to induce great performers like Miles Davis, Wayne Shorter, and Steve Lacy to discover new depths in themselves.

Evans is currently in London working with a British orchestra. It featured the cream of local musicians – including John Surman and Don Weller on saxophones, Guy Barker and Henry Lowther among the trumpets, and John Taylor on keyboards. Despite that, any collection of players coming to grips with Evans's music for the first time is trusting itself to a form of free-fall guaranteed to shake anybody's resolve. The repertoire was pure Evans, much of it material featured on his last visit here and on recent recordings, blending relaxed mid-tempo rock, old jazz tunes twisted into new shapes, spacious journeys through eerie landscapes in which the rhythm is sometimes barely hinted at, insinuated through whispers and asides from all the instruments.

The early solos sat squarely on the beat as if mesmerised by the magnitude of the occasion, but John Surman broke the spell with such inventive splicing of the soprano saxophone and the resources of the synthesiser that the musicians with one accord played with a new looseness, particularly guitarist Ray Russell – whose mixture of ingenuity and singing tone made him sound as good as anyone Evans has used on the instrument.

It lacked the magic of the Evans band's Bracknell performance and the leader's simplicity of raw materials was occasionally made to sound almost prosaic, because the inflections that make it shine were just missed an unthinkable notion for an Evans performance. But to hear him spring joyous brass sounds out of voids, setting horns tangling lazily with each other, is his trademark and there was just enough of that.

Old Friends

The Guardian, March 1983

One of the heartening things that jazz music can do is to remind you of what it is that's precious about your closest friends. It is, par excellence, an art of subtle and delicate inflections like the expressions of a face, rather than portentous, crusading journeys through the universe in search of general philosophical illumination.

The music of Chet Baker, the thin, hunched and reticent trumpet player who looks as if he's stepped straight out of a Jack Kerouac novel, is a perfect example. Baker made his comeback relatively recently, having dropped out for years through ill-health and 'personal difficulties'. A brilliant remoulder of the soft and evaporating trumpet style of Miles Davis, Baker's performances have nevertheless not been invariably happy events, since the subdued nature of his playing sometimes makes it all but vanish altogether, like a flame starved of oxygen. His opening at the

Canteen on Monday, however, was a revelation and a relief.

Performing with the John Horler trio (Horler on piano, with Jim Richardson on bass and Tony Mann on drums) Baker – who was seated throughout – blew every note as if he had hand-picked it, and demonstrated the confidence rare in modern jazz musicians to play slowly without sounding lost.

It was a classic example of how infinitely reworkable old materials can be – and how seldom they are reworked with originality. Chet Baker is currently playing as well as he can play now, and that's saying something.

Hard Cop

The Guardian, March 1983

Sometimes music appears to belong almost desperately to the jumpy, angular urban present, and the effect is generally like being hit on the elbow with a baseball bat. It was audible in the Miles Davis electric groups of the late Sixties, and it is as clear as a bell (or maybe an automobile smash) in drummer Ronald Shannon Jackson's Decoding Society, a six-piece electric band of the most scalding vitality.

On the surface the ingredients sound straightforward enough – slamming percussion effects played on a massive sculpture-like kit festooned with cymbals and tom-toms; loud, fast, electric guitar playing, a crunching two-bass underpinning which acted virtually like another drummer. On top was a horn section (Zane Massey on reeds and Henry Scott on trumpet) that would fitfully hurl into the mêlée sleazy, street-corner melodic ideas which sounded like warped versions of the themes to some interplanetary cop show.

Working at times on similar principles to the old Mahavishnu Orchestra but with more bizarre and unearthly twists, the Jackson band delivered these full-blooded exercises in flat-out ensemble playing with such fury that they created the effect of careering through the eventful landscape of the Camden Jazz Week like a speeding vehicle with sirens wailing.

Massey sometimes produced a sound on the saxophone that took on a keening quality halfway between a Middle Eastern *shenai* and the bagpipes and Scott produced a wild, bubbling confection of brassy assertiveness and electronic effects which compounded the overwhelmingly urgent, adrenalin-ridden speediness of it all. The group's softer moments seemed oddly purposeless and confused by comparison, though you would have thought they would have come as a relief. A wild, rugged, frantic explosion of a band.

INFIGHTER

The Guardian, March 1983

People waiting outside Ronnie Scott's Club for the late performance by Buddy Rich's big band were asking those leaving after the first show what the veteran drummer's act had been like. Rich's performances have operated on much the same replenishable mixture of showmanship, phenomenal drumming skills and ordinary, not to say mediocre, musical content since he reformed his orchestra in 1966.

The drama was added by the fact that Rich, a gritty, volatile and indefatigably energetic sixty-six-year-old had a heart attack earlier in the year, which seemed almost certain to slow down his frantic Olympic-sprinter exertions. But Rich has simply set his distinctive jaw in an aspect of even more lugubrious determination, and after a ten-week layoff 'to give the band a rest' has come charging right back.

All Rich's legions of fans know the repertoire of gleaming arrangements fine-tuned to spotlight the drums, the obligatory pose of profound respect that the sidemen have to adopt while the leader is soloing, the rat-tat-tat left hand and whiplash cymbal smacks and Bill Reddie's now famous *West Side Story* medley. Rich still crowns this with his showstopping accelerating press-roll solo which eventually soars into a blur of sound punctuated by cymbal splashes and born aloft by the whole orchestra careering back into the fray with a brash rendering of 'Something's Coming'.

KALEIDOSCOPE

The Guardian, March 1983

Cecil Taylor is a hard man to please. He once failed two-thirds of his students at Wisconsin for 'lack of seriousness' (a judgement that a nervous faculty hastily adjusted to 'satisfactory'). His audiences over the years have usually felt themselves to be under the same scrutiny. Taylor's music, after thirty years of more or less remorseless devotion to the same packed, swarming playing style, bridging contemporary classical vocabularies and jazz, is about as challenging an experience as anything in modern music.

Taylor's band played the last night of the Camden Jazz Week at the Roundhouse in the company of New York's Dianne McIntyre Dance Company – five black performers who have frequently worked with Taylor before, as well as developing jazz ballets to accompany the work of Ellington, Eubie Blake and rock music.

But unlike Taylor's solo performances, often volatile introversion, this one was an open book. Initially in twilight, the dancers (in violet with red headbands), began with everybody hitting hard objects quietly. A sound like clapping hands kept emanating from the area of percussionist Andres Martinez, which confused the audience into thinking it should applaud, which fitfully it did. The piece, which ran for two hours and was called 'Eye of the Crocodile', amounted to a succession of episodes of varying intensity – some amplified by the uncoiling movements of the dancers, some featuring the sonorous, operatic voice of Brenda Baker, some collective improvising, some the saxophone of Jimmy Lyons, who has by now developed an unshakeable empathy with Taylor's kaleidoscopic concept of time.

Most really spontaneous music makes you imagine movement. The fact that it was here before you – the stretching between intervals, the whirlpools of rhythmic flurries, the nervous reverberations from Taylor's drum-like keyboard style, all expressed in the patterns of limbs – revealed the coherence and shape in Taylor's music that is often buried by its awesome intensity. Not only that, but the combination of jazz influences (mainly rhythmic) and vocal and visual ideas from other sources entirely revealed a version of what 'new' music really can amount to. And in a vigorous, if more monochromatic, opening set, British pianists Howard Riley and Keith Tippett did much the same.

STALKER

The Guardian, April 1983

Miles Davis's reputation has been that of an imperious and self-preoccupied man, yet his music bears hardly a trace of these qualities. This is not an accident. By their very nature, many jazz performances hover on the verge of going seriously off the rails. Davis, by a combination of charisma, precision, taste, technique, disconcerting determination and uncanny choice of partners, has simply developed the means to minimise the dangers without destroying the element of chance. Patience has governed his return to concert performance and recording, which was interrupted by a layoff that lasted more or less from 1974 to 1981.

When he returned to Britain last year, with a young, vigorous and typically percussion-dominated band, his music sounded more spare than in his early days and even revealed a tinge of uncharacteristic sentiment. From the start of last night's show at the Odeon, Hammersmith, something was altogether different. Not that you could have told from the way the band began, with a barging clamour of sound. But it was the trumpeter's first few notes that did it – a sound immediately clear and silvery, vibrato-less, dimming the glare of the opening section to a glimmer, and

Davis immediately took to playfully intensifying and softening the music's dynamics.

One of the most notable features of Davis's current playing is a return to clearly telegraphed chord-changes and song-forms, a development that has brought his music full circle, with all the innovations of the past thirty years now hanging in elegant balance. This more open idiom has deprived the music of some of its ethereal, ambiguous quality, but Davis's glancing way with the ballads of his early career has resurfaced. The band is much the same as last year, though the excellent John Scofield has come in as guitar support for Mike Stern – and the latter's more brutally metallic extravagances have cooled to smooth linear variations. By the time the proceedings had reached the spectacular Mino Cinelu's drenching conga solos, the whole outfit was rolling at a headlong pace. Davis, normally indifferent to the press, took to crouching in the footlights and inviting the photographers to shoot straight into the bell of the trumpet while he played little feathery, skittering noises. When the set ended, Davis shook the horn in the air with a gesture that was very nearly genial. It was a memorable moment in a career that has known more than a few.

DIZ

The Guardian, May 1983

The inimitable style of Dizzy Gillespie is a direct inheritance of the fervent, boiling directness of trumpeters from the earliest years of jazz like King Olivier and Louis Armstrong. Gillespie, however, delivers it with a melodic sophistication and complexity of construction that not surprisingly made him and Charlie Parker the dominant figures of the Forties musical revolution.

Gillespie's recent trips here have not been infallibly marked with that distinction. Inclined to coast on superlative technique if he chooses, sometimes over-inclined to backchat, he has often taken the not unreasonable course of resting on the laurels that his reputation and the advance into his mid-sixties entitle him to. The result has been that his playing has sometimes wilted into a rather muddy, indecisive bluster. But, as ever in jazz, the presence of powerful partners makes the world of difference, as it does on this trip to Ronnie Scott's.

The first thing you notice is that Gillespie is playing with more restraint and less bravura, a sure sign that he's feeling at home and engaged. On a Latinish tune called 'Tanga', his vigorous tendency to bend the resolutions of phrases into notes that are slightly off the chords jerked an otherwise lush and predictable idiom into a jangly dislocated feel. On Don Redman's 'Gee Baby Ain't I Good to You', Gillespie initially sounded unsettled, wandering rather vacantly over the bluesy chords like a blindfolded man try-ing to find his way out of a room – a tendency compounded by the contrast of the clean, lithe Wes Montgomeryish chords of guitarist Ed Sherry. But the trumpeter steadied himself, and was soon composing a stream of explosive and glittering phrases, hung mischievously behind the beat and attacked with a masterful clarity.

BLOW OUT THE OLD, BLOW IN THE NEW

The Guardian, May 1983

In November 1968, a cardboard sign was to be seen outside the entrance to a Berlin music club called the Quartier von Quasimodo. It proclaimed: 'Double entrance price for critics'. The occasion was the first Total Music Meeting, which Germany's leading experimental musicians mounted as a counter-attraction specifically aimed at the country's biggest and most respectable jazz festival, the Berlin Jazz Days.

Several current events bring the episode to mind. A season of concerts at London's Institute of Contemporary Arts, starting tonight, features Company, a kind of international repertory troupe of improvisers, some drawn from jazz, some from academic and art-music circles, some from performance art. Another growing phenomenon is the unlikely stream of startlingly original music from Russia – some of it jazz-derived, some not – now coming into the country through the offices of a British label, Leo Records. And then there is Germany's Moers Festival, taking place this week and demonstrating, as in past years, how far American jazz truly coexists with European. There is mutual respect, but at last an evident sep-aration.

In 1968 when the young German players made their demonstration, fuses were, after all, blowing everywhere. The sign at the Quasimodo reflected many pressures: fury at critical indifference; determination to get out of America's shadow, the desire of the practitioners to sort out their problems by themselves without relying on the whims of record com-panies or promoters. A German critic wrote, with the unselfconscious optimism only possible at the time: 'Free jazz was the musically expressed quest to make living together bearable.'

Fifteen years later, some significant victories have been won. Public funding for the music had improved immeasurably in Holland, Germany, Britain, Italy and France, at least until the recession. And the compara-tively healthy climate of the middle Seventies did bring audiences. British player Evan Parker, one of the world's leading saxophone innovators, observes: 'In a way, there's always an economic recession for unconven-tional musicians. But it makes them wily survivors, and very nomadic. If you hear there's work in Italy then, sooner or later, a lot of musicians will wind up in Italy. Things are going well in France at the moment because there seem to be sympathetic characters in the cultural departments of the new administration. In Holland there is a stability of support for this music which is hard to beat.'

Even the most perfunctory look at the social role of the music around Europe reveals intriguing differences – differences that are camouflaged by the readiness with which performers from all over the world come together to make music whenever opportunities arise. In spite of the Heath Robinsonian manner of its dissemination, some version of free-music is now to be found in most of the world's major cities – from New York to Tokyo via Leningrad, London, Helsinki, Rome or Budapest. A sizeable majority of practitioners have been influenced extensively by orthodox jazz – mostly those modifications of it twenty years ago in which the likes of Ornette Coleman, John Coltrane or Albert Ayler brought the vocalised tone of the blues back to the music to interrupt the often deadening treadmill of the cycle of chord changes. European players like Evan Parker, Peter Brötzmann, and the current members of Company, E. L. Petrowsky, Zbigniew Namyslowski, and Willem Breuker, have all done time with this particular source.

On to this platter of Sixties free jazz, improvisers have latterly grated bits and pieces of the vocabulary of electronic music. Company performer Hugh Davies was a member of Karlheinz Stockhausen's first live music ensemble. The random and chance philosophy of John Cage appeals especially to percussionists, in their appetites for whistles, klaxons, toys, rattles and general paraphernalia in addition to the conventional drum kit. Even the moods and vocabularies of quite dissimilar musical cultures, especially those of India and the Far East, have a place. Performances almost anywhere in the world by musicians of this persuasion might therefore suggest, sometimes in the course of a single evening, post-Sixties jazz, Dada-esque performance art, spacious, trance-like episodes of minimalism, or intricate and detailed twistings and turnings of the same fragment of a phrase that might be the embryo of a composition. In terms of modern composers, the preoccupation of artists such as Stockhausen concerning the duration and erosion of clusters of sounds more than their harmonic relationships has appealed naturally to improvisers; so has the enthusiasm for cyclical forms – often operating around tonal centres – of figures like Philip Glass and Steve Reich.

But if there are close musical ties between the world's free musicians, the social and cultural positions occupied by them vary widely. In Britain, despite an increasingly knowledgeable and interested public in recent years, the music still occupies a marginal position, in relation both to the jazz and the straight worlds. In Russia it is a passionate sideline of academics and orchestral players. In Holland it has a wild, vaudevillian quality, and a degree of municipal encouragement. In Czechoslovakia, jazz players, engaged in a running battle with both the Musicians' Union and the Ministry of Culture, are in the forefront of counter-cultural activity, producing *samizdat* publications dealing with all the arts.

Voice of America's Willis Conover broadcast some 25,000 shows since the end of the Second World War. This may have been as much a part of cultural imperialism as the distribution of Coca Cola, but for a good part of Europe it was the only opportunity to hear one of the century's few vital and inspirational musical departures. Latterly, there have been opportunities for the musicians to influence each other at close range. The upshot has been the most intricate, varied, subtle and culturally crossfertilised musical development currently being made. Sergei Kuryokhin, a brilliant classically-trained Russian improvising pianist, considering the phenomenon in an interview in Leningrad in 1981:

'Avant-garde is the name given to some sort of creative music, which has developed over the last seventy years . . . serial music, dodecaphonics, new jazz, musique concrete, electronic music . . . how can one classify the music Stockhausen is writing today as distinct from the English group Company? Some of the Company's records are, in a European sense, much more serious music than, let's say, some of the records of Kagel or Luc Ferrari.'

There is, nevertheless, a Catch-22 in the ambitions of improvising musicians, one that Kuryokhin, as an *enfant terrible* in the Russian music world, undoubtedly understands. Material survival and the need for audiences and backers invite the players to dispel their loony fringe image. But musical survival may lead the opposite way. Evan Parker again:

'These musicians are not much interested in packaging the stuff as high culture. It's just . . . what it is. They don't pretend that it's based on the latest discourses in high energy physics, or a prose poem by Kafka, or reinterpretation of *Antigone*. Straight composers often do it, hoping that a dressing of ancient cultural values will give their work an appearance of substance, which it may have or not. After all, how can you go wrong with The Cosmos? If you call the music *Jamming at Eddie's Place* or something, the music may be just as interesting but the name won't inspire Great Thoughts. Respectability may be useful for getting finance, but music attempting to be creative and innovative should be careful of it.'

When the impact of the Total Music Meetings all those years ago in Berlin finally sank in, the establishment promoter George Gruntz made a startling admission to his challengers: 'With you,' Gruntz said, 'music is made. With us, it can only be performed.' All over Europe today the point is being resoundingly confirmed.

CLASS ACT

The Guardian, July 1983

It had to happen. With the dust barely settled from the Wynton Marsalis Festival Hall performance, a British trio in the decidedly modest surroundings of the Covent Garden community centre performed music of comparable panache and intensity last Thursday. The group featured the saxophonist Alan Skidmore, with Dave Green on bass and Tony Oxley on drums.

It was a heartwarming event on a number of counts. Skidmore himself, a Coltrane fan with a powerful, muscular sound, was as eloquent as at any time in his career – and overcame his occasional submersion into the technical intricacies of the style. Dave Green, normally a firm but unspectacular player, combined a resonance worthy of Charlie Haden with that rigorous care for the beat which has made him such a popular ensemble player.

And Tony Oxley, one of the world's great percussionists, was able consistently to lift the melody instruments into another dimension by combining his audacity as a straight-time player with the innovations he has made as a free musician. Oxley is a drummer of extraordinary flexibility and relaxation, qualities not always immediately apparent from his awkward demeanour at the drums, which he plays like a man trying to get out of a jacket without undoing the buttons.

He will play a stream of timekeeping patterns with his right hand hovering between the snare and the cymbal, breaking up the inexorability of the cymbal pattern as Elvin Jones did. Mostly the repertoire involved either Coltrane tunes or original pieces that sounded very like them. On 'Weaver of Dreams', a Skidmore composition, the saxophonist wound up the tune with a feverish coda in the celebrated 'sheets of sound' manner, trancelike repetition of fast runs bursting out into off-the-instrument whoops. A world class band, that deserves a world class exposure.

SAL

The Guardian, July 1983

Sal Nistico, the rugged, barrel-chested tenor saxophonist from Syracuse, is the perfect example of how the spirit of jazz is not exclusively borne along by its front rank stars. Nature has made Nistico a figure of character anyway, who looks like a fight referee and who tucks the mouthpiece of the saxophone into the corner of his mouth like a cheroot. His sound, though it is a blend of the approaches of Charlie Parker and John Coltrane in about equal quantities, also possesses at times a bleached and hollow quality quite unlike either of them and more reminiscent if anything of Warne Marsh. Fast and agile in execution and offbeat in phrasing, Nistico's favourite behaviour is the building of long melodic lines that bridge several choruses of a solo – an enviable foresight that marks out the stronger soloists from the many performers who adopt a kind of halting, painting-by-numbers manner.

The mood of the band veers from the brittle sound of a Gillespie-Parker group to a stylish hard bop somewhere between a Gerry Mulligan band and the Jazz Messengers – long expositions swelling out of flimsy, functional compositions. The other musicians maintain the quick-thinking eloquence, particularly Horace Parlan on piano and Dusko Goykovich on trumpet. The Yugoslav, a performer capable of both contemplativeness and bravura, was the ideal foil for Nistico's brusque, rolled-sleeves approach.

The band was at its sharpest on modern jazz classics like 'It's You or No One' and 'Woody 'n' You' and the excellent drumming of Alvin Queen, accents exploding on the cymbal like water hitting a hot plate, was a cornerstone of the band's vigorous and authoritative demeanour.

RAISING AN EYEBROW

The Guardian, September 1983

The playing of Art Farmer, the dapper, jowly, bloodhound-featured improviser, mostly revolves around a cool, poised, Miles Davis-influenced bop. Intelligent and balanced, its generally muted and refined effect is compounded by Farmer's preference for the velvet-sounding flugelhorn over the trumpet. Farmer is currently on a short British tour, in the company of Brian Dee on piano, Len Skeat on bass and Alan Ganley on drums.

All of the leader's graceful, nonchalant mannerisms were on show on Monday night at the 100 Club. Farmer, though he can handle the teleprinter-like style of uptempo bebop, is at his best at a medium-paced lope in which his phrasing takes on the characteristics of a lugubriously mobile Jacques Tati-like face – equivocal phrases like raised eyebrows, sudden bursts of assertion, hovering, preoccupied sounds.

Also on the bill was the Tommy Chase quartet, an excellent young British bop outfit dominated by the saxophone playing of Alan Barnes. Barnes is clearly a highly educated soloist, thoroughly familiar with the methods of men like Charlie Parker and Art Pepper, and garnishing the confection with a few well-modulated avant-gardisms. They all look like vacuum-cleaner salesmen but play the daylights out of a very sophisticated bebop. It is, of course, a fairly archival style for a young band to be adopting, and its premeditation was reflected in how unadaptable it was to an unexpected interruption from the irrepressible South African saxophonist Dudu Pukwana. But it is a band to watch.

TIME AND MOTION

The Guardian, October 1983

A bloke at the next table in the Pizza Express, observing your correspondent struggling to make the odd mark with a piece of burnt stick on the back of a pawn ticket, passed over a note which read: 'Jazz critics are as necessary as a time and motion expert in your bedroom when you're . . .' Well, you can guess the rest. All I can say is, don't knock it till you've tried it – thanks to science, I now average seven-and-a-half minutes extra sleep a night.

It's not surprising that this view surfaced in Vi Redd's season in London. It's a line that you often find applied to jazz, usually by musicians – that the music is the business of the passions and the heart, and thus needs no apologies. Ms Redd, the alto saxophonist and singer whose track record has included work with Count Basie, Dizzy Gillespie and Roland Kirk, is a player of just the kid of old-fashioned bottle to make the music-speaks-for-itself theory faintly practical – until you think how much publicity her work could still do with.

Vi Redd is performing with a trio led by the British pianist Eddie Thompson, and her opening night was full of surprises. To begin with, her sound, which is roughly based on the melodic ideas of Charlie Parker, is of no regular dialect. She imparts to notes a rubbery, half-formed quality reminiscent of Ornette Coleman. She is also endlessly willing to experiment, dropping into 'Summertime' midway through 'The Shadow of Your Smile', and playing a firm, raunchy mid-tempo strut as the back half of an otherwise plaintive and faithfully delivered version of 'I Can't Get Started'. 'Autumn Leaves' was also done at a gentle lope, full of breaks – which Ms Redd would sometimes mischievously toy with by holding the delivery of notes back so that they would emerge as swallowed, squeezed off sounds.

As a blues singer she is capable of bringing the house down, a skill she amply demonstrated despite, as she said, being clearly travel-weary. The Thompson Trio played with sympathetic verve, the leader being a very high class piano player indeed.

POISE

The Guardian, October 1983

The great days of Bill Evans and Scott LaFaro take some matching. Though they could sometimes resemble a well-modulated debate between two equally eloquent and urbane dons, the overall effect subsumed their instrumental skills into an articulate and passionate music that transformed the introverted format of piano and bass. So it is with Joanne Brackeen and Clint Houston, who are at Ronnie Scott's for this week.

Enthusiasts have been eagerly awaiting Ms Brackeen's visit. Her recent album *Special Identity* created a stir, revealing her as occupying a style midway between Paul Bley and Chick Corea, but the cumulative effect of her playing is a musical switchback ride, full of unexpected turns, cliff-hanging bravado but above all a freshness and gusto that is like heading straight into a sea breeze. She hits the keys with a piston-like force, appears to be playing well within herself even when the notes are spraying about like confetti, and plays many self-penned tunes that – in a particularly Corea-like manner – hold a number of contrasting melodic and rhythmic idea in tension with each other.

In the case of 'Special Identity' itself, this takes the form of an offbeat, sidelong figure reminiscent of an early Carla Bley piano tune, switched with a broad, chuckling, fiesta-like melody. Houston, a brilliant bassist from whom the notes snap like whiplashes and who is comfortably able to run neck and neck with Ms Brackeen on the most convoluted excursions, pursues all the twists and turns of the tune like a defender marking an unpredictable striker.

Left to herself, Joanne Brackeen unleashes floods of sound from the piano that never lose their graceful, coherent poise. Her music is intelligent, elegant, free of cliché and repetition and delivered with a whirlwind force. Such panache surprised the punters, discovering in a piano show the clout of a saxophone player at full belt. A great pianist, and a living definition of what jazz improvisation is all about.

1984-86

By the middle of the decade, the new cultism that was beginning to surround old bebop players had grown increasingly audible and visible. In London, young DJs had been playing classic Sixties soul-jazz and hard-bop records to even younger dancers, so veterans like Art Blakey suddenly found themselves performing for audiences who had worked out dance steps to music they had started playing thirty years before.

On the avant-garde, the cross-culturalism that had begun in the 1970s and been buttressed by insufficient but definitely detectable public arts funding activity subsequently reached its highest general profile in Britain when a Russian jazz group, the Ganelin Trio, began a tour in an era when a representative of the KGB always came along for the ride. The band subsequently visited the United States – and though its collage-like mix of Western and Eastern musics, and its approach to improvisation were more formal and premeditated than West Europeans generally favoured, it symbolised a perception of 'jazz' as an attitude to creative music-making, rather than as a prescription for obligatory techniques. London also seemed, for a while at least, to be on the verge of securing a home for the music in the form of a National Jazz Centre building, but though its capital requirements were small compared to an opera house or a theatre, a mixture of enthusiastic but amateurish planning and over-cautious funding policies finally left it dead in the water in the middle of the decade.

But a gradually returning audience for the flexibility and forthrightness of jazz was detectable in London on appearances by a variety of volatile legends – like the singer/pianist Nina Simone, who packed Ronnie Scott's Club on several memorable seasons, and the trumpeter Chet Baker, a James Dean look-alike of the Fifties and a poetically lyrical performer whose career hung by a tantalising threat after a lifetime of self-destructiveness. The triumphant optimism of South African jazz surfaced in the continuing creativity of expatriate musicians, including pianist Abdullah Ibrahim (Dollar Brand) and trumpeter Hugh Masekela. The *breadth of the spread of African music to the New World was represented in the playful, unruly energies of Brazilian multi-instrumentalist Hermeto Pascoal (an inspiration to Miles Davis) and the gleeful, glowing professionalism of Machito's Cuban band (a survivor of the period when Cuban jazz was first embraced by Dizzy Gillespie in the Forties).*

Signs that a new confidence was abroad in the British jazz scene became unmissable after the mid Eighties. A young big-band, Loose Tubes, emerged to join avant-garde orchestral jazz, bebop, African music, fairground and marching-band themes, and surrealistic comedy. And a new name appeared in the credits of a handful of workshop jazz groups performing around London – that of saxophonist Courtney Pine.

Hypnotist

The Guardian, December 1983

The trumpet playing of Chet Baker, on a good night, remains one of the most thoughtful and shapely manifestations of the improviser's art. Though peppered with long lay-offs, during which periods it seemed likely that jazz was to be forever deprived of one of its foremost lyricists, Baker's career has nevertheless seem him sustain most of the melodic inventiveness he started out with in the Fifties.

Baker is performing at Ronnie Scott's Club in a quartet that comprises local players John Critchenson (piano) Kenny Baldock (bass) and Martin Drew (drums). Unusually, he opened proceedings by singing – an activity he pursues by the unconventional method of hanging the whole business on phrasing and rhythm alone. In other words, though his pitching is shaky and he reduces lyrics to rubble, he nevertheless manages – like a true jazz singer – to hypnotise an audience by the sheer swing and dynamics of his work.

The song was 'Just Friends', taking at a fast clip and featuring a long trumpet solo that elegantly combined a subtle and elaborate lattice-work of runs which bridged several choruses uninterrupted, with Baker's inimitable burnishing of a single note to make it flicker with life. Early on in the game, it was clear that the group would not allow the trumpeter's famous lassitude in performance to get a grip on him. Martin Drew's drumming, heavily dependent on a bright, buzzy cymbal beat and an insistence on doubling up the time on the snare (it's a way of playing that puts you in mind of two relay racers endlessly accelerating out of each other's reach) leaned against Baker's languid ruminations and at times the leader's playing became almost shrill in response.

Baker is at Ronnie Scott's for the rest of the week. Almost everything he does is musicianly, and hearing him do it is not only a pleasure but an education. In the nicest sense of the word, that is.

WATERS' MUSIC

The Guardian, February 1984

The all but forgotten British jazz scene – of the Fifties – and its audience were at the 100 Club for the benefit for incapacitated pianist Alan Clare. There was Beryl Bryden, smile as wide as a keyboard and voice to match, drummer Tony Crombie, looking as ever like an irascible taxi driver, trombonist George Chisholm, looking mischievous and delivering some of the most succinct solos of the night.

One of the outsiders in this venture was the remarkable veteran saxophonist Benny Waters, a box-like man with a face like a walnut and a wild, thrilling sound. Waters is now eighty-two, having enjoyed a spectacular career that took in the bands of Fletcher Henderson and Jimmy Lunceford in the Twenties – and he still managed to make several of the participants on this show seem as if they were his grandparents.

British trombonist George Chisholm was playing in the band that supported Waters, having already made his point guesting with an all-trombone front line in a version of 'Creole Love Call' in which he was able in a few short choruses to make the instrument seem agile, invigorating and witty all at once. The general knees-up mood was sustained in a galloping rendition of 'Strike Up the Band' by which time even the laconic Crombie – who normally plays drums as if he was swatting flies with a dishcloth – was playing fit to pop a button. Waters looked to be enjoying himself hugely, which was, as you might say, the feeling of the meeting.

RENAISSANCE

The Guardian, March 1984

Something fascinating has happened to the career of the effervescent veteran drummer Art Blakey, and it was born out by a representative of Ronald Scott's organisation reflecting, 'I've been getting some very funny calls this week.' In other words, it wasn't the usual coterie of buffs and night-owls, but part of that new audience for Blakey's music which accounts for his records being played to congregations of boppers and breakdancers at formerly non-jazz venues like the Electric Ballroom.

If any of this was surprising Blakey he wasn't letting on. His band played with its usual aplomb and brisk and businesslike vigour and had a couple of familiar faces in saxophonists Jean Toussaint and Donald 'Duck' Harrison, two men who complement each other admirably, given the former's dry, understated style and the latter's twisty, rather Dolphyesque brittleness.

The musical director this time – Blakey has always been open to entrusting the arrangements and repertoire of the Jazz Messengers to virtuosi much younger than himself – was Terence Blanchard. Blanchard's spare, leisurely, early-Miles trumpet style helped to build the usual intriguing tensions and contrasts of a Blakey outfit: in this instance phlegmatic and reflective soloing pitched against the leader's customarily flushed and tumultuous style at the drums.

The repertoire featured those catchy originals that always remind you of early Sixties Blue Note albums. Blakey, uninhibitedly revelling in his work as usual, seems younger by the day.

IN FROM THE COLD
The Guardian, March 1984

Russian jazz! The very notion of it has struck such a vein of curiosity and incredulity that the first concert of the current tour by the USSR's Ganelin Trio was a sell-out days ago, and musicians and punters alike have been fascinated to discover at first hand what the sound of surprise from a country so distant and so shielded from the jazz tradition might actually be like.

The Ganelin Trio features Vyacheslav Ganelin on keyboards, Vladimir Chekasin on reeds, basset horns, flutes and sundry odds and ends, and Vladimir Tarasov on percussion. They come from Lithuania, they've been a regular working outfit for twelve years and they play a brand of free improvisation within carefully considered structures that is both unusually deliberate for what is clearly avant-garde jazz, and strikingly flexible considering the extent of the forethought.

At their London concert at the Bloomsbury Theatre they played two pieces that have formed the basis of records recently available here: 'Non Troppo', a taut, dense, anxious composition that begins with tiny, tinkling treble keyboard effects and ends with the sound of a wooden flute skimming across a snowscape, and 'New Wine', a percussion-dominated gallop that had much in common with the derisory, clowning style of the Dutch school of improvisation.

'Non Troppo' was inventive but restrained, and for a while it seemed as though one of the most unsettling dilemmas of the avant-garde – being able to conceive of a way of improvising that can be hinted at in performance but which is not explicit – was going to cloud the whole show.

The band would veer between open sections in which Chekasin – a veritable Jacques Tati of the saxophone but with a formidable technique for either Ayleresque yearning or a Rollins-like irony in manipulating familiar materials – would pitch his raw, hoarse intonation against Ganelin's elegant ruminations, or they would slip into an outrageously cool cruise through conventional bop, the leader accompanying his scurrying right hand with a counterpoint coaxed from the basset, a small electric keyboard that replicates the bass. 'New Wine', the second piece, started audaciously with a long drum solo, which Tarasov littered with hushed, chopped-off sounds as if trying to restrain his own exuberance. Chekasin, who bends straight from the waist as if wearing a corset, stomps like a matador, and warily approaches the microphone as if about to throw a net over it, delivered a sardonic and frequently impassioned mixture of whirling note clusters and cantankerous, Brotzmann-like honks.

As highly organised 'free' music, it will have its detractors amongst improvising purists; it uses so many conventional devices as to be in danger of subjection to them. But it is a kind of jazz that is vital, alive, funny, committed, virtuosic and assembled in a manner quite untypical of either European or American variants of the music. The Ganelin Trio's Arts Council tour is currently under way.

CHERUB

The Guardian, March 1984

Han Bennink, the massive, cherubic-faced Dutch drummer, is not so much an instrumentalist as a Cecil B. De Mille-scale event in his own right – and many of his visits to Britain, by scrupulously avoiding the fetishes of the smooth and impeccable 'performance', are guaranteed to be a breath of fresh air.

A brilliant drummer behind all his antics and gallumphings, Bennink played a kit that simply consisted of a single snare drum and a cymbal hanging on a cord from the ceiling – which item he proceeded to deploy like a conventional bop-style ride-cymbal, as an offensive weapon that would swing menacingly around his ears and which he would fight off with wild swings of the sticks and spine-chilling yelps, and at one point as the victim of the attentions of an enormous bolt-cutter which he found whilst rooting amongst the ICA's props backstage.

His deliberations were therefore a mixture of straight-ahead drumming that would have catapulted any jazz band in the world into orbit, thunderous clatterings and hammerings at a multitude of objects lying around his feet, general yelling and gesticulating, and some very lyrical soprano saxophone playing somewhat in the manner of Lol Coxhill.

Guitarist Derek Bailey, as usual, played imperturbably throughout this barrage, but his style is clearly on the change. Normally exhibiting a vocabulary of pinging harmonics and harsh, scrambled chords, Bailey has reintroduced much of the chordal texture he started out with three decades ago, but rejigged in a fascinatingly wayward manner. He has also recovered the desire to close episodes with something close to orthodox resolutions – normally a heresy for one of the great iconoclasts of improvisation.

But the beauty of the pairing is that the expected ingredients never fit together. If Bennink plays a ballad on soprano, Bailey makes a noise like somebody dragging a sack of broken bottles. If Bailey exhibits a limping swing, Bennink will break his sticks and throw them at the kit. It has all the perversity of life as we know and love it.

ALL UNDER CONTROL

The Guardian, March 1984

It's not what you do, and sometimes not even the way that you do it, but the way that you appear to be doing it that can make the difference between an average performance and the kind that builds a reputation. Steps Ahead, the pioneering American jazz-funk band, has the knack of being able to sound much more spontaneous than for the most part it really is. Since many far more literally spontaneous ensembles often generate a great deal more heat than light, it's nevertheless no mean feat.

The group is a five-piece that delivers a stylish confection of many of the more mainstream ingredients of recent commercial jazz and funk. Both the principal soloists (Mike Brecker, saxophones, Mike Mainieri, vibraphone) play with composure and balance, and though Brecker has a mixture of that broad, billowing tone favoured by jazz-funk artists like Wilton Felder and Ronnie Laws, he combines it with a rough and raucous quality drawn from Coltrane, and a remarkable ability to avoid repeating himself. Mainieri plays like a less florid version of Gary Burton, but with the same relaxed sense of form.

The band's versatility was demonstrated on a Mainieri original by the name of 'Oops' in which the theme was unfolded in two tempos pulling against each other, the middle section involved key changes and the improvisatory passages took place in a straight-ahead jazz time in which Brecker played some spectacular high-speed excursions. A rather pretty, studied outfit for some – but at least the labour of the premeditation paid off in compositions of real maturity and flair.

QUICKSILVER

The Guardian, March 1984

The demeanour of saxophone players, who have dominated jazz since the 1930s, is a many-splendoured thing. Some are cool and diffident, holding the instrument as if examining a Ming vase. Some swing it as if it was a jiving partner. Some ignore the audience, some proudly parade their dexterity. And a few, notably Sonny Rollins and the brilliant ex-Art Blakey altoist, Bobby Watson, rhapsodise ingeniously while staring straight at the punters with raised eyebrows as if to say, 'Now where the hell is all *this* coming from?'

Watson is a young man but a player of the old school, a celebrater of past glories as Wynton Marsalis is – he shared Blakey's front line with Marsalis in his days with the Jazz Messengers. But although Watson's work is infused with the quicksilver lyricism of Charlie Parker, he is many leagues away from the standard bebop remould. His tone is very pure and clean; his lines have a fiery and imperious passion, even when their construction seems too complex and intricate to sound anything but algebraic.

At the Bass Clef on Wednesday, Watson was playing the first gig of a nationwide tour, which will take in a Camden Jazz Week performance on 22 March. He is appearing with a British group featuring the trumpeter Guy Barker who – in both the modesty of his on-stage conduct and the unexpected intensity of his playing – strongly brings to mind a young Kenny Wheeler. The band played a repertoire of distinctly Messenger-like pieces of hard bop, Latin tunes and ballads. 'Orange Blossom', opening as a piece of pure *film noir* music, accelerated through an increasingly animated trumpet solo by Barker, which ended in little prodding phases that Watson gleefully took up and unravelled into a series of incandescent, comet-like swoops. Andy Cleyndert played a beautiful bass solo on the same theme, mostly in the deepest register and with sepulchral slowness, full of throaty slurs.

And on the bouncy, mid-tempo Messengers' tune, 'Time Will Tell', Barker demonstrated his determination to keep up with the leader with a solo that veered wildly from shouts to whispers and swung fiercely. He never loosened up enough to unbutton his jacket, for all that.

LAST BOW

The Guardian, April 1984

Machito, that puckish and genial defender of the Afro-Cuban style, appears to have been recently struck, like all the rest of us ordinary mortals, by the need for economies. This has imparted to his current band a shriller and faintly over-reaching edge because a distinctly pared-down version of his usual reed and brass section is having to achieve the outfit's obligatory (and all but inevitable) finale of bringing the house down wherever it works.

Initially it was a disappointment even to see a shrunken version of this ensemble, and the combination of Machito's joyous, arrangements, without the sheer clout of the full complement, made you wonder if things could be quite the same. But Machito has allowed them all to cover the gap by playing more loosely and eccentrically as individuals. The opportunity for longer solos brought some attractive reflections from veteran trumpeter 'Chocolato' Armentierez, whose manner of improvising fits salsa music like a glove, being entirely composed of mischievous upturned phrases and gentle humour, infectious as a broad grin. Collectively the effect was wilder, and compellingly spontaneous.

Percussion is always to the fore in the band and the opening of the third tune to their Monday night set at Ronnie Scott's was a long exchange between the two drummers, the congas flooding the room with rich and jostling sounds, some soft, fleshy sounding, some booming and resonant, some crisp and hard and driving the rhythm. Machito's own singing, a semi-spoken, exultant-sounding monologue that resembles somebody telling their friends that they've just won the pools, reveals just how acute his understanding of the idiom and his own players actually is.

(*This was the last review to be written of a Machito performance. The band-leader, Frank 'Machito' Grillo, died in London during the run. An even more irreplaceable loss in the same week was William 'Count' Basie.*)

URBAN BUSHMEN
The Guardian, June 1984

The urban bushmen are back. The Art Ensemble of Chicago, one of the few groups playing improvised music in a contemporary manner that has achieved something like world-celebrity status, was performing at the Festival Hall as part of the Greater London Council's London Against Racism events. It was an apposite choice. In its power to win over audiences with little experience of jazz through sheer force of musical personality, the group has for years been a living embodiment the notion that cultural differences are not as unbridgeable as they look.

An Art Ensemble performance has a strong whiff of ritual about it. Trumpeter Lester Bowie sports an intern's white coat, others wear grease-paint and have various forms of vegetation growing out of their hats. They all begin by standing, heads bowed in silence, and wait for inspiration. On this occasion it was Bowie's horn, making a sound like an approaching piston-plane running out of fuel. The band joined in with bright streamers of sound that eventually died away into a tinkle of bells and marimbas.

Bowie returned into this sunnier climate, leading a piece of breezy, street-band swing through which the entire group eventually soloed in turn. Altoist Roscoe Mitchell started stiffly, but the length of his solo gave him an opportunity to loosen up into an increasingly relaxed exercise of guttural squawks, reflective warbles and slithering runs. It brought the band close to what you might call its operating temperature, and was a good example of how the patience born of confidence enables them to find a groove that many improvisors search vainly for all night.

Joseph Jarman's tenor solo took the best from the mood that had been painstakingly sought out by the others. Though his elaborate headgear made him look like a studious moose, the rich, lubricated quality of his sound began to give the music a sensuous, purring intimacy. It culminated in a volcanic drum solo from Don Moye, which led to all the performers taking to the vast array of drums that adorned the stage and establishing a rhythm that lapped and washed like the tide, and which set the audience breaking into incredulous whistles and whoops.

Now's the Time

The Guardian, June 1984

Jazz festivals often occasion deep foreboding, being mostly opportunities for predictable caravans of bored artists to practise their scales and demonstrate the full dynamic range between loud and hysterical. The Now's The Time festival, an ambitious GLC/Jazz Centre venture running throughout last weekend in various parts of Brixton was, though not without its ups and downs, a frequently inspired illustration of both the ethnic and the stylistic variety loosely encompassed nowadays by that remarkable tolerant word 'jazz'.

Friday night was a good example. It began with a performance of free-playing and visual aides from the British group Coherents, a loose limbed performance of Caribbean music and dance from the Martinique group Dede St Prix and wound up with a classic display of nihilistic kitsch from the Sun Ra Arkestra. As usual, this band comes on sporting a wardrobe apparently culled from a combination of *Flash Gordon* and a village hall production of *Camelot*, plays a baited-breath intro until the leader steams impressively on to a semi-darkened stage waving flashlights, his considerable bulk wrapped in a glittering red cape and with wraparound shades.

Much other-worldly reverence has been attached to Sun Ra, who is now in his seventies and still maintains that he is a space traveller who has gathered much of his inspiration from a species other than the likes of you and me. Even if you choose instead to view him as a kind of avant-garde Liberace, a performer with a genius for packaging a difficult production who has stuck resolutely to his story for thirty years, it remains the case that a performance by his band is like nothing else in jazz.

Sun Ra, amongst his other achievements, was one of the first jazzmen to use synthesised sounds and the band, in awaiting his arrival, pumped a steady supply of rumbling electronics into the cavernous auditorium of Brixton's Academy. They then all roared into a hit-and-miss vocal chant of 'You Are Children of the Sun' and a consideration of the disadvantages of nuclear war as symbolised by bangs, thumps, flashes of light, squeals and hurried pirouettings by a small, lithe dancer who traversed the stage with anxious flappings of vestments.

Then followed a rattling mid-tempo blues, a demonstration of Sun Ra's fondness for the swing music of the Thirties, and a tongue-in-cheek foray into 'Mack the Knife'. As has been previously pointed out about Sun Ra, a reprise of earlier styles in his hands is worth more than all the college-boy note-for-note revivalist bands put together.

Saturday's show was even more of a mishmash, but patchier in its achievements. A large Caribbean outfit called Ellie Matt and the GI Brass offered a peculiar mixture of exclamatory swing-band section playing and reggae and inventively applied it to a repertoire that included Boy George's 'Chameleon' and Bob Marley's 'No Woman No Cry'.

Eric Burdon and Zoot Money then came on to remind you of all the reasons why the white hard-rock music of the late Sixties mostly now sounds like somebody driving a milk float into a brick wall, and the evening was headlined by a band led by the Cuban trumpeter Arturo Sandoval and a hard bop group fronting tenorists George Adams and Archie Shepp.

Sandoval, a thick-set, moon-faced man who looks as if life mostly strikes him as pretty droll, played a spectacular set in a trumpet style partly dependent on jazz, partly on classical precision, and partly on Latin extroversion. Though he plays everything as if it were 'Flight of the Bumble Bee' at 78 r.p.m., the extraordinary effusiveness of his sound, the absolute control of the most ambitious effects, and the cool logic and virtual absence of jazz clichés from his phrasing even at the most blustering tempos all gave his music an irresistible charm. Two episodes in his set – a scat-singing babble of bebop lines culminating in a mock drum solo in which the trumpeter waved his arms about frantically as if hitting cymbals, and a pocket-trumpet encore of 'Green Dolphin Street' that ended in almost everybody on stage playing a stormy Latin percussion interlude – will live on in the memory.

George Adams and Archie Shepp wound up the proceedings with a performance of raucous tenor extravagances from Adams, a bit of obeisance to Charlie Parker, and some rather murky originals. It was a

disappointing finale because Shepp was discreet and Adams – as he sometimes is – unable to detach himself from his omnipotent, overloaded
tenor-hero style. Shepp, though he didn't play much, nevertheless demonstrated the sly and knowing manner of building a solo and the pliable,
sinewy sounds that have remained so consistently his strengths.

A Prayer Don't Need No Visa

The Guardian, July 1984

Hugh Masekela, South Africa's most famous trumpeter and a musical revolutionary in many senses, is a man whose every turn is sure to be
scrutinised from all sides of the political spectrum for signs of softening
up. Some are already muttering that his act is too multi-cultural now he
has signed himself to a major record company. But on the evidence of his
concert at Ronnie Scott's, Masekela would have no trouble claiming cur
rently to lead one of the world's great bands.

The trumpeter's presence in London had clearly caused a stir, and it was
standing-room only before much time had elapsed in his long, melodic,
shrewdly-paced set. He began it without his full band, getting the measure
of the audience with a lightweight selection of African township music,
permeated with a professional gloss that threatened at first to undermine
the warm spontaneity of the style.

The tunes are mostly structured on bubbling brass intros (Masekela
adopts the voice-like flugelhorn throughout, and plays with a pure, ringing tone) that give way to African vocal chants. But lately Masekela has
adopted a mixture of styles for his band in which the African origins are
diffused with the mannerisms of Western pop and Latin American music
as well as jazz. Having once got the audience where he wanted it,
Masekela did not waste his chance to cut deeper. The middle of his set was
occupied by two slow pieces, the first a song in prayer for rain ('A prayer
don't need no visa') and the second a slow, exploratory interplay between
the musicians that brought a complete hush to the house.

By this time the band featured three female singers in addition to the
regulars, and saxophonist Barney Joel Rachabanc, who wrapped a
staggering collection of tumbling arpeggios with pealing cries and sardonic remonstrating interjections around the elegant edifice of Masekela's
flugelhorn. Rachabanc is a man who will surely hit the world's jazz stage
in a big way, if there's any justice. An extremely moving, heartening and
spectacular show.

BACK TO THE FUTURE

The Guardian, September 1984

It has often been remarked of Reuben 'Ruby' Braff, the stocky, wisecracking white cornetist from Boston, that he was overlooked in the Fifties because his role as a youngster preoccupied with the ebullient, unbookish styles of men like Louis Armstrong and Bobby Hackett made him out of date before he began. Now that most of the music's pioneers have passed on, Braff has become precious – a souvenir of a jazz age more optimistic, open handed and in some ways ingenuous than the ones that followed. He is fifty-seven now, and looks as if he will be safeguarding the jewels for many years.

He is the guardian of jazz's domination of popular culture before the war – characterised by artists with very little interest in technique for its own sake, a love of good songs, a sense of humour, gracefulness, immense self-possession and the sense of unity between the instrument and the idiom to construct a dialect with it as natural as speech. Braff has looked after his childhood heroes particularly lovingly, because he has consistently captured the atmosphere as well as the procedure. Most replica musicians of the period today sound as if they were taking an exam.

Braff was appearing at the Pizza on the Park in the company of a local pianist, Brian Lemon. Unusually for brass players, the American has frequently favoured drumless ensembles, since he is a master of controlled excitement in a curious, *sotto voce* manner. Lemon, a restrained and unshowy pianist of remarkable sensitivity, was perfect for the job, cooing and massaging his partner through a collection of well-thumbed classics.

'Sweet Georgia Brown' was a typical Braff rendition, introduced as a casual riffle through the theme, interrupted by audacious squirts into the upper register, the melodic variations a mixture of soft, humming sounds, sputtering, valve-fluttering runs and brassy blares as sharp and surprising as throwing open the shutters on a sunny day. 'Tea for Two', 'S'Wonderful', and 'I Cover the Waterfront' were included in a string of evergreens, though both men were at their best at a straight, unfussy middle tempo, Braff performing like a man expertly dealing cards. He is around for some weeks, so keep an eye open.

GIL EVANS

The Guardian, October 1984

Considering its orchestral complexity and hairsbreadth dependence on nice timing, any Gil Evans orchestra gets under way in such a manner as to suggest that the stage is simply occupied by a lot of aimless roadies who happen to be wandering around carrying instruments.

Then from somewhere you hear the distant chug-chug that might be a guitar playing a funk riff, and a gathering insistent shuffle comes from the drums. Keyboards sidle in, adding little afterthoughts of muttering, throw-away phrases. When the trumpets come galloping into the foreground, you suddenly know it's Evans's adaptation of Jimi Hendrix's 'Stone Free', one of the staples of the legendary seventy-two-year-old's perpetually engaging repertoire.

Evans is at Ronnie Scott's Club for two weeks with an eleven-piece band of British musicians, some of whom played with him on his tour here last spring. He has brought his dependable trumpeter Lew Soloff, who on the opening night had his work cut out keeping the whole craft afloat. In the opening set the band delivered a kind of wing-and-prayer version of 'Stone Free' through which both Don Weller on tenor saxophone and Lew Soloff negotiated convincing individual forays – Soloff's solo playing was as sure-footed as was his ringmaster's role throughout.

Thelonious Monk's 'Friday 13th' followed – a melody that sounds as if it was written for a child – often played by Evans at a threatening drawl but which eventually works up a wild contrapuntal fury against an almost matter-of-fact cycle of chords. By the time the orchestra got to the popular, swaggering swinger 'Up from the Skies' – another Hendrix tune – it was beginning to relax and enjoy itself.

Very little new music emerges from the old master these days, though he has never been prolific and the British band, though excellent, is a little tentative and studious to liberate all the exuberance that lies within the music. But any dose of it, in whatever concentration, is worth hearing.

BLACK PIAF
The Guardian, November 1984

Nina Simone, a kind of black Edith Piaf, is a fierce sculptress of popular song far wider in scope than that of the blues and gospel tradition alone, transparently galvanised by it though she is. On a good night, her relationship with her audience can be so direct as to make everyone present feel that they have a unique line to her soul. It is a great entertainer's knack, achieved by immense stage presence, presence of mind and an unpredictability of phrasing and control of dynamics that – even though her voice is not all that it was – can achieve intimacy in the twist of a phrase. It is also achieved by an apparent lack of artifice which makes each statement seem unequivocally a personal revelation.

For her third visit to Ronnie Scott's this year – she is back by public demand until Saturday – Nina Simone is accompanied by British drummer Paul Robinson. Her performances are legendarily unpredictable, but this was a generous, forthright and often downright effusive encounter, particularly towards the end of the first set.

The opening was solemn, Simone working her way powerfully through a *Mahagonny* medley ('There's No Returning', sung in her great desolate voice, was lifetimes and heartaches away from the cleanly-enunciated, defiant manner in which Brecht/Weill is often performed). The delicacy and flickering lyricism of her piano playing highlighted the grainy realism of the performance all the more. 'Moon over Alabama' and 'Mississippi Goddam' followed, Simone running songs into each other, splicing in remonstrances with the audience, autobiographical adaptations and achieving such a level of audience participation in 'C-Line Woman' that she eventually took to leaning, with a look of comic resignation, on the piano while the crowd got on with it. 'I Sing Just to Know that I'm Alive', Simone crackled out, the piano ringing like bells. No one doubted it.

HAZARD AND HOPE

The Guardian, November 1984

If ever a music made the world seem a smaller and warmer place, it is that of Abdullah Ibrahim, formerly Dollar Brand (solo at the Shaw and the Albany Empire over last weekend). It is a characteristic of Ibrahim's music – and of music of African original generally – that is intriguingly remarked upon by Wilfred Mellers in his notes to the pianist's latest album *Autobiography*.

Mellers maintains that the music of the New World, embodied in its purposeful, assertive linear constructs, expresses the impulse of Western civilisation to appropriate and conquer, while Southern African music has represented empathy and identification with the surroundings. 'Ibrahim, a musician of the old world and the new, is on a razor edge between hazard and hope.'

This is always typical of his solo performances. The first set at the Shaw on Saturday was a rounded and reflective series of variations on many of Ibrahim's best loved themes, in which his favourite and tireless device – the sharp contrast of extremes of dynamics and rhythm – was deployed with more nerve and panache than is usual even for him.

In addition, Ibrahim's single-line improvising, which has sometimes taken on a tortured, halting quality in previous performances, possessed a ringing clarity and an inclination to develop ideas at length. The first set was a more balanced performance, the second more of a mixture of all of his mixed antecedents, blending Ellington ('In a Sentimental Mood') and

Thelonious Monk tunes in a way that – as he often does – reminds you forcibly of the intimate relationship between the work of those two jazz giants. Asked what is the first music he heard, Ibrahim will say without any affectation 'my heart'. His performances continue to confirm it.

DAVE HOLLAND

The Guardian, November 1984

The Dave Holland quintet took a catholic selection of the innovatory jazz ideas of the past twenty years and shook them to the marrow in the opening concert of its Contemporary Music Network tour. Despite being a performance that was very nearly too densely packed with ideas for its own good – the lengthy first half was so scorchingly intense as to be almost as exhausting to listen to as it must have been to deliver – it was clear from the outset that this ensemble is not only as inventive as the reputations of at least three of the performers would suggest, but that in drummer Marvin 'Smitty' Smith it possesses a musician capable of galvanising the most laconic of improvisers.

Holland himself is the British bassist who was spotted by Miles Davis in Ronnie Scott's one night in 1968, invited to the States and then proceeded to play with just about anyone of any significance in contemporary jazz – from Thelonious Monk to Lee Konitz, Stan Getz and Chick Corea. In addition to Smith and Holland himself, who plays the bass with a beautiful precision and remarkable lyrical imagination, there are Kenny Wheeler (trumpet), Steve Coleman (saxophones) and Julian Priester (trombone).

Marvin Smith helped set the pattern in the opening piece – a fast, Ornette Coleman-like theme full of teasing, oblique resolutions – by performing at the drums as if he were about to carry the show singlehanded and filling out the work of the melodic instruments with a torrent of loose, buzzing cymbal sounds and urgent, restless accents, endlessly doubling the time, adding clattering punctuation, detonating explosive thumps and hammerings all over the kit.

Coleman, a young saxophonist of modest demeanour and startling fleetness, made perfect use of this ferocious support, skiing and weaving effortlessly through the avalanche and demonstrating a precociously mature grasp of the development of the long and coherent spontaneous line. Priester, an ex-sideman of Herbie Hancock, is a delicious trombonist, performing in a mixture of blurred, yawning sounds, little clucking phrases and urgent sounds like running feet in an upstairs corridor in the freer passages, but also capable of some delicate swinging with a soft and yielding elegance.

Holland's own bass solos possessed his customary sparkling clarity, and only in the ensemble passages surrounding his foray into cello playing did the music become fussy and momentarily desultory. But it's generally a band of the highest class, vibrant and emotional, but as logical as a game of chess.

JAZZ DANCE

The Guardian, December 1984

While cardboard stars and wooden clouds hung from the ceiling for the Deptford Albany's *Peter Pan and Wendy*, the country's more headstrong young musicians were rumbling through the second of two fund-raising drives for the National Jazz Centre.

Topping the bill was Working Week, which now plays an attractive Latin-tinged mixture of danceable jazz and soul music to a growing young non-buff following. Also on the roster was John Stevens's Dance Orchestra, the membership of which was so immense on this occasion that a few members of the audience and a couple of passing drunks from the local could have been accidentally shanghaied into it, for all anyone would have known. A modestly-named but thoughtful group called Dwarf Steps – composed of students from the Jazz Centre's Outreach scheme – opened the show with a sharply played hard bop repertoire.

The Dance Orchestra played the middle set, delivering one long, fitfully shambolic, but ultimately uplifting piece, based modally on the playing of part of a scale. John Stevens's drumming was inspirational, as it often is, and though the whole huge, thrashing, glowering mishmash of noise veered at times towards the relentless, it was nonetheless a heartening demonstration of the virtues of collective improvisation, and one in which soloists like Simon Picard (tenor), Annie Whitehead (trombone), Harry Beckett (trumpet) and John Etheridge (guitar) revealed how inventively they could go about embroidering the same transparently artless theme.

Courtney Pine, an effervescent and inventive twenty-year-old black Londoner who sounds like a cross between the American hard-boppers Joe Farrell and Billy Harper, took as decisively subversive an approach to this event (wailing volcanically throughout his solo) as he had been gracefully disciplined through Dwarf Steps' set earlier on.

Brand of Love

The Guardian, January 1985

Even the most skinflint dispensers of human warmth acknowledge that Abdullah Ibrahim, formerly Dollar Brand, is a man of some presence. He is tall and graceful, the possessor of a magnificent physiognomy of arching cheekbones, an imperious nose and haunting eyes. He was born Adolph Johannes Brand in Capetown in 1934, with strands of African, Afrikaner, European and Malaysian in his makeup, his father a Basuto tribesman, his mother leader of a Methodist choir. Since his discovery in Zurich by Duke Ellington in 1965, Ibrahim has slowly become one of the best-loved pianists in the world today to have emerged from as unpredictable a stable as jazz. The name 'Dollar,' which stuck until his conversion to Islam, was an acknowledgement of his love of American as well as African music – particularly Ellington's.

If you ask him what was the first music he ever heard he will answer without affectation 'my heart.' Ibrahim's performances are frequently sell-outs and his fundraising concerts for a variety of causes (the Ethiopian famine for Dutch television, African National Congress work everywhere in the world, this country's unemployed at the Albert Hall tomorrow) often record-breakers.

Though a Muslim, and a self-proclaimed conduit for a plan not of his making, he is no disdainful ideologue. A practitioner of Japanese martial arts, a teacher of karate, a student of Chinese medicine, a producer of his own records and other people's, he is a man of both contemplation and action.

Ibrahim's conversation is not greatly different from hearing him at work. He speaks in slow, doodling speculations infused with Dutch inflections, explosions of chuckling, rolling his r's like the rumbling left hand at the piano, peppering it all with images of old Africa, quotes from the prophet, jokes about Miles and Duke and Monk. For all that, he insists:

'I've never called myself a jazz musician' (Ibrahim always refers to 'so-called jazz'), 'and Duke Ellington always said the same thing. Most of the musicians you talk to would say the same.' In his childhood and for his ancestors, music was an accompaniment to planting, harvesting, weddings, funerals, and even now he looks for the connections and ignores the divisions.

'Whenever I hear Scottish folk music,' Ibrahim says, 'I always hear African lines in it. When I was in high school and they were saying Stravinsky was difficult, I found it natural except maybe the rhythms were too stiff. When I met Thelonious Monk, who people said was weird, I couldn't understand the problem.

'When I started to play Bach I thought that was beautiful too, and if people turned away from it, it could only be because of interpretation.

When you start off doing something, you have to really believe it with all your heart – which means love, you have to love this thing you're doing.'

Very many more musicians claim that pious cause than practise it, but Ibrahim's impact in concert is unambiguously committed, which enables him to reach outside the perimeter defended by the dedicated jazz enthusiast. His best work exhibits a combination of celebratory vigour, soulfulness, fierce idealism, melodic strength and transparent simplicity that makes it a language easily grasped by intuition.

His first influences were undoubtedly contained in the hedonistic gusto of South African township music. From the townships he learned swing, and communal song, the virtues of unambiguous celebration even in servitude, of traditional pleasures unhesitatingly embraced. From America, where he lived, initially under Ellington's wing, from the mid-Sixties to early Seventies, he learned obliqueness, dissonance, contrariness. The two influences shook down side by side.

The Soweto riots of 1976 were a turning point for him and for his singer wife, Sathima Bea Benjamin. Over 600 died, many of them children. The African National Congress wanted him (as a 'cultural freedom fighter') to make a stronger contribution. Soweto convinced him. He left the country for good and redoubled his efforts outside.

Nearly all of his record titles since have featured the word 'Africa' and many of his songs the word 'freedom' too. When American record companies worried that politics were bad for sales, he started releasing his own and sold more than ever, particularly in his homeland. 'Oliver Tambo' (of the ANC), says that we have run out of cheeks to turn.' In the freedom song 'Tula Dubula' – sung in his inimitable husky, half-spoken tones, Ibrahim suggests anything but a gentle solution. 'The end of dialogue has arrived,' is his description of it.

Ibrahim speaks with offhanded deliberation about the future, as if apartheid is already dead, a murderous zombie railing at the avalanche of rebellion that is rolling inexorably toward it.

'It is inevitable. My Japanese karate teacher says to me' (he lapses into an outrageous Afrikaans-Japanese accent) 'many people say weapon is hand and foot. Not true. Weapon is time, space, change.' He guffaws uproariously, then switches into a hypnotic stare.

'For *everything* there's an appointed term, and when the end of your time comes, there's nothing you can do about it. But it is incumbent upon you to speak up in cases of injustice wherever they happen, until injustice doesn't exist any more. It is the quality of falsehood that it must vanish when the truth comes.' Less abstractly, he will wearily say, 'I have never had the right to vote in my own country.'

Ibrahim is shrewd at identifying the power of song to the cause and its closeness to African hearts. The thrust for liberation of the disfranchised, put into song, is a rallying force where few other kinds of communication exist. And the humanity and sensitivity of his own music is a deliberate affirmation of gentleness, a confounding of the primitive stereotype so beloved of apartheid.

'The problem for so-called jazz musicians is that the society does not really allow any kind of home for those that are spiritually endowed as musicians. When the community was still intact they had support. Most of the friends I started playing with I met in the church choir. Traditionally even bebop wasn't an elite form, something separate. Even at those break-neck tempos' (claps frantically) 'they could be used for dancing. People are always looking for secrets. There are no secrets, there are only basics.'

NOT CLOSE ENOUGH FOR JAZZ

The Guardian, February 1985

It was an organisational catastrophe such as to transform the Dardanelles into a tactical masterpiece, and Lady Di and, by extension, a Fleet Street flotilla had to be there to witness it. The National Jazz Centre, scheduled to open in Covent Garden in May and still in need of funds, was to be the beneficiary of Sunday night's gala at the London Palladium, at which music fans rich and poor could make their contribution to an ambitious and enterprising project that's been a dream since 1968. Eleven acts were scheduled to represent the diversity of the music in Britain, from dance-able pop-jazz, through celebrations of the rich tradition, and a few brief scatterings of the avant-garde. So far so good.

Unfortunately, no one had had the foresight to anticipate that time passes while performers are getting on and off between sets, and that a succession of compères – Spike Milligan, David Rappaport, Graham Chapman and Moira Stuart – might have been given some idea just what they were letting themselves in for. Frantic busking by these luckless individuals pulled some of the enterprise out of the fire (Milligan opined that the show must be run by the same people who run the economy), but couldn't avoid giving the proceedings a tension and insecurity that the event needed like a hole in the head.

In the opening half, notable mostly for a performance of characteristi-cally lugubrious dementia from Milligan and Chapman, the audience was confronted with the crisply nostalgic swing of the National Youth Jazz Orchestra,some punchy if rather predictable fusion music from saxo-phonist Barbara Thompson's Paraphernalia and snatches of genuinely exhilarating inventiveness from tap-dancer Will Gaines and the classical-jazz hybrid violinist Nigel Kennedy.

Kennedy shrewdly convinced this somewhat conservative-looking col-lection of punters of his credentials by a sublime rendition of Bach pieces, before bringing on two sidemen who looked like refugees from the Stray

Cats to deliver a torrent of disco-funk, mixed with atmospheric, dewy electronics over which Kennedy rhapsodised a harsh and brittle poetry on a bugged violin. Singer Alison Moyet then demonstrated why she's currently the classiest and most mature of the new pop singers digging out the old swing records, and Juliette Roberts, the young black singer with the excellent Latin-jazz ensemble Working Week, brought the most spontaneous applause for a performance of massive clout and passion.

Pianist Stan Tracey played Ellington and Thelonious Monk with mischievous energy and a swing that sounded like an entire rhythm section, which made his work, and not for the first time, a definition of jazz better than any words. Few words either, except unprintable ones, could describe the mishandling of such a crucially high-profile event. 'It'll be all right on the night' won't be good enough for a National Jazz Centre.

FRESH AIR

The Guardian, February 1985

Benny Golson, the veteran saxophonist who still exhibits a tone that purrs like a Rolls, is currently appearing at Ronnie Scott's with his quartet. Golson is a past master in the art of making progress by stealth and ingenuity rather than bravura and, like the best improvisers, never sounds as if the rules of the game are leading him by the nose. Some jazz musicians fit the phrases into the spaces of the chord structure as if they were working on an assembly line.

Golson's tone on slow pieces is inimitable. It is, to adapt Lewis Carroll, somewhere between a drawl and a rumble, with a kind of affectionate chuckle in the middle. By the time the band had flexed its muscles through a series of elegant, witty revelations on principles as old as the hills and reached 'Are You Real?' (a prodding swinger that Golson used to play with Art Blakey) the leader was also demonstrating his ability to gently invert most melodic and dynamic expectations. He plays breaks by spiralling down into the low register rather than the more customary agitated ascent, a notable instance of the kind of thing that sets you raising an eyebrow with pleasure. Golson's talent rarely produces indecent extremes of elation – this reserve makes him at times such a breath of fresh air.

The presence of the Ronnie Scott quintet in the club this week makes for an interesting contrast with Golson's unflappable *savoir faire*. The group has a fondness for that loping jazz-funk of the Sixties Blue Note period – and though it is sometimes prone to rather phlegmatic and monotonous soloing – frequently demonstrates how suitable a vehicle it is for the enduring skills of Scott himself. Though liable at times to sound as lugubrious and downbeat as his own announcements, he continues to perceive a solo as a whole, to construct it as a series of logical events and lace it with a strong flavour of the blues.

JEHOVAH

The Guardian, March 1985

The worst job in the world is being the act that has to follow Hermeto Pascoal on to the stage. In the second concert of the Camden Jazz Week at the Logan Hall, the forty-nine-year-old Brazilian multi-instrumentalist got the opportunity to present his extraordinary act to a British audience for the first time.

Pascoal's entrance alone was worth it. The announcements were made and then – nothing. Just about coinciding with the fidgets starting, the doors of the auditorium burst open and the band, waving bells, came on from the side. Pascoal himself looks like the principal boy from *The Ten Commandments* – he has white hair almost to his waist, a massive white beard and looks every inch the father of Brazilian modern jazz.

The band promptly sailed into a thumping electric keyboard riff reminiscent of early 1970s Miles Davis (a period in the trumpeter's career Pascoal significantly influenced), supporting a high-pressure mixture of whistling flutes, driving percussion and wild, cackling laughter from the musicians. Pascoal began on keyboards, then adopted a low-register curved flute, shaped like an umbrella-handle, on which he delivered a series of increasingly heated variations, some sung, some gabbled, and some played as straight bebop lines, mostly at a galloping double-time.

The music, though clearly founded on Brazilian roots in its vigorous percussion and glittering, danceable tunes, was always pitched askew to the mainstream Latin American idioms, and thus was almost entirely free of cliché, partly compounded by the inclination of the band to break into hoarse exchanges of atonal playing at times.

The contrapuntal flute piece, 'Baptismo', had a tingle of oblique, third-stream classical music about it and on an uptempo finale, the leader took up a bizarre, guttural-sounding horn like a mammoth's tusk, through which he not only played manic snortings and ravings, but guffawed sardonically at key points in the saxophone playing of his excellent reed partner, Carlos Malta.

CATHARSIS

The Guardian, May 1985

The century's great American singers have all wrestled, coolly or desperately, or both, with the drive to keep the soul alive under the avalanche that was the emerging New World. If Frank Sinatra's secret lay in the collision between his laconic, cocky maleness and teen-dreams vulnerability, or Betty Carter's dynamism is the territory between sensuality and irony, Nina Simone's is the grappling pressures and pleasures of womanhood, blackness, love, and the urge to be loved. What heightens the impact of all those volatile forces in performance is that the suspense with which they hang in each other's balance is more taxing than most. Ms Simone contends with life so close to the edge of the world that part of the fascination of her work is the voyeuristic uncertainty that she may fall off.

Nina Simone is in London for the rest of this week, in the most recent of a series of highly successful visits to the city. She was spirited away to the seventh floor of a Mayfair hotel, and though it was five o'clock in the afternoon the room was still dimly lit – and the singer sat quietly, dressed only in a short white shift, access to her inner sanctum prefaced by a chorus of indications from her assistants as to what she might say, or not say, or enjoy, or be distressed by.

Though she has returned to the performing world with a bang after a semi-retirement that began in the mid-Seventies, it is clear that since she knows what slings and arrows feel like she wants to protect herself from all the avoidable ones.

'I was trying to settle down,' she says of her long lay-off, which took her from Liberia to Switzerland and then to France. 'I was trying to get out of the music business. Because it's too *hard*. It's a hard business. And it's not *fair*. So I was trying to settle down and have a life apart from this.' But the man she was engaged to in Liberia, who would have been her third husband, died suddenly. She missed the affection of the public, even if she still feared its voraciousness. And she found business partners she thought she could trust.

Nina Simone was born Eunice Waymon in Tryon, North Carolina, in 1933. Her mother wanted her to be the world's greatest classical pianist – and the first black one. Ms Simone herself still insists she would have preferred it – with the implication that not only would the seriousness of her art be better recognised but that she would have been less vulnerable to the showbiz racketeers who have hovered over her.

'I would rather have been a classical pianist, yes.'

All her statements have a brusque finality about them. The words usually used about women in her line of work – words like 'blues', 'soul' and 'gospel' – induce that response with particular sharpness. It's not that she distrusts the tradition from which the blues have come – it is one of the cornerstones of her work and burns with as fierce a flame as ever – but she knows that it comes from a vocabulary also used by whites to keep black artists in their place.

Revealing messages about the twentieth century is her primary occupation. It makes her draw in European culture, and sail it on the dark undercurrents of being a black American woman. She loves the work of Brecht and Weill for its prophetic force, has recorded 'There's No Returning' and 'Mr Smith' from *Mahagonny* – making the former song a spine-chilling feature of her concerts.

It is more diffuse and general appraisal of an unwelcoming world than the one that aligned Nina Simone with the civil rights movement of the 1960s, when 'Mississippi Goddam' was virtually an anthem. As the years have passed, the urge to protect herself has clearly grown. She says, more resigned than bitter, 'They didn't change the world' – but there is a bleakness in her injured defiance on stage that sends shivers up the spine.

Like many of the great female vernacular singers of the century – Bessie Smith, Billie Holiday, Judy Garland, Edith Piaf, Janis Joplin – Nina Simone's is a very revealing kind of 'entertainment', ironic, discomfiting and cathartic. On the face of it, she is loved – as her entourage will simply put it – 'because she is a great artist', an interpreter of good songs in ways that illuminate the emotional chords they strike. She is also crucially *someone else* – an intimate stranger reliving the trials of life before your eyes, vibrating like a tuning fork, and because it is her and not you, you can wince, and then breathe a sigh of relief.

Nina Simone points to a photograph on the wall. It shows her and a girl in each other's arms. The girl is beautiful and vibrant, her face in profile, looking out of the picture with confidence. 'It's my daughter. She's twenty-two now. Lorraine Hansbery, who wrote the book from which "Young, Gifted and Black" got its name, was her godmother.' Do Nina Simone's hopes for her daughter extend to hopes for the world? 'I don't know. I don't have the answer, that's for damn sure'.

GRANDIOSITY

The Wire, April 1985

When the National Jazz Centre admits the first paying customer and the first band plays the first note of the first tune to be reflected off its acoustically engineered and expensively refurbished interiors, all the little firsts that will happen on that day will roll up into a very big first for arts funding in Britain. The National Jazz Centre is the first all-round, purpose-built, seriously-intentioned non-showbiz home for jazz music in this country. It is the fulfilment of a dream that came to life in 1968, and is now jazz folklore, when Ronnie Scott's Old Place finally closed and there was no longer an appropriate establishment for adventurous local musicians to go.

The NJC is also likely to be a 'last' – certainly for the near future. As a building-based arts project which has absorbed a seven figure sum – much of it public money – it is inconceivable that such a thing could be repeated in the present climate. The Jazz Centre's organisers jumped over a draw-bridge already in the process of being lifted, the one that connects the nation's cultural life to the public purse. In the circumstances, they have almost certainly done the right thing. In an era in which the elected repre-sentatives don't appear to give a damn about living art, the next best thing to be in is real estate.

A cool £1.5 million has gone into resuscitating a Victorian warehouse in Covent Garden's Floral Street to produce not just a performance space or a concert hall, but a range of facilities for students, musicians, the dedi-cated and the passer-by, the buff in search of arcane information, the casual listener intrigued and welcoming enlightenment. It's what the administrators call a 'vigorous open-house policy', open from breakfast-time to midnight. As a way of building for the future (since the music has never seemed entirely at home grafted on to Britain's nostalgic, class-based and museum-oriented cultural life), the Centre wants education to be a priority. British Petroleum has already come up with money for the enterprising Outreach scheme.

Currently the organisers are holding forth about the project in a manner that recalls the style of arts administrators in the early Seventies. They pro-ject a picture of community arts which is now difficult to visualise through the prism of the 'new realism'. It is, nevertheless a vision that has kept the organisers going through a painful succession of reverses. The Arts Council and the Greater London Council were the original supporters of the means by which the Jazz Centre Society (which had existed from 1968 in a series of temporary homes) could establish its real objective. The GLC, with Tony Banks as arts supremo, earmarked the Floral Street building for arts use and gave the jazz organisation the option on it. The Arts Council similarly put aside funds from the now defunct Housing the Arts scheme.

In the early 1980s, the Jazz Centre got seriously down to business. Charles Alexander, the principal administrator under whose charge the Society had garnered increasing amounts of Arts Council revenue fund-ing, became the man who went out in search of backers – the public bodies, not surprisingly, wanted to see their commitment matched. But Alexander, working on his own, found the going hard. Amidst consider-able acrimony, he was replaced in 1982. Escalating costs of the initial structural work already underway in Floral Street were causing panic at the Jazz Centre, by constitution a promoting body and not an organisation geared to speculative building. If the Floral Street scheme foundered, the debts could drag the Jazz Centre Society down with it. After considerable hand-wringing, pressure was put on the board to separate the functions and the liabilities; the National Jazz Centre thus became a company on its own, touring promotion being taken over by an organisation that came to be called Jazz Services Ltd.

Despite the knocks, imagining the Centre in full swing was enough to keep the organisers going – and in the nature of capital projects, the more concrete went into Floral Street, the less likely it became that the backers were going to pull the plug. Though some purists were disturbed at the trend towards further 'institutionalisation' of a living and changing art form, many jazz buffs were tired of pub back rooms, massive and alienating concert halls, tatty, crowded basements, and were anxious for a place that would symbolise confidence about the music. But in Covent Garden, with Central London overheads and a timid Arts Council, not to mention a possibly departing GLC, things are going to be tough. Can the NJC keep its priorities intact in the worsening weather to come?

John Cumming, one of the steering group of three masterminding the scheme, is an optimistic man by temperament but a highly experienced arts administrator too, with a background in theatre as well as music. His view is that 'The strength of the project is that several different components are involved in it. The NJC has created "new money" partly through the Outreach scheme. There is also Gulbenkian money, Greater London Arts Association money, BP money. The Musicians' Union has been very supportive. And there's certainly no reason why we can't make money at the box office.'

But isn't the pressure on at the moment to make the box office the arbiter of whether an arts project is worth doing or not? Jazz has always been a vociferous minority art, but attempts to make it popular on a grand scale more often than not produce very bad jazz. Surely when you massively increase the overheads of presenting a non-mainstream art form, you also increase the obligation on it to become more orthodox to survive?

'The jazz world is somewhere between the commercial world and the subsidised world,' Cumming opines. 'And in some cases the heavily subsidised world, if you take the avant-garde and experimental ends. But you have to remember that jazz as an art form appeared only this century and already its influence on other arts has been immense. The Centre should take a lead to draw all that together. Musicians like Lol Coxhill, Phil Minton and Maggie Nicols have worked with theatre for years, Steve Lacy is currently doing experimental work with dancers in France, Anthony Davis is writing an opera about Michael X. That cross-fertilisation is going on all the time, and the Centre should reflect it. If the status of jazz in this country is not substantially higher in ten years' time, then we won't have achieved much.'

Though some of the impetus to bring this about is for the pragmatic purpose of enabling jazz to shelter under the umbrella of some of the higher-status arts in a time of cutbacks, Cumming's desire for integration is impelled by a genuine desire for stimulation of all the arts through making unexpected connections. He will talk enthusiastically about video projects, collaborations with organisations like Dance Umbrella, links with community projects. He admits, 'There's strength in numbers.' But the National Jazz Centre will almost certainly need such friends – because if money gets tight, it would be infinitely more desirable for other forms of adventurous activity to be presented in the building than that it should find itself rented out as some kind of upmarket bingo hall in five years' time.

Detractors of the scheme include some jazz musicians, a breed not undisposed to dog-in-the-mangerism, but doubts expressed about the programmers' view of the avant-garde are not entirely unreasonable, considering the old Jazz Centre Society's past record and the current pressure, as Cumming acknowledges, to preserve the established art forms. One prominent free-improvisor sees the scheme as dedicated to 'widening the scope to something that jazz can never be'. Others from the more commercial end of the jazz world worry about the Centre's lack of a can-carrying 'boss' – someone who might have accelerated progress in the floundering early stages, or maybe even resigned in embarrassment at the chaotic mishandling of the Centre's Royal Gala fund-raising show at the Palladium in February. Collectivised or centralised, firmness is going to be crucial in the difficult times ahead.

But though good intentions rarely solve crises or anticipate mishaps, they do impart the will to carry an unfashionable, audacious, and farsighted scheme to a conclusion. As John Cumming says: 'The purpose of the Centre is to change things for the better, for this country's musicians, once and for all.'

COUNTRY BOY MAKES GOOD

The Wire, May 1985

Twelve years ago, guitarist Pat Metheny, the country boy from Kansas, began to make what he would call a 'serious' impression in jazz circles and it was the kind of impression immediately likely to extend beyond the borders of jazz alone. Now, still on the admissible side of thirty, Metheny is already ahead of what many musicians would be obliged to regard as the peak of a career, and still rising. His records sell 100,000. He has scored several films, the latest being John Schlesinger's *The Falcon and the Snowman*, which took Metheny's collaboration with David Bowie into the pop charts. Along with Miles Davis, Wynton Marsalis and, to a lesser extent, Weather Report, his band is that rarity – a jazz-based outfit of improvisers who can guarantee themselves a gig somewhere in the world most nights of the year.

Metheny still bears the same old rag-mat haircut, battered sneakers, boyish grin and drawling Jack Nicholson intonation that he undoubtedly had kicking his heels on the Kansas City sidewalks as a teenager. He continues to play a wide variety of music, much of it in the company of the Jarrett-like pianist Lyle Mays, and characterised by conventional song structures, imaginative use of electronic technology, ethereal use of voices, a strong sensation of mid-West open spaces, and the capacity to be either background music or serious listening. This last is a surefire guarantee of popular success and a surefire guarantee, moreover, of a chorus of complaints from purists about abandoning the One True Path of jazz.

One indispensable fact confounds much of this aggravation and that is the immense respect in which Metheny's work is held by exactly the kind of jazz players whom the hard-core fans most admire. Metheny's current partnerships with drummer Billy Higgins and bassist Charlie Haden, which produced the ECM album *Rejoicing* (a blistering confection of Ornette Coleman tunes, bebop and semi-quavers flying around like ping-pong balls), has continued to flourish. There is every prospect of a European tour with that ensemble, an event to gladden the hearts of all guardians of the Coleman faith.

Metheny was in England in March, on a pre-tour publicity run for a two-month string of European gigs with his regular band, which ends in Britain this month. We had met two years previously, and at that encounter I had asked him all the customary questions about his musical origins. He had been a rock fan in the hippie era when, to him, hippies were grown-ups.

'I saw *A Hard Day's Night* fifteen times when I was twelve,' Metheny had said then. '"She Loves You" came out when I was nine or ten, and it was like all those moments in your childhood when you suddenly notice something you've never noticed before. It was the first time I really got chills after hearing music.'

The experience had the curious effect of making Metheny's teenage rebelliousness, when it came, expend itself on the pop orthodoxy he had already absorbed.

'When I got to fourteen or so,' was his explanation, 'I went the opposite way, rebelling against rock and roll completely. I didn't want anything that wasn't Miles or Coltrane or Sonny Rollins.'

It made Metheny 'a very sophisticated fourteen-year-old'. When other kids of his age were hot-rodding cars, Metheny – having learned to play jazz guitar with indecent haste – was starting to play professionally with jazz stars visiting Kansas and mixing with musicians more than twice, and sometimes three times, his age. His big break came when he persuaded vibrahapist Gary Burton to let him sit in. Metheny immediately joined Burton's band and his brand of lilting, lissome single-line improvising jaunty country-music chords and effortless swing (the latter strongly reminiscent of the late Wes Montgomery) soon made him a guitar celebrity.

He was immediately absorbed by the idea of producing music of his own, though, a music that owed as much to pop and country music as jazz and which, in its early stages, closely resembled a more muscular, technologically inclined and less fastidious version of Burton's own work. It took the roots of Burton's popularity – melodiousness, rock and roll time, catchy tunes, sophisticated improvisation – and magnified them. Yet, for all the fact that Metheny has committed himself to a middle road, he speaks as obsessively as a man of his relaxed demeanour can of the crucial significance of doing things his way.

'I refuse to be intimidated by success,' Metheny says. 'And I don't think I've even for a second played down to people. The musician has to be playing at his peak for the music to really sound right. You have to feel that the person is playing the best they can play, and what they really want to play. When I listen to my early records, I might want to take a lot of it back now but at the time we played it, that was it. In some parts of the hard-core jazz community they will say things like the only reason Charlie Haden would play with me is because he's a nice guy. A record company president, on the other hand, might say, "Sell half a million records or we don't want to know about you." I'm not interested in either position because they're political/economic points of view – they're both wrong, and they have nothing to do with music.'

Metheny's work with Billy Higgins and Charlie Haden has proceeded in parallel with the activities of his own band and has developed from being a casual try-out to a working ensemble which has now toured extensively in the States. There is now enough live material on tape to make a new trio record which in Metheny's words will be 'serious business'. It is the counter to all the carping about Metheny that he is a jazz-inflected MOR player who produces music to calm your nerves in the dentist's.

The trio represents a genuinely musical partnership between three improvisers sharing a deep and wide understanding of the post-bop innovations of Ornette Coleman. Metheny is a rare example of a player absorbed in Coleman's work, who is nonetheless rooted in conventional harmony. Like Coleman, he loves music that swings. Like Coleman, he is a highly rhythmic improviser. But Metheny's fondness for pop music means that he likes songs, too, which leads him to admire the saxophonist's early compositions, the melodies of which positively dance. Metheny believes that bassist Charlie Haden had more of an impact on Coleman's early progress than is generally acknowledged.

'I've learned from Charlie a whole bunch of Ornette's tunes that have never been recorded, some of his hippiest ones, and we may even do a quartet record with Ornette, who's been to hear the band several times and likes it. Ornette's harmonic thing is unbelievably advanced but the unsung hero of it is Charlie. He had an incredible ability to make up harmony as he's going along. My mother could sit there and bang random notes on the piano and he would play a bass part that would make it sound as if she were thinking of a line. It imparts an inner logic that you don't get when Ornette plays with other bassists. Interestingly, *Rejoicing* has sold almost as many in the States as the group record, *First Circle*, that's over 100,000. We get kids coming to the trio gigs who only know the band stuff, and they still dig it.

'I don't buy the theory that there's got to be a heavy backbeat on everything for them to follow it. That said, I'm well aware that there are some things going on for me that definitely help – one being that I play the guitar at a time when the guitar is *the* instrument, another is that what I play is extremely melodic and develops a tradition that goes back to Lester Young, of telling a little story when you play, and of course we tour relentlessly, which is an incredible promotional aid.'

Metheny's favourite guitar players, and the strongest influences on his own approach, are Jim Hall and Wes Montgomery – even though Montgomery died when Metheny was a child. He admires improvisers who, as he puts it, 'think like drummers'. It is, he says, 'the most attractive thing about Wynton Marsalis, that rhythmic feel. He'll play some phrases on top, some behind, he can put it in a lot of different places – most guys have only one way they can phrase and they'll phrase it that way, no matter what, fast or slow.

'I loved all that Jimmy Smith organ stuff when I was a kid and the way Wes would play with him. It makes you think of a rhythm for the phrase first and the notes later. Jim Hall has that, Wes had it, Bill Evans had it, Miles has it, and Keith Jarrett is very rhythmically sophisticated, too, I think, though I would question some things about his attitude and I wish he wouldn't sing when he plays. But the players who have that quality have it no matter what else they do, and it doesn't leave them.

'People put down Herbie Hancock a lot less these days but, if you went into a room with just him and a piano, he'd blow your mind. George Benson, too – he could go out and make two jazz records a year, if he wanted, and be on top of the polls for ever . . .

'I have to say that of all the New York jazz heroes at the moment, very few of them work with me, with the exception of Wynton and his brother. I don't have a feeling with many of the others that they have the basic grammar of improvising under control. Ornette's got something that enables him to bypass the Charlie Parker tradition but he's the only one who could really do it. Coltrane, even in the later stages, was always relating to some kind of harmony. Those records of the great Miles quintet in the Sixties – they sound like they're playing free, but the structure is there. That's what it's supposed to sound like.

'My big qualm, and I would say this even about Wynton, is that people are saying, "Here we are, back in the tradition", and all that; when you think back to the major innovators who were strongly aware of their traditions too, but some part of their personality made them say, "Yeah, but I want to do it like this", or just, "Well, fuck it". When I see somebody being too reverent about the past it makes me sceptical. And when I see somebody my age, or younger, or maybe just a few years older, playing as if they've never heard a note of rock and roll, it makes me wonder, where have they been? When I see somebody twenty years old with a suit and tie playing early Sixties and late Fifties music, well, it's puzzling.

'But one other thing I can attribute to Wynton's popularity is that his presentation is incredibly good. It's rehearsed, it's sharp, here are our tunes, bang, bang, bang and that's not just a small detail when you may be asking these days for people to shell out ten, fifteen bucks to get in. I'm aware that if a guy brings his girlfriend out to hear me, it could be a quarter of his income that he spends on that one night, and I ain't going to let that guy down. I know these time are rough. Also in the Sixties there were very few TV stations. Now there are sixty, broadcasting twenty-four hours a day. You're competing with that. There's less tolerance for unprofessionalism.'

Hard competition is the characteristic of the era; Pat Metheny is too sharp an operator not to realise that it seriously affects jazz, as an art-form unpopular with much of the press and traditionally regarded as of minority interest and very little mass-appeal. Metheny views the current fashions as ominous.

'I'm as American as you can get, coming from the mid-West, but that's exactly where the real problems in America are building up. There's this lack of imagination and growing ignorance, Reagan keeps cutting the arts and education budgets and getting us involved in countries we have no business being involved in and we're growing this nation of stupid, prejudiced people.'

That sounds close to an angry statement. Isn't that out of character?

'Well, I'd be the first to admit that I have a kind of loose wire in this department, I definitely hear things funny. Jim Hall sometimes sounds angry to me. Some of the people characterised as really angry free players often sound totally passive and not very free. I had a group at high school that was tenor, guitar and four drummers that used to play Albert Ayler and Ornette tunes and that was pretty angry at times. When people talk about James Blood Ulmer, I say, "Have you ever heard Hendrix or Sonny Sharrock? If you listen to "The Calling" on the *Rejoicing* record, and turn it up as high as you can go, I think you'll hear what you mean in that."'

And the future?

'I want to do a project with Milton Nascimento – he and Miles are *it* for me. And a solo project. And surviving. Doing what I want to do, which is playing every night. When I wake up in the morning, I just thank my lucky stars. Some of the best players I know can't work.'

SOBRIETY

The Guardian, June 1985

Sonny Rollins is one of the few jazz stars for whom an album title like *Saxophone Colossus* could be simply a sober evaluation of the facts. Arriving like a whirlwind in the 1950s his style out of Coleman Hawkins and Charlie Parker, Rollins's tone eschewed vibrato, his sound was more like a bark than a purr, and in constructing solos of exhaustive length as if examining his materials from every possible angle, he virtually came to define the phenomenon known as hard bop.

But unlike a pure bebopper, he remained fascinated by the tune, however functional – endlessly returning to it, distorting it, mocking it, turning it into other tunes like an illusionist. At the Dominion on Saturday – pacing the stage as ever, stomping on the spot as if he were treading grapes, swinging the horn to the heavens – Rollins swept without ceremony into a booming rendition of 'I'll Be Seeing You', which he then dissected and reworked over the course of a twenty-minute solo.

The audacity with which Rollins pours out bubbling torrents of new tunes from the fragments of old ones is – and this is what marks him out from many other resourceful improvisers – significantly dependent on his skill at dividing a solo into phases and moods so that each improvisation takes on a concerto-like poise.

The band is very much better than the succession of rather ordinary performers with whom Rollins has been associated since the Seventies, particularly ex-Dizzy Gillespie drummer Tommy Campbell, a performer of slow, graceful movements, whose features on the mid-tempo 'No Problem' elegantly blended tom-tom accents that resembled hand-drum sounds with taut, emphatic figures on the snare.

Guitarist Bobby Broom played some delicious tributes to Wes Montgomery in 'My One and Only Love' (Rollins introduced 'Greensleeves' into the same thing), the leader played the obligatory rather colourless funk on 'Real Life', and wound up with a barnstorming 'Don't Stop the Carnival' which he concluded with an earth-shaking foghorn-like honk. The show is geared to him being the boss, which curtails the unexpected, but Rollins remains one of the greatest living improvisers.

PROSECUTION

The Guardian, July 1985

Most of the audience for Miles Davis and his band in the first show at the Festival Hall on Saturday was on its feet by the end – not, this time, in simple appreciation that one of the twentieth century music's giants is still at work after a crippling illness, but because playing for over two hours non-stop is something he doesn't have to do now, though he appeared on this occasion to want to.

The current ensemble is the most exciting and empathetic Davis has been involved with since before his six year lay-off. It is very much looser in approach than the new pop-flavoured album (*You're Under Arrest*) lets on, and the leader is clearly enjoying himself with it. Fascinatingly, though some observers turned up their noses at the trumpeter's new affection for pretty and probably pretty lucrative tunes after years of bulldozing funk, the caressingly delicate side of Davis's ballad playing has come to life again under the temptations of themes like 'Human Nature' and the undulating, soft-reggae Cyndi Lauper ballad 'Time After Time.'

No amount of griping about the opportunism of his motives for that recording can obscure the fact that Davis has tried to balance the lyrical, the swinging, the improvisatory and the commercial facets of his work of late. Certainly this doesn't reveal his old spontaneous genius but it is a long way from the aridity of much of the early Seventies funk period too.

Davis began with an adapted theme from his two-year-old *Star People* album, an oblique, skidding theme taken much faster than the original and featuring an excellent tenor solo from new recruit Bob Berg – a performer with both the wide, scorching sound of Gato Barbieri as well as the sleekness of a mainstream hardbopper.

The second tune was slow and bluesy, for which Miles came out of his corner and meandered the stage blowing a series of quiet, burnished phrases that ended in a splintering exclamatory chord from the band which triggered the audience into a burst of applause. As Miles raised his trumpet in acknowledgement the piece accelerated into an oscillating mixture of slow blues and medium tempo bop, which extracted a steely and inventive solo from John Scofield, the most impressive guitarist currently operating in this idiom.

The band then moved into its *You're Under Arrest* material. Much of this phase of the concert brought wonderful things out of Davis. His style has always represented a distillation of his materials rather than elaboration of them and such is his instant grasp of good melody and swing that opportunities for more space are blessings he has not always appreciated. Crouching, the horn facing downwards to the floor, he would release a vibrating spiral of descending trills, bright, blurted sounds, then a series of stuttered, hesitant notes followed by a flight of tuneful phrases that could have dated from almost any period in his history – his variations on 'Time After Time' being delicious evidence of that.

OLD BOPPERS NEVER DIE
The Guardian, September 1985

There is a much-handled 1947 story to the effect that Ronnie Scott, then twenty years old, was playing a plush, polite-society job for the band-leader (subsequently DJ) Jack Jackson one night, when the inspiration of Charlie Parker overtook him and he launched ecstatically into chorus after chorus of that tumbling, feverish, high-octane music known then as rebop. Jackson, appalled, asked his guitarist what the hell was happening. 'Ronnie's got the message,' came that hipster's reply. 'Well, I've got one for him,' returned the exasperated maestro. 'Tell him he's fired.'

On Sunday night at the club that the erring tenorist subsequently made into a London landmark (not least as an escape from Jackson's Tin Pan Alley world) a reunion of its forerunner the Club Eleven was filmed by the BBC in a rare but welcome show of enthusiasm for the music. It was a phenomenon long overdue for tribute, and due in large part to the energies of the jazz chronicler, Jim Godbolt.

Ronnie Scott, John Dankworth and many others, refugees from Stepney and Whitechapel and Highams Park, visited the States in the late 1940s and were instantly convinced that one of the century's cataclysmic musical upheavals was going on in New York's 52nd Street clubs. They were dumbfounded by the musical fertility of the black iconoclasts – Parker, Dizzy Gillespie, Thelonious Monk, Miles Davis – who had reacted against the schmalz and clichés of the swing bands. The British players returned to open their own version of a 52nd Street dive in a basement in Great Windmill Street – now a peep show – called Mac's Rehearsal Rooms. Mac's became the city's first full-blown 'modern' jazz club, run by the eleven men who played in it.

Drugs were naturally part of the scenery. For musicians united by the desire to crash through the sound barrier into paradise, the dangers then seemed remote and the promise was a shorter journey. The police raided the Club Eleven in April 1950 and it folded not long after. Protests by the felons that the cocaine was for toothache were received unenthusiastically.

But the Club Eleven became a musical legend. The music that was forged there was derivative – its practitioners acknowledged that – but it laid one of the foundation stones for a Europeanised jazz that could survive on its own. It could also be played with immense verve and passion, as Sunday night's reunion bands demonstrated. The only deceased founders were the pianist Tommy Pollard and Denis Rose, the bop guru who made harmonic sense of the flights of Parker and Gillespie and wrote it all down for his disbelieving colleagues. As much as anything, the whole show was dedicated to Rose's memory.

Ronnie Scott's sextet charged through a bop repertoire including 'Ornithology', 'Billie's Bounce' and 'Groovin' High'. Hank Shaw on trumpet, unsettled at first, eventually rolled with ingenious precision through the darting chords of 'Billie's Bounce'. Scott played as well as he has in years – his solos a mixture of Coltraneish gravity (he resisted the temptation to play a replica of his 1950 style) booming tone, and hard, clattering runs.

John Dankworth led the other ensemble, delivering 'Body and Soul' as a series of airy swoops over buoyant bass playing from Joe Muddell; scudding through Parker's 'Donna Lee', and propelled throughout by the drumming of Laurie Morgan with a touch almost as light and mischievous as Art Blakey's. Nostalgic it may have been, but it was a real musical event, not a rose-tinted replica. All those sixty-year-old delinquents played their hearts out.

Honsinger

The Guardian, September 1985

For eccentricity to be marketable you have to be sure that it resides in repeatable behaviour – rather than a genuine compulsion to discern whatever the audience is expecting, and then head resolutely in the other direction. The Dutch cellist Tristan Honsinger, who first surfaced here through membership of Derek Bailey's international improvising troupe Company, has many of the qualities necessary to be a cult figure – passion, expertise, subversion of an existing genre, immense stage presence. But his performances are different every night. This compulsion alone drives his work to the outer reaches of acceptability, at least in Britain.

Honsinger – a frenetic, sharp-featured, bird-like man – played at the London Musician's Collective in Camden Town. He is a fascinating artist. His behaviour in performance involves much ecstatic breathing, flapping about of feet as if they were on wires, huffing, puffing, periodic perplexed deliberation and muttering to himself. A former classical player who took to busking and then to free-improvisation, Honsinger displays an unrelenting determination to reshape the orthodox practice of conventional arco cello playing, as if he were continually feeding the phraseology of his previous experience into some kind of ghostly musical blending machine.

He played unaccompanied at the outset, making full use of his arsenal of half-finished classical cello licks, tumultuous flurries of sound, percussive thumps and bangs. Pianist Alex Maguire and drummer Steve Noble later formed a trio with him.

SUBTLEST, SUBTLIST

The Guardian, October 1985

Much of the effort that Wayne Shorter has found himself obliged to expend in the past fifteen years has been that of simply making himself heard. A gifted saxophonist with a remarkable lyrical imagination, who has been one of the genuinely original inheritors of John Coltrane's legacy, Shorter has actually missed out on a good many opportunities to make a real impact as an innovator.

The reason has principally been his absorption since the beginning of the 1970s into the pioneering fusion band, Weather Report – an ensemble in which he was often obliged to occupy the role of special effects man, and one with a substantial audibility problem when sharing a stage with those panzer divisions of percussions and electronics.

The effort seems to have blunted none of Shorter's ability to play the horn in an immensely subtle and intelligent fashion, but seems to have severely affected his sense of the right setting in which to feature his best attributes. He played two performances at the Logan Hall on Thursday with a quartet that worked its way through a good deal of the material from a new album (*Atlantis*), mixing arrangements strongly reminiscent of Weather Report with the histrionics of a band not unlike one of Chick Corea's funk outfits.

Almost exclusively, Shorter plays soprano saxophone – an instrument on which he exhibits a piercing, trumpet-like sound mingled with shy, wriggling doodles of noise that are surprisingly like Steve Lacy's meditative approach. Only in the wistful passages of a repertoire mostly delivered in a series of haunting crescendos did this contemplative side of Shorter emerge – it was almost captured by some of his ambivalent, themes at times, but the tendency of the band to accelerate everything into a burn-up made these impressions infuriatingly brief.

Tom Canning's keyboard playing – he frequently approached the job as if he were in a heavy metal band – contributed a lot to this. He worked on the basis that if an idea was good then it was worth repeating – and then repeating louder. In the Latin-flavoured tune, 'The Three Marias', Shorter did get a chance to play a beautiful solo, full of breezy puffs of sound and discreet flourishes over a quiet piano accompaniment, but the impatience that flavours this kind of band still couldn't leave that mood alone. Shorter's drummer behaved as if he hoped he might ring a bell and win a prize if he hit things hard enough.

Loose Tubes

The Guardian, December 1985

The British big band Loose Tubes, which recently played a successful London season, is made up largely of young performers, and has now released a record, simply called *Loose Tubes*, produced under their own steam and edited from sessions in September this year and December 1984.

From its opening keyboard solo by leading member Django Bates (a tracery of feathery runs) through repeated instances of its mischievous tendency to pitch cosy jazz clichés against the wrong harmonies, tumbling written sections yawing wildly between massive intervals like transcribed Eric Dolphy solos, lilting lute-and-brass themes that might have come from *Sketches of Spain*, sardonically fancy deployments of Quincy Jones-like orchestral licks, Loose Tubes represents the most striking British orchestral jazz to have emerged in many a long year. It looks outward to its audience and avoids the laboratory-like self-examination that characterised much of the jazz of the generation before it, and it isn't guilty about enjoying itself. A startling and memorable debut.

Azimuth '85 is a quiet, chamber-jazz recording of the British trio that features John Taylor on piano, Norma Winstone on vocals and Ken Wheeler on trumpet. Early versions of the band were always as musicianly as the line-up would suggest but were hampered by a pallid, cloistered atmosphere insufficiently punctuated by sharp insights in the soloist, apart from fitful fireworks from Wheeler. With the startling development of Taylor from a Herbie Hancock and McCoy Tyner disciple into a performer of graceful and original imagination, Azimuth has acquired colour in its cheeks.

If it has a drawback, it is probably the rather dated-sounding canyons-of-your-mind quality of some of the lyrics, but Ms Winstone's breathy scat-singing against the brittle, nervous energy of Wheeler's horn is a compelling contrast.

New Blood

The Guardian, January 1986

Chances to witness the striking emergence of the young saxophonist Courtney Pine on the London jazz scene have mostly been restricted to his occasional appearances on other people's gigs – notably the startling contribution he made to a free-for-all led by drummer John Stevens at the Albany Empire last year, and latterly as part of the front line of the Charlie Watts Big Band.

Pine has already shown that the great traditions of jazz have seemed far from an irrelevance to a young black Londoner. His playing – a powerful and driving sound strongly influenced by John Coltrane but with forays into the ghostly harmonics of Albert Ayler, and the dry, clattery vocabulary of hard bop specialists like Hank Mobley or Joe Farrell – is at a compelling stage where much of what he will ever need to know technically has already been absorbed. Experience is very likely to introduce Pine to a music all his own.

Pine was performing in the company of a trio on a soul and jazz night at the ICA, the bands being the choice of Working Week singer, Julie Roberts. The repertoire partly consisted of a collection of salty and muscular originals (in which new pianist Julian Joseph attractively displayed a gravelly and angular piano style not unlike Mal Waldron's) and tunes by Wayne Shorter and Thelonious Monk – and on the latter piece Pine switched to soprano saxophone and played his best-shaped solo of the night.

The band didn't swing as much as the music invited, which sometimes left it sagging when the rhythmic propulsiveness of the leader's own style was taking a rest, but it was a heartwarming set for all that.

Look No Hands

The Guardian, February 1986

Considering that so many good musicians (including last week's Star People band at the Bass Clef) fall depressingly over the same hurdle that countless groups of the past fifteen years have done in sounding like a Billy Harper band out of John Coltrane, you approach exponents of the up-and-coming with some cynicism.

But the Iain Ballamy Quartet, featuring the boyish, shock-haired leader on saxophones, with a genuine British jazz genius (that rare species) in Django Bates on keyboard, Mick Hutton on bass and Steve Arguelles on drums, played a set of such vivacious invention on Sunday night as to lead the thoughts to the notion that a new generation might truly have arrived for whom an inferiority complex about American jazz is not so much an obstacle to be overcome, but an incomprehensible hang-up.

Bates, as ever, has much to do with this, being a soloist of lightning reactions, immense wit and disguised delicacy as well as an excellent supporter of other people's efforts – this last through intelligent use of the scope of electronics to create unexpected sound effects that vary from the surging of a cinema organ to the splinter of a car smash.

On his own composition 'Freely' – an erratic, clowning theme like the incidental music to a Laurel and Hardy sketch, suddenly coloured by bluesy howls – Bates performed the introduction with a sound like a squeezebox from the left hand and lissome, flute-like melodies from the right. Iain Ballamy, who has a hard, rubbery tone that grows hoarser and more urgent as the temperature rises, sounded thoroughly distinctive on tenor – a virtual impossibility these days – and even his Jan Garbarek-like melancholy on slow pieces was more of an association of idioms than inflexion. He demonstrated both moods on 'Further Away,' a typical Bates mixture of a ballad and a free-form barrage.

The group also subdivided into Human Chain, the duo that Bates has with drummer Steve Arguelles (they played a stunning blend of dark, baleful wanderings like rhythmless sitar music and crashing percussive keyboard sounds like electro-funk) in which the latter abandoned all the tentativeness that sometimes overcomes him in a time-keeping role for a series of deep and sonorous drum rolls executed tantalisingly in slow motion, like the beating of enormous wings.

TAXING QUESTIONS
The Guardian, February 1986

'What took you so long?' inquired George Russell, the wry and energetic sixty-three-year-old American jazz composer. It was a fair question. Until this Contemporary Music Network tour which visits eight towns over the next fortnight, Russell has never been heard here before, despite his unique skills having emerged on the jazz scene as long ago as the beginning of the 1950s. At the end of that decade, Russell staked his career on a war against the over-simple harmonic principles of jazz, but where some musicians threw formal construction to the winds as their escape route, Russell went deeper in.

The American began his opening concert, fronting a mixed European and American band by delivering a retrospective of some of his most memorable pieces, from 'Cubano Be, Cubano Bop' for the Dizzy Gillespie band at the end of the 1940s, through to 'New York, New York' in the 1960s. Russell sprang a spectacular surprise early on by splicing into the band's Cubop rendition a tape from Gillespie's old Carnegie Hall performance of the same tune, with percussionist Sabu Martinez.

'All About Rosie', a justifiably celebrated three-part composition from 1957 was a highlight of the first half. Russell conducted it by describing angular geometrical shapes in the air like a mime trying to represent the Pompidou Centre – so you could very nearly have heard the music just by watching him. The piece deploys big band licks as old as the hills but pitched against other sections playing phrases of different lengths, overlapping in such a manner as to not only revitalise them but render them structurally essential.

Russell's triumph was always to have built a sophisticated compositional theory out of the materials of jazz rather than import an alien one and hope it would stick. Kenny Wheeler, Courtney Pine, Chris Biscoe and the excellent young trombonist Pete Beachill played solos of rumination, bravura, poignancy and hard-hitting clarity according to their respective dispositions, and the composer's regular drummer Keith Copeland was superb. The second half features a longer, and fitfully ponderous newer work called 'The African Game,' based on the composer's studies of polyrhythm of recent years. Courtney Pine revealed the range of saxophone tonalities he is currently exploring – from dry, pebbly, Coltrane effects to wide and rolling sounds that sometimes recall the Texan soul-jazz tenorists. He is tending to give all his solos the same dynamic shapes however, and got stranded once or twice by Russell's changes of gear.

Trumpeter Palle Mikkelborg however played a rich, plummy flugel-horn solo that reduced the hall to total silence. For a pick-up band, it was a striking first night with some of the most demanding compositions in jazz.

COURTNEY PINE

The Guardian, March 1986

The cover of the March issue of the elegant British jazz magazine *Wire* features a young black man in a red beret and a natty grey overcoat, holding a tenor saxophone. Unusually for a jazz performer, the figure has lately become very familiar in younger music circles in this country, through a TV appearance, local press coverage, and even that barometer of current tastes, *The Face* magazine. The recipient of all this attention is Courtney Pine, the twenty-one-year-old British-born son of a Jamaican carpenter and a local government official, who has suddenly shot to as much stardom as you can get on the jazz scene this side of the Atlantic.

Though the pioneers of almost every major departure in jazz music have been Afro-Americans, black practitioners of the art in this country like Pine have been a rare breed. Most of the West Indians who came to Britain in the Fifties and Sixties found a musical outlet in calypso, and then in reggae. There was hardly any local jazz tradition of any kind to latch on to in the early days, least of all a non-white one. Now all that is changing.

Courtney Pine has lately guested with the Charlie Watts Big Band, on the recent tour of the veteran American composer George Russell, and is due to appear in various guises at the current Camden Jazz Week including – and this is a recognition accorded to very few British performers, certainly of Pine's tender years – an appearance in an augmented Art Blakey Jazz Messengers at the end of the week.

Pine is a fine saxophonist in the manner of John Coltrane and Wayne Shorter, but on his own admission he's in the foothills of finding his own voice as yet. But as a young black Londoner of charismatic appearance and immense confidence and momentum about his work, his image fits the times like a glove – and provides a powerful inspiration to this country's small but potentially dynamic black jazz scene into the bargain. His predecessors – like the West Indian trumpeter Harry Beckett – have often been excellent players who have adapted their talents to the tastes of other leaders. Courtney Pine, young as he is, has no intention of letting such grass grow under his feet. There will be an authentic British black jazz style, he believes.

'When you listen to a band like Wynton Marsalis's,' Pine says, 'you hear something deeper than most of what's available here. No black person has really been able to find their own way in jazz in this country except for Joe Harriott.' Harriott was the brilliant Jamaican altoist who came to England in the early 1950s, cut some pathfinding records a decade later, and died in obscurity on a circuit of beer-money gigs in 1973. Life in Britain doesn't look so much rosier today, so will Pine fare better?

'Some things have changed,' he insists. 'There's a lot more interest now in black music of all kinds than there was then. British funk is big. Look at magazines like *Blues and Soul*, *Black Echoes*. The conditions aren't the same.'

Gerry Barry of the IDJ Dancers, a London-based black dance team, shares Pine's optimism. He is part of the movement among young British blacks that has brought dance back to the world of jazz in a way that hasn't seemed so natural since fans jived to it in the clubs of the 1950s. IDJ will be dancing with Art Blakey during the festival, and through it finding an interpretation straight from the street art of British cities for the music of an American musical legend.

'Some music stays unique regardless of its era,' Barry says. 'Blakey sets a jazz standard. We all got bored with hip-hop, and breakdancing is really a form of gymnastics where you reach a peak and that's it. Jazz dancing is an individual expression, even in a group like ours. You can be yourself.'

SONG X

The Guardian, June 1986

Of all the steadfast characteristics of Ornette Coleman, the wild man of the new jazz of the early 1960s, one of the most striking has been the saxophonist's resolution about staking out his ground, pitching his tent on it and waiting for everybody else to come to him.

The current collaboration between Coleman and the popular young guitarist Pat Metheny – whose music, though lyrical and frequently beautifully written and played, has occasionally veered towards a super-sophisticated MOR – has unquestionably required the younger man to move a good deal further than the older one.

The result is a really thrilling collaboration, and finds Coleman in magisterial form. His consistency is a perpetual reproach to those who first thought him a joke. Coleman's horn sounds now as it always did – as passionate, bluesy and bristling with elegantly counterposed ideas as the solos of Louis Armstrong or Coleman Hawkins. As for Metheny, his profound understanding of jazz has always been one of his strengths.

Song X finds the two in collision and collaboration, accompanied by bassist Charlie Haden and Coleman's son Denardo on drums. Some of the tunes resemble the saxophonist's most playful and abrasively skittish early compositions.

LET'S JOIN HANDS AND CONTACT THE LIVING
The Guardian, June 1986

In 1947, young British jazz players were floundering. Their high priests – Charlie Parker, Thelonious Monk, Lester Young, Dizzy Gillespie and others – were in America and a union ban meant they couldn't play in Britain. The answer, for Ronnie Scott, Johnny Dankworth and friends, was to go to New York. For Ronnie Scott, it was the experience that completed his transition into a natural frontman for his musical generation.

Introduction from *The Guardian* (June 1986) to an extract from *Let's Join Hands and Contact the Living* (Elm Tree Books, 1986; republished as *Jazz Man* Kyle Cathie 1995).

When the young players came back off the boats they were, as Laurie Morgan would later put it, 'boiling with music'. The problem was that there weren't many places to let off steam.

One solution to the problem was a tatty basement called Mac's Rehearsal Rooms in Windmill Street, opposite the Windmill Theatre. Since it was so close to Archer Street, the young boppers would book the room on Monday afternoons and pass the word – surreptitiously – that playing would be going on there for anyone who fancied a little animated relaxation. Regulars there were Scott and Dankworth, Tony Crombie, Laurie Morgan, trumpeters Hank Shaw and Leon Calvert, bassists Lennie Bush and Joe Muddell, pianists Tommy Pollard and Bernie Fenton, altoist Johnny Rogers, with occasional visits from Denis Rose. It rapidly became a focus for jam sessions. And it caused a stir in Archer Street. Laurie Morgan would keep his drumkit in the Piccadilly left-luggage office, available for use at the drop of a hat. Secret messages would be passed. And when they would play, curious faces would pop round the door, anxious to listen or blow.

So much curiosity was aroused that the ever-vigilant Harry Morris convinced the others that a golden opportunity was being missed by neglecting to charge the listeners for the privilege. Events at Mac's Rehearsal Rooms became more frequent. Both Dankworth and Crombie led bands there, augmented from time to time by visitors. And because there were ten musical 'regulars' plus Morris, who became the unofficial manager and doorman, the establishment was dubbed the Club Eleven on its opening on 11 December 1948. It was the first club in Britain to present an all-jazz repertoire, with a policy devised entirely by a cooperative who were also themselves practitioners.

At night, life in the club was the perfect definition of bop style and exclusivity. Much of the dress was American-derived, for those who could afford it. There were the drape-back jackets with aggressive shoulders, pegged cuffs, Billy Eckstine shirts, lurid ties with a big knot. Cecil Gee's was the outfitter that specialised in the genre. Detractors of the lifestyle – and that was almost everybody not intimately involved with it, in particular the adherents of the new cult of traditional New Orleans jazz which was gathering steam in South London and Kent – spoke disparagingly of it all, sardonically dismissing the hipsters and their 'fruit salad' ties.

There were plenty of other variations. Corduroy bags were popular, prismatic sweaters, waistcoats. Theolonious Monk's polka-dot bow tie was also much imitated (the two bands at the Club Eleven had red and blue ones respectively) and so were cravats. Music was for a more sophisticated young clientele, taking unintentional advantage of the fact that the university population at the end of the 1940s had reached an all-time high, partly due to the return to studies of forces personnel.

There was nothing prepossessing about the Club Eleven in those days. Visitors descended the wooden staircase opposite the Windmill to find themselves in a cramped low-ceilinged room with a bandstand at one end, dimly lit by bare bulbs. A few battered sofas passed for the soft furnishings. But on a good night the Club Eleven could be the wildest place in town. Young women who became regulars at the club developed their own half-speed dancing momentum to cope with the breakneck tempos of bop, dirndl skirts elegantly twirling, backs straight, cooler and more distant than the jitterbuggers who had preceded them there.

Other implications of bebop were emerging on either side of the Atlantic. For Louis Armstrong's generation, a white-run entertainment industry, frequently racist, and full of humiliations and compromises, nonetheless seemed the inevitable world of work. In the generation that followed, Lester Young symbolised a sidestep, a Bohemian retreat into another world with its own language, its own ethics, its own mode of dress – the beginnings of hipsterism. But though the beboppers idolised Young, they were different. The sound of the music was fierce, urgent, where Young was a pretty, mellifluous storyteller. Pioneered by Kenny Clarke, bop drumming took the beat from the bass drum to the top cymbal (a more varied, flowing and sensuous approach) and left the bass, tom-toms and snare for accents. The metronomic quality of the swing bands was thus disrupted at a stroke. Thelonious Monk, an unorthodox and untrained pianist immersed in church music and hymns, played percussively with his fingers splayed, used unconventional chords, and welcomed bop as a way of freezing out strangers, musicians who, by his standards, weren't really serious.

In early 1949 Ronnie Scott and Johnny Dankworth got a chance to sample Parker's work at even closer range. They were invited to the Paris Jazz Festival, where many of the heroes were scheduled to appear. Scott nearly didn't make it at all because he discovered, whilst waiting to leave at the airport, that his passport was out of date. 'We can let you through,' said the customs officer to Ronnie Scott's frantic pleading. 'But you'll never get off at the other end.' As with the invitation to join the army, official obstacles were not always impenetrable to musicians who knew the ropes. In an unstable postwar world, it was often only necessary to know the right phone number. Scott eventually tracked down a passport official after hours. It took a fiver to get the passport problem fixed. The delay made him a day late, and put him on to a plane heading into the worst storm he was ever unfortunate enough to fly in. But by the time Scott, altoist Johnny Rogers and Dankworth found themselves in a small club in St Germain, busking gently through their semi-bop repertoire, all the effort started to be worthwhile.

The word came that Charlie Parker was on the way. When he arrived – a large shapeless young man with a fitfully angelic look that dissolved the world-weary impression of his shambling appearance – he was followed by an entourage of acolytes. He joined the band, borrowing Dankworth's alto, roared through an uptempo bebop standard, insisted on playing no more choruses than his fair share, to the chagrin not only of those who had come to watch, but to those other performers on the stand who would have been happy for him to go on all night.

Dankworth discovered, standing next to Bird, that the saxophonist hardly needed a microphone, and could – as bandleader Thad Jones once remarked – 'seal every crack in the wall' with his sound. Ideas tumbled from him, even when he was exhausted, in bad mental shape, or drunk. Dankworth said later that his alto felt as if it had been transformed by Parker's handling of it, seemed as if it had somehow been 'opened up'. Parker's wind came up from the gut, his stomach muscles could be made so taut that he could resist a full-blown punch in the midriff as if it were a playful tap. Moreover, Dankworth was aware that

Parker had served an apprenticeship with the orchestras, was used to making a big sound in big venues.

Back in London, Club Eleven continued to be the place to be. It wasn't only a jamming and socialising haunt for local players, it was a refuge for visiting musicians as well. Benny Goodman, Ella Fitzgerald and the composer Tadd Dameron all appeared in the audiences there. Dameron was returning a social call that Scott and bassist Pete Blannin had made on him during the cruiseship *Caronia*'s stopover in New York – when Miles Davis had arrived in the middle of the evening, taken one look at the two Londoners and growled to Dameron, 'What you doing with these ofay cats?'

Club Eleven was so popular, and yet so poorly endowed, that a move was essential. In April 1950, they took a bold step, shifting the premises to Number 50, Carnaby Street, one of the hippest thoroughfares in London, as it was to be again a generation later. It moved into a disused night club, as shabby as Mac's, but it was somewhere to take the music to, and somewhere to hang out. The doorman was Charlie Brown, a black ex-boxer and the landlord of 10, Rillington Place, an address that became one of the most famous in English criminal history as the location for a gruesome string of murders. Musicians and fans ate at 50, Carnaby Street, played cards there, drank there, played music.

New premises occasioned thoughts of a new policy. It might be worth trying to get some of the passing international celebrities to actually perform at the club to raise its profile. But the whole subject was a minefield at the time. The legendary saxophonist Sidney Bechet had illegally played a concert in defiance of the Ministry of Labour's and the Musicians' Union strictures in November of the previous year and the men who brought him in were convicted and fined in June 1950. Nevertheless, they figured if they got a big fish on the hook, they could then argue the pros and cons later.

They sent an invitation to Billie Holiday. The optimistic young proprietors of Club Eleven sent an offer for $250 for a week's work and accommodation. They didn't mention the air fare, had no idea they were supposed to. They didn't know the singer's whereabouts either, and sent the request care of the American jazz magazine, *Downbeat*. Knowing Lady Day was involved with drugs, they dropped various hints about being able to meet her more exotic requests. But, unsurprisingly, they never got a response.

Ronnie Scott continued to grow as a British musical celebrity. The saxophonist (and subsequently writer) Benny Green later recalled the day at Sherry's Ballroom in Brighton when he was playing his first professional assignment and discovered that Ronnie Scott had arrived on the balcony of the hall. Scott's reputation made the saliva dry up in Green's mouth and he couldn't play a note.

Back in Club Eleven, trouble was brewing. Ever since the war years and the American 'invasion', drugs had been part of the scenery. For those living from day to day in a city under attack, edging along a high-wire of nerves, it was bad enough. For musicians in that same world, driven moreover by a boiling desire to crash through a sound barrier to the sublime, to play as well as their heroes, to play as well as each other and better, some drugs seemed an aid to stamina and concentration. They could, as Laurie Morgan put it, 'shorten the distance between not knowing and knowing something'.

Most of the problems associated with this centred on the pianist Tommy Pollard, who was one of the first of the circle to become dependent on hard drugs. Pollard was a brilliant musician, who understood the circumlocutions of bebop as well as Rose did and was genuinely 'inside' the music rather than simply covering its mannerisms. But he was already a heroin addict and the habit was leading him towards the fringes of the underworld.

The night of 15 April 1950 promised nothing out of the ordinary. Ronnie Scott was playing Parker's 'Now's the Time', with his eyes closed as was his frequent habit. When he opened them he found that the club was teeming with police. A massive uniformed sergeant almost blocked his vision.

The scene was chaotic, close to farce. Ronnie Scott had cocaine in his wallet, and no chance whatever of disposing of it. Denis Rose headed frantically for the stairs, hoping to escape through the club's lavatory window, and Scott saw him again a few seconds later being carried back down by two policemen, his feet not touching the ground. Rose already knew he was in big trouble, since his unannounced absence from military service wasn't going to go down well, whatever else he might be charged with. Everyone was carted away to Savile Row.

It all looked more serious in daylight. The magistrate knew nothing about the jazz life, or about jazz clubs, and in fact he seemed to feel that he was standing on the bridge between the nation's moral welfare and the assault of a collection of dangerous Americanised subversives. 'Musicians and Seamen in Early Morning Raid', trumpeted the *Evening News* in alarm. 'Police Swoop on a Soho Bebop Club!'

'What's bebop?' the magistrate enquired of the officers of the law.

'It's a queer form of modern dancing,' Chief Inspector Brandon of Savile Row replied. 'A Negro jive.'

'This sounds a queer sort of place to me,' the magistrate reflected. 'A very rum place.'

In the end they were all heavily fined and told to shape up. But even if nobody went to jail, Club Eleven didn't really recover. The place closed a few months later. Somehow, the heart had gone out of it and no one was especially surprised. The explosion of the discovery of bebop was already three years into the past. They had all discovered how much they wanted to play it. But they hadn't yet worked out *why*.

SEX IS POWER

The Guardian, August 1986

This is a bad period for singers who cultivate images of uninhibited sexuality and project as much eroticism as the out-takes from a *Carry On* movie. Annette Peacock, on the other hand, really sings about sex (or sings about real sex), as well as about optimism and cynicism, meanings, revenge, euphoria – and being a woman. She made a rare, welcome and well-attended one-off appearance at Ronnie Scott's on Sunday, partly to promote her new album, *I Have No Feelings*.

Peacock hardly surfaces these days, and contents herself with the occasional record release. During the late Sixties she was absorbed by hippie culture (associated with guru Timothy Leary), moved from acting to music, experimented with synthesisers when they were still space-age technology to most musicians in rock or jazz.

She also developed a kind of angry wistfulness as a singer that sounded like no-one else. Coupled with her adventurousness with electronics, the nearest point of comparison was that Peacock had become a fierce local (and largely unrecognised) version of Laurie Anderson.

After slow beginnings, her Sunday night performance showed her old distinction and force. The last two words of 'I've Been in the Streets Too Long' erupted in a scream out of a matter-of-fact preamble, the parenthesis of 'I Have (So You Can Use My Body) No Feelings' spoken in a voice of resigned flirtatiousness. In her self-preoccupation, skewed romanticism and assertion of sexuality as a force of human transformation, Annette Peacock is a child of the Sixties. But her originality as a performer is not tied to any date, which a predominantly young audience instantly grasped.

HUMAN CHAIN

The Guardian, October 1986

'Strangely horrible, wouldn't you agree?' Django Bates enquired mildly of the audience as the closing notes died away from an eccentric and convoluted item from the repertoire of Human Chain, much of which sounded like organ music being played backwards. Bates takes a quietly challenging attitude to both his music and his fans.

Human Chain is normally a duo, for Bates on keyboards and the drummer Steve Arguelles – but for this performance at London's Bass Clef it was augmented by bassist Stuart Hall. It is also one of the oddest, and most original contexts in which to hear Bates, who has emerged in the past couple of years as one of the finest improvising piano players in the country, as well as being a composer of considerable punch.

Frequently deploying pop-derived electronics, funk, free-playing and chunks of other-worldly explorations that resemble the soundtracks to Gothic horrors (Bates even has a tune simply called 'Death'), Human Chain is a substantial example of the ways in which many of the old musical alignments of the Seventies have changed.

In the course of their work on Sunday night, the ensemble played its own version of funk, which sounded like Herbie Hancock of the Maiden Voyage era put through a tape loop and then turned into a scything synthesiser solo by Bates, who in the space of a few minutes did a good deal to discredit most of the flabby and vulgar expositions made on the machine in the past decade.

'Death' was a short vignette, of ghostly choir-like organ over slow-motion drum patterns. On the oriental-sounding 'Relax', Bates made the organ sound like a concertina, while Steve Arguelles played pans. They completed the picture with a galloping Rollins-like calypso – Arguelles maintained a strange, rattling momentum, elbows akimbo as if he were frying eggs.

WE LOVE PARIS

The Guardian, October 1986

The Town and Country Club (a vast establishment distinctly unlike its discreet-sounding name) is now going into jazz promotion in a big way, with a barnstorming performance by Lester Bowie's Brass Fantasy last week and shows by other illustrious artists in the next few weeks, including Brazilians Airto Moreira and the extraordinary, Methuselah-like Hermeto Pascoal.

This week, the beneficiary was the Paris Reunion Band, a collection of hard bop players who congregated around the late Kenny Clarke's circle in Europe and which includes some of the most unsentimental exponents of that most unsentimental of genres currently in business. The group is effectively led by Woody Shaw with Nat Adderley on cornet, Joe Henderson and Nathan Davies (saxes), Idrees Muhammed (drums), Jimmy Wood (bass), and Grachan Moncur (trombone). The regular pianist, Kenny Drew, was replaced by the excellent British keyboard player, John Taylor.

From the outset, it was obvious that the relatively small crowd in such a big venue was going to affect the sound in a way that Lester Bowie, playing to a packed house, hadn't been inconvenienced by. The result was that the ensemble playing frequently sounded as if it was coming from a distant radio station, and soloists created the impression of playing in a bathroom. This, to some extent, blunted the edge of the performers' highly individual styles, though the ears did attune to it after a while.

Grachan Moncur's trombone sounded as grandiloquent as an ocean liner hooting its way into a dock as the band shunted through a collection of sidelong, mid-tempo themes; a honking blues developed out of a stirring double-bass intro, and a rendition of 'My Funny Valentine' by Adderley, which zig-zagged with warmth and geniality between the familiar landmarks of the tune.

Taylor led off the blues impressively with a chiming, percussive solo that developed into a series of churning crescendos, and Joe Henderson stepped imperiously into the ebb tide with a series of hollow, gargling figures that precisely defined the hard bop tenor style. Nathan Davies, also on tenor, turned the same piece into very nearly a rock and roll song.

HOME BOY

City Limits, November 1986

'They're standing in line for *Round Midnight* in the States,' Dexter Gordon says with some satisfaction. Since the movie turned into an opportunity to pay a tribute to artists ('my heroes, your heroes') who forged *the* twentieth century music but frequently died young, were rooked of their dues or disappeared into obscurity, the recognition in the land of jazz's birth is something to feel satisfied about.

As Dale Turner, the fictional character whose life is drawn from those of Lester Young and Bud Powell, plus a good deal from the actor who plays him, Dexter Gordon is (at sixty-two) about to receive quite a lot of the public recognition that has been insufficiently afforded to him as a player. But Gordon, a bebop hero and a spectacular exponent of both a tumultuous uptempo saxophone style and a bruised lyricism in ballads, is a cornerstone of postwar jazz.

'Just a kid' in the big band era when he worked with the legendary Billy Eckstine band that included Dizzy Gillespie and Charlie Parker, Gordon left his homeland in 1962 to live and play in Copenhagen and later Paris. Dale Turner's life is as familiar to him as the keyboard of his horn – the rounds of hotel rooms indistinguishable from one another, the hovering pushers, the love affairs with a beautiful foreign city and the fatal magnetism of 'home'.

'I thought the guy was nuts,' Gordon says of the original suggestion by Tavernier with much the same drifting, laconic preoccupation he displays in the movie. 'I mean, Bertrand explained the idea to me and I thought,

"You want to *what*?" But then I realised that nobody had ever had this opportunity. I wanted to tell people all about my heroes.'

But most of the portrayals of jazz players in films have been an embarrassment. Not only are they stereotypes, they don't even move their fingers in the right places. 'All the attempts to film jazz characters have been like that. So we tried to open it out. That's why we couldn't do a story just about Bud (Powell) because Bud was *tragique*, you know. And Lester was *dramatique* (chuckles).

'The sources I used were guys I've known all my life. I would show another side of those cats, the interest in symphony music, the evolution of their playing, the dedication, almost to the exclusion of everything else. That's a big point. Anybody sees the film, maybe it will open their consciousness a little. It's a *human* story.

'All that stuff about jazz musicians being self-destructive . . .' (Gordon looks mildly disgusted) '. . . well of course, everywhere you worked there was booze, all the temptations that one could want (laughs). But a lot of those guys who died early didn't die from that. They died from broken hearts. Having to worry about a gig every week, "Where you workin' next week?", "Dunno, man." *That's* what killed them.'

Gordon is hurt that the jurors at the film festivals thought it wasn't serious acting for a musician to play himself. 'It was hard work. Everyone says, "It seems so natural", well maybe. But all the thought and concentration that went into getting that. Not that it's Shakespeare or anything, but you know . . .'

MELANCHOLIA

The Guardian, November 1986

For three decades, American saxophonist Lee Konitz has been the most active member of that clan of white experimentalists who founded what came to be known as the 'cool school' – other key players, like Warne Marsh and Chet Baker, having been prone to long spells of marking time. The characteristics of the genre have been delicate quavering tone, an avoidance of histrionics, and a fondness for ballads – which has led to it being typecast as a cerebral, passionless music somehow at odds with 'real jazz'. *New Yorker* critic Gary Giddins however, has described white jazz as 'swinging with melancholy,' which is a much fairer summary of just how distinctive much of the music has actually been.

Konitz opened a London season on Monday night, performing with Dave Green on bass, John Taylor on piano and Trevor Tomkins on drums, and his opening set was a surprise on several counts. One, that he should have entered into such an open-ended, freely-associative style with unfamiliar partners; two, that he should have risked it in a nightclub where the audience often prefers more straight-ahead activities; three, that his manner of playing should produce the spin-off effect of making so much everyday jazz playing sound as if it's taking place between musicians who aren't listening.

Konitz is a stocky, slightly grumpy-looking individual whose public manner asserts that he's just there for the music. He began his set by adjusting the mouthpiece with quiet blurts and honks, drifting without a break into his opener as if the accompanists had been faded up on a mixing desk. The piece, which swayed between walking bass figures and delicate, out-of-rhythm embroidery, emerged – and only in snatches of phrasing – as 'Green Dolphin Street', interpreted by Konitz in high, fluting sounds and gruff low-register murmurings. He did much the same with Monk's 'Straight No Chaser', inviting the band into brief episodes of swing (just enough to make the audience nod) and then drifting wilfully out of it again. John Taylor was an excellent foil for Konitz, though the technique that the saxophonist employs is in fact a cool school trademark of long, quavering runs that endlessly delay their resolution and craftily serve to disguise the chords. Taylor's assertion of the latter sounded, by contrast, almost verbose.

Hip

The Guardian, November 1986

Not many things can drag a rational being to Wembley on a wet November Sunday afternoon, but a Miles Davis band – almost regardless of the personnel – is high on the list. At the very least, there will be a point in the show at which he will hit a single note that has an encyclopaedia of definitions of rhythm and musical passion hidden in it. It is a gift that, through a multitude of tribulations, has never deserted him.

On the first of three performances at Wembley, the newly-amiable jazz superstar, the sixty-year-old walking definition of hip, played an exciting and fast-moving set mostly based on the repertoire of his last two albums (*You're Under Arrest* and *Tutu*) and, at times, hit sublime levels of spontaneity. This is a difficult achievement with such an outfit, which is very loud, very mechanised, performs complicated arrangements, and has – since 1981 – given too much space to a succession of long-winded guitarists.

The band played for two hours, plus twenty minutes or so of encore. It was an eight-piece, strongly featuring guitarist Garth Webber and the excellent Bob Berg on saxophones, who has visited Britain with Miles before. The trumpeter led his men on, sporting a black rhinestone jacket and gold lamé trousers, and lifting his shades to peer at the audience as if examining an unfamiliar species.

They all then erupted into fast funk, as if somebody had thrown a switch, phased it into the kind of jaunty blues with which Davis can tantalise his audience with that nostalgia for his early style that he has so little time for himself, and then shifted into 'Perfect Way' from *Tutu*, and Cyndi Lauper's 'Time After Time', a beautiful song in which Davis went into a huddle with Berg (playing soprano) and delivered a series of taut, veiled, whispering phrases. The brooding and dramatic opening of the title track of *Tutu* then followed – but where it's used, Gil Evans-like, on the album as purely a vehicle for Davis's lyricism, it became an opportunity for an interminable solo from Webber.

Davis played with the mute on almost throughout the gig, which made the brief flare in the middle of the poignant, lyrical 'Human Nature' suddenly ring out like a church bell. When Whitney Balliett wrote of Davis, over a quarter century ago, that he seems to play lines distilled from much more complex melodies inside his head, it was an insight that has become ever more applicable to the trumpeter's work.

Much of Davis's own playing – a tapestry of baleful and enigmatic runs, squirts into the upper register, shy, evaporating sounds and unexpected fierceness – has been almost pure rhythm ever since his decision to line himself up so intimately with contemporary black pop, but in a way it always has been. The lyrical Davis can still make fleetingly moving appearances, as he did on the gorgeous ballad 'Portia', which the band shrewdly saved for its encore.

1987–89

During 1989, Ronnie Scott remarked that it had at last become possible to hear more jazz on the TV commercials than you could on the programmes. If he was right, it was a symptom of how much jazz had come to symbolise chic discrimination and taste – more or less the exact opposite of what it had signified less than a decade before, though Scott's own establishment had proved its durability and faith in its original convictions by celebrating its thirtieth birthday the same year. The stalled and bankrupt National Jazz Centre project in London had been finally abandoned in 1987.

The great composer-arranger Gil Evans died, having mystified and delighted audiences for years with a gentle, all but undetectable conjuror's mastery of his materials (the musicians, and a loose, almost doodling deployment of a palette of mistily colourful harmony) and his most famous partner, Miles Davis, grew increasingly communicative and open-handed in his trumpet interpretations of pop ballads. Though Davis threaded these delicate interludes through a generally storm-tossed tapestry of fast disco-funk, other jazz stars who had embraced fusion in the late 1970s were moving back to an increasingly fashionable classic jazz. Saxophone virtuoso Mike Brecker was one.

The new British jazz aristocracy of the mid-1980s consolidated their careers with a different kind of fusion – the outward journey to 'world music', which Courtney Pine (whose debut album Journey to the Urge Within *sold an astonishing 75,000 in its first year) pursued through his West Indian origins towards Africa and the Caribbean, and new saxophonist Andy Sheppard did through Coltranesque hard bop mutated by Latin and dance ideas. Meanwhile, European jazz had by this time become a fixed part of the scenery of serious music, so much so that American piano virtuoso Cecil Taylor (a contemporary of John Coltrane and Ornette Coleman and almost as famously innovative as both) came to Europe to work with the best local players, and Miles Davis's illustrious former record producer at Columbia, Teo Macero, travelled to London to produce a Loose*

Tubes album. Macero expressed the opinion that Duke Ellington would have appreciated the adventurous British band.

The surest signs that jazz had returned to the mainstream came not through music but through film. Before the decade was out, the hard bop tenor veteran Dexter Gordon had starred in the jazz movie Round Midnight as a played-out but still dignified expatriate musician, and Clint Eastwood (a jazz fan of old) had made Bird!, a biopic of Charlie Parker.

Meanwhile, the classic jazz reissue business continued to boom. Record companies scoured their archives for almost anything that might earn a label proclaiming a piece of indispensable jazz memorabilia. New electronic resampling techniques were constantly applied to old masters, in attempts to salvage ever more 'natural' sounds from the crackle of the 78s. Wynton Marsalis went on resampling too, carrying his investigations of jazz history back way before Miles Davis now, and exploring the ensemble sounds and instrumental techniques of some of the earliest jazz. It was an obsessive mission, but the young trumpeter was not to be diverted from it.

PRO

The Guardian, March 1987

Mark Murphy, the forty-five-year-old jazz singer from Syracuse, once played Jesus Christ in a film. The notion is hard to square with Murphy's jazz style, which is worldly, sophisticated, pragmatic and cool. Once a regular performer in London – he lived here in the Sixties and early Seventies – his appearances at the Bass Clef last week were a reminder of how neatly Murphy can splice the traditions of jazz improvisation.

Murphy's characteristics are a light, firm voice, an understanding of improvisation so that his scat singing does not sound like someone in the midst of an asthma attack, an endearing stage presence and intelligent variation of lyrics. In 'Stolen Moments', the last surfaced in a tangent into which Murphy veered that involved stolen time in the romantic sense, turning into stolen time in the jazz sense.

Herbie Hancock's 'Maiden Voyage', with its jumpy, prodding rhythm, was hard work, and Murphy did not find an answer to it. 'Misty', however, brought out the best of his microphone technique, as he varied the distance from the instrument to his vocal chords with the effect of someone playing with a volume control.

Not all Murphy's rapping was exactly advanced in content ('All you little girls look in your mirror'), but his mock confusion about how to fade out of a song without the help of low lighting, which forced him to drop to a whisper and pretend to hide behind Peter Ind's bass, was a classy exercise in stagecraft. A pro in his prime.

RIVE GAUCHE

The Guardian, March 1987

If Dexter Gordon wins an Oscar for his role in *Round Midnight*, it won't just mark a revival of interest in classic jazz that's already in the fast lane, but a boost for the old favourite, bohemian Paris, as well. Bertrand Tavernier's film, as well as being an honest and respectful look at the jazz life (if faintly inclined to nourish its stereotypes), must equally have been a big hit with the French Tourist Board. It told you that Paris is a city with a heart, a city capable of healing those injuries sustained by New York hustle, a city that art's most outward-bound travellers could believe to be a port in a storm.

In Paris now, *Round Midnight* is still much talked about as the catalyst that has done wonders for the French jazz scene. Currently in the city there are more than fifty clubs presenting some form of jazz. On one night recently Chet Baker, Art Farmer and Woody Shaw were playing within a mile of each other around the city centre, and the Polish altoist Zbigniew Namyslowski did a one-nighter in Chinatown the evening before.

Baker was performing to a young, left-field audience in a big, informal barn-like club near the Gare de l'Est, Farmer was blowing his rounded, affable variations in a tiny basement behind the Châtelet in a club so small that reaching for your handkerchief could constitute an improper suggestion to the piano player. Shaw, doing his jazzman's Lee Van Cleef routine, was working below an elegant brasserie in Les Halles, with moody pictures of Nina Simone and Elvin Jones adorning the walls.

If you were even more of a traditionalist, you still wouldn't feel deprived. You could have heard a barn-storming French swing orchestra in Montparnasse while you were rolling cocktails called 'Doctor Jazz' or 'Sweet Georgia Brown' around your palate, or you could have jived to a Benny Goodman-like outfit in the legendary Caveau de la Huchette, a fifteenth-century grotto that's been running as a jazz dance hall since the liberation of Paris. As the man at the Centre d'Information du Jazz said with a hint of weariness: 'I could go out five nights a week and still miss things.'

But though Paris has certainly retained more of its postcard bohemianism than cities that have taken one look at the twentieth century and rolled over on their backs, the jazz clubs don't really look like Tavernier's sets any more.

In the days when Bud Powell was a local, jazz mostly happened in the Latin Quarter. It was a refuge for artists on the run, and for cognoscenti cheering them on. Nowadays, the scene divides into that part of jazz (swing, fusion, bebop) that can be comfortably absorbed into the country's civilised drinking and eating patterns, a small but significant representation of the avant-garde, and a degree of state involvement (now shaky again with the arrival of Jacques Chirac) that extends to the funding of a national jazz orchestra playing a far from conservative repertoire.

The first sector, which more or less embraces 'the jazz revival', thus takes place on a strictly commercial basis in the bars and the restaurants. The music may not be bursting any dams, but its quality is high – as is the quality of the food, which in Paris is what you expect.

At *Le Jazz Hot*, the legendary French jazz magazine founded by critic Charles Delaunay in 1935, the new editor Philippe Adler echoes the sentiment that the town is buzzing. 'Sales started to fly when we did a special on *Round Midnight*,' Adler says. 'There's a new audience for jazz now – for the French and Europeans, as well as the Americans. Young people are turning to it because there's nothing interesting happening in pop, which is eating its own tail.'

Under Adler, sales of *Le Jazz Hot* – at around 30,000 – are better than at any time in the paper's fifty-two-year run. But Adler is very much a part of the 'jazz revival'. A tough, rugged ex-*L'Express* music journalist who keeps his raincoat on while sitting at his desk, Adler has been brought in by a new owner to give the one-time buffs' magazine a downmarket jauntiness ('We're sorry Samantha Fox doesn't play jazz') which occasions raised eyebrows from purer souls and supporters of the more analytical rival publication, *Jazz Magazine*.

Adler shrugs at such reservations. 'If we don't sell the paper, we die. If I put a young French avant-garde musician on the cover, the magazine doesn't sell. If I put Dizzy (Gillespie) on the cover, it does.'

At the Rue Dunois, a long, twilight street in the 13th arrondissement, where the only patches of light are the Chinese and Vietnamese restaurants, it is a different story. In the warm-up to the main attraction (Zbigniew Namyslowski, on this occasion) at a club simply called 28 Rue Dunois, the audience may be entertained by video screens displaying the deliberations of free-improvisers, and show no visible signs of exasperation. The atmosphere of spruce seediness and a youthful and involved audience is faintly reminiscent of a small-scale progressive arts venue like London's Almeida Theatre.

Sylvain Torikian, a leading light of the ten-year-old venue who also happens to be the administrator of France's Orchestre Nationale du Jazz, is less interested in a jazz boom that is principally for one kind of jazz – vintage bebop, or repro-vintage bebop. 'We don't do so much of that,' Torikian says. 'I think some of the most interesting improvised music these days is European, especially East European. They're technically very good, and their attitude is different.'

The club, because of its campaigning spirit and the breadth of its general arts policy (it even puts on children's theatre during the day) was popular with the Ministry of Culture under its charismatic former boss Jack Lang, and has been getting thirty per cent of its revenue from the government, as well as a useful five per cent from City Hall. But the Chirac grip is tightening. At the Rue Dunois, they fear cuts in their budgets next year.

For many of the others, signs of prosperity are in the air, and at this time of the year unquestionably fuelled by young Parisians, not by tourists – as in London, where Ronnie Scott's can get a packed house on a Monday night for Joe Henderson when five years ago he would have been playing to his own echo.

Le Petit Journal in Montparnasse (where a moving neon of a trumpet player beckons you own an otherwise unprepossessing high-rise street alongside the Gare de Montparnasse, and the frontage looks rather like Peppermint Park) attracts an audience of both fledgling and adult yuppies (a noticeably different crowd to the Rue Dunois), keen on swing and bop.

The club books high-quality acts – Art Blakey and Cedar Walton are on the billboards – and though its entrance fee isn't cheap by London standards (around £12) you can get drinks and food rolled in, with supplements for some items.

The equally smart Magnetic Terrace (bop and Brazilian music) in the Rue de Cossonerie uses the same system, as do many of the Paris clubs – some of the smaller bars, like the Sunset at Rue des Lombardes in Les Halles, or the Petit Opportun in the Rue des Lavandieres adapt it to hit you for £8–£10 for your first drink with reduced prices thereafter. Pascal Anquetil, the Centre d'Information du Jazz's administrator observes 'many of the new places are really bars and restaurants that also present jazz' – that is reflected in the entrance deal.

The New Morning, in the Rue des Petites Ecuries, a far more louche and unaffected establishment in spite of its illustrious roster of international guests, charges a straight entrance fee of £8–£10. So does Le Caveau de la Huchette (Rue de la Huchette) at Saint Michel. Looking just the way a jazz club looked in the rollnecks-and-reefers imagery of the 1950s, it is really a subterranean dancehall, relatively cheap to get into (£5 or so) with an upstairs bar and a clientele of kids who look like extras from *Absolute Beginners* energetically shaking a leg to swing bands.

Though the high profile aspect of Paris jazz centres on the international imports, this flourishing scene is founded on local talent. 28 Rue Dunois will feature many of the more experimental practitioners, but all the clubs confirm the new confidence of non-American jazz players today.

In the basement of the Sunset (a pleasant place, but designed for leprechauns) I heard an excellent Herbie Hancockish pianist, Allie Delfau, in a quartet where the bassist was also female, plus a black American drummer and a French guitarist. At Le Petit Opportun, a superb bop pianist, Georg Avanitas, buoyed up and teased out the rumination of Art Farmer.

André Francis of ORTF (French national radio), *the* jazz broadcaster whose work over the years has done much to nurture a mature jazz consciousness among the regular populace that's far ahead of Britain's, says: 'There are two thousand jazz combos, twelve regular big bands, three jazz schools in France. There are four jazz programmes on radio a day, two of them for one and a half hours each. Jazz on the radio is very important in France.'

To deprived British enthusiasts, the situation looks as healthy as jazz – which is only uneasily and inconsistently a popular art – could ever hope to be. The French schools are pumping out a new generation of young performers who are not just escaped classical players but fully versed in the arts of jazz. Paris hosts a massive jazz festival every October, paid for by the city and featuring local and international bands, and the communist departments of the suburbs do the same throughout March.

The radio stations acknowledge the music's significance, and the state-backed Orchestre Nationale appears (so far) to be secure in spite of a less accommodating government. The Salon du Jazz, an international recording and distribution trade fair for the music, staged in Paris in 1983 and 1985, was an event unique in the jazz world – and the organisers want to do it again in 1988, but this time much of the state cash will have to be replaced by sponsorship. Most of the music this complex infrastructure generates will occupy the mainstream but some – if for no other reason than the sheer numbers of emerging young players and the sophistication of their awareness of jazz – will gravitate toward the avant-garde.

Actuel magazine, the bible of hip Parisians, ran a list of sixty essential jazz records last autumn – for those who knew little of jazz, or maybe actively disliked it. FNAC, the record and video store, instantly reported a forty per cent increase in sales of the titles. But if it's *à la mode* right now, can it stay that way?

Pascal Anquetil: 'The new audience is in two groups – the young ones who have come to jazz through pop, maybe Miles Davis, and discovered how rich it is. And the thirty to forty year-olds whose first love was jazz and who have come back to it. That audience won't disappear.'

Well, it might. But in France, with its radio shows, club life, festivals, jazz schools and all the other trappings of a culture that takes this art very seriously indeed, it'll be harder to just wake up one morning and forget that jazz exists.

ALICE IN WONDERLAND

The Guardian, July 1987

When John Coltrane died twenty years ago this month, aged forty, the event triggered not simply a series of heartfelt valedictions from all over the world, but composers like Phillip Glass, LaMonte Young, and Terry Riley cited his influence. So did Sixties rock artists like the Byrds, the Allman Brothers and Carlos Santana, and latterly almost every magazine-cover style-conscious young jazz player seems to be re-running his licks as if the intervening two decades had never happened.

His widow – formerly pianist Alice McLeod, now Alice Coltrane to most and Turiyasnagitananda to some, following her adoption of Buddhism – has followed her late husband's path, and appears in London on Friday with a band that mirrors the one John was involved with not long before his death. That is, Alice on piano, Reggie Workman on bass, Rashied Ali on drums, and the twenty-year-old altoist Oran Coltrane, who was four months old when his father died, taking the saxophone parts.

Ms Coltrane has rarely appeared in public in recent years, nor on record, though her recorded work features much spacious, meditative and unusual music which some have regarded as an authentic extension of Coltrane's musical mission. She plays an unusual organ which predates modern keyboard technology and often sounds like McCoy Tyner playing the sitar. Coltrane had wanted to bring Indian music into jazz more, had studied with Ravi Shankar before the pop aristocracy of the Sixties took to doing it, and even named his elder son after the sitarist.

Since Alice Coltrane's conversion to Buddhism, much of the past has been taken up with religious teaching, at the Vedantic Centre in Agoura, California, where she now lives. Only benefit concerts have tempted her out. But since this year is the twentieth anniversary of John Coltrane's death, the pressures to play have been stronger than usual.

Ms Coltrane, who hails from Detroit, is fifty now. She was the pianist in the band of vibes player Terry Gibbs at the beginning of the 1960s, and was extensively influenced by the work of Bud Powell and later McCoy Tyner, John's pianist. In 1966 she joined Coltrane's band after the bust-up over artistic direction in which the saxophonist declared his intention to delve further into the dissolution of orthodox jazz form. She married him later that year.

She recalls: 'I had a deep belief in God because I came from a religious family, and my parents had performed with church choirs which influenced me musically. 'But John had done a lot of research into world religions and the spiritual dimension and said to me, "take a deeper look".'

John Coltrane's influence on young players has been so extensive that – like Charlie Parker – virtually every horn player of his son's age either sounds like a clone of him or clearly owe an immense debt. But Coltrane was the explorer, and many of his imitators have taken his lessons straight, which has come to impart an oddly static and muscle-bound feel to an idiom that started life as furiously dynamic as the first bop outings of Parker, Gillespie and Monk.

'Young musicians instead of going forward and exploring spiritual heights have gone back,' Ms Coltrane reflects with regret. 'It's demonstrated by the music they play – it has no spiritual message. John wanted to go beyond all limitations in music and if he had lived he'd still be doing it today. He always thought there was something else to do, something else to create.'

LONGEVITY
The Guardian, July 1987

The current era is now seeing some of the best all-round jazz virtuosi for years and since those confirming this phenomenon are young enough to have decades ahead of them to refine their art, doubts are stilled about the longevity of jazz.

At the Bracknell Festival this weekend – still one of the most adventurously programmed events in the British jazz calendar and this year featuring George Russell, Mike Gibbs and the Brecker Brothers, among others – two saxophonists will be present to demonstrate it. One is British, one American, and both are thirty.

Steve Coleman, the brilliant New York-based altoist who recently raised eyebrows here with the Dave Holland band, was the 1986 *Downbeat* alto poll winner. America's *Musician* magazine described him as 'one of the more singular thinkers to emerge on the jazz scene in recent years.' Andy Sheppard, from Warminster, also appears on several Bracknell billings. He was the runner-up in the Schlitz up and-coming jazz musicians contest at Heaven last year, and in the opinion of many should have won it outright. A superb technician, his originality of concept and approach puts him in the same class as Coleman but using contrasting materials.

Coleman's playing with his own band, Five Elements, is quite different to the fast, beautifully-turned work of the Dave Holland group, one of the most mercurial and resourceful ensembles to have hit jazz in the last ten years. Where Holland's music was brisk and boppish, and the improvisers crossed horns with all the precision and dangerous delicacy of fencers, Coleman's own outfit mixes a kind of earthily operatic vocals, synthesisers, rap, funk and bop.

It has a wider and less surgical quality than Holland, and the audacity of the mixture is a welcome change, considering the rather formulaic affairs jazz and pop often share. Coleman has been saddled with a reputation for wanting to combine the influences of James Brown and Charlie Parker, which is a simplification he laughs about but wouldn't disown.

'I was a Charlie Parker fanatic,' says Coleman, a fast-talking individual whose reflections on life and art come at you like snaredrum rolls. 'But music was everywhere when I was a kid and it couldn't help but be a big influence. I was playing on the streets in New York not so long ago, and being influenced by James Brown made a lot more sense than playing "Lush Life" or something. I know all those tunes and some of them are good, but they don't mean anything to me as far as my background goes.'

Coleman didn't have to stay on the streets long. His skills had already landed him jobs with orthodox bands like Slide Hampton's and Mel Lewis's in his native Chicago, and the busking period in New York was soon followed by the invitation to join Dave Holland. He dislikes current jazz nostalgia ('for lack of something to play they're looking back at the past') but is inspired by jazz to find a contemporary language that isn't about the work of earlier heroes.

Andy Sheppard, being currently Bristol-based and having lived in Europe for most of his twenties, finds his influences come from different sources. On recent showings, however, he has shown himself to be a player of great imagination. There is a reflectiveness in his playing even at high pressure, and he is able to mix so many inflections of jazz that his solos can pass through phases of Coltraneish urgency, Ben Webster-like plushness, and feats of circular breathing and harmonies reminiscent of the free-musician Evan Parker within the space of a few minutes. He is the most complete British player of the current crop of new soloists here.

A puckish and unhurried individual, Sheppard is untroubled by whether what he does will be in or out of fashion. 'It's pretty normal for people to take twenty years to catch up on changes in music,' he says, echoing a comment of the late Thelonious Monk. People are already catching up on Andy Sheppard significantly quicker than that.

Diva

The Guardian, July 1987

George Wein, the founder of the Newport Jazz Festival and the touring package of which the current JVC/Capital Jazz Parade on the South Bank is a part, has gone to considerable lengths to present Sarah Vaughan in much the same way that Maria Callas probably came to consider right and proper over the years.

In 1979 at Carnegie Hall Ms Vaughan had three consecutive concerts devoted to different aspects of her immense contribution to music. American critic Gary Giddins called her the most creative singer working in the pop-standard repertoire, as well as a great jazz 'instrumentalist'.

Ms Vaughan's repertoire would sound a bit staid to Beastie Boys fans maybe, but she is blessed with the most beautiful (and at times, the most moving) voice currently devoted to jazz and jazz-inflected music. Other jazz singers may at times be more adventurous or more surprising, but for range, accuracy and timbre she sweeps the board.

Sarah Vaughan's concert at the Festival Hall represented a ceremonial broadside to open this year's Jazz Parade, following a first set in which Georgie Fame sang some jauntily bluesy material in front of the Jack Sharpe Big Band, a cinema-style presentation not quite suited to the singer's intimate, mischievous, Mose Allison-influenced musical persona.

After the interval, Ms Vaughan swept on in a billowing pink creation, to rapturous applause, after two tunes by her deft, businesslike trio (George Gaffney on piano, Andy Simpkins on bass, Harold Jones, drums), and launched into a two-paced version of 'Fascinatin' Rhythm', which started lazily, hung tantalising on a scattered break midway through, then galloped frantically to a close.

Having performed a quick musical triple-somersault to make sure everyone was listening, Ms Vaughan then unfurled her effortless array of gifts. She sang 'Summertime' unaccompanied, at first softly, then unexpectedly delivering a lark-rise ascent on 'one of those mornings you're going to wake up singing', that caused audible intakes of breath in the stalls. She opened 'All of Me' yearningly, then sidestepped it raffishly into swing; handled the wordless 'Chelsea Bridge' as a series of high, sighing sounds sweeping down into dark reverberating vibratos, and then rolled the entire works together in the erotic love song 'The Island', which steamed like a sauna.

Sarah Vaughan's remarkable technique guarantees her concerts, but her power to move audiences with emotions other than admiration varies widely. On this show she was stylish, witty and sharp. She blew opportunities for a full hypnotic effect by the 'thank you so much' after ripples of applause greeted opening bars, or the playful instructions to get the spotlight back in the opening of the anxiously passionate 'To Say Goodbye'. But even with those showbiz diversions, she can rescue what seems to be a missed chance. At the end of the song, her first 'goodbye' descended into the throbbing near-baritone of her voice as if in resignation, but the second rocketed into a desperate wail that tingled the spine.

BALLET

The Guardian, July 1987

You could mistake the hush of expectation on the premises when Stan Getz is due for simple anticipation of pleasure in the company of a great artist, but there's more to it than that. Getz's music has, at its best, had a bloom on it, a petal-like flawlessness and symmetry that always seems too vulnerable to survive. But, unlike many ascetic 'cool' players, his work also represents 'purity' of an unmistakably impure and jazz-inflected kind, which is why he was an inspiration even to such a dissimilar player as John Coltrane.

Each time Getz returns you fear this secret formula may be lost, and this is a source of seductive anxiety. Unlike most saxophonists of the post-war period, Getz has the confidence of his maestro status to be certain of that – his strongest suit is playing sparingly. This enables him to reverse the standard horn player's tactics and perform fast passages as impressively as anyone in the music, but as throwaway lines at the ends of phrases, brief fillers between pealing sustained notes as lustrous as a clarinet, casual codas. It's as if a trapeze artist performed an act of almost pure ballet and delivered the triple back somersault as an afterthought on the way out.

At the Festival Hall, Getz was performing with an excellent piano trio of considerable sensitivity to his needs. But he began tentatively, even pausing in mid solo for his water bottle, and looked uncomfortable – a disquiet that may have partly stemmed from his opening dedication to Al Cohn, a recently departed player from a similar school, and partly from his recovery from major surgery. But from the opening notes of his first ballad – an idiom of which he is an undisputed master – Getz located his muse. The solo displayed all his artistry with dynamics, alternating between shimmering notes hovering like bubbles and wincing cries on louder sounds bridging the chord changes and it also displayed his sense of the shape and momentum of a solo.

Getz huffed and mumbled a little on the uptempo tune 'Voyage', and returned to sensuality with Duke Ellington's 'Warm Valley', into which he also introduced a plush, trembling vibrato. After an uneven middle period in which he introduced Joey Alamera, a capable but nervous student from his master class, he then picked up speed on the up-tempo numbers and began treading together a tracery of bubbling mid-register runs and sounds like suppressed exclamations, which he uses like sudden adjustments of a steering wheel to drift into a chord. All the sidemen were experts at sympathetic support, and pianist Jim McNeally – a mixture of Herbie Hancock, Bill Evans and Red Garland – was superb. Getz played his encore ballad without the mikes. The crowd wouldn't let him go.

INDIAN SUMMER

The Guardian, September 1987

John Dankworth celebrated his sixtieth birthday on Sunday with a concert at the Barbican featuring the massed bands of the LSO, classical pianist John Ogden, various jazz and classical partners and ex-partners, and a repertoire covering his contribution over forty years, from precocious bebop soloist after the war, through bandleader, film-score writer, musical ambassador and all-round purveyor of eclecticism.

Though not intending to, Dankworth is actually very good at producing jazz-inflected music for people who don't really much like jazz, at least the part of it that Whitney Balliett called 'the sound of surprise'.

Dankworth's 'Pavanne' sounds like film music, as does his rather soupy arrangement of 'I Dream of Jeannie with the Light Brown Hair'. The full orchestra nevertheless did sound surprisingly swinging on an arrangement of 'Caravan', in which the theme stole softly up behind a deep trombone riff reverberating like a cathedral organ.

Kenny Baker, the sixty-six-year-old trumpeter, then bounded on stage to play Bunny Berigan's 'I Can't Get Started'. His tone slashed through the hall with the opening theme, dropped back to an amiable growl, and proceeded through this alternation of gleaming sounds and puffs of smoke until the penultimate climax – at which point he stopped, cracked a gag about his age, then went back and hit the note right between the eyes and brought the house down. Then they all charged into Benny Goodman's 'Sing Sing Sing', the orchestra beginning to sound like a superannuated Buddy Rich band. But the reconstruction of the old Johnny Dankworth Seven with all the original members was a neat stroke. It was delightful, not only as a reminder of the popularity of that kind of accessible bebop in the Fifties, but also because of the real relish of the players for the occasion – particularly tenorist Don Rendell, who has retained a wild, unruly eloquence, and Dankworth himself, who played some fluid alto on a mid-tempo blues.

Cleo Laine, the band's original vocalist, came on to sing 'Easy Living' with her customary voluptuous low-register sounds and breathy, flute-like falsetto.

YOUNG FOGEY
The Wire, September 1987

I went to a Ruby Braff gig a few years ago, and was surprised by how much I loved it. The trumpeter's expansive tone, his affability and his lyricism were irresistible. I didn't think of it then, but maybe his journeyman matter-of-factness was a pleasure too. You couldn't imagine him ever becoming 'an issue'. What brings him to mind now is the 'debate', as you might say, in the jazz world about Wynton Marsalis.

Hence Ruby Braff. For all his shrewd adaptation of the style, Braff was of course never a contemporary of the people whose styles he affected. He was twenty-seven years younger than Louis Armstrong, and twelve younger than Bobby Hackett. If the definition is that a twenty-five-year-old has a moral obligation to play the music of most other twenty-five-year-olds in the same business, Braff should have been a bebopper. He decided instead to be a mainstream classicist, and sounded just fine doing that. But there is difference, which is not Marsalis's fault. The machine never took up Braff, somewhat also to his chagrin. He became a buff with technique, a man making a modest living pursuing an obsession. Marsalis is part of an industry that wishes musicians like him, who don't want to change jazz more than by the odd telling twist and tweak, would come along more often. Consequently he's welcomed like a messiah. The notion that players might also feel that part of their work is to search for a radically different music not yet made, as Parker, Coltrane, Ornette and Miles all did, is not a currently popular theory. Marsalis of course doesn't have a duty to be visionary if he isn't one – the problem is that he's being heralded as if he were.

Standard Time features twelve tunes, including 'Caravan', 'April in Paris', 'Cherokee' (twice), 'Foggy Day' and 'Autumn Leaves'. The band is technically astonishing, as it demonstrated at the Festival Hall this summer, and its interpretative devices are often dazzling – like 'April in Paris' played as if it were to be a Monk tune at first, with a limping, dirgey intro, then opening out and swinging into a drenching Marsalis trumpet solo, where his lines bridge the bar breaks endlessly and keep coming back at intervals to explosive sounds on the accents to remind you of the beat. At the end of a Marcus Roberts solo on the same tune, the pianist seems to hide in a series of *sotto voce* variations of porcelain delicacy before returning to the swing and ending up on a hanging, unresolved phrase. Then the band comes back in, Jeff Watts playing a circling, breathless acceleration of the rhythm in the displaced way that Tony Oxley would use.

Marsalis opens his first version of 'Cherokee' over the most spare of backdrops – Watts's headlong brushwork, Bob Hurst's surefooted bass lines and occasional stabbing chords from Roberts. Marsalis then plays the living daylights out of the chord structure with the mute on, rocketing through it with a mixture of balance, eloquence and agility of mind and touch that any of the legendary figures of bebop trumpet would have been gasping to match. Even Dizzy Gillespie in his prime might have had a problem with it. But Marsalis doesn't restrict his show to speed and rhythm. He plays 'Goodbye' with the emphasis on the purity of his tone, particularly in the sustaining of long, yearning sounds with the rounded, fleshly quality that Miles Davis would play a ballad with. My favourite on the disc is 'Soon All Will Know', a cruising mid-tempo tune, again featuring Watts's superb brushwork and full of hovering trumpet sounds mixed with zipping ascents into the high register and hung fundamentally around that Miles-like ability to coast effortlessly in the middle register – but Marsalis alters this by sustaining a single line longer than Miles would do and occasionally treading water on curious off-pitch notes which throw the correctness of everything else into relief.

The close of 'Foggy Day' is full of accelerations and decelerations of the time, Watts being a shrewd and original drummer with a delectable cymbal sound, like running footsteps fading in and out of earshot. 'The Song Is You' is played with slightly sinister-sounding piano chords in the theme, Watts adding a Tony Williams-like slapping snare sound to the climax of 'Memories of You', and 'Autumn Leaves', arranged by the drummer, is performed in a blur of tempo changes, Watts adding a beat to the metre every bar of the theme. This undoubtedly produces an entirely distinctive version of it, and breaks down the customary monotonous and cyclical quality of the structure which conventional bop approaches tended to be stuck with.

So it is a dynamic album, full of hard, serious playing, and full of intelligence. But Marsalis is one of the most gifted musicians of the new generation – and he is playing standards. It is hard not to feel that a man who can clearly play anything he can think of – a gift restricted to all but the best improvisers – would not be playing different music if he had come to the business in any other era but this.

WOODY

The Guardian, September 1987

With the 27-year-old Wynton Marsalis releasing his new album of jazz standards and demonstrating that those who follow in the footsteps of pioneers sometimes perform the ironic trick of seeming to improve on what the pioneers did, the position of a man like Woody Shaw is a curiosity.

Still only 43, but looking frail, Shaw made his reputation in the Sixties when he played with most of the leading jazz artists, including Eric Dolphy, Hank Mobley and Jackie McLean.

A hard bop trumpeter, Shaw's sound came to resemble that of Freddie Hubbard, a model for all technically-skilled brass players at the time who wanted the opportunity to sound more flash than Miles Davis's reflectiveness permitted. And though not at his best, he certainly left his stamp on proceedings at the Bass Clef. He played a series of well-known tunes, including Monk's 'Well You Needn't', which he hurled himself into with such force that his distinctly tentative approach to the stage was instantly obliterated from the memory.

He then dropped to a Latin-tinged slow tempo and accelerated again for the tune, 'If I Were a Bell' – made famous by Miles Davis's rendition of it and given considerable verve by the relish with which Peter Ind's trio attacked it. Shaw started his solo like a shorthand version of the tune and blew a string of effortlessly-fresh phrasing on it, eventually developing an empathetic relationship with pianist John Pearce as the latter delivered a back-up of chiming chords behind the trumpeter's rat-tat-tat tongued effects at the close of his solo. Everybody sounded more familiar with each other than they actually were.

CHERRY IN BLOSSOM
The Guardian, October 1987

Through the squeaky, nervous sound of the pocket trumpet, phrasing that nudges clumps of notes around like the bubbling of a kettle, and a method of construction that makes his solos principally a mixture of exclamations and question marks, Don Cherry is a trumpet master of an inimitable type.

In a world in which there are hundreds of dutiful sub-Coltranes, and sub-Miles Davises, sub-Don Cherrys are hard to find. And since he genuinely has the receptivity of a shortwave radio for world music influences, he can't be typecast and is therefore almost impossible to market. This feature makes Cherry relatively safe from plagiarism.

Cherry is currently on an Arts Council Contemporary Music Network tour, the opening concert of which was at the QEH on Wednesday. It was one of the most satisfying jazz events in years – the kind that doesn't still leave you imagining some other kind of playing that would have made the gig just perfect. This occurred despite the absence of a cornerstone of the band, drummer Ed Blackwell, who is currently ill in the States, obliging percussionist Nana Vasconcelos to play both his own part and Blackwell's, which he appeared to do with ease.

Inevitably, the presence of Ornette Coleman, Cherry's old employer, hung over the show. But since all of the four members of the band have their own distinct trademarks, Coleman's spirit simply supplied the rough sketches and they did the rest. Some of the pieces were harmonically 'free' in the Coleman sense, but tied to a beat and often to a repeated bass figure as well. In the second half the band also played some conventional bebop, Cherry playing with the mute on, and sounding like vintage Miles.

What was so special about the show was that the level of improvisation and the quality of the compositions was equally high, and that the qualities of both reminded you more of the players themselves than of the sources of their vocabulary.

From the opening drone, sprung on a regular bass pattern and illuminated by a dazzling alto solo from Carlos Ward (who played with blazing passion all evening) through two Ornette-like pieces, a bass solo mingling buoyancy and soulfulness from the excellent Mark Helias, Nana Vasconcelos's chanting-and-percussion feature, and a series of Third World musical references, the band proved repeatedly that accessible new frameworks for improvising can always be found, without retirement to the musical laboratory.

Cherry's own improvising style – a mixture of wild squeals, clusters of notes played deceptively in a monotone before wriggling escapes into the upper register, and a primitive, bugle-like sound – contrasted neatly with Carlos Ward's which is clear, direct and jammed with blues and gospelly drive.

MONK'S MAN

The Guardian, October 1987

For many people, Thelonious Monk *was* modern jazz – even more so than Charlie Parker, whose rebelliousness was more intense but less eccentric, or Gillespie, who stage-managed it more carefully. Monk spoke no more than necessary, often wore a fez, pottered around the stage when not playing, and left behind a music unique in its elbowing, dissonant charm.

Charlie Rouse, the American saxophonist currently on tour here, was Monk's saxophone player for much of the 1960s. Stan Tracey, the British pianist, has spent many years trying to shake off the label of Monk disciple but in recent times has increasingly played Monk material.

Since Monk left a prolific selection of memorable compositions, it's a certainty that musicians will go on rediscovering his material as long as jazz is played. Tracey and Rouse, with Art Themen on saxophones, Roy Babbington on bass and Tony Crombie on drums, played the second gig of Rouse's tour at the 100 Club on Sunday.

Since virtually all of Tracey's gigs are musically entertaining and the only sin this spritely sixty-year-old has ever committed is the unavoidable one of being taken for granted on his own turf, the additional element of a second Monk specialist was always likely to produce a music at once dynamic and nostalgic. A wild card was dealt by Tony Crombie, substituting for Tracey's son Clark, and delivering an utterly personal form of accompaniment, Crombie's mixture of a Zutty Singleton-like sensitivity to whichever instrument he's backing – constant variation, frequently deafening volume and outrageously deliberate casualness – remains one of the enduring pleasures of British jazz.

This volatile ensemble thus rumbled delightfully through an assortment of Monk tunes including a sinewy version of 'Nutty', and also explored an attractive piece of Rollins funk and a grittily rhapsodic 'In a Sentimental Mood'. Rouse demonstrated his closeness to the Monk method by rarely straying far from the tunes but accumulating variation by a quirky, interrogative phrasing just like his mentor's, letting the harmony work by playing sparingly off it, and leaning the considerable weight of his powerful, penetrating tone against the materials.

ALONE AGAIN, UNNATURALLY

The Wire, November 1987

Those with little time for him would say that Mike Brecker, the thirty-eight-year-old musician, plays just enough sensuous and raunchy saxophone to sound soulful without being vulgar, just enough almost-free saxophone to sound adventurous without obsessiveness, and just enough modest, elegantly executed tributes to jazz heroes to sound like a man of cultivated and balanced tastes. But his current album, simply called *Mike Brecker*, is something of a surprise. After twenty years in the business it is, strangely enough, his first album as a leader.

Brecker is accompanied by an excellent band comprising Charlie Haden on bass, Jack DeJohnette on drums, Kenny Kirkland on piano and Pat Metheny on guitar. The album reflects more of the jazz lineage than Brecker recordings often have, and imaginatively stitches together a wide contemporary vocabulary. Brecker goes through a remarkable variety of musical styles in the space of a few minutes, and doing this in what seems to be a deceptively unpremeditated way is his secret.

A tall, relaxed, studious-looking man who might be an up-and-coming East Coast literature don, Mike Brecker was preparing for the evening's work on the Capital Jazz Parade when we talked in July, pressed for time, but courteous and thoughtful, with a deliberating conversational manner like the attorney his father is. He's very proud of his new album – not just for the music that is played on it, and the illustriousness of the sidemen, but for a culmination of efforts to produce music that he could feel was truly his after the years of self-effacement.

MCA/Impulse, the phoenix that arose from the ashes of the old Impulse Records, offered the saxophonist the opportunity to make an album of anything he fancied. Brecker thought about what he had most enjoyed doing, and knew it was the tour he had played on in 1980 with a Pat Metheny group that had included Jack DeJohnette, Charlie Haden and, on that occasion, Dewey Redman. It would be a band like that, and with a similar confection of musical elements.

'Since they'd said I could do what I liked, I started to think more seriously about doing a jazz record, which I had always wanted to do if I made a record of my own. I've always worked collaboratively before, like with Randy in the Brecker Brothers, or as a sideman, and I'd never felt the desire to make my own record, or to feel that it was a necessity. But with this opportunity, I thought of the recording I had done with Pat Metheny and that tour with him in 1980. We had done an album together called *80/81*, which basically consisted of these people, including Dewey Redman. I had a great time with the rhythm section and it had always been a pet dream of mine to get them together. The great thing about a band that has that rhythm section but also Pat in it, is that it can then both make colours and swing.'

This long-postponed step into space was harder to take because of those years of slipping and sliding around the requirements of employers as different as the late John Lennon ('I don't recall him liking jazz particularly, but he had such a great sense of humour that hanging out with him was a real pleasure') or Yoko Ono, or Eric Clapton or Mike Gibbs, or even Don Sebesky. But Brecker had been able to measure his feelings about all this against the practice of working in blowing bands like the guitarist John Abercrombie's, and like Steps Ahead, the ensemble Brecker co-led with vibes player Mike Mainieri over the course of a decade. These contrasts made Brecker adaptable either to situations where spontaneity was sacrificed to composition and attention to form, or to ensembles where the solo space was opened up.

'As far as fusion and straight jazz are concerned, I'd been doing both all along, though the main thrust for me was Steps Ahead, which got started around 1978. For years Eddie Gomez played upright bass in it, and it was an acoustic band which originally consisted of Eddie, Don Grolnick, Steve Gadd, Mike Mainieri and me. We played original compositions, and a couple of standards reorganised. But since we were all refugees from fusion at that time – well, not from fusion maybe, but from more electronic settings – we brought that approach to the way the band played. Different rhythmic approaches, the interaction of the brass line and the drums, the function of the melody, the development of texture. It changed as time passed, and became electric itself. Eddie Gomez eventually switched to electric bass because the music called for it, slowly the lean began to be towards the compositional elements, and as that happened the freedom in the playing began to be diminished. I don't mind that at all if other things are working, and I really liked the compositions we were playing and the way we were delivering it.

'And at the same time I was playing with other groups, particularly John Abercrombie's, which was much looser. I found there that there's something about the sonority of the tenor with an upright bass that makes it a little easier to play freer – you're not dealing with all that volume, and that wall of sound effect, and anyway the tenor saxophone's a low instrument.'

There isn't much outright nostalgia on the disc, but there is a lot of down-the-line blowing on it, sitting confidently alongside the synthesis of popular and jazz inventions of the past twenty years that now makes up Mike Brecker's musical unconscious. After the blend of styles on 'Sea Glass', for instance, Brecker launches into a saxophone soliloquy accompanied only by DeJohnette's bursting drum sounds that demonstrates not only how diligently he pursued the technical innovations of Coltrane (no big surprise) but how much his understanding of the details, the slurs and tonal variations and sense of space, makes sense of the primary compulsion to play very fast arpeggios in several registers, which is where most imitators leave it.

Mike Brecker's father and his sister are both pianists. Brecker Senior, a lawyer, was a professional musician briefly and was 'good enough to remain one, but he took another direction for financial reasons'. Mike's brother Randy, four years older, is a trumpeter who similarly got involved in late Sixties rock music, performing with Blood Sweat and Tears and Janis Joplin, as well as with stars like Stevie Wonder.

Mike Brecker declares his earliest influences to have been Miles Davis, Clifford Brown and Dave Brubeck. He took up the saxophone in his teens, and studied in Philadelphia with Vince Trombetta, a saxophonist on the TV chat show run by Mike Douglas which ran for seventeen years. Drummer Eric Gravatt, later to join Weather Report, was a playing partner and friend during Mike Brecker's teens.

By his late adolescence Mike Brecker was a fully functioning pro and his brother had already moved from Philadelphia to New York.

'One thing led to another and we found ourselves in different situations both individually and together, played with a lot of groups and eventually ended up forming the Brecker Brothers,' Brecker says. 'That led to a bunch of albums for Arista and at the same time when we were in New York we found that we did quite a bit of studio work, and a lot of touring.' Critic Gary Giddins thought that Mike Brecker's most convincing playing was to be heard on one of the studio jobs that had a special place in the saxophonist's memory – a recording with Charles Mingus, by 1973 in a wheelchair with multiple sclerosis. Brecker had certainly felt inspired by the opportunity, though realised that it had come too late for a musical relationship with Mingus to be quite what it might have been.

'I recorded with him,' Brecker recalls, 'but you couldn't really say I played with him. He was producing it, but he was already ill and working in a wheelchair. There was another bass player there, Mingus was conducting. He was very nice and still quite lucid but very weak and I think you'd have to say it was only really one colour of the old Charles Mingus. I had all his records and I was a fan so it was a thrill for me just to be kind of half playing with him. He died shortly afterwards.

'But he was a wonderful mixture of sophistication and earthiness. And that's true of quite a lot of players like him, including Sonny Rollins and Trane and Charlie Parker and Clifford – an incredible earthiness and soulfulness, yet all that intellectual depth, absolute brilliance, harmonic brilliance. Which is often overlooked, which surprises me. Charles Mingus had that same thing.'

And in the case of Coltrane, it has been an influence that has buoyed up but also overshadowed two generations of musicians who have followed him. Alice Coltrane says she is surprised that more horn players have not emerged who have taken the instrument in other directions, or built more imaginatively on what her husband left to the world. Like Parker, he has produced many followers whose playing, whether as an act of devotion or opportunism, appears virtually to shut out original thought. Mike Brecker did not share Mrs Coltrane's surprise at the omission.

'I'm not so surprised, because he was way ahead of his time, and covered such a wide field – I think there may be players, including myself, who have gone off in other directions, but he had a very pervasive influence. Not just on tenor saxophone players but on the whole realm of jazz – that quartet had a very far-reaching influence.

'But I think you have to recognise that music has grown in many other areas – particularly pop music and R&B and digital stuff and techno stuff and everything. And there are also great new young players as well as players like Joe Henderson who are still carrying the torch in their own way. Steve Coleman is great, Branford Marsalis is wonderful, Dave Liebman and Bob Berg too. Then there's Kenny Garrett who I believe is playing with Miles right now. And Dave Sanborn has been an absolutely monstrous influence.'

Brecker was due to go on the road with his own band last time we spoke in September, and had just returned from a Japanese tour with Herbie Hancock, Ron Carter and Tony Williams. Next spring he's scheduled to return to the studio with a project of his own, which is still at the gestation stage, though it may involve some of the same players as on the current album. At the end of the second conversation, I pitched him the hard question – was the reason for that twenty years of silence as a leader because after all that work for other bosses he had lost confidence in the idea that he might have something to say himself?

'There was an underlying amount of fear, you could say,' Brecker said in his dispassionate way. *Mike Brecker* is not an album that will change the course of jazz but, just the same, he needn't have worried.

UPTOWN
The Guardian, November 1987

Since jazz is an art-form with both a history of being marginalised and a parallel tendency amongst some of its practitioners and fans to see the ghetto as a natural home, Sunday night's British Jazz and New Music Awards at the Waldorf Hotel were nothing if not a gauntlet thrown at such self-deprecation. The venue was flash, the audience was chic, and a variety of celebrities including Linton Kwesi Johnson, Joe Orton's biographer John Lahr, avant-garde writer Kathy Acker, *EastEnders*'s Judith Jacobs and Amen Corner star Clarke Peters were there to present the fetching pieces of metalwork that now constitute British Jazz Music's Oscars, voted by the readership of *The Wire* magazine.

The whole affair was a monument to the arts in the 1980s – the Carlsberg company paid for the Waldorf and the punters were liberally supplied with its products, the science of marketing was working overtime, and the music (Jazz Train playing Blakey-like hard bop, the Jiving Lindy Hoppers jitterbugging) was an expert celebration of some period around 1956.

But if there were all of the trappings of arts mastering nostalgia and vaudeville to make a living, there was also an enthusiasm for jazz that only the most churlish ascetics could write off. Getting noticed is an incalculable nourishment – and though this year's winners were predominantly young, there were among them a number of players who have already made an indelible mark and who clearly have the imagination to develop rather than disappear once their haircuts go out of style. Jazz Train supplied the live accompaniment, being the hard bop band led by Simon Purcell and Julian Arguelles.

After Jazz Train's set, the award ceremony was then embarked on at such a furious pace due to the brevity of the speeches that it was over almost as soon as it had begun – even these days, the taciturn habits of jazz players hasn't much changed. The new generation virtually swept the board. Itchy Fingers, a contrapuntal all-saxophone band of stunning virtuosity but cramped spontaneity won the Best New Band category. The eccentric and ingenious young keyboardist Django Bates won as Best Composer, Jazz Warrior Cleveland Watkiss found himself Top Vocalist, and the Warriors themselves were voted Best Band – after being in existence for probably a shorter time than Itchy Fingers has. Loose Tubes' *Delightful Precipice* received the Best Album award (another indirect tribute to Bates), and Andy Sheppard Best Newcomer – an irony since Sheppard is now thirty and is only a newcomer because he's been working extensively abroad.

Ashley Slater of Loose Tubes won the Best Haircut Award (he's as bald as a coot) and sent his barber to collect it, and the diligent and dedicated enthusiast and trumpeter Ian Carr won a much-deserved prize for Services to Jazz. As top dog of the lot, *The Wire*'s readers picked Courtney Pine, whose first album was a runaway success this year and who is now promoted like a pop star, as Best Instrumentalist. Nobody was very surprised at the award.

BET'S BEST

The Guardian, December 1987

They were queuing down Frith Street in the rain for Betty Carter this week, because Carter is not only a singer with both artistry and presence, but one with the urge in her blood to improvise, and this is a quality that is enjoying something of a comeback. A small, lithe fifty-eight-year-old with alert, mobile features, Betty Carter is both intent and playful on stage at Ronnie Scott's, physically balletic, and capable of reinventing songs in ways that enhance the good ones and wickedly caricature Tin Pan Alley's excesses –

and her mercilessness with the latter draws a razor so slowly and gently along their veins that for a while it seems like affection.

Carter comes from Michigan originally, and was borne Ella Mae Jones. She appeared on stage with Charlie Parker in Detroit in the Forties (playing hookey from school and altering her birth certificate to avoid the club's 'No juveniles' rule), a period in which she was hypnotised by both bop and its lifestyle. The legend then goes that she maintained a stormy relationship with the Lionel Hampton band for a couple of years, being fired seven times by the boss and rehired seven times by Hampton's wife Gladys, who was an unshakeable Carter fan.

'Hampton was the band leader and I was a little snot,' she says cheerfully. 'I loved the Dizzy Gillespie world – I wanted to be in his band, but he wasn't hiring females – and I didn't realise that the man upstairs had put me in the best band I could have been in. Disciplined, well run, well paid, and a place where I could learn.' Hampton wanted her to improvise all the time – he dubbed her 'Betty Bebop', which she hated. But though she was a fine big band singer and later an inspired and inspiring collaborator with artists such as Miles Davis and Ray Charles, it has always been in small groups that she has been at her best. So it continues this week, with Betty Carter winding together and picking apart a tapestry of vocal invention that is quite unlike both the widescreen heart-on-the-sleeve emotionalism of the torchy jazz singers, or the metallic, disembodied scatting of bop vocalists who pretend to be instruments – a practice that she nowadays dislikes.

Like Art Blakey, Betty Carter relishes working with musicians much younger than her – her current pianist, Steven Scott, is eighteen, and the last one wasn't much older. And, as with Blakey, the attraction is both the opportunity to teach and to learn.

'You get energy, inspiration and eagerness from them. They don't watch the clock, they just want to play. I won't have it any other way but this kind of trio nowadays, because you're working with a bunch of kids who haven't been over-exposed to the standards but are hearing them for the first time. Steven didn't *know* "The Good Life" [Carter recorded this song before Tony Bennett, and has only recently rejuvenated it] before I taught it to him. So he doesn't know how it *goes* [Carter asserts this with considerable irony]. He's still flexible enough to do it different. I can teach them what jazz really is [this with a thumping emphasis], and I'm so glad that kids everywhere, musicians or not, are learning that again.'

Ms Carter's current delivery of 'The Good Life' – a brittle and close to ominous rendition of a song that normally sounds as if it is emerging from a jacuzzi – is one of the triumphs of her current act. Her work alternates between sounding unfinished and restless, skidding away from notes half-formed, a rhythmic bounce as infectious as a drummer ('What a Little Moonlight Can Do'), and a kind of sensuous assertiveness when she stops running, as on the brooding 'Make It Last'. At fifty-eight, Carter still takes more chances than anyone in big-time vocal jazz.

The Guvnor
The Guardian, March 1988

Ken Colyer, the most unwavering and dedicated of British jazz traditionalists, has died at the age of sixty. Born in Great Yarmouth, but a Londoner
for most of his professional life, Colyer's place on the jazz circuit seemed
unshiftable by fashions, economics or mortality. From the early 1950s,
when the civil war between the factions of modernists and traditionalists
was gathering steam, Colyer led bands that behaved as if Louis
Armstrong, let alone Charlie Parker, had never existed. It was a form of
musical fundamentalism that was never so assiduously observed by any
other British bandleader, and precious few anywhere else in the world.

Colyer's preoccupation was with the sound of Bunk Johnson, a trumpeter from the pre-recording period of jazz whose music enjoyed a
resurgence in the 1940s as part of the backlash against bebop. Louis
Armstrong had liberated the role of the soloist in jazz with an abundance
of spontaneous melodic ideas that inevitably led to the creation of star
improvisers fronting rhythm sections. Colyer was devoted to the New
Orleans music that *preceded* Armstrong, a collectively improvised contrapuntal music in which no one stood in the spotlight. It was also
rhythmically far closer to the marching bands and funeral bands of turn-
of-the-century New Orleans than it was to the driving tempos and
unpredictable placing of accents that coined the term 'swing'. George
Melly wrote in *Owning Up* that Colyer 'intended to sound like an old man
who had never left New Orleans when they closed Storyville'.

He began performing like this at a time when even the addition of a saxophone to a New Orleans-oriented revivalist ensemble could occasion
heated abuse from purists, but to less obsessive fans a more modernised
remake of the early style was attractive. Colyer hated such mutations. He
formed the Crane River Jazz Band in the early Fifties, which he named
after a stream running near his home in Hounslow, was nicknamed 'The
Guvnor' by all the serious adherents of the idiom, and rejoined his old
service, the Merchant Navy, in order to wangle a trip to New Orleans. He
deserted once he got there, played with many of the surviving veterans of
the music, was jailed and deported back to England, to a hero's welcome
from the cognoscenti. Chris Barber and Monty Sunshine formed a band in
readiness for his return, but characteristically Colyer rejected it, com-
plaining that it was too commercial. When the skiffle craze and
subsequently the 'trad jazz' boom of the late 1950s happened and Chris
Barber was highly influential in it, Colyer was probably the only major
British practitioner of early jazz who didn't benefit from it.

Colyer acted as curator of a style now recognised as a cornerstone of jazz
music's development and one that, because of the lack of recording facilities at the time, few people had the chance to hear live. Even the veteran

Americans recognised his dedication as an invaluable living history lesson for younger jazz fans, and more open-minded British jazz musicians like Humphrey Lyttelton, listened with kind of reluctant admiration to Colyer in the 1950s. His devotion to purely musical values and his indifference to compromise were an example even to players light years away from his style.

CELESTIAL DISSONANCE

The Guardian, April 1988

The elegant Greek notion of the harmony of the spheres wasn't the first time that musicians felt their work to vibrate to laws beyond the doings of mere mortals, and two millennia's worth of such convictions have followed it. Particle physicists have even gone on record as claiming the universe to be more like music than matter. And even in jazz, an art form practised by individuals obliged to be pragmatic, there have been many dedications of the music to the pursuit of one or another kind of god – particularly in the modern era. But few modernists have taken it to the lengths of Anthony Braxton, the forty-two-year-old Chicago-born saxophonist and composer who has contented himself with nothing less than the development of something akin to his own solar system, in which spheres of sound identified by his meticulous researches wheel and spin according to principles laboriously worked out over two decades of study.

Braxton's systematic speculations, influenced by the ideas of John Coltrane, Ornette Coleman, Eric Dolphy, Karlheinz Stockhausen, John Cage, unfashionable jazz geniuses like the late Warne Marsh and Paul Desmond, Egyptian mysticism, physics and astrology, have resulted in a massive body of work bearing his name, both in composition and musical analysis. Braxton is the most prolific composer ever to be a master improvising saxophonist, and the most inventive improviser ever to have conceived 300-odd compositions in twenty years, let alone to have simultaneously been a potential chess master and a pretty effective pool hustler into the bargain. Many of his pieces, particularly for larger ensembles, have remained confined to the drawers of his desk, but his solo and small group performances are savoured by a small but appreciative group of fans world wide. Years of uphill struggle have not significantly dulled a boyish enthusiasm linked to a scientist's rigour. In his own words, 'the challenge of creativity is to move towards the greatest thought you can think of'.

Braxton was in London recently, delivering a recital of solo saxophone pieces to a packed ICA. The concert demonstrated not only his startling command of saxophone techniques old and new, but also the firmness with which he maintains separate improvisatory moods for each composition. Sometimes they would recall Albert Ayler, sometimes Lee Konitz, sometimes an attempt to condense Charlie Parker's legacy into a single breakneck solo. The concert celebrated the launch of *Forces in Motion*, a book on Braxton's remarkable life and thoughts, written by *Wire* journalist Graham Lock as a result of a fortnight in Britain in 1985, during which Lock accompanied Braxton's band on a Contemporary Music Network tour. Lock's book is an absorbing conjunction of anecdote and road gossip with a sympathetic and penetrating study of Braxton's own labyrinthine world views. The former encloses such dissonances as Braxton's mysticism and euphoria at visiting Stonehenge and his vigorous defence of McDonald's hamburgers in the face of militant vegetarianism, and the latter is a close study of Braxton's personality and convictions, complete with footnotes on Pythagorean numerology, the affinities between chess and music, appendices on music and the mystics and an analysis of the artist's remarkable home-grown notation.

Lock's book is, by design, no highly polished 'appraisal', for which some may criticise it as a high-flown fanzine with academic trappings. Moreover, Braxton's terminology (despite Lock's elucidations) often reflects the light, however deftly the chronicler projects it, and using the term 'meta reality' in the cover line some would say was downright foolhardy. But as a description both of the circumstances of a square-peg collection of uncommercial 1980s virtuosi on the road, and the state of modern music as viewed by a cussedly independent practitioner, it is a compelling read.

Anthony Braxton went to school with two other prominent Chicago jazz artists, Roscoe Mitchell and Joseph Jarman, who later came to prominence through the Art Ensemble of Chicago. Though it was the New York 'high energy' idiom – often a furious, unrelenting, free-for-all – that came to characterise 'free jazz', the Chicago musicians were adapting Coltrane, Coleman and Ayler's languages into forms far more forgiving in their attention to space, dynamics and silence. But already Braxton's tastes were quite different from those of his contemporaries.

'I had problems with my heroes since high school,' Braxton says wryly. His discourse is a mixture of crisp anecdote, high-speed prose which philosophises in a mixture of communal and self-generated terminology, and sudden explosions of laughter, like escaping steam.

'I think it was in the sophomore year when I called for Brubeck's "Take Five" at a jazz session we had and everybody went "WHAT?" I was shocked by that reaction. And then when I adopted Schoenberg as one of my daddies I got another set of responses to that. Somehow it's seen as strange for an African man to have affinities with Europe, or Asia, or women composers or whatever. It seemed as if all of my heroes were unacceptable. So by the time I was eighteen and fell in love with Stockhausen, for instance, I knew what would happen – of course they hated

Stockhausen. By 1966 the concept existed of Braxton's music as not a proper reflection of being an African American, and "not swinging" and being too interested in science. Only in jazz can you not be interested in the scientific aspects of music. Somehow it's a violation. You're supposed to have all this great feeling, it's all supposed to emanate from feeling as opposed to thought processes.'

Braxton reports being devastated by the death of John Coltrane, his greatest jazz hero, in 1966. Coltrane, moreover, was a musician whose passionate playing, at first dismissed as 'neurotic' but later widely embraced, was most certainly the result of systematic and obsessive research. 'Mr Coltrane was able to create a body of work in spite of the jazz establishment and the weight of his work would transform the disciplines. I made the decision after he died to stop, and get out of modal music first of all, to rid myself of his devices because I was learning that what I liked about my heroes was that they were not afraid to find their own way. So I found myself at this point backing away from what is called "jazz", looking at tonality from another perspective. John Cage's work really helped me in the last part of the Sixties. The philosophical aspects, and the music, I might add, I think the music is incredible. So I tried to create my universe in the cracks.'

Braxton is now a music professor at Mills College in California, and observes that 'this is the first year when the telephone has only been cut off one time, which is real breakthrough for me', but life in the cracks has been tough. Too subversive of jazz improvisation and orthodox swing to become a neo-Coltraneist hero, too interested in jazz to be a conservatoire cult figure, a compromised would-be European to some black Americans and a black man with no sense of rhythm to some whites, Braxton has fitted no niches. He recalls with some irony how Pierre Boulez welcomed Frank Zappa to perform a symphonic work at IRCAM, but that such an opportunity would still be denied to him. The teaching job secures his livelihood and his family (Braxton is married, with three children), though he retains an old suspicion of the lecture rooms, intensified by the current 'bebop boom', which has come to music colleges and nightclubs alike.

'The universities and institutions are now teaching the processes and devices of the music in the same way and spirit that they destroyed the forward thrust of Western art music starting at the turn of the century, after the period of Wagner and the romantic period, where the great European creative musicians and mystic intellectuals had built up a continuum. It's the technocrat sentiment, glorifying the process and draining the lifeblood from it at the same time, and suddenly you have generations and generations of incredibly talented people who cannot play a note if you take away the music from them.

'In every other discipline, whether we're talking of mathematics, physics, or the new sciences, people are looking at extended forms. We're in a period of extended technology, new possibilities are opening up, scientists are plotting and learning more about planets and their orbits and star systems, and this information will probably be part of the next order. Then there's what Coltrane talked about, which is music as a vehicle for understanding spiritual consciousness, music as a vehicle for helping to clarify motivation, music as not separate from health. I was interested in all of that in terms of what I learned from my teachers, the daddies and mummies who went before me. The beautiful thing about creativity is that you can go as far as you want to, because there's always something. That's why I'm a professional student of music.'

LOOSE

The Guardian, July 1988

It's not just the enduring talent but the offbeat dignity of a man like Dizzy Gillespie that elevates events like the JVC/Capital Jazz Parade from the three-ring circuses they lean towards. This year, the week's package at the Festival Hall includes no less than five jazz/rock fusion acts so, ironically, the conviction of the organisers as to the hipness of that style seems to be growing now that it's twenty years old and the midriffs of its leading practitioners have reached the loose shirt stage.

It was appropriate, though, that the seventy-one-year-old Gillespie should have headlined the opening night, even if he did have to come on after trumpeter Chuck Mangione. Mangione's technique and tone remain as good as they ever were, particularly on ballads, but the music – a crazed confection in which ballads suddenly find kettle-drum barrages reminiscent of *Thus Spake Zarathustra* charging through them and singers totter through half a dozen personae in the space of one song – got the better of the trumpet player, and some of the audience, in a challenging, eighty-minute first set.

Dizzy Gillespie's big band came on after the break and, just like last year, it was marvellous. If anything, the leader was more secure in his own playing, possibly assisted by the late adoption of a trumpet bug instead of a mike. Jon Faddis, Gillespie's brilliant trumpet protégé, was less crisp and more showy than last year but the grizzled and professorial Sam Rivers got some solo space for his guttural, rattling eloquence. On the Forties classic 'Emanon' Gillespie played a lovely oblique solo, mixing steely ascendant runs with wild off-pitch shouts and abrupt changes of volume, and the four-piece trumpet section with its scalding, high pitched answering riff set the audience applauding. 'Night in Tunisia' mixed a baleful mid tempo with flag-waving swing, and on 'Round Midnight' Gillespie's solo seemed to stalk alongside the piece rather than inhabit it, as if injecting the Monkish ambiguity that this arrangement leaves out. Faddis pulled himself together with a superb solo on 'Things to Come', each new phrase developed in a higher part of the range. Technique and form hand in hand.

STEEL AND VELVET

The Guardian, August 1988

'I was once on a panel discussion with Pierre Boulez,' reflects Cecil Taylor, the nervy and mercurial fifty-six-year-old jazz piano virtuoso from New York, 'and I was asked, you know, "What do you think the future of jazz is?" First thing I remembered was the Thelonious Monk answer, "I don't know what the future of jazz is, it may be going to hell, for all I know."'

It is at least a certainty that Monk himself would never have been asked on to a panel discussion with Pierre Boulez. For Taylor, whose apprenticeship in the 1950s took in Stravinsky, Bartok and Elliott Carter inside the prestigious New England Conservatory, and Monk, Bud Powell and Duke Ellington outside it, the belatedly accommodating response he now receives from the academic music establishment is no more than what might have been his due a quarter century ago. Mikhail Baryshnikov, who danced to Taylor's music in a series of concerts in the States at the end of the Seventies, spoke glowingly of the pianist revealing to him 'another dimension about dancing to music'. He has also been called 'the Art Tatum of the avant-garde'.

Taylor is due here on Saturday for a keenly awaited duo performance with the British percussionist Tony Oxley at the new Crawley jazz event, called Outside In. On the panel discussion that involved Boulez and the thoughts of Chairman Monk, Taylor had gone on to say that he believed the present era to offer more opportunities for the understanding of other cultures than at any previous time, and that this ought to augur well for music. If it's true, Taylor has not lacked patience and fortitude, for all his legendary prickliness. He is of the generation of John Coltrane, Ornette Coleman, Charles Mingus and Albert Ayler, the musicians who treated bebop as a starting point rather than a destination thirty years ago and who reforged jazz history with a boldness that has not been repeated by any movement since. In some respects, because of his scalding speed, melodic density and the relentlessly high pressure of his attack. Taylor came to be regarded as the hottest potato of the lot. This status meant that for years the principal employment he was able to find for his lean and graceful hands was as a dishwasher, ironically enough in the very New York jazz clubs that wouldn't let him on the bandstand.

For a while, it seemed only the fulfilment of the inevitable. Though he had been able to play difficult classics at seven, and his mother was a devoted Duke Ellington fan, Taylor had always been told at home that a career in music was no life for a favoured son. 'I can still remember the colour of the sunlight, the way it permeated the furniture at the moment I asked my mother for piano lessons,' Taylor recalls. He is a trim and youthful man, but with the preoccupied demeanour of someone waiting outside an operating theatre. His speech is often laced with a counterpoint of contrasting statements, in which pieces of philosophising, forms of stage direction of his own or others' responses, and incidental commentary on the beauty of a passing cat will merge as seamlessly as one of his own improvisations.

'Mother asked why I wanted the lessons,' he continues. 'She wanted me to be a lawyer or a doctor or a dentist.' Taylor's mother died of cancer when the boy was thirteen. Her illness was diagnosed the day after she had caught him playing hookey at the basketball court, and the nightmare that his disobedience might somehow have triggered his mother's decline haunted him so much that he had ulcers by the age of fifteen. 'I even thought, much later on, on the rare occasions I got jobs playing music, that it was continued disobedience that would cause me to get ill and die myself.' But the intensity of this unintentional legacy of his mother's was balanced by another one – an unshakeable conviction that what he was doing (in this case modifying the notion of swing, improvising without chord patterns, spontaneously composing with the timbres and intonations of jazz but some of the devices of conservatoire music as well) was right, no matter what. Taylor still affectionately recalls the advice of pianist Freddie Redd, when the young man was just starting out. Redd said, 'Cecil, whatever you're doing – and I'm not sure I know what that is – don't let anybody tell you not to do it.'

'For special family occasions mother dressed me in velvet,' Taylor observes of his childhood, and without either affectation or apparent irony. 'I was raised to be a prince.' (His father was head chef in a sanatorium.) 'So the difficulty that I had with certain major jazz impresarios on the rare occasions they claimed they were going to make me a star, was that mama had already made me a *galaxy*. So I knew those people don't really give you anything. They say we will give you money, but we want you to play this, or that. And I always thought, if I'm going to do that, I might as well go back and be a dishwasher.'

For a man who has long had a reputation for defensiveness and scorn, Cecil Taylor has become almost mellow with the pleasure of working through the summer with European avantists, and discovering through them that the torch he and the others lit in the Sixties is now being triumphantly borne all over the world. The experience borders on the pleasure that the exploratory virtuosity of younger Americans who have followed in his footsteps gives him: 'It's like I could feel a tremendous weight being lifted. All these voices, Han Bennink, Tristan Honsinger, Derek Bailey, Paul Lovens, have been saying, "We hear it".' Taylor believes that the depth of these roots will outlast the present retro-jazz and bebop boom. He recalled an exchange of postcards he had with sympathetic promoter friend at the end of the Jimmy Carter era, which had begun with the incoming message: 'Bebop is the music of the future.' Taylor had mailed back: 'If that is so, then Reagan is our president of the future.'

But no amount of idolisation of the past can successfully lock the door against ideas too powerful to package. 'After playing, you know,' Taylor says. 'After all those forces of nature have passed through, you lose your sense of specialness and egocentricity and just explode like a flower.'

In concert, Taylor is often assumed to have exploded more in the manner of a landmine than a flower, though lately there have been stretches in his music (notably on the brilliant Leo Records *Bologna* concert) where he seems positively tranquil. It is likely to be the rip-roaring side that surfaces on Saturday with Oxley. Either way, the prince will continue to retain his gracious pedigree.

CASHFLOW

The Guardian, September 1988

'People in boardrooms are happy to write out a cheque for Glyndebourne with a lot of noughts on the end,' says Chris Hodgkins, the pugnacious, energetic director of tour promoters, Jazz Services, with some resignation. 'They haven't woken up to the fact that the image of jazz has changed.'

The subject of Hodgkins's address is the feasibility of commercial sponsorship for jazz in the UK, largely uncharted waters at the present time, though the sound-equipment business and youth-oriented brewers like Schlitz have toyed with it. Hodgkins believes that the business world would be astonished if it took the time to digest some of the findings of a piece of 1986 Arts Council market research into who consumes what art, and how often. Based on attendances by the sample group over the previous year, jazz, unsurprisingly, came in behind theatre, children's shows, visual arts, classical music and musicals, but more of the sampled attendances had been at jazz than ballet (5 per cent), opera (4 per cent) or contemporary dance (3 per cent).

Over a quarter of the regular jazz attenders declared salaries of more than £20,000 a year. According to the poll, the average age of the opera punter was fifty-three, that of the jazz fan, thirty. It all went to endorse the widely held view in the jazz world, that when it comes to the arts the senior officers of British industry continue to prefer to take the unbusinesslike course of only investing in the badges of their own social elevation, or that being a 'minority interest' doesn't exclude an art form from enthusiastic backing as long as the right minority likes it.

Now Hodgkins, who runs the only offspring of the old Jazz Centre Society to have emerged without blushes from the expensive affair of the capsized National Jazz Centre, is currently helping to float a cross between a marketing exercise and an artists' agency on behalf of nine of this country's most eminent modern jazz musicians. Hodgkins is a rare bird, an ex-jazz musician with a business head and a pragmatic comprehension of the economic climate of the 1980s. He is convinced not only that the nine members of this conglomerate, christened Jazz Directions, are all sufficiently exciting performers to drum up much more work than they currently get if a full-time professional promoter were to be on the end of telephone every day, but also that a sponsorship deal would be far from a one-way ticket.

The best jazz virtuosi believe that many of their equals in age and experience in the dinner-jacket arts would find associate professorships, lecture tours and master classes their rewards after two or three decades on the stump, and the means to these ends would not be box office receipts but subsidy, of one kind or another.

The operation is set up to offer the business world precisely the standards of excellence in the jazz field that attracts sponsorship to other arts, as well as the opportunity for companies to get their branding on events which, to judge by the market research, reach a young, educated and well-heeled audience. Received wisdom in the boardrooms, however, still seems to be that jazz is marginal activity, patronised by subversives who will spit on their products. At the Association for Business Sponsorship of the Arts (ABSA), they're cautious about just how quickly a young and unruly art will be able to claim the hearts and minds of the business community wedded to more formal and traditional ones. 'A major consideration for businesses,' reports ABSA's Director Colin Tweedy, 'is being seen to be associated with quality. Business people are, after all, just members of the general public and general concepts about art, whether accurate or misleading, pervade the whole of society. If people associate excellence or upmarket status with some arts rather than others, putting that right is a matter of arts education.'

OUTSIDE IN

The Guardian, September 1988

The third day of the Outside In festival of new jazz at Crawley's Hawth Centre was a showcase for British bands, including the most celebrated and fashionable of them in Loose Tubes and the Andy Sheppard Sextet. The usual shambolic logistics of such events resulted in Sheppard (head-lining the Sunday roster) coming on half an hour after the programme maintained he should have gone home, but such is the current charisma of this boyish and undemonstrative saxophone hero that the majority of the audience gritted its teeth, forced down another drink, and hung on.

Sheppard eventually appeared, to play a fierce and heavyweight set (its roots were in the Sixties American free scene, but it strayed wider, particularly in the saxophonist's exchanges with his Sierra Leonian percussionist) and conclusively proved that he bridges the world of the atonal and the orthodox with an eloquence and logic uncommon not just on the British scene but on the world jazz circuit. Sheppard's whirlwind drummer Simon Gore is big bonus, as he was on the Schlitz Young Jazz Musicians' contest in 1986 when Sheppard first came to general notice, and the vibraharpist Orphy Robinson added his own particular glow.

During the afternoon Robinson appeared with a good quartet of his own, including the young pianist Joe Bashorun, whose over-the-ears hat made him resemble a black Chico Marx. Though some colourless material and the rather thudding bass lines of Gary Crosby impeded Robinson's lissome swing and drumlike attack, the vibist clearly has an illustrious future. Another Englishman who can effect Andy Sheppard's blending of centre and left-field techniques is the keyboardist and composer Django Bates, who in the end contrived to make a bigger contribution to the last day than even Sheppard did.

Bates appeared in the afternoon with his trio, Human Chain, and later with Loose Tubes. Human Chain's set was the most musical and yet adventurous of the day. It moved through an oriental delicacy, Blakey-like excitement (drummer Steve Arguelles performed throughout with a clarity that made some of the day's drummers sound bemused), a brilliant, ecstatic tribute to the South African altoist Dudu Pukwana in which Bates adopted a headlong, Jimmy Smith-like organ sound, and finished up on an exquisite slow calypso.

Parallel with these grand-slam performances, Derek Bailey led a four-hour session of free improvisation in the Hawth Centre's Studio, a mixture of that taut and dramatic exploration of sound and space which free playing can illuminate as the basis of all music, and the usual desultory scratchings and hesitation. German guitarist Uwe Kropinski dazzled the audience in the main theatre with an unaccompanied recital which successfully spliced superlative technique, world music references and improvisation, but which fell back too often on repetition of ascendant pinging octaves. Loose Tubes, the penultimate performers, sprawled a lot (Django Bates imperiously cut one piece short with an explosive keyboard full stop that none of the band could misinterpret) but wound up with a feature which started out like an Edwardian music hall song and finished as a storming calypso that unleashed dancing in the aisles.

BEACHCOMBER

The Guardian, November 1988

If you've ever had a nagging fear that much of what currently goes under the name of 'world music' is not much more than a Cheshire Cat exercise in removing the stuffing from the musics of the globe and leaving only an exotic grin, the work of John Zorn is instantly rejuvenating. Zorn is the 35-year-old New York composer and improviser who erupted to public notice (after nearly 15 years underground with the avantists and performance artists of the Lower East Side) with a captivatingly personal interpretation of the movie music of Ennio Morricone in 1987.

Morricone – who not only penned all those hot, baleful spaghetti western themes for the Sergio Leone/Clint Eastwood partnerships, but also scored *Battle of Algiers*, *Once Upon a Time in America* and a raft of others – said admiringly of Zorn: 'My ideas have been realised not in a passive manner but in an active manner which has recreated and reinvented what I have done.'

Reinvention is the name of Zorn's game. He is a tireless beachcomber of contemporary culture and his reference points are movies, the line of blues and jazz that run into pop, and urban soundscapes. He is devoted to Japan because he admires that culture's openness about borrowing and mixing ingredients from elsewhere. Though Zorn's written works appear superficially to function on lines of Cage-like randomness, it is quickly clear that they are sharply honed and orchestrated. But, like a jazz composer (though he restricts himself to no single school of composition), Zorn now constructs works that are both hooked to an overall theme and open to the eccentricities of spontaneous players.

Though he freely acknowledges the accomplishments of the many great musicians who don't improvise, Zorn finds improvisers – with whom he has regularly worked since 1974 – represent a special breed of player, a type independent yet collaborative, working outside the traditional composer/conductor hegemony, 'who accept improvisation as part of the palette of what they do'. But they may be improvisers of different kinds. On his Morricone album (*The Big Gundown* on Nonesuch Records), for instance, Zorn not only used the train-crash guitar effects of modernists like Fred Frith and Bill Frisell, but the jaunty amiable chucklings of Toots Thielmann's harmonica as well.

Zorn's own playing (he is an excellent saxophonist but perversely camouflages it) mixes bop alto, duck calls, heavy metal music and pounding, horror-movie clichés. Mix it all with an obsessive absorption in the world of spaghetti westerns, and latterly *film noir* B-movies for his recent Spillane album, and you get some idea of his collage techniques with sound. 'When I listen to music at home,' says Zorn. 'I make cassettes of my favourite tracks from all my favourite records. Then I take them on the road with me. There might be Japanese pop next to Bobby McFerrin, next to reggae, next to hard-core punk. I listen to music in this way all the time, and that's what I'm trying to present in my work.'

Zorn was born in 1953 in New York. His first musical interests were in Cage and Ives, but a period of his life spent in St Louis attracted him to jazz, particularly bebop and the post-bop avant-garde. He has described the music for kids' cartoons as being a significant influence with him (Bugs Bunny melodist Carl Stalling is a hero) and his work is often a restless confection of jump-cuts, like an insomniac endlessly switching TV channels.

Zorn's music was described by the *New York Times* as being composed the way a computer would do it – a process of split-second decisions and recalculations – but if it is packed with nervous energy it is also packed with explosive humour and a sly wisdom about the fast, disposable media culture it feeds off. He has said, 'I've got an incredibly short attention span. You've got to realise speed is taking over the world. Look at the kids growing up with computers and video games which are ten times faster than the pinball machines we used to play.'

Zorn's band Naked City will be performing his customary virtuosic Frankenstein job on popular culture on Sunday with a repertoire that includes a John Barry tribute featuring the James Bond theme and *Zapata*, Henry Mancini's *Shot in The Dark*, Ornette Coleman's 'Lonely Woman' and what Zorn calls his own mixture of 'cartoon music, reggae, punk, blues, jazz and improvisation'.

As for the audience reaction, 'I try not to think about it. I concentrate on the people I work with, the music I like, and keeping it on the edge and adventurous. If it isn't there, I'm not interested in it. You can't second-guess people, work out what the public will want, this year or next year. All that's so fickle, because one year you're popular, and the next year you're not. I'm just making music for the today that I live in, which is different from the one you live in, or the one somebody in Tulsa lives in. I think it's a live one and rich one that I present, and if you like it, fine.'

CHAN

The Guardian, July 1989

On the trip back from Paris last week to meet the late Charlie Parker's last and closest wife, Chan, there was a busker playing tenor in the subway. The tune was 'Are You Lonesome Tonight?', delivered in the bleak, querulous tone of the inexperienced reed player. But at the end of each chorus of the theme, with an unsteady flourish like an amateur conjurer, the busker unfurled a high-pitched double time improvised run that fluttered optimistically through the echoing corridors. The execution was erratic, but the phrasing was pure Charlie Parker. It has been that way in the streets, in clubs, on records, in concert halls and in the minds of anyone who has heard more than a few bars of postwar American music since the late 1940s.

Thirty-three years after his death at thirty-four from a mixture of cirrhosis, heart failure, stomach ulcers and pneumonia, and after a life of dizzying creativity and equally dizzying indulgence, Charlie Parker makes it into the mainstream cinema via Clint Eastwood's biopic *Bird!* The story has been based on a script by Joel Oliansky, largely drawn from the writings and reminiscences of Chan Parker, the woman with whom the saxophonist shared an intimacy rare for him, two children, some brief glimpses of economic success, and most of the last five years of his life.

Formerly Chan Richardson, the daughter of a vaudeville producer and a Ziegfeld Follies dancer, she was a professional dancer herself by her late teens. Attractive, effervescent, musically educated and eventually a tireless proselytiser for the revolutionary bebop music of the 1940s, she was constantly listening to it in New York's 52nd Street clubs. Chan and her mother bought a house on 'The Street' and it became a free hotel, social club and office for passing jazz musicians of every description and inclination.

Since the early 1960s Chan Parker has lived in France, eventually marrying the alto saxophonist Phil Woods, an early disciple of the Parker method. Now a small, neat, bony woman in her late sixties, with a sudden, gleaming smile, measured and laconic tones that you have to strain to catch and a mischievous wit that has survived age and tragedy, she remains in dignified service to the memory of a man she worshipped. Charlie Parker's flight across the twentieth-century firmament has been likened to those of Dylan Thomas, Jackson Pollock and James Dean – comparisons that capture the saxophonist's frantic rebelliousness but not the massive musical logic and lightning improvisational reflexes of his gift to the world. *Bird!* doesn't really get to the impact of Parker on the vernacular music (and some of the conservatoire music) of the late twentieth century, nor does it really escape the 'tortured genius' trap to account for what his apprenticeship was like, but it is a serious commercial film about an African-American jazz artist, and that's a substantial achievement in itself. Chan, who has waited for such a film about Bird for years, is more than comfortable with it.

'Joel Oliansky, who was a Columbia staff writer then, wrote the original script around 1981,' Chan recalls, as if slowly moulding the story out of clay. 'He interviewed me, quoted my words directly in it, used my memoir *Life in E Flat*, and altogether gave me a lot of involvement. But other things didn't look too promising. Columbia said, "Who's heard of saxophones, let's turn the main character into a singer and we'll get Prince". Then there was talk of Richard Pryor playing Bird, which I wasn't crazy about. Other directors have wanted to make a Bird film too, including

Louis Malle, but nothing came of them. Then I heard Clint Eastwood was interested. That terrified me, because I didn't know he was a jazz fan and just thought "Dirty Harry"! But as soon as I spoke with him on the telephone about it, I realised that he wanted to make the best film about Bird and jazz music that he could, and had complete confidence from then on.'

Chan first heard Charlie Parker in the Three Deuces Club in 52nd Street in 1943. Bebop, though denounced by older jazz stars like Louis Armstrong and Cab Calloway, was captivating young audiences with its musical challenges (Parker had both an extraordinary harmonic ear and the ability to manipulate rhythm) but was also an emblem of a romantic, and sometimes nihilistic bohemianism. 'Chan was hip and beautiful,' wrote Ross Russell in *Bird Lives!* She also understood where the music had come from, and where it was going.

'I'd heard about Bird from other musicians, of course. Since I'd been brought up on Duke Ellington and Johnny Hodges, his sound took a little getting used to. But what he was playing just blew me away. I had played the piano since I was five, our house was full of music and I'd always heard modern sounds. My piano teacher was giving me Bach and I'd bring in George Gershwin, and later got into Bartok and Stravinsky. I wanted something not to resolve into the tonic, you know, and that was Bird.' Chan emphasises this with a straight-in-the-eyes, that's-how-it-was laugh.

Some of the territory the movie deals with is out of her ken by choice, or because it was before her time. It ignores Bird's adoring mother Addie, his Kansas city adolescence, his three former wives ('You'd have a movie six hours long,' reasons Chan). It does handle the death of her child Pree, at three years old (Bird sent a stream of incoherent and helplessly grief-stricken telegrams from the West Coast) but not the litigation over the saxophonist's chaotic estate, which left her with very little to show but memories. These matters, and the subject of narcotics, bring a set to her jaw and a wordless look into the middle distance. The actress Diane Venora, who sensitively plays Chan and spent hours talking to her about the role, says, 'Chan's a person who takes anger in quietly. She also viewed Parker as a god, and those two things are the key to the part.'

For her part, Chan is delighted with Venora's interpretation, and the probing that got her to it. 'After all, I didn't want to see Jean Harlow up there,' she says with some acidity. For both women, a memorable moment of the making of *Bird!* was hearing Parker's own solos, the rhythm section bleeped out, coming over the speakers to be accompanied by the jazz musicians of 1988. Venora, who speaks in a fast, shorthand rat-tat-tat, recalls, 'I was chilled from my head to my feet. These guys sitting there, playing chord changes and suddenly in would come Parker. And the musicians would be shouting, "Go Bird, go!" They were completely flipped around by it. You'd see guys with a new tone to their skin, new quickness in the step, saying, "Amazing, amazing, all these years go by and he's still ahead!"'

Chan was also moved by the scenes of Bird working with strings, a move that had preoccupied him in his last years. 'I saw this full string orchestra in the studio and thought, "Bird, it's just what you always wanted." He wanted to get out of saloons, you know. He wanted to write for a larger format. He played classical music all the time at home. He adored Bartok. His head was into modern harmonies. He wanted to stop being spat on in nightclubs and being thought of as just a bebop musician. After all, if you were Bird and you had to go out on the road as single and work with local rhythm sections who didn't even know altered chords, it must have been just hell for him. Of course, the work with Varese never quite happened because Bird used to say, "Well, you can't just drop by, you've got to take a nice bottle of wine, a bouquet of flowers."' Chan Parker chuckles to herself. 'Procrastination,' she mutters. She has remained a listener to the jazz that came after Parker, enjoying Eric Dolphy and early Ornette Coleman, enjoying Coltrane less.

'Bird was conversational, he loved words, I don't think he ever would have played those sheets of sound that Coltrane did, space was too important to him. I hear that in Dolphy, I don't hear it in Coltrane.' Chan Parker admires Forest Whittaker's performance as Bird, a distinctly tall order. Musically knowledgeable himself, Whittaker regarded the saxophonist's notoriously chameleon-like personality (often interpreted at the time as a sign of mental disturbance) as part of an overwhelming musical personality, an effort to harmonise. It was a key to Bird always retained by Chan, who in life and in the movie rejected the ECT therapy offered to Parker as a choice between having 'a husband or a musician'. The child was also alive in him to the end, an aspect both of his creativity and his defencelessness. It is a quality Chan Parker shares to this day. 'Childlike, not childish,' she admonishes, carefully. That slow, knowing chuckle unravels around the statement, to be sure you took it in.

WOMAN TALK

The Guardian, August 1989

This Sunday, the Oldham-born trombonist Annie Whitehead leads her dynamic percussion-based new band The Dance in a performance at the East End's Half Moon Theatre. And on Monday Cheryl Alleyne, the powerful twenty-eight-year-old West Indian drummer who first came to general notice last autumn in the drum chair on the Jazz Warriors' UK tour, appears on the first night of the Loose Tubes week at the Almeida Theatre. Both events signal the extent to which women instrumentalists have become more visible, and audible, in the jazz world.

Whitehead is now a seasoned professional, who went on the road with the Ivy Benson band at sixteen and has since worked with some of Europe's most creative jazz musicians, recorded with Elvis Costello and Jerry Dammers, toured with Fun Boy Three – and Alleyne, an instinctive musician with a history of grasping the rudiments of most instruments virtually at the first touch, is at the gateway of a career that will almost certainly be as substantial and admired as Whitehead's. What unites them as much as their membership of a growing force of high-class women instrumentalists in what has until recently been a man's profession, is the originality and independence that they have developed through exposure to a mixed musical culture, in which definitions of musical differences have never made much sense.

Whitehead, a thoughtful, persuasive and youthful thirty-four-year-old, never inhabited a world in which jazz or any other idiom had exclusive territorial rights. 'When I used to go and call for my best friend at school in Oldham,' she recalls, 'I would hear ska and stuff, because she was West Indian and that's what her mum and dad played. I used to love it. Our street was poor working class, racism was rife because of the pressure on jobs and housing, but because I was a kid it only seemed good to me, nice music and colourfully painted houses, it was such a change from the drab Oldham I knew.'

Cheryl Alleyne is a brisk and practical twenty-five-year-old of first generation West Indian parents, with whom she lives on a North London estate. She learned clarinet from the age of twelve, and subsequently violin, but was absorbing the material of the Royal School of Music's grading system alongside her father's record collection, 'which meant early reggae, ska, Percy Sledge, Desmond Dekker, all that'. Both women gained confidence early on from precocious talent encouraged by teaching. Alleyne walked music exams, and her playing in her short career has consistently been singled out by everyone from college teachers to the presenters of the wall clock she won at a miners' gala as top percussionist with the Ashington Colliery Brass Band while a student on Tyneside. Whitehead was also a star of local brass bands while student in Oldham, 'and the music department was so proud of me it used to use me as an example to the boys. I don't agree with all that now, you know; "If a girl can do it, why can't you?", but it gave me a lot of confidence at the time.'

Neither woman was discouraged at home. For Annie Whitehead's parents, both millworkers, prospects in Oldham were grim enough for them to be happy that she could find a career that took her out of it. 'They're proud because I've managed to achieve something I've always wanted to. My mum's always been musical anyway, and if I want to know the middle eight to a standard I can just ask her and she sings it from memory. They support me even though they know I've had my ups and downs and my life's not that steady, and they can't expect grandchildren and things like that. After all, as an itinerant musician, I find just keeping myself together is hard enough, filling in tax forms and all that. I'd much rather be just wandering around the place dreaming all the time, but I can't. I've never regretted doing this, even though I don't think people think enough about the importance of music in our lives, think about what life would be like if we all stopped doing it, you know.

'I suppose I sometimes kick myself for not trying some things earlier, for needing somebody else to tell me to do it, which is something I don't think men get so much. I know some people are put off by a woman playing trombone, thinking it doesn't look very glamorous going bright purple blowing it, but so what?' Whitehead laughs gleefully. 'But I don't play saxophone, so I can't stand around looking really cool.' Alleyne has encountered the same story probably more times already, because she plays what's often considered a macho instrument.

'But I'm not playing drums to prove something, I'm doing it because now it's the only thing I really want to do. When most guys realise that, and realise that I can do it, they usually back off.' But the old song still gets sung, even when the singer thinks he's being really helpful. 'I came across a classic example just recently,' Alleyne recalls. 'I was doing a gig with Ashley Slater's funk band Microgroove, and we were playing opposite a soul band whose name you'd certainly recognise if I told you. Of course the musicians all get introduced to each other, and I usually get over-looked because they think I must be somebody's girlfriend. But as it happened I had to borrow the other drummer's kit for the gig, and when Ashley introduced me he couldn't believe it. He even asked me if I'd remembered to bring my sticks, which is about as sensible as asking a guitarist if they've brought their guitar. After the gig he went to Ashley and said, "That girl's good, isn't she?" Ashley just said, "Well, that's why we've got her in our band."'

VOICES

The Guardian, October 1989

Coming hard on the heels of a more high profile piano trio performance on the South Bank, Geri Allen on piano, Charlie Haden on bass and Paul Motian on drums delivered a performance on Tuesday night that rivalled last month's Keith Jarrett concert for authority, and at times exceeded it for taste and surprises. Ms Allen has quickly come to be an accessible young jazz keyboard star, her work sufficiently rooted in Fifties and Sixties jazz piano history to fit the requirements of the current classicism, but also a sufficiently idiosyncratic synthesis of her enthusiasms to amount to a genuine reconstruction of the past.

Geri Allen's work seethes with recognisable voices elegantly dovetailed, the quiet, seamless insistence of Bill Evans apparent in it, as well as Monk's jangly downward runs and jolting chords, and at times the poignant monochrome of Paul Bley. She began with a piquant and dolorous slow original that turned into typically unfussy and incisive improvisation (Ms Allen is constantly busy and businesslike, eschewing rhapsodic effects or flagwaving climaxes in favour of logical advancing of the musical argument), revealed her Monk and Evans allegiances in Ornette Coleman's bluesy piece 'The Blessing', and proceeded with a mixture of remoulded bop, blues and soft, evaporating slow pieces.

Though the band was tentative at the outset, and the leader lost some of her steely sharpness at the highest speeds (as well as playing the theme of the Coleman piece as if she had somebody else's glasses on), it was rapidly apparent that most of her improvisations were going to be handled with the same economy and absence of flab or repetition, particularly as the concert wore on. The success of the enterprise was also significantly dependent on Haden and Motian, two of the finest small-band practitioners in the business. Motian's preference for building fragments of disparate rhythm against each other in solos rather than hammering the daylights out of his kit, plus a selectivity in accompaniment bordering on diffidence, have always marked him out. And Haden, though less song-like and reverberating than usual, shared the inclination to play essences rather than embroidery. His progress on his own 'Blues in Motian' from mere hints at the tune, to percussive thunder and then to the most sublime of walking patterns was a triumph of creative bass playing. This was a gig of real musicality.

CASSANDRA

The Guardian, November 1989

That group of radical young black New Yorkers going under the collective name of M-Base (currently producing some of the most unexpected departures from the long traditions of jazz and the shorter ones of hip hop and rap) includes in its ranks one of the most powerful emerging talents in the world of jazz singing in the Mississippi-born and Brooklyn-bred Cassandra Wilson.

And whetting the appetites of British admirers through the trickle of imports of her own formidable records (featuring her handling both of contemporary materials and latterly Tin Pan Alley ballads on the album *Blue Skies*) and work with the dynamic alto saxophonist Steve Coleman, Ms Wilson made it to Britain on Monday for a single show as part of the Half Moon's Jazz Lunarcy Festival. It was worth the wait. Cassandra Wilson, a declared campaigner for the continuing cause of black rights in America and an attentive listener to the barrage of sound from the street that assails her apartment in Brooklyn, has breathed the kind of influences that produce independence, depth, flexibility and technical assurance, and the abundance with which she possesses all these rather undercuts the manner in which she's now being touted in hip circles as a 'jazz artist for the Nineties'.

Cassandra Wilson is more than ready now. She worked with a crisp and impressively self-editing trio on Monday, featuring Rod Williams on keyboards, Kevin Bruce Harris on bass, and Mark Johnson on drums. The sharpness of the young accompanists and Ms Wilson's swerving, bent-pitch phrasing thus more than once suggested a less fanciful and more muscular Betty Carter, mingled with an abrupt and spinechilling mid-register fierceness that even brought to mind Nina Simone. She opened with 'Blue Skies', followed by a displaced, reflective 'Polka Dots' and 'Moonbeams', shifted into emphatic, exclamatory scatting on a street-beat piece of her own and followed pianist Williams's exquisite opening to 'Round Midnight' with a mixture of meditativeness and blistering, almost accusatory statements.

This led into an epic in which Johnson pursued a driving Tony Williams-like hi-hat beat against a spectacular thumbed funk solo from Harris and brusque, darting interjections from the piano, Ms Wilson performing in a mixture of spacey, wheeling sounds and yodels. It would be tempting to say that the jazz world doesn't have to look any further for its next Betty Carter, except that what it has is the distinctive identity of Cassandra Wilson, through and through.

1990s

The 1990s

In 1990, *Time* magazine ran a cover picture of young trumpeter, Wynton Marsalis. The headline heralded 'The New Jazz Age'. They were late catching up with this story: the signs had been there since the early 1980s – some would even say 1974, when the Village Vanguard club was unexpectedly overrun with fans of emigré bop saxophonist Dexter Gordon on his return to New York. But a jazz renaissance still came as news to many. After being all but unmentionable in a record store for almost a decade, jazz had risen from the grave.

Time Magazine could hardly contend that jazz was enjoying a public status it hadn't known since the last 'Jazz Age' – no jazz artists were doing enough business to cause Madonna or Michael Jackson to lose sleep, or having the kind of popular appeal that gained Paul Whiteman his 'King of Jazz' title sixty years before. But jazz had undoubtedly acquired an influence outside music again, though maybe not in the way Scott Fitzgerald had meant it. The word, particularly in Europe, could be found adorning cars, perfume and clothes. Jazz seemed chic and, by implication, upmarket or already there.

(From *Jazz* by John Fordham, Dorling Kindersley, 1993)

The early years of the 1990s were overshadowed by the death of Miles Davis, who had long seemed a permanent, if elusive presence on the jazz scene. Less than two years after Davis's death in 1991 Dizzy Gillespie, the other founding father of postwar jazz trumpet music followed. The evocative voices of singer Sarah Vaughan and saxophonists Stan Getz and Dexter Gordon were also silenced. As if to facilitate their transformation from unpredictable living artists to back-catalogue legends, it seemed as if many of the prime catalysts who had helped make jazz music what it triumphantly was were just getting helpfully out of the marketing departments' way.

After the public-funding advances of the late 1970s and 1980s, and the briefly incandescent commerciality of jazz to the funders of wine bars and bistros in the 1980s boom (investment had even extended to the launching of an all-jazz radio station in London in 1990, though it quickly trimmed its programming sails) recession was reversing the tide.

Yet the gains of the revival of interest in jazz could not be erased completely. Young musicians took to learning jazz techniques alongside other disciplines, even if they were primarily classical or pop performers – the bolder classical interpreters even took to including jazz materials in their repertoires, as did rap artists on the pop scene. Female jazz instrumentalists, formerly a rarity, grew in numbers. Jazz history, perhaps for the first time, seemed to be standing on the brink of general recognition as one of the fundamental forces in the development of twentieth-century music of all kinds.

1990

Though that Time *Magazine cover looked promising, claiming the ascent of jazz to its rightful throne in the cultural firmament of the late twentieth century, many jazz musicians who had been around for longer than Wynton Marsalis's generation didn't believe it would last. Jazz was too mercurial and unruly, too devoted to the spontaneous to be easily packaged, which was why the record companies generally preferred to concentrate on the lucrative 'all-time classics' reissue market. Greatest-hits music, whether in the pop or classical worlds, achieved the audience-levels it had because the merchandise either involved celebrities repeating familiar and much-loved material, or great recordings by deceased giants, for which the only remaining creative leeway lay in redesigning the artwork.*

But in Britain, there was certainly just as promising a sign as Time's *endorsement of a jazz resurgence – a radio station secured investment and a licence to broadcast nothing but jazz around the clock. If anything symbolised a fundamental change in listening habits (at least for Londoners – it wasn't a national station) Jazz FM seemed to be it and though it broadcast a good deal of blues, funk and jazz-pop vocals to broaden its audience in the daytime, it seemed at the outset as if it represented a seachange in the British media's attitude to the music. But would it last? Could it attract big enough listening-figures to generate the advertising revenue that its overheads and its ambitions required? Eighteen months had to pass before the answers became clear.*

But if Jazz FM's young broadcasters didn't always appear to know who was who in jazz, some sensational performances occurred in 1990 for those who knew, but who were still open to surprises. One of the most memorable was guitarist Pat Methenys informal appearance at a West London club better known to rock and country audiences, to display the unfettered force of his jazz improvising technique rather than his glitzier showbiz-fusion persona. Metheny appeared in a jazz trio with bassist Dave Holland and drummer Roy Haynes, and Haynes also delivered a movingly theatrical tribute to the legendarily indestructible percussionist Art Blakey, who had that year defied rumours of his immortality by finally dying at the age of seventy-one.

Another star drummer and one of Miles Davis's most dynamic percussion partners, Tony Williams, also played an astonishing show, with all the whiplash rhythmic power, imperiously wayward solo timing and balefully restrained steaminess that the 1965 Miles band had displayed, and with Williams's own ingenious compositions on top. Wallace Roney, the most creatively respectful of Miles trumpet clones, was to repeat much of this mix with Williams two years hence, but for an even more deeply felt and evocative reason. Other ex Miles-men, guitarist John Scofield and bassist Dave Holland, contributed to the addition of a new catchall term – 'postbop' – to the jazz lexicon, addressing new balances of older ensemble writing (Charles Mingus reborn), fusion's raunchy directness and bebop's ambiguous fluidity. Scofield in particular brought out a brilliant 1990 disc, Time on My Hands.

The great South African jazz musicians Chris McGregor and Dudu Pukwana died young, and within months of each other, during the summer of 1990, though at least in time to have seen Nelson Mandela begin his journey to reunifying the country they had been forced to leave. Both men had had an incalculable effect on the wider perception of the turbulent optimism of South African jazz, and brought a unique vitality to the European jazz scene in the process. Tenorist Dexter Gordon, a voluntary expatriate from the States for much of his life and probably a more significant instigator of the renewed interest in classic jazz and bebop even than the inheritor, Wynton Marsalis, also succumbed. A short-lived but ground-breaking British big band, Loose Tubes, didn't die but exploded into many glittering fragments – its finest players, Django Bates, Iain Ballamy, Eddie Parker and Steve Buckley, separated to illuminate new territories of their own. Two other one-off British big bands, Andy Sheppard's Soft on the Inside and pianist Django Bates's own group, blended Irish jigs, bop and circus music (in Bates's case) and abstract free music (in both) with the compositional approach of Carla Bley and George Russell, to spectacular effect.

LET'S GET LOST

City Limits, February 1990

When Bruce Weber's documentary feature *Let's Get Lost* opens at the Metro it will be the third opportunity for the movie-going public to watch serious jazz artists going seriously on the skids in four years – the size of the audience has been changed, but the derelicts remain the same. This is maybe a better deal for jazz than all the years in which the very idea of a mainstream jazz film was a joke, but is an indication of how deeply attached writers and movie-makers are to the irresistible symmetry of saxophones, syringes, and stumbling idols kept upright only by music and by devoted admirers holding their elbows. It is a picture loved by older jazz groupies (the new generation seems to have successfully exorcised it) and loathed by most musicians, and this time the late Chet Baker gets the treatment, a Doomed Youth who might have been made for Hollywood. But unlike the two fictionalised features, Bertrand Tavernier's 1986 *Round Midnight* and Clint Eastwood's 1988 *Bird!*, what you see this time appears to be the real thing – as much as the expression means anything in the context of Baker's perfect suitability for white postwar myths of the passively rebellious, self-destructive and gifted outsider. Looking like James Dean was the worst thing that ever happened to him.

The arrival of Weber's film at the end of the last decade was an appropriate culmination to a movie period that, if it wasn't perfect, at least substantially lifted the spirits of jazz followers. Throughout the Fifties and Sixties most jazz in the cinema was a grisly mixture of sanitised jive-talk and badly mimed instrumental playing by Hollywood stars who looked about as much at home performing jazz as Noh theatre – like Robert Wagner's unintentionally hilarious impersonation of a jazz trumpeter in *All the Fine Young Cannibals*, which gets a quote in the Baker film. Good jazz documentaries did get made – but hardly anybody saw them because the outlets were few and TV programmers thought jazz was self-indulgent or morally threatening or both.

Against this background the arrival of three major films in the Eighties – three films that all take the music seriously, and with an unprecedented respect for technical accuracy – is indisputable progress, and an indication of how far the ripples of the current 'jazz revival' have travelled. In pursuit of authenticity, Bertrand Tavernier used the saxophonist Dexter Gordon instead of a regular actor to portray *Round Midnight*'s Dale Turner, a *mélange* of real-life wasted heroes Bud Powell and Lester Young. Clint Eastwood used authentic Charlie Parker solo recordings grafted on to the playing of a contemporary rhythm section to convincingly reproduce the live sound of Parker at work, combined with a performance of rigorous detail from Forest Whitaker, himself a long-time Bird fan.

Bruce Weber, the fashion photographer (the Calvin Klein underwear ads) turned film-maker, says of *Let's Get Lost*, 'I made the film with Chet because I wanted to have my own story about him.' Baker's aura depended on his indifference to the past and resignation about the future so that his identity – even to himself – became a collection of stories without narrative, snatched images. A lighted match illuminating unmistakable cheekbones in the back of a car, a rare grimace of pleasure at the wheel of a fairground dodgem, a tired seated figure with a trumpet pointed towards the floor, and a collection of hazy and contradictory memories in the minds of people who loved him. You can't find some parcel called Chet Baker's character through all these investigations, you can only find dislocated fragments of mingled recollection and legend, which is the essence of *Let's Get Lost*, and why it is a reflection of Weber's own rather myopic obsessions as much as Baker's. But Weber's conclusion that the only whole and integrated element in this painful and dislocated life is the unique and enduring character of Baker's music is hard to avoid.

The movie looks as beautiful as you'd expect, and has already won accolades such as the critics' prize at the Venice Film Festival. Shot in black and white, it is a documentary *film noir* to portray what it is hard to avoid representing as a *life noir* – Baker, the James Dean youth, the romantic ballad-singer, the trumpet lyricist who made notes into falling petals, and Baker, the junkie, the itinerant with no forwarding address, the manipulator, and finally the corpse on an Amsterdam street, one Friday the 13th, at the age of fifty-eight.

Weber had to fit the making of his film around Baker as he found him – there was never any prospect of getting the trumpeter to run to a timetable. Some days the crew would set up for shooting in the States and the star would turn out still to be in Europe. Crucial facts about his life – like a wife and son he forgot to mention until late in the shoot when asked if any of his children were musical – would emerge as if only incidental to his real preoccupations, music and heroin. In his accounts of events he was often proved to be forgetful, selective, or downright dishonest. But presenting all this became Weber's intention, reproducing the contradictions of an already unreal relationship, that between audience and artist. And having made a fortune out of iconography as an adman, Bruce Weber can't leave it go as a documentary maker.

Let's Get Lost is nevertheless a hard film to turn away from, and is often bleakly funny too. A deadpan Baker describes the collapsed junkie who opened one eye after he had given him thirty minutes' artificial respiration to complain, 'You guys messed up my high.' Trumpeter Jack Sheldon, a frequent associate of the young Baker and clearly an aspiring stand-up comic, relates laconic accounts of how difficult it was to hang on to a sexual partner once Baker was in the vicinity, even if you were actually having sex with the person in question at the time. But Weber, in his devotion to Baker, is merciless with women, and in handling the pain as well as the pleasure experienced by those who were, or thought they were, closest to him. In this respect it sometimes invites a kind of seedy, tabloid newspaper-like complicity on the part of the viewer. A series of separate interviews with wives, ex-wives and girlfriends (by the look of it not all intended to be on the record) splices together to amount to a distinctly tacky picture of competition between them for who had come closest to understanding Baker, while at the centre of all their claims and prognostications the genie himself impassively provides his own perspective – impassive, indifferent. He is filmed at one point discussing his former wives whilst leafing through nude photographs of women, and when asked what he reckoned the best day of his life was, replies, 'The day I got my Alfa Romeo.' Weber even takes the trumpeter's respectable and respectful mother Vera Baker to breaking point with the question, 'Did he disappoint you as a son?' (Long pause.) 'Yes, but let's don't go into that.'

'Everybody has their own story about Chet Baker,' runs *Let's Get Lost*. But if Weber was driven by that perception, the payoff of which is that the music is the only coherent image in a hailstorm of disparate fragments, then recording as rich an account of Baker's art as possible ought to have been inevitable. Instead of which, *Let's Get Lost* presents a picture of a battered but poignant singing voice and almost sidelines the trumpet skills that survived far better into Baker's middle age than his vocal chords did. It wouldn't have meant turning the romantic *film noir* that the director clearly found irresistible into a jazz buffs' movie – simply coming more fully to terms with the one thing that rises above the evasions, alibis and myth-making which pepper the participants' memories of Baker and Baker's accounts of himself – the subtle, inflected, balletically poised sound of one of the great artists of postwar jazz.

LOVE YOUR ENEMY
The Guardian, April 1990

There's always evidence for the continuing passion of a section of the audience for the kind of jazz that reworks 'The Shadow of Your Smile' – the proof lies in the hail of unmentionable substances that periodically fall upon reporters who endorse versions of the music in which that song, or something like it, plays no part.

But coming up under this group, without whose devotion to the song form the history of jazz's great lyrical improvisers might evaporate, is a new audience with different assumptions. Though its enthusiasms are for fundamental jazz values – improvisation, collective energies, subversiveness – it is hearing them now through new, or at least reprocessed, materials. On 15 and 16 April, several bands associated with the cult New York avant-garde club The Knitting Factory will be performing at the

South Bank. Some recent preview discs include the Jazz Passengers (due to be among the April visitors), a septet who mix scrambling violin passages, fitful stretches of breezy jazz time and bricks-through-windows electric guitar eruptions; violin-led trios that play as lyrically as if they were trying to sell Elgar to East Side street gangs; soloists who improvise on Albert Ayler tunes country-style on steel guitar; plus electronics, banshee chanteuses and much more.

The second volume of Knitting Factory discs, featuring sound effects guitarists Sonny Sharrock and British expat Fred Frith, is more abstract but more dramatic than the first. Sharrock also appears on an album of his own, also recorded at The Knitting Factory, *Live in New York*. 'Dick Dogs', which appears on the compilation, is a blistering thrash that starts off sounding like Cream, then the old Mahavishnu Orchestra, then abandons notes and takes off into spearing treble sounds and fusillades of bottleneck squeals. But, as with recent Sharrock albums, the full deal is nothing like so vicious. *Live in New York* includes stretches of genial funk, R & B, and a poignant, country-tinged sway on 'My Song'. It calms the nerves of the fearful, but it sounds like other people, which Sharrock at his delinquent best, such as with 'Last Exit', never does.

And just to show that the place for 'Shadow of Your Smile', or something like it, remains honourable and eternal, some of the best known playing of one of jazz music's surviving lyric poets, Stan Getz, has been reissued on a Verve cassette (or CD) package devoted to his bossa nova hits of the Sixties. Few of these sessions tugged at Getz or required more from him than the petal-like fragility of his sound and you'd need to be a Latin obsessive in a big way to need all four albums at once but the graceful walking-on-water songs, and Getz's ability to attach the flimsiest of lace to a tune and transform it have preserved the shine on these golden oldies. Astrud Gilberto debuts here, letting those feathery syllables out as 'Girl from Ipanema'.

Praising the Genie

The Correspondent, April 1990

When the volcanic tenor saxophonist Dexter Gordon made his 1974 comeback to the New York clubs after a five-year absence in Europe, the *Village Voice*'s critic, Gary Giddins (in a tribute fittingly entitled 'Long Tall Dexter Bites the Apple'), wrote: 'His sound is incomparable, capable of robust clarity on fast tempos and dark sobriety on ballads. He can honk so powerfully in the lower register you expect walls to crumble before him, and his husky cries in the hidden register can be chilling. It is a sound with depth and authenticity, something you want to reach out and touch.' Gordon's massive, shambling form came into focus for a wider audience than the cognoscenti through his artless but heartfelt performance in Bertrand Tavernier's 1986 feature film *Round Midnight*. Gordon played the part of an alcoholic tenor saxophonist called Dale Turner, thereby representing that popular piece of jazz-life mythology, the self-abusive intuitive artist fitfully visited by sufficient bursts of sublime music making to sustain the commitment of the martyred friends and admirers who keep him alive.

That Dexter Gordon's fame outside the coterie of jazz fans should have depended on such a road-weary theme was a pity. By the time the movie was made, Gordon's musical powers were already waning, with the result that the swirls and breakers of his sound were mostly reduced to a dignified but hesitant murmur, though the blend of tenderness and force that had always marked him out as a ballad player was still audible. But the mannerisms of the character of Dale Turner – child-like playfulness in the midst of confusion and pain, gentleness all the more affecting for residing in the frame of a giant, loyalty to friends, obsessive and consuming love for creative music – were all true of Gordon too.

Like all jazz musicians of his generation, Gordon knew how heavy an emotional price African-Americans were paying for expressing themselves through an art form in the hands of so many hit-and-run promoters, tin-eared record executives, racist agents and philistines in general. He would listen patiently to the objections about negative jazz imagery in *Round Midnight*, smiling quizzically at you, his knees under his chin on a hotel sofa he made to look like a piece of doll's furniture, the occasional syllable slowly welling up from his chest with a slow rumble like an approaching aircraft. But ultimately, he came back with the unsurprising but also undeniable reply. Too many of the people he had loved as players and as human beings – Charlie Parker, Bud Powell, Lester Young and many others – had lived and died like Dale Turner, and Tavernier's was at least a knowledgeable, technically authentic and unpatronising story, made by a jazz lover for a change. For Gordon's generation, the world had changed its mind about jazz too late.

By the end of the 1940s, Gordon's skills were consolidated into a style of immense melodic variety, freedom from cliché and repetition over even the most prolonged extemporisations, mischievous enthusiasm for rampant quotation from other tunes, and an arsenal of boneshaking special effects warbles, hoots, honks and hoarse, ascendant cries. The style awakened the gifts of a man who was to become far more of a cult figure than even the star of *Round Midnight* could become – John Coltrane, who always acknowledged the depth of his debt to Gordon. The route from Gordon to Coltrane was a connection that overwhelmingly influenced the direction of jazz music from the 1960s onward, and remains everywhere audible in the sound of the 'jazz revival' today. Mention Gordon's name to anyone who ever saw him play and it's likely they'll recall both the headlong inventiveness of his tenor solos at their best, and his characteristic gesture of both triumph and wonderment at the end of a gig, raising the tenor aloft with both arms outstretched, as if offering it to the wayward genie of jazz improvisation. He never lost that gratitude, despite the ups and downs of his career, and neither did we.

Dexter Gordon, born 27 February 1923; died 25 April 1990.

FIRECRACKER

The Guardian, July 1990

That Dudu Pukwana, one of the most moving and distinctive of all South African jazz musicians, should have died only weeks after the early demise of his long-time musical partner Chris McGregor may be just vicious coincidence. But anyone who witnessed the best moments of that creative empathy which once had Pukwana described as the Johnny Hodges to McGregor's Ellington, might have guessed that the wrench of the latter's departure was likely to be profoundly dispiriting to Pukwana, whose health was already doubtful. Now only one member of the original South African Blue Notes – drummer Louis Moholo – survives out of the quintet that left the Cape (all in their twenties and bursting with music) for Switzerland in 1965. It lends support to the contention that the disequilibrium of exiles, a chronic condition for anybody forced from home, may be even more undermining to South Africans driven from a dazzlingly beautiful country by the scourge of such a malignant system.

Pukwana lived in England from 1966, when the Blue Notes – then playing a kind of unruly hard bop laced with townships dance music and New York free playing – settled in London. The whole band made a vivid impression (nothing they did was cool, restrained or apparently calculated) but Pukwana was always especially memorable. A short, vivacious man, built like a rain-barrel, he was a firecracker both as a performer and a human being – his arrival anywhere was impossible to play down. Given to abrupt detonations of laughter, a mixture of bear-hugs and occasional suspicious fury (usually short-lived), he translated all these mannerisms into musical parallels – wild swoops of sound on the alto saxophone ending in cantankerous honks, tender, vibrato-laden rhapsody, raucous guffaws turning into sly, knowing seductiveness. His closest musical relative was the early saxophone style of Ornette Coleman, which he both admired and understood, but if Pukwana was a gifted thematic improviser who didn't need chords to tell a story, he was also a master of the breathy romantic quiver, a rich and billowing sound worthy of Hodges or Ben Webster, that in Pukwana's case was a relic of accompanying the late-night clinch at a thousand townships dances.

Dudu Pukwana came from Port Elizabeth originally, where he was born in July 1938. His mother was a singer, his father a singer and pianist, and it was as a piano player that Pukwana first made headway. He was visiting Cape Town as a pianist in 1962 when music student Chris McGregor, then looking to form a band, noticed him. Around the same time, after he had been playing the alto saxophone for six years, he won the Saxophonist of the Year prize at the Johannesburg Jazz Festival, and it was as an altoist and composer that Pukwana helped McGregor form the Blue Notes – a band that became famous not just for the vigour of its music, but also for its then unique mixed-race format. In the Seventies in England (after successes with various McGregor groups, including the spectacular Ellington-meets-*kwela* big band Brotherhood of Breath) Pukwana began to form groups of his own. One of his first, Spear, toured South Africa with Hugh Masekela, and then toured the States. But Pukwana's musical interests ranged wide. He also liked reggae, and even the distinctly unsonglike sounds of the European free improvisers, with many of whom he shared some bizarre and often astonishingly fertile evenings. In 1978 Pukwana formed Zila, a sometimes ragged but unfailingly exhilarating band with which he has regularly worked ever since.

Dudu Pukwana was one of the most gifted, wayward, inspirational and exciting jazz musicians ever to have lived and worked in Britain. He was not calculating or mean-spirited or parsimonious with his capabilities as a player. As a result, his optimistic assumption that every band wanted him to sit in, his occasional tendency to ask for his fee twice (having genuinely forgotten by the end of the gig that he'd taken the money upfront and deposited most of it in the bar in the course of the evening) or his erratic timekeeping were usually taken to be a small price for access to such a life-force, on or offstage. He will be much missed.

Dudu (Mtutuzel) Pukwana, born Port Elizabeth, South Africa, 18 July 1938, died Notting Hill, London, 29 June 1990.

SUPERGROUP

The Guardian, July 1990

The band that opened this year's Capital/JVC Jazz Festival was a supergroup in every respect. Drummer Jack DeJohnette, guitarist Pat Metheny, pianist Herbie Hancock and bassist Dave Holland are all major celebrities of the international jazz scene who emerged in the Seventies and are leaders in their own right. Bands tailor-made for the festival circuit frequently do little more than trade clichés at a permanent crescendo, but the reputations for intelligence, ideas and curiosity that accompany these musicians suggested that musicality would get the upper hand.

The first of two shows by this quartet at the Festival Hall on Monday night – an hour and three-quarters non stop – more than supported the assumption. The band played old and new funk, ballads, and some roaring up-tempo neo-bop, displayed a lot of mutual rapport, and set a level of improvisational flair and high drama that will be hard to beat all week. After a Jack DeJohnette opening of quiet, brooding drumrolls that expanded into his characteristic mixture of offbeat, exclamatory blows and garrulous bass drum patterns, the band fell one by one into an insistent, repeated vamp until Pat Metheny took off on a guttural, distorted guitar solo, followed by Herbie Hancock's keyboards unleashing a sound like Miles Davis's trumpet. At this point the gig promised a high pressure, rather self-congratulatory fusion music. A typical Metheny mid-tempo piece of poignant lyricism followed, Holland's string-slapping bass-guitar funk reverberating the gently lapping waves of the guitarist's style, but it was on the third tune, a dragging blues, that DeJohnette's devastating repertoire of rolls, abrupt halts, wrong-footing pauses, sudden cymbal crashes and echoing snare drum explosions began to shake the players' inclinations to play what they knew.

Though most of the strong thematic ideas from then on were provided by Metheny's flair for memorable pop-jazz orchestration (swaying country songs, jaunty, whistling guitar timbres, chord-rooted improvising style) and the weaknesses came from the same source's tendency to slide into New Ageisms, the ensemble spontaneity was mostly thrilling for the rest of the set. Hancock played a superb solo of churning runs and chiming chords on one of his own older funk compositions, 'Canteloupe Island' (though such hard edged, choppy music undid Metheny, who prefers a legato style unsuited to the idiom), and late in the set Holland played a devastating slow solo of thumping low register sounds and slurred chords once left entirely to his own devices. Metheny seemed belatedly to gain striking power up against Hancock's yelping electric keyboard in a breakneck chorus-swapping finale that brought the crowd to its feet even before the last slamming chord.

Multi-Kulti

The Listener, August 1990

They danced the rhumba in the 'bottle party' clubs off Piccadilly in between air raids, but they didn't call it World Music. Maybe 'the world' is anything outside a twenty-mile radius of a record company's head office, because they never used the term to include the musics of the familiar immigrant communities of London (Asian, Caribbean), Chicago (Caribbean) or New York (Latin) but pumped it up when they wanted a name for more 'mysterious' parts of the globe like Mali or Senegal.

Yet before the current chart driven corporate raiding for new faces and new sounds ever got moving (closer to home and seventy years ago the majors were doing it to the American descendants of slaves for what they sold as 'race records') some of the more broadminded of jazz players had been on the case for years. Saxophonist Yusef Lateef (using Eastern instruments in his work from the 1950s), the post-Parker altoist Charlie Mariano (adopting the Indian double reeded *nadaswaram*) and John Coltrane, John McLaughlin and many other improvisers long ago perceived Third World music as a catalyst for spontaneity not requiring variations on the chords of 'I Got Rhythm'.

One of the most imaginative and unpredictable pioneers of this investigation has recently returned to England for his first performances in three years, and a new album with his distinctly worldbeat quartet Multi-Kulti is due for release at the end of the month. The artist is Don Cherry, the fifty-four-year-old trumpeter and multi-instrumentalist from Oklahoma via Watts, Los Angeles. As a trumpeter, Cherry is hard to categorise by most known jazz practices. He plays pocket trumpet (which looks as if it has been run into at the mouthpiece and the bell by two speeding trucks) to produce a high, rubbery sound, he phrases in impacted clumps of notes like the bubbling of a kettle, and he avoids regular chromatic runs in favour of infant-like exclamatory and interrogatory noises. This independence of approach has led Cherry to work with an unimpeachable array of contemporary musicians including Ornette Coleman, Sonny Rollins, Gato Barbieri, Carla Bley and Lou Reed, and to be as likely to perform nowadays a John Lee Hooker blues played on a Malinese hunting guitar (the *doussn'gourni*) as a postbop Ornette Coleman trumpet outing.

Cherry's arrival on the world's jazz stage began to roll in the winter of 1958, when the Ornette Coleman quartet rehearsed for its impending revolution – the one greeted effusively the next year by hip straight music authorities like Leonard Bernstein and Gunther Schuller – in Cherry's mother's garage in Watts. Cherry, who is of both African-American and Indian-American descent (his grandmother was a Choctaw) has a simple definition of world music, 'the music of people who have been listening and travelling'. If that's what a world musician is, then Cherry has qualified since around 1966.

He left the States for Stockholm then (having met his second wife Moki, a painter, and mother of now famous singer Neneh Cherry, whilst on a European tour with Sonny Rollins) and spent the early months of his new life in that city's Ethnograhic Museum, studying ethnic instruments. Cherry's next move was to take off through Europe, Africa and the Middle East with his new family, a camper, and no plans – never being the type to exactly budget for his retirement, he has always reckoned not being in hurry to be somewhere else is an essential prerequisite for truly listening to what a total stranger is telling you. In this mood (subsisting on savings and local hospitality) Cherry thus sat in with village musicians on three continents and began to perceive his jazz background in a new light, as providing a set of improvisational inflections and timbres that could be introduced into spaces within an overall sound quite different from jazz. Though before he left the States Cherry had achieved what the *New York Times* called 'the respectful obscurity reserved for important jazz players who didn't die young and who aren't Miles Davis', lack of interest in his expressionistic style didn't hold him up. He formed an audacious small group with Argentinian tenorist Gato Barbieri, producing classic albums such as *Complete Communion* and *Symphony for Improvisers*, worked with ethereal ingenuity with Carla Bley and the Jazz Composers' Orchestra on the Indian-influenced *Escalator over the Hill*, explored Tibetan and Japanese music with the late sitarist Collin Wallcott in the band Cordona.

Latterly, after upheavals in his personal life but renewed interest in his work by a major label (A&M, which wrested the delightful Ornettish jazz album *Art Deco* out of Cherry last year but has now let him record the eclectic Multi-Kulti) he has returned to the States and even found himself invited to compose and perform a mass for all the world's religions for a San Francisco festival, in partnership with the Brazilian percussionist Nana Vasconcelos. Since Don Cherry's avowed affection for the raga form is a generalised empathy with a music of 'no endings, only beginnings', it is likely to be a mass of unorthodox shape. Since, in addition, improvisation is not a career but a spiritual imperative in him (sometimes to the mystification or exasperation of family and friends), Don Cherry's progress through his fifties is almost certain to mean that 'World Music' is in safer hands than the ones currently counting the takings.

CABARET FOR ELEPHANTS

The Guardian, October 1990

It often seems as though the style of the German saxophonist Peter Brotzmann – something akin to the sound of a herd of elephants fleeing from a bush fire and about three times as loud – is impervious to the idiosyncrasies of any type of accompaniment, any audience, any venue. But three opportunities to sample this extraordinary phenomenon live in London within six months (at the Crawley Outside In Festival, at Stoke Newington's Vortex and on Sunday at the Jazz Café) have conclusively proved that Brotzmann isn't unshakeably devoted to doing only what he overpoweringly feels like.

This time he was in the company of B Shops for the Poor, an ensemble drawing on jazz, contemporary classical and what often sounds like Thirties European cabaret music, and featuring the distinctly unjazzy and often Kurt Weillian vocals of Louise Petts. As an opportunity that both cast

Brotzmann in a different light and loosened the sometimes rather formal B Shops, the gig was an exhilarating, if deafening, business. Its last forty-five minutes consisted of rapid scene shifting between strutting contrapuntal horn ensembles, quirky, dislocated fusion reminiscent of the old Henry Cow, and admonishing, martial rhythms.

Brotzmann, a man who took the abrasive post-Coltrane methods of Pharoah Sanders to the limits of turbulence and has then kept them there for twenty-five years, ironically became the unifying factor in a band usually notable for the dislocated and fragmentary character of its works. B Shops is dedicated to maintaining discord as realism rather than seeking the softened up fusion of many eclectic bands, and on Sunday night Brotzmann, crown prince of discord, curiously became the underlying harmony. B Shops is about to release a record of collaborations with him in which it will presumably be a lot easier to hear the subtleties. It will be fascinating to discover whether or not this is an advantage.

1991

In 1991 Miles Davis died. The event overshadowed the year, obscuring much excellent work on a still fruitful jazz circuit, and even eclipsing the same year's valedictions for another departed giant of improvisation, Stan Getz. Local radio stations in the States ditched hours of scheduled broadcasting time after the news broke, and replaced it with album after album of his recorded work.

Why was Davis regarded with such awe? For all the frequently repeated reasons, and a few more. He had refused to coast on earlier successes, constantly sought to reorientate jazz, allowed his music to evolve in organic transaction with favourite soloists as Ellington did, and his trumpet sound was utterly unique.

But maybe what all this boiled down to was that Miles encompassed all those qualities of the term 'hip' that aren't just about modishness and style – qualities like uncanny timing, an ability to make profound statements by ambiguity and implication (and thus with the element of constant surprise), the knack of making a personal artistic order seem both inevitable and unexpected at the same time, all of them aspects of beauty. In jazz terms, he could swing with the most minimal of statements, in which respect he was a walking definition of the unique contribution of African-American music to the modern world, a vocabulary shaped by rhythmic insights quite different to anything developed in Europe.

Meanwhile, there was a deepening economic recession all over the world. The proprietors of jazz clubs reported in 1991 that it was affecting the frequency with which punters would purchase food and drink, but in general the healthy expansion of audiences that had occurred in the late 1980s was not noticeably declining – a characteristic frequently observed of recessionary periods, that consumers might not renew their car or their carpets, but they'd be damned if they were going to be cheated out of a little creative escapism from the grind until no other alternative economy was left.

On the British jazz scene, the growing authority of the black musicians of Courtney Pine's generation was visible all over the place. Pine himself, having *learned to live with his overnight status, continued to search among his influences for a music of his own, as did the guru of the young-jazz movement, Wynton Marsalis, on the other side of the Atlantic. Pine's one-time pianist, Julian Joseph, was on his way to being one of the finest jazz keyboard artists ever produced in Britain, and demonstrated it by performing with a gleefully astonished Johnny Griffin, that grizzled American tenor veteran, at London's glitzy new Jazz Café. Saxophonist Steve Williamson, who had emerged in the largely black and Asian big band, the Jazz Warriors, demonstrated that he was covering the funk-influenced New York M-Base territory in his own way, and using an American record producer and accompanying musicians too.*

Abdullah Ibrahim's sax partner, Carlos Ward, played a sensational show with his own band in the same year, extensively featuring the blistering drumming of Pheroan Aklaff – and singer Cassandra Wilson suggested she was taking her rich and dramatic voice away from the cutting-edge American fusion repertoire (M-Base, again) toward jazzier and more standards-oriented material. And the septuagenarian American bandleader George Russell, working with a mixed group of American and British players, showed he still had one of the most powerful and audacious jazz orchestras on the road. Its full-blast account of a transition of Miles Davis's famous trumpet improvisation on 'So What?' had to heard to be believed.

LITTLE GIANT

The Guardian, January 1991

Johnny 'Little Giant' Griffin, now sixty-one, and forced to live down the reputation of being one of the fastest tenor saxophone players in jazz, has been playing three nights at the Jazz Café. All the best things about star soloists with rhythm sections they've never met before – freshness, creative accidents, exuberance – vibrated around the room during his second set with the Julian Joseph trio on Thursday night. Since the worst things are tentativeness, unconstructive competition, and the repetition of clichés to fill space, this was an all-round relief.

But Griffin with the Joseph band didn't simply hit it off with musicians who understood his enthusiasms, making the event just a high-quality impromptu collaboration. The four musicians blended into a quartet that sounded as if it had been touring for months, clearly to Griffin's satisfaction, and he allowed his accompanists at least as much playing time as himself, and maybe more. Griffin's own playing, which in earlier times never strayed far from impeccably accurate and intense fast bebop, has become more abstract with time, and more creative with a battery of devices (fleeting descents to bell notes, squiggly doodling figures half-locked to the chords, Dexter Gordonish warble) that have come to substitute for a lot of the wall-to-wall semiquaver onslaughts he used to go in for. He was thus meditative and elusive, alternately full bodied and oblique on his ballad 'Woe Is Me' (picked up by a crystal-clear Bill Evans-like solo from Joseph), initially evasive and eventually ferocious on a funk outing that sounded as if it had been written by a combination of Herbie Hancock and Thelonious Monk, and flat out on Monk's 'Rhythm-a-ning', which closed the set. Joseph's opening piano solo on the funk piece, 'Call It What You Wanna', was a tour de force of glittering single note runs and chordal figures – sometimes on top of the beat and some-times delaying it, and it brought Griffin to feverish clapping, grimacing and egging on at Joseph's side. The applause was long for an encore that never came.

FLIMFLAM

The Guardian, February 1991

For most of the past decade, the massive, lurching, white-bearded figure of Slim Gaillard was a fixture in the London jazz clubs, and with the mix-ture of musical adventurousness, geniality and opportunism that propelled his career from the late Thirties onwards, he became as affec-tionately regarded a part of London's youth jazz and club scenes as he had been of Hollywood's when still a youth himself. Gaillard was a more than competent guitarist and pianist, but it was as a completely unclassifiable vocalist that he made his name.

Gaillard's roots were in the 'novelty' songs of the 1930s, but the lateral imagination that he brought to singing an inspired gibberish, coupled with an awareness of the bebop scene, gave his work an edge that distinguished it from the frequently cosy wackiness of the vaudevillian jazz of a previous era. Gaillard performed as a solo variety act in the mid-Thirties, playing guitar and tapdancing at the same time. With the bassist Slam Stewart, Gaillard formed a successful duo that made him a radio star, and during the early Forties (influenced by bebop's early tendency to make virtually all music resemble saxophone playing, and by the survivalist surrealism of the war years) he evolved a mixture of scat singing and jive talk that he chris-tened 'vout', for which he even furnished his own dictionary.

Gaillard, having had a big hit with the record 'Flat Foot Floogie', would veer from jazz singing to staccato high-speed sound effects, demolitions of Latin torch singers, outrageous impressions of Chinese as the critic Gary Giddins put it 'could fashion an entire scat sonata around his favourite word, avocado'. All available materials went into the meat-mincer of his style, including in the case of 'Yip Roc Heresy' the contents of an Armenian restaurant menu. Gaillard continued to flourish through the Forties with hits like 'Cement Mixer', 'Moto Cikkle' and 'Laughing in Rhythm', and also appeared in movies such as *Star Spangled Rhythm* and the cult comedy hit *Helzapoppin*. As well as more exotic forays into showbusiness, aeronautics and amorous encounters with Hollywood stars, Gaillard also explored the motel business and farming as the pressures on his personal economy intensified, and he recorded more infrequently until he was rediscovered in the 1980s. He appeared in the *Roots* series on TV, toured the UK with much of his old material and eventually had a multi-part *Arena* series on Channel 4 devoted to his extraordinary life.

Though few jazz singers have shared an appetite for headlong lunacy that quite rivalled Gaillard's, his blend of a fundamentally jazz-driven swing and improvisational flair, and an uninhibited bravura about reshaping the language, helped pave the way for many more 'serious' jazz vocalists, all the way up to Bobby McFerrin.

IT DOESN'T HAVE TO BE PERFECT

The Guardian, March 1991

In the remaining days of the excellent Camden Jazz Festival, one of the two front-running female performers on the programme is a pioneer instrumental virtuoso from the days when it was highly unusual, the other operates in the more conventional role of bandleading vocalist. The first is Irene Schweizer, the brilliant Swiss pianist who is fifty this year and performing the birthday-present composition *Theoria*, written by composer/bassist Barry Guy for Schweizer and his London Jazz Composers' Orchestra. And New Yorker Cassandra Wilson, the jazz diva for the Nineties, as they say, returns to Camden after a week at the Jazz Café, where she packed the place to the doors. Wilson's singing is a powerful mixture of imperious steeliness and a knowing delicacy of graceful elisions and evaporating sounds (deriving from Betty Carter) hung on joltingly contemporary street beat ideas drawn from the fashionably inventive Brooklyn M-Base musicians, and sometimes on rhythmically audacious adaptations of jazz standards.

Irene Schweizer is ostensibly from a different jazz world. Wilson travels with a manager and dressmaker, Schweizer with nothing more than optimism that the piano will be in tune. But they are united by good deal of shrewdness both about their position as women within jazz, and the importance of improvisation. Irene Schweizer taught herself piano at twelve, learning boogie and ragtime music. Later classical training didn't divert her from a certainty that she wanted to play jazz ('although I didn't know how I could live from it, but was sure I wanted to do it somehow') and she wasn't long turned twenty when she won first prize in the piano category at the annual Zurich jazz festival. Her trio operated in the soul jazz style of Bobby Timmons and Junior Mance, and later in the mould of Bill Evans and McCoy Tyner.

Then, inevitably in the mid-Sixties, the magnet became John Coltrane. 'Gradually we started to get more and more off the beat,' Schweizer recalls, 'and away from chords and standards, but we never decided to, it just happened through playing and rehearsing, and a lot of other people in Europe at that time were doing it too. Unlike today, where people are more into revivalism.'

Schweizer's choice of music has meant that she has to travel widely for work. Barry Guy, who composed the tribute piece she plays on Thursday, similarly finds that he can book his orchestra on prestigious festivals throughout Europe but concerts here are a struggle. Any opportunity to play with Schweizer, however, is a bonus. 'She's so constructive,' Guy says. 'She comes up spontaneously with so many counter strategies to whatever you're doing, she has an amazing imagination, and she's totally different from one night to the next. You see jaws drop within the band, let alone the audience.' As a woman, Schweizer mostly found herself the odd one out on the European jazz festival scene. 'Not only was I usually the only woman playing an instrument on the festivals, at that time there were hardly any in the audience either. That's changed now. When I joined the Feminist Improvising Group at the end of 1978 [including Britons Lindsay Cooper, Maggie Nicols and Sally Potter] it was a great challenge, because we had very different levels of playing, and technique wasn't so important any more, so I relaxed. I didn't have to prove how good I was, how fast I could play, how much technique I had, it wasn't important in that group, it was more about expression and how you could communicate your feelings, and extend musicality through simpler things.'

Cassandra Wilson, who stands to become a much bigger jazz star than Schweizer ever will, came of age in an era where such flexibility was more common, though she believes there's still work to be done. She announces in her almost-whispered Mississippi drawl that since 'women of colour' are in numerical supremacy on the globe, it's only residual bigotry that makes their achievements occasions for surprise. Wilson's father is a musician, and the fellowship and private language of musicians attracted her at first, almost as much as the material. 'Musicians would come to the house and rehearse, and I loved the kind of communication they had, the language they had, the music being created around me.'

Though she intended to go into television originally, and took a communications degree, the company of musicians of her own generation, like adventurous saxophonists Henry Threadgill and David Murray, changed the course of her life. And the underlying force of the music she heard founded devotion to ambitious jazz not a million miles from Irene Schweizer's. 'Jazz is meant to be open to the personalities of the people playing it. I couldn't imagine trying to arrive at the perfect form of something. If you don't have surprises you don't stay interested yourself, and when you're interested it draws you and the audience into the music together.'

DRIFTING TO THE BLUES

The Guardian, March 1991

The word association game with Jimmy Giuffre (outside of the cognoscenti, at any rate) goes 'Train and The River', with maybe 'Four Brothers' as a close runner up. Multi-reed player and composer Giuffre helped the Woody Herman Orchestra learn bebop with the seamless, close-formation 'Four Brothers' score, but it was the buzzing, insistent clamour of 'The Train and The River' from the *Jazz on a Summer's Day* movie that guaranteed him a place in the folk memory of people otherwise barely bothered by jazz.

Giuffre is seventy next month, and appeared at the Jazz Café as part of the Camden Festival with two of his most appropriate and long-term associates, Paul Bley on piano and Steve Swallow on bass. As an exercise in left-field, low-key and at times faintly ethereal spontaneous composition it was a delight, featuring three of the most resourceful of melodic improvisers at their inventive ease, both independently and collectively. It must have been the quietest music yet played at the Camden Jazz Café, but to the quietest house, barring the endless maddening squeak and slam of the kitchen door.

Steve Swallow, one of the few musicians to have made the electric bass a thing of traditional beauty, played an opening overture of ringing low notes and violin-like sustained high sounds, which Giuffre gradually joined on clarinet with a gathering accumulation of curling wisps and warbles, intensifying into bursts of clamorous double time. All the musicians hinted at the blues that the piece eventually became.

Giuffre, looking like a thin owl, briefly drew the music into New Orleans-like raucousness and then away to floating impressionism, Paul Bley's accompanying piano sounds spaced out and glistening like snowflakes. Giuffre then turned to soprano for a circuitous route into 'All the Things You Are,' which flurried more than the opener and ended sublimely on bubble-like soprano notes drifting over a gently strummed chord from Swallow. 'I Can't Get Started' was just as graceful, Swallow sounding like a low register zither behind it and Bley demonstrating the immense impact of unambitious effects by suddenly zipping up the strings inside the piano lid behind Giuffre's poignant and smoky resolution of the theme.

Expertise, but so long matured as to be completely at the service of music.

Gentlemen and Artists

The Guardian, March 1991

With the departure of Bud Freeman and Jimmy McPartland within days of each other, the 'Austin High School gang', which unintentionally founded that brisk, bustling ensemble style that came simply to be known as the sound of 'Chicago jazz' has now passed into history. Though often sidelined by comparison with the furnace burning in the Twenties and Thirties bands of Louis Armstrong, the Chicago school produced much eloquent and exciting jazz and, in Bix Beiderbecke, a founding father of the cool movement of many years later.

Freeman and McPartland were at opposite poles in lifestlye – Freeman fastidious and deliberate, a faintly disapproving outsider amidst such fast-lane tearaways as Eddie Condon and McPartland himself. Since they both lived well into their eighties, both men proved their points in their different ways – McPartland that a little indulgence never hurt anybody, Freeman that taking care of yourself paid off. McPartland actually stopped drinking at the end of the 1960s, after a lifelong love-hate relationship with booze – he started going to Alcoholics Anonymous after the war and thereafter carried two thermos flasks with him everywhere, one for coffee, one for tea.

A big, bluff, foghorn-voiced man, Jimmy McPartland was a boxer originally (he and Beiderbecke once floored three hoodlums in the street who tried to take their instruments), but music gradually pulled him away from the gyms. He hit the big time when he replaced Bix Beiderbecke in the Wolverines in 1924. McPartland's sound has always been urgent, breathless, a tousled blend of Armstrong's fierceness and Beiderbecke's shapely tone. McPartland's favourite quote is Beiderbecke's opening words to him, 'I like you, kid. You sound like me, but you don't copy me.'

Along with other students of Chicago's Austin High (Bud Freeman, Frank Teschemacher and others), McPartland had discovered jazz by playing records on a wind-up machine after school, and hearing the New Orleans Rhythm Kings led them to form a similar band, soon joined by drummer Dave Tough and later a clarinet prodigy who turned out to be Benny Goodman. Even after the invitation to join the Wolverines,

McPartland was still toying with a boxing career, and his prospective employers told him he had to chose one or the other, on the grounds (as he reported to writer Whitney Balliett) that 'a cornet player needs all his teeth and a boxer doesn't'.

After the Wolverines, McPartland worked with Ben Pollack and with Eddie Condon, including some key recordings with the McKenzie-Condon Chicagoans. He toured extensively in the 1930s, joined the army and won a medal on D-Day (though some musicians skipped the draft, McPartland observed, 'I was a patriotic drunk'), and met his British pianist wife Marian whilst performing for ENSA. After the war, the two performed together frequently, and McPartland's vivid and affable sound was in demand all over the world. In 1970, Jimmy and Marian McPartland divorced, and at his seventieth birthday party (thrown for him by his former wife seven years later) McPartland declared, 'I suggest that all married people get divorced and start treating each other like human beings.' McPartland once described the ideal playing circumstances, in congenial company, as being 'like fine conversation. Whatever emotions you have that day go right to the edge, and then come out. You forget about yourself, because you're too busy treating the other musicians like gentlemen and artists, which they are.'

Jimmy McPartland, born 15 March 1907, died March 1991.

You've Got to Have a Hobby
Q Magazine, May 1991

If there was a musical equivalent in a rich eccentric's hobbies to the Howard Hughes wooden flying boat (born in the wrong era, dependent on old technology, briefly airborne, mostly hinting at getting out of the hangar tomorrow, or next week, or next year) it was the Charlie Watts Big Band that bulged the walls of international jazz haunts from the middle to the late Eighties.

Well, to be fair, that immense aggregation of three generations of British jazz musicians (including a three-man drum section of Watts, plus Bill Eyden and John Stevens for moral and technical support) did enjoy a few more triumphant flights after its 1984 debut than Hughes's one-mile one-off. On a bad night it was a mess, players of completely different allegiances getting in each other's way as if simultaneously trying to walk through a revolving door. On a good night it was riot, like a cross between Woody Herman's Orchestra and Sun Ra's.

Charlie Watts is currently on the jazz beat again, one of his oldest and deepest loves. The incentive is bizarre one. In the mid-Sixties the Rolling Stones and the Beatles competed not just for record sales, but over who was better at demonstrating a previously unnecessary skill – that a rock and roll musician could breathe in and out and write at the same time. John Lennon supplied the Beatles version with the art school surrealism of *A Spaniard in the Works* and *In His Own Write*. Watts published a tribute to Charlie Parker, a book of drawings and a short but heartfelt biography about a musician most of the Stones fans of the time would never have heard of.

Now *High Flying Bird* is republished, and an accompanying CD (featuring a quintet with Watts in the drum chair) provides a soundtrack to it. Watts intended to ghost the sound of the Parker quintet that included the trumpeter Red Rodney and – a little unexpectedly – the music is delicious. Peter King, one of the best saxophonists ever to have developed in Britain and a man who preceded the 'jazz revival' by twenty-five years, wrote the arrangements and represents Bird's voice. Gerard Presencer, a blazing teenage trumpeter, soars over the music with almost as much certainty as King. Though he keeps his head down, Charlie Watts plays with a soft, lissome swing. Unlike most of the bebop remakes currently bending the CD racks, Watts's hobby music exudes surprising warmth.

Charlie Watts prepares himself fastidiously for what is plainly the taxing prospect of talking about a personal preoccupation rather than contentedly thumping away at the back of a stage in front of 90,000 people; Jermyn Street shirt studded and pressed to a razor's edge, tie arcing so decisively from between the jaws of his collar it could have been whittled from timber, waistcoat as taut as he is himself. 'Don't like talking about myself,' he mutters. 'Makes me paranoid.' But start to turn the subject around with him – is all music the same, does jazz have a special song, was this a slow burn affair or an overnight rush, what was the Sixties Soho jazz and blues scene like? – and he stops perching and stretches back on the sofa, inspecting the ceiling for the distant sounds of the three or four bands a week he played in before he joined the biggest rock and roll phenomenon ever.

'Good rock and roll shouts what it is, and ends on a shout, that's what I've always thought. It may be an old way of looking at it, but the people I've always played rock with just lock in and stay there, and that's it. With jazz it's a much looser thing, it breathes, it stretches. If you try to bring things down in volume on the drums in a rock band, like you do in jazz, it just disappears. I always wanted to sound like the loosest drummers originally. Keith Moon used to say that he loved Gene Krupa, but never wanted to sound like that, used to sound like the first bebop drummer, Kenny Clarke. Kenny Clarke was the best rider of the cymbals [Watts demonstrates here with lazy rocking of his wrist, making a noise like rain on a metal roof], and the nearest to him is Billy Higgins, who has the sweetest ride of anybody alive today, and that includes Tony Williams. Tony's ride is an instrument in itself, but Billy's just floats. That's jazz to me.'

Charlie Watts made a saxophone out of rolled-up newspaper when he was a kid (and painted it bright orange) after he bought his first horn record, an Earl Bostic blues set. Gerry Mulligan followed, and then Bird. 'I fell in love with it. I still don't know what it was that got me, but if I play "Just Friends" now, or "Dancing in the Dark", anything like that, I just go cold and it still means the same thing now as it did then. It's improvisation, it's an amazing thing to do. I love the people who can do it, same as I love being around painters and sculptors. They seem like amazing things to do with your life.'

But Charlie Watts didn't do that with his life. He claims he was never good enough, and the Stones picked him up and swept him away before he ever got the chance to learn to be, though he worked frequently with jazz musicians in the active all-night scene of Sixties Soho, in Alexis Korner's blues band, and in a group with Stan Tracey's orthopaedic surgeon/tenor saxophonist Art Themen. Believing it was impossible for any band to last more than a couple of years, Watts kept his day jobs in graphic design ('commercial artist, they called it then'), sat in the flat he occupied on weekdays with Mick Jagger, Keith Richard and Brian Jones, reading the jobs section in *Advertising Weekly* while Jones crafted high-flown letters to *Melody Maker*, proclaiming how unbelievable the Stones were. But after a while, they all found that the band just couldn't shake audiences off. 'One week you'd play in a pub and there'd be ten people,' Watts says 'Next week there'd be thirty. After few years, ninety thousand. We never wanted for an audience, whether they were laughing at us or clapping us.'

Eventually it convinced Watts he could leave commercial art without starving, but not before the skills of his apprenticeship had made *High Flying Bird* possible. He was on his own in the Stones as a jazz fan though, and still is. 'Keith likes Louis Armstrong because he's a great blues player, and he's got good ears so he can't put any of the musicianship down. But basically I think Keith would sum jazz up as "toodly toodly".' Watts is the personification of self-effacement when he discusses his book and his record. ('I can't see many people playing it, but it was a nice thing to do.') A big part of his motivation when he put his Eighties big band together was exposure for British jazz musicians, some of whom (like bassist Dave Green, who he's known since he was ten) are his own age, some either side of it. CBS Records suggested augmenting the band with Wynton Marsalis when they went to the States, and Watts declined, insisting that he was showing Americans what Don Weller, or Bill Eyden or Annie Whitehead could do, not telling them something they knew already. This was a rejection of a public relations gift that only a showbiz star could afford. What he gets from making the Parker tribute, apart from glee at how well it panned out, is the thought that it might germinate more jazz lovers. 'These are just little cameos illustrating a book, though Peter put it together beautifully, and put himself into it much more than I had any right to expect. But if somebody likes it, then they might listen to Parker and go on to other things. You know, "Did he really, was he really, did he play like that?" That would be the best thing that could happen to me.'

KEEPER OF THE FLAME

The Guardian, May 1991

When Bill Evans died in 1980, a gaping hole opened up in the jazz world. There were plenty of pianists who could play fast bebop, quite a few (in the wake of Horace Silver and Evans himself) who could play with an emphatic, percussive sound, even one or two who had his firm, uncloying romanticism and improvisational vision. But someone who could knit all these qualities together and sound like a commanding and distinctive musical personality – that was a lot harder. Even Keith Jarrett, with his Standards Trio, would falter on the treacherous ground of an unseemly self-importance.

Downbeat magazine rightly regards Joanne Brackeen as one of the top five pianists on the world jazz scene, and though McCoy Tyner is a closer musical relative than Bill Evans, this remarkable California-born keyboard artist (a one-time collaborator with Stan Getz and Art Blakey) does convey much the same confidence that Evans occasioned, of consummate control, perfect taste, and bounding clear-sighted energy without hyperbole.

Tuesday's performance at the Bass Clef called up a lot of these echoes. Like Evans, Brackeen is too fastidious and tasteful to tolerate cliché, which she made deliciously evident through a mixture of surging chords, delayed accents and splashing Gershwinesque arpeggios on 'Tenderly'. Like Evans, she revealed in the same piece her skills in adopting the elements of a cliché and giving it a new twist, inquisitive where it was formerly bathetic, assertive where it was coy. And like Evans, too, she has a storming all-round technique and melodic imagination, that enable her to orchestrate simple themes into furious broadsides, suddenly spin clean, limpid melody out of chordal typhoons, and keep up long, twisting lines regardless of the beginnings and endings of the bars. A ferociously complicated funk original called 'Curved Space' (crisply negotiated by Andy Cleyndert on bass and the irrepressible Mark Mondesir on drums) erupted from a quirky left hand figure and fragments of Latin sounding chords, a reverberating unaccompanied version of 'Foolish Heart' displayed all Brackeen's rhythmic adventurousness and the subtle gradations of her touch, and the fast bop of 'Seven Steps' crackled with fresh phrasing and vibrant chord work.

THE COG SLIPS ON

The Guardian, May 1991

In recent years the long, loose frame of Cleveland Watkiss has regularly ambled on stage to collect the annual *Wire/Guardian* UK Jazz Awards for Best Vocalist. Watkiss, who, unlike many younger players, occupies a stage as if it were the most comfortable place on earth, usually takes the opportunity to draw attention to the sources of his inspiration – Africa, America and the blues. Watkiss's new album (*Blessing in Disguise*, on Polygram) and his recent show opposite Tania Maria at the Festival Hall certainly tell that story, with the tradition that spawned singers from Nat King Cole to Bobby McFerrin and Cassandra Wilson audible in it. But there are other strong undercurrents, notably of reggae and Indian classical music.

They're there because of the kind of London citizen Watkiss is, which is what makes his generation different from those earlier British jazz-based players who lived vicariously in New York and treated the realities of Hendon or Streatham as bad dreams. Watkiss is a one-time electrical engineer and sometime actor (he played the lead in a European touring production of *Hair* in the early Eighties) who lives in North London's Stamford Hill, one of a family of nine born to Jamaican Britons. 'If you do the bus journey from Seven Sisters through to Bethnal Green,' Watkiss says, 'you'll see every walk of life as well as original English – the communities of Sikhs, Jews, West Indians – and I saw all that growing up. So I didn't feel only part of West Indian culture, but part of a lot of different people.'

Watkiss arrived on the scene with bang, as a prominent figure in the rapidly risen black jazz scene of the mid-1980s, which had as its most spectacular vehicle the Jazz Warriors big band. His jazz leanings were clearly towards Bobby McFerrin, and smatterings of soul and Ray Charlesian blues (the last two favourites with Watkiss's DJ father). The young singer had a little of McFerrin's light, fluid sound and easy swing, and the American's relaxed and humorous stage presence too, the latter often making him the informal MC for the Warriors. But fast music unsettled him, scat singing and improvisation often pressured him (like a driver using too much throttle for his experience and technique) into running out of road, and he clearly hadn't yet found his feet. In the late Eighties he made an uneven DIY album called *Green Chimneys*, recorded at Pete Townshend's studios. Watkiss had been one of the backing singers on the 1989 Who tour of the States, and Townshend, a jazz lover with a saxophonist father, recognised the seriousness of the young artist's intentions, and his raw talent.

But despite exposure, on the London scene at least, though the record, through the Warriors, an early group of his own, and good deal of media interest following the jazz awards, Watkiss stepped back from the scene for a while in search of his personal lost chord. He thought a lot about the kind of Briton he really is, and *Blessing in Disguise* and his current repertoire are the result. McFerrin still pads gently around some of the music ('Be Thankful for What You Got' has recent McFerrinesque overdubbed harmonies), and Cassandra Wilson's three-stage downward-sliding notes are also there in the Indian influenced 'Don't Waste my Time'.

But much of it is pure Watkiss, a deftly chosen display of internationalism, improvisation and determination to be regarded, as he says, 'as a musician, not a "vocalist", to know as much as I can about music of all kinds. Monk didn't call his music jazz, neither did Ellington or Charlie Parker. It's a term of convenience, and today it might mean Bird to someone or Acker Bilk or Sade. I want to make music out of what's important to me – the M-Base in New York, Monk, reggae, Public Enemy, Billie Holiday, it's all there. And I can't help thinking of Africa, where it all came from. African drum and vocal improvising is very much like Monk's idea of improvising – if you listen, take an idea, and every chorus it will go like that [Watkiss makes twisting motion with his hands] the cog slips on a little bit, the shape keeps changing. It's very deliberate, and you have to understand black history and black culture to work it out.'

ESSENTIALIST
The Guardian, May 1991

Maybe the majestic seventy-year-old Pittsburg-born vocalist Billy Eckstine was making a point by performing a marathon opening set at Ronnie Scott's on Monday in which he wasn't off the spotlight for moment, but it's more likely he was just enjoying himself. As Eckstine glided smoothly through a repertoire of the kind of witty lyricism that made him the first black pop star in the pre-rock era, it was clear that virtually all of his considerable technique, with the occasional exception of projection, was in perfect shape.

Ballads have always been Eckstine's speciality, delivered in a vigorous, vibrato-laden baritone, and his versions of 'The Very Thought of You', 'Lush Life' and 'Good Morning Heartache' were gems of precision, tenderness, and the ability to make the smallest sound count in a manner that Harry Connick, for instance, still has to learn. And in combining a manner both startlingly youthful in firmness and rhythmic bounce with the rugged, phlegmatic, occasionally wistful qualities of his age, Eckstine was at one with his materials, engaging the music with a relish and commitment that captivated the house.

Eckstine got through an immense amount of material, without instrumental solos and without extensive embroidery, editing each song to its essentials. Tributes to Duke Ellington, Billy Strayhorn and Billie Holiday were highspots (without melodrama, Eckstine made the tenuous hold on sanity in 'Lush Life' achingly audible, and disconcertingly peeled back the shaky pragmatism of 'Good Morning Heartache') and the singer's long-time accompanist, Bobby Tucker, anticipated his every move with graceful fills and echoes at the piano as if thumping the cushions and dusting the furniture for his boss's every lustrous note to have a fitting place to land on.

Bassist Chris Laurence and drummer Tony Crombie performed with an emphatic confidence as if they were regular Eckstine sidemen. The resourceful young local pianist, Jason Rebello, is playing opposite Eckstine for this week with a fairly routine fusion band. In direct opposition to Eckstine, Rebello's group plays a great many notes and not all of them seem to crucially matter, but his solo strength and the guitar playing of Tony Remy still count for a lot.

CAPTAIN MARVEL

The Guardian, June 1991

That John Coltrane, one of the most explosive and impassioned of saxophonists, should have been an admirer of Stan Getz, one of the most reserved, is a measure of the respect accorded to the Philadelphia-born tenorist by musicians of every kind. At its best, Getz's music had an evaporating bloom on it, a petal-like fragility mixed with just enough hard swing and rough inflection to make its roots plain. Getz's elusive methods gave his listeners the right to expect something close to perfect symmetry in a music so often associated with the unfinished, the interrupted, the raucous and the fallible.

A master of ballad playing for nearly five decades, Getz often made the tenor saxophone sound more like a clarinet, or even a flute. And although his technique was remarkable, it was mainly put to the service of polishing and refining qualities of timbre and intonation rather than speed. It wasn't that Getz couldn't play fast when he felt like it, it was just that, with a throwaway dominance, he would hang a lightning arpeggio at the end of a coda, or as a dazzling fill between his habitual long silences and trembling sustained sounds. He wanted everything he played to have balance, dynamic logic, and above all meaning in the context of the song. . . . Getz didn't change the course of jazz, but his taste, storytelling skill and capacity for self editing are rare qualities in jazz today.

DEEP WATERS
The Guardian, June 1991

Maybe alto saxophonist Carlos Ward isn't leading one of the best jazz bands in years and Wednesday's first set at the Jazz Café was a fluke, but I doubt it. Ward, who is usually perceived as Abdullah Ibrahim's eloquent but essentially accommodating partner, is at the venue until Saturday right with an astonishing quartet featuring Michele Rosewoman (piano), Kenny Davis (bass) and Pheroan Aklaff (drums).

The band's performances this week are already a certainty for those 'Best of 1991' lists, but in searching for comparisons I was put in mind of an Ornette Coleman quartet show with the likes of Charlie Haden, Ed Blackwell and Dewey Redman which played in London back in the 1970s. Aklaff is a towering virtuoso, Ward displays a warm, emotional tone and all but perfect pitch control on both alto and flute, and the other two are a great deal more than supporting acts, though Rosewoman suffered a bit from being mixed down.

But the fact that they were all virtuosi wasn't the secret – in the 1990s, who isn't? The force of Ward's band lies in its deeper musicianship, a virtuosity under the control of an uncanny group empathy. Aklaff is phenomenal performer, a descendant of the Elvin Jones/Tony Williams line, endlessly shifting the focus of the beat around the kit, turbo-charged by the ferocity of a Ronald Shannon Jackson. His accompaniment is a typhoon of cymbal sounds of various colourations (bell-like at the centre, swishing rivets at the edge), hissing hi-hat flurries, rising and falling intensity in the snare offbeats and tireless stretching of accents towards and away from the beat, all the while maintaining a song-like coherence of shape.

Some of Ward's repertoire has the melodic quirkiness of Wayne Shorter tunes, and at times his alto approach took on an Ornette Coleman-like squawky urgency. But on slower pieces his remarkable tone is a gripping mixture of poignancy and defiance and his flute solo in the uptempo section of a piece that had begun as a Coltraneish dirge had a feathery lightness and the purity of a tuning fork. For those nervous of the sharp end, there was a delicious bluesy stomp to wrap up the set.

HEAVEN AND HELL
The Guardian, July 1991

The Rumanian born violinist Alexander Balanescu and the New York alto saxophonist, duck-call virtuoso and thrash metal dilittante John Zorn, meet at London's Place Theatre this week (from 23 July). They won't rehearse, and as yet have no idea what they'll play. They're brought together by one of the world's leading festivals of improvised music, Company Week, which has similarly spliced many performers of utterly disparate persuasions in its fourteen years of life. Yet Balanescu and Zorn are related by an energetic curiosity about music in their own time that transcends their differences, and they're also both Houdini-like about being packaged by anyone, friend or foe.

Balanescu, whose associations with Michael Nyman's music are widely celebrated, has also performed with his string quartet with the Pet Shop Boys at Wembley, and worked with film-maker Jim Jarmusch's musical partner, John Lurie. Zorn, one of the Eighties architects of deconstructivist music propelled by jazz, cartoon and movie soundtracks and European free improvisation, has become a commercial proposition through left-field but saleable recordings remoulding Ennio Morricone's spaghetti western themes, music for Mickey Spillane stories, even Ornette Coleman tunes reprocessed as impacted cough-and-you-missed-it thrash-jazz jams. Zorn loved jazz and remains a fluent and startling bebop altoist as well as an abstract impressionist and hardcore metal player. But as powerful as his teenage affection for bop was his absorption in American TV culture as a bedroom retreat from the constant domestic duelling of his parents, he says. Balanescu was the opposite, a solo violinist at nine who went through the classical mill, winding up at New York's Juilliard and then in one of Britain's most respected contemporary string quartets, the Arditti. But Balanescu in Romania, and Zorn in New York, both needed their escape routes.

'When I was a teenager living in Romania I listened a lot to jazz and I guess it represented some kind of image of freedom for me, but it faded,' Balanescu says. 'Lately I've got very interested in it again, but in the context of the whole range of improvised music, not just chord-based jazz for instance.' Britons John Surman, Andy Sheppard and Keith Tippett, and American jazz drummer and pianist Jack DeJohnette, all of whom Balanescu has recently worked with, exhibit that breadth of imagination too. If they had just been interested in variations on 'My Funny Valentine', or Balanescu in variations on Mozart, the connection would never have happened.

'When I studied at the Juilliard, I learned a tremendous amount but also learned to fight against people being trained to be machines,' Balanescu says with a glimpse of a smile. 'There were so many violinists of such high standard, trained to play loud, fast and in tune, but they left me cold. I would think about those older, pre-marketing era classical records, which didn't have the aim to do something perfect but to offer more of a conception about the work, like Bruno Walter's or Furtwangler's. They gave performances that jumped off the records, and I felt you had to expect something extraordinary from live performances too, where you don't know what's going to happen and it might be absolutely heavenly or absolutely hellish, but if it isn't like that you might as well listen at home. That's why someone like Menuhin, who maybe doesn't play so well any more, still has an attraction, he's unpredictable.

'Sometimes it's a question of context. Andy Sheppard's quintet is quite conventional in a way, but when he plays with Keith Tippett he's a different person.' But is a combination of personal unpredictability and a radical repertoire or a spontaneous one another phrase for seats without bums on them?

'Maybe so, but nevertheless I think it's important – it happens as a kind of lab for things that get into the mainstream later. And it doesn't have to be completely uncommercial. Look at John Zorn. He's an experimenter, yet he's managed to do things that are fairly direct and quite popular. He's communicative through adapting familiar material, blues or film music. I use memories, sometimes of ethnic music I've absorbed. An improvising situation is a wonderful feeling, but also terrifying, like being faced with a blank page. But I enjoy the mental process that starts happening, that all kinds of ideas and images come and sometimes they come together in a cohesive statement and sometimes they don't. But it's got to be almost instantaneous, and it depends a lot on what you're getting back from the others.'

KEEPING UP
The Guardian, July 1991

In his sixty-fifth year, it might be supposed that the whirlwind pace of an Oscar Peterson performance might have given way to more autumnal ruminations. But though Peterson now looks a little weary negotiating the distance from the dressing room to the piano stool, Monday's concert at the Albert Hall confirmed his old reputation for keyboard hellraising (rarely poetic but often thrilling in its way) to be firmly intact.

Peterson performed in the kind of band that doesn't permit an altogether unobstructed view of his skills – a quartet featuring Herb Ellis (guitar), the great Ray Brown (bass) and Jeff Hamilton on drums. Trios have generally suited him better, and unaccompanied performance best of all. The more musicians there are in a Peterson group, the more they all try to keep up, and the result can leave you feeling as peaky as being trapped in a group of non-stop talkers.

The standard Peterson offering – and there was plenty of it on Monday – is the uptempo tune (either a standard or an original that sounds like a standard) that starts either solo or with light accompaniment, grows in volume from both keyboard and drums in the second chorus and by the third is an unbroken cascade of keyboard-length runs resolving in thump-ing chords, thumbs-down-the-piano ripples and churning repeated phrases that even now exert an undeniable thrill of admiration.

On Monday Peterson applied this treatment to tunes that invited it – like 'Anything Goes' and 'Sweet Georgia Brown' – and those that conclusively didn't, like the dewy and delicate ballad in the first half that turned into this kind of burn-up and then bizarrely relapsed into caresses at the end. The best pieces on the show were the slow tunes that came later (presum-ably Peterson feels his audiences need reassuring with fireworks first) in which the band dropped back behind some deliciously liquid arpeggios and arching, drawn-out piano phrasing – spaciousness that also brought out the best in the majestic tone and time of Ray Brown. These ingredients made the bossa nova 'Tranquila' a delight.

ELLA

Q Magazine, July 1991

It's a routine observation that you don't learn much about Ella Fitzgerald from listening to her sing. The woman with one of the most flexible, pin-sharp and hard-swinging of all jazz voices hasn't got big by imposing a dominant personality on her songs, but by burnishing their inherent virtues to a gleam. Jim Haskins, however (*Ella Fitzgerald – A Life Through Jazz*, Hodder & Stoughton), has also proved that you don't learn much more about Ella Fitzgerald from writing her biography either.

This is a workmanlike book about Ella Fitzgerald's achievements, but she hasn't collaborated in it, and her friends and colleagues have been cagey and protective. Haskins hasn't made the pursuit of an elusive and private subject any easier by adopting a rigid one-damned-thing-after-another chronological approach that by the 1960s becomes a relentless sequence of awards, citations, patchy domestic fill-ins (decorating houses, cooking meals) and world tours.

Just why Ella Fitzgerald has been so popular for so long, and just what her consummate musicianship resides in, Haskins has clearly regarded as too slippery for his book, and he also has a fondness for bolt-on clichés like 'the gathering clouds of war'. It is useful on a reference level, aware on racism, and touching about her childhood and relationship with Chick Webb, the bandleader who discovered her, but it is stiff and formal, list-like by the end, and doesn't come close to mirroring the subject's famous onstage verve.

Too Wonderful
Q Magazine, July 1991

The American writer Francis Davis came out with the astute observation that Harry Connick's secret fear is that he's not as wonderful as he's certain everybody else thinks he is. It is a source of exasperation to some that a man so much stronger on showmanship and all-round amiability than the musicality and technical authority of his heroes (Sinatra, Nat Cole) should be treated as such as big deal, but as Davis notes, it is also part of his appeal that he hasn't really done anything wrong except be a self-confident kid with a relaxed stage style, and everybody else has done the rest.

You get all the pros and cons on this video (*Harry Connick Jr, Swinging Out Live*, CBS), which to Connick fans is over an hour of punchy big band music, a good many standards such as 'Nice Work if You Can Get It', 'Don't Get Around Much Any More', 'How Deep is the Ocean', 'Do You Know What it Means to Miss New Orleans' and twelve other pieces. Connick accompanies himself sporadically at the piano, but his piano playing has never been his greatest gift to music, a blend of Herbie Hancock, Errol Garner and Thelonious Monk, plus a confection of boogie and Latin music which brings the house down but generally doesn't have a fresh phrase anywhere in it.

Connick gently sends up his work (he mocks himself as a hoofer and as a crooner on 'All I Need Is The Girl' and even gently nips the audience for wanting him to keep the tempos up) and on 'How Deep Is the Ocean' turns in a genuinely affecting performance. But he is a long way from making every sound count like Sinatra, and a lot of his work simply sounds sloppy.

Time After Time
The Guardian, July 1991

I don't know how many members of the audience at the Festival Hall last Friday wished they could have been hearing Quincy Jones's epic Montreux rematch between Miles Davis and the Gil Evans orchestra instead of Davis's regular funk sextet, but it would be worth betting that those who did wouldn't all have been reliving a lost youth. After all, some young artists' chemistry between jazz and pop is now so much more sophisticated than the Davis group's sometimes rather headbanging version of it, that younger audiences might well be starting to say (to rearrange Miles's own quote) 'they don't play that way any more'.

Yet still nobody plays like Miles, cracked notes and more frequent latter day passivity about fitting into the structure included. About half of last week's unbroken two-hour set was good, and that's more than enough for most pilgrimages to the shrine of a sixty-five-year-old jazz giant. Davis delivered the material mainly from his recent WEA recordings, and the two ballads he first recorded on 1985's *You're Under Arrest*, which have become both favourites with audiences and vehicles for some of the most poignant remnants of his slowest improvising style.

In other words, it was more or less an all-funking evening, with the contrasts coming mostly from dynamics – big thrashing climaxes giving way to tiptoeing minimalist backings to Miles's diffident muted trumpet, ascending to ferocity again and back to whispers. Of the band, lead bassist (often effectively lead guitar), Joe Foley McCreary was his now familiar self – an inventive contrapuntal accompanist and rather melodramatic soloist; second bassist Richard Patterson applied jet propulsion to the bassline on fast funk and played a couple of breathtaking solos; pianist Deron Johnson was imaginative with texture, especially on organ; and drummer Ricky Wellman was a surprisingly dated-sounding snare-banging fusion player, really only at ease in furious crescendos. Davis's themes (particularly from the *Amandla* album) have grown more cryptically lyrical in recent years and the effervescent opener 'Jo Jo' is one of the strongest examples of it.

The first hour went by in kiss-and-punch extremes (Miles played a set of delectably curling variations on a slow organ-backed blues) but the band didn't really ignite until he unfurled his best solo of the night on Cyndi Lauper's 'Time after Time' – a mixture of fluttering double tempo runs, quietly clamorous fanfare-like sounds, and descending dolorous figures of soft, yearning yelps that one couldn't help thinking might have lodged in his brain from his celebrated *Sketches of Spain* get together with the Gil Evans band at Montreux the week before.

The band shifted into a steady, laid-back ticking funk beat which Kenny Garrett then dug into as Wayne Shorter once did with Tony Williams, playing much the same pulse, and they all wound themselves up around an eventually flamethrowing atonal tenor blast that would have been a credit to Pharoah Sanders or even Peter Brotzmann. This concentrated energy snapped the rhythm players into a groove which lasted for the rest of the set.

WILDFLOWER

The Guardian, September 1991

When Carla Bley, the bony, wire-haired, charismatic composer and pianist arrived on the jazz scene nearly thirty years ago, she was a rarity in a musical community that mostly bracketed women with sex, catering, sometimes finance and, at a pinch, singing. Bley's arguments for breaking loose were exclusively the quality of her work, since she dislikes gender debates, but her composing originality quickly made her one of the few women composers, in any area of music, to be accepted as a major creative force worldwide, a maverick with an instinct for avoiding the obvious.

She uses waltzes, Spanish civil war songs, marches, tangos, ragas, odd glimpses of Kurt Weill in her work, and quotes Erik Satie and the Beatles as influences alongside Charles Mingus and George Russell. She once said that her music set out 'to tickle tonality, not to overthrow it'.

Carla Bley was a church organist, competitive roller skater, cinema usherette and nightclub hat-check girl before she was a composer, she has married twice (both times to musicians who became close artistic partners), she is rarely seen in anything other than black, and she has a twenty-five-year-old daughter, Karen, who is a dead ringer for her and now leads her own band. She has won every kind of award, helped found artist-run record labels, distribution services and promotional organisations (she once wrote about herself and her like-minded contemporaries: 'we were the weeds, the wildflowers, the ones who had managed to survive without care'), played at Carnegie Hall, written for classical ensembles as well as jazz bands and been able to attract the finest interpreters including Keith Jarrett, Julie Tippetts (formerly Driscoll), Gato Barbieri, Robert Wyatt and Gary Burton.

This weekend (on Sunday, 1 September) she appears in a trio at Crawley's Outside In festival with bassist Steve Swallow (a man whose surname couldn't better reflect the motion of his electric bass lines, and with whom she now lives) and the British saxophonist Andy Sheppard, a musician whose idiosyncracies she empathises with. She was born Carla Borg in Oakland, California, in 1938, the daughter of church musicians (her father was a Swedish immigrant who met her mother at the Moody Bible Institute in Chicago) but her childhood piano lessons ended early when her technical wilfulness drove her father crazy and she bit her mother on the arm for good measure. She quit school at fifteen to work in a music store and by her late teens she was a jazz lover, taking jobs as a cigarette salesgirl at New York's Birdland club to get close to the music. She married an expatriate Canadian piano prodigy, Paul Bley, and travelled the States with him (she once told the writer Margo Jefferson that 'marriage was one of the few ways of locomotion for women' in those days).

Paul Bley, for his part, realised that this whimsical, ironic, poetic and musically freewheeling young woman had at least as much to offer him as the other way around. She started writing for Bley's group (strange, off-beat, rainy-streets pieces with titles like 'Floater' and 'Ida Lupino') and pretty soon for a queue of jazz luminaries, notably George Russell, Jimmy Giuffre and Art Farmer, and later Gary Burton, all of whom started recording her work. In the Sixties, with her second husband, trumpeter Michael

Mantler, she helped found the Jazz Composers' Orchestra Association (they had both given up on the commercial music business) and wrote and recorded a massive opera, *Escalator over the Hill*, which made her name. Bley is both a worrier and a reflexive, hedonistic California dreamer, which may be something to do with growing up in a Nordic domestic and religious culture rehoused on the West Coast. But it makes Bley's music what it is too, the same mixture of playfulness, dark broodings, *film noir* foreboding and hair-down exhilaration she herself emits.

Though she is showing the odd sign of bandleader's anxieties now, Bley's daughter Karen has never really been the same. 'I was never nervous about her,' Bley says. 'I knew she'd be all right. She was in my band when she was six or seven, and she played glockenspiel then. We took her on a tour of Europe for five or six weeks and she'd bring a book on stage and read it until it was time to come in, and then put it down and play.' Many of Carla Bley's current anxieties come from the financial state of the organisations she devoted much of her life too, now hit by recession economics. But the retreat the Eighties forced much exploratory art into hasn't diverted her conviction about writing what she knows. 'When I get down about things, Steve [Swallow] tells me I'm lucky there are fifty thousand people in the world who are interested in what I do, who'll buy a record or come to a gig. And he's right. I'd rather have my fifty thousand than a bigger audience that wanted me to do something different to what I do.'

But she opted for commercial music at least once, in the 1970s, when she joined Jack Bruce and Mick Taylor's road band as a pianist. 'I did that just for fun,' she observes matter of factly. 'All that stuff that bands are supposed to do in hotels, you know, changing the breakfast orders people would leave outside their rooms at night from coffee and yoghurt to coffee and seventeen bananas, that kind of thing. After it was over I decided to have my own road band, and once you do that of course, it stops being so much fun.' Being a bandleader isn't fun? 'I don't mind going up on stage but I long for the day when it would be okay for the composer to go on stage looking like a hag and not talk, not do all that artifice. I ask Steve, is this the tour for that, and he says, "not yet, not yet".' (She chuckles.) 'But since I've been teaching more, I've realised again that the music I loved back in Birdland in the Fifties is the music I love now. I know now that this music has stood the test of time, and it will turn out to be the great music of the age.'

MILES

The Guardian, September 1991

On those sultry early evenings a few weeks ago, the anonymous trumpeter who lives a street or two away from me had abandoned the classical exercises and the periodic blues and bebop he usually went in for, and was coaxing into uncannily perfect life the muted half whisper of Miles Davis's late Fifties ballad sound. I had heard Miles was in coma around about the same time as that sound drifted gracefully across the gardens. Somewhere on the planet, most hours of the day and night, a trumpeter picks up a horn and does just that, probably a lot more of them this past fortnight when it seemed that the always softly flickering candle of Miles Davis's artistry was finally about to go out.

He was truly a giant of twentieth-century music, and his admirers and imitators have laboured lovingly in pursuit of his secret since the late Forties, and increasingly in every corner of the globe. That distilled and restless sound was the essence of one of Miles Davis's finest and most influential records, the 1960 *Kind of Blue*. I gave it to myself as a Christmas present around 1966. Since nobody I knew then with thirty-two shillings and sixpence to spend on seasonal goodwill would have had the first idea where to look for a copy, or know who Miles Davis was, I thought it was the safest course.

For years afterwards, it was the jazz record I returned to more regularly than any other. It wasn't just the delicate, private, at times wounded poignancy of his sound, his sensitivity to timbre, the graceful swing achieved through space and delay as much as through his oblique utterances, his uncanny intimacy with the qualities and harmonic movement of the chords his improvisations were wreathing through, not even the presence on that disc of John Coltrane and Bill Evans. There was always something more elusive. When Spike Lee said 'do the right thing', it always brought Miles to mind.

For most of his life he did just that in his music, with a consistency astonishing for an improviser. It would often be a glancing statement, a cluster of notes and a pause, a ricochet off the rhythm section buried so deep in your expectation of what the right thing is that you would be astonished to your fingertips and find yourself exhaling '*yeaah*' at the same time.

There's a moment on *Kind of Blue* which all jazz fans recognize, one of the great here-and-gone moments in a music for which the evaporating instant is central to the attraction. It is an object lesson in perfect timing, one that's quoted by many jazz musicians and fans as the instant in which they truly fell in love with the music. After the stealthy, whispering ensemble theme of 'So What', drummer Jimmy Cobb makes a split-second switch from brushes to sticks, Miles hangs a single note out over what for an endless moment seems an unbearably long drop, before Cobb sets the rhythm rolling with a shimmering cymbal splash, the rivets sizzling on under Davis's suddenly swaying and weaving trumpet.

You could still be surprised by the audacity of that sudden devastating acceleration even after countless listenings – the inevitable and the astonishing at once. Miles Davis seemed to confirm inner symmetries, rhythms inside the heartbeat that transcended all differences of cultural and generational taste, and for his universal poetry he found an audience all over the world. My memories of Miles on record include the drawn out, evaporating, often imperfect trumpet lyricism of *Birth of the Cool* (Miles's identity was elusive enough to capture the switched-off ironic, Bomb Culture white beats of the Fifties, but lovers of the more vibrant qualities of jazz at the same time, because he was never cool inside), the quirky phrasing and urgent bop swing of the subsequent Fifties Blue Note recordings, and almost anything from *Kind of Blue*. They'd also take in the heat haze shimmer of 'Saeta' from *Sketches of Spain*, a breathtaking ensemble interplay with Wayne Shorter and Herbie Hancock through the Sixties (some of the greatest moments in postwar small group jazz interplay), and the increasingly cryptic lyricism and unexpectedly growing jauntiness of some of his jazz funk exploits (notably from the WEA *Amundla* album) of recent years.

He could still turn it on in his remarkably long single set live shows too. In July this year, Miles unfurled a delectable solo on Cyndi Lauper's 'Time after Time' that mingled fluttering double tempo runs, quietly clamorous fanfare-like sounds, and descending dolorous figures of soft, yearning yelps that went all the way back to *Sketches of Spain*. The latter echo might well have come from a made-in-Heaven reunion of the trumpeter with a replica of Gil Evans's *Sketches of Spain* band at the Montreux Festival the week before. One of my profound regrets will always be that I didn't hear that show. A profound relief is that Miles Davis finally agreed to perform on it with only months to live, because it probably gave him more pleasure than he would admit to, and gave its witnesses a memory to burnish for ever. But then, maybe he knew all along.

SVENGALI: (MUSICIANS' TRIBUTES TO MILES DAVIS)
The Guardian, September 1991

Dave Holland (Miles Davis's bassist, 1968-70)

Miles taught me that the more naturally the music develops the more real it is, and he was a master of creating the conditions for something to happen. That's why it was way off line for Wynton [Marsalis] to have shown disrespect for a man who's made it possible for him to be what he is. Miles did a concert in Vancouver once and Wynton came on stage in the middle of the show, to sit in. Miles just stopped the band. He gestured Wynton over, and then said in his ear in that big hoarse whisper, 'Come back tomorrow night.' Miles wasn't going to be there the next night, of course.

When I joined Miles, I didn't get a bundle of music in the mail, or a rehearsal, or any idea of what to do. One day I was a London bass player, next day I was opening with Miles at the Count Basie Club in Harlem. But he knew that if somebody's right for a situation, you're not going to have to tell them a lot about what to do, because if they're right, they already know, even if they don't realise they know.

We hear the result of music, but the process is what's important. And since Miles is a connection to Bird, who's a connection going back into the fundamentals of jazz, that faith in the process gets handed on.

Andy Sheppard (saxophonist)

I think Duke Ellington called Miles the Picasso of modern music and that's how he seemed to me. Some people only like him in a certain period, but I like all of it, it's a monumental achievement. He had an amazing ability to seek out new talent and get the chemistry right in his bands, and he had a sound like you could recognise halfway through the first note, which was true from the Fifties through to last month. Incredible.

Mike Gibbs (composer)

I met him a few times and he scared the hell out of me, you felt he could see through everybody. But at Montreux this year when he worked with Quincy Jones on the *Sketches of Spain* collaboration with Gil Evans's musicians, it was different. He was painfully thin but he had these lavish clothes on, which hung off him and he was surrounded by a heavy entourage which kept people away.

There was a noon rehearsal and he arrived at eleven that night, and clearly couldn't get his fingers round the written parts. Next day he was a little better, then they shooed everybody out of the hall and said he wanted to rehearse in peace. I don't know what happened between then and the concert, but it was phenomenal. Wallace Roney was playing his written parts and sounded great, but like the Sixties records – but Miles's solos were nothing like the records, they sounded completely new. It really lifted the hairs on the back of my neck. After Charlie Parker he had to be the greatest giant in jazz for me.

John Harle (classical saxophonist)

For someone like me, interested in adapting jazz materials in my own way, it's like him dying has suddenly released *Porgy and Bess* or *Sketches of Spain*, it snapped me out of romantic attachment to that material the way he and Gil Evans did it. Those records for me remain the highest attainments in music that is almost uncategorisable. And, while he was alive, they seemed untouchable.

Steve Swallow (bassist)

I heard about his death driving my car around midnight, and the announcer broke it gently to the listeners, and then started playing his records from the Charlie Parker band onwards. I slowed down to around 40 m.p.h. on a 65 m.p.h. road so I wouldn't get home until I'd heard it all. I remembered that when I was sixteen and came to New York I used to keep visiting Eugene O'Neill's *The Iceman Cometh* with Jason Robards, and after the show I'd run around the corner to the Café Bohemia where Miles was trying out various versions of what became the great Fifties quintet that included Coltrane and Red Garland. I heard several versions, one with Tommy Flanagan and Sonny Rollins, and it was all so fantastic that it made me decide to be a jazz musician there and then. I owe Miles that. A lot of people owe him something like it.

John Scofield (Miles Davis's guitarist, 1983-85)

It was the perfect example of going with your gut instinct. He drove it home more than anybody, and if he had an idea it would almost always be the thing that made everybody fresh, spark things off, even if he only brought it up just before you were about to start recording or something. And he was smart enough to know you work with people for what they can do, you can't get them to be something they aren't. I really liked him a lot, but of course there was a lot of idol worship from all of us who worked with him. He could be very charming, and he was also one of the angriest people I ever met. I'm not sure what that came from, but I'm sure he had a reason.

EPITAPH

The Guardian, October 1991

'My music is evidence of my soul's will to live,' said Charles Mingus, that active volcano of a jazz composing genius who packed such an incendiary mixture of blistering and lyrical music, convivial and delinquent behaviour, personal politics and hyper-sensitivity into his career years 1945 to 1979 as to make many high-output jazz artists seem semi-conscious.

Mingus was behind a number of the most enduring compositions in jazz, but in the Eighties the world came to hear work on a different scale even by Mingus's or his hero Ellington's remarkable standards. The work was

Epitaph, a two-and-half-hour epic written over twenty years, abandoned undiscovered in a box in the Minguses' apartment until 1979, and unearthed after the composer's death by Montreal musicologist Andrew Homzy.

It was lovingly reassembled by Gunther Schuller – for over three decades one of the most energetic and scholarly of all academia's pro-jazz campaigners – and immediately poleaxed the cognoscenti. Blending improvisation and composition more ambitiously than anywhere else in the Mingus canon, splicing styles as diverse as Dixieland, a Jelly Roll Morton tribute and uncategorisable sections revealing the composer's interest in twentieth-century non-jazz composers such as Schoenberg, Stravinsky and Bartok, it's a fearsome challenge to improvisers, most of whom rarely stray from one style. All of Mingus's moods, from the darkest to the most exuberant, are contained in it.

The work turned up only because Mingus's widow Susan located the box in a cupboard when Andrew Homzy was collating her late husband's scores and notes. Homzy found a stack of yellowed sheet music, a foot and a half high, containing themes he didn't recognise. When he discovered that each bar was numbered from one to over three thousand the penny dropped that this was huge integrated work. They called Gunther Schuller, an old friend of Mingus and the expert who unquestionably understood the mechanics of the composer's work best.

'I nearly jumped through the ceiling,' Schuller recalls. 'Because though I was a very close friend of Charles Mingus, he's never mentioned in our long association that he'd written such a piece.' There had been a disguised attempt to record at least some of it, on a live concert at the Town Hall, New York in 1962. But Mingus was so far behind with the arranging on that occasion that the copyists were still working on the parts at a desk on stage during the gig, he was about to be sued by Jimmy Knepper for knocking one of the trombonist's teeth out during a discussion over the arrangements, and liaison with United Artists' engineers was so ill-organised and intrusive that many of the listeners demanded their money back. Gunther Schuller believes Mingus's sense of bitterness and humiliation about the fiasco led him to make a secret of it for the rest of his life.

Schuller believes the very early *Self Portrait* (also called *Chill of Death*, which supports the contention that Mingus already intended this to be his valediction even when barely out of his teens) to be among the composer's although it was written without space for improvisation, reflecting Mingus's interest in modern classical composers. 'There's also multi-layered activity with seven or eight strands of music all in different metres, that's very Charles Ivesian,' Schuller observes. 'Though I don't think he knew much about him. He absorbed other people's concepts and renewed them through his own music, and the reason they come out specifically different because he was finally a jazz musician and he translated these materials into jazz language.

'Pieces like *Pithecanthropus Erectus* or the *Fables of Faubus* are masterpieces for small groups, but you can't get very multi-layered with five instruments. Once he had this conception of a thirty-one piece orchestra he fully exploited it the way Ellington used his orchestra, or Brahms used his. That's why I would say this is one of the most monumental achievements in the history of jazz in terms of composition, and in specific musical, conceptual and even technical ways even going beyond Ellington. Most jazz is a tune, usually based on somebody else's changes and then a bunch of improvisations and then you play the head again, and ninety per cent of it is still done that way. This piece stands almost alone in the scope and vision with which it tries to break through all those bounds, and that's where Mingus is the true heir of Duke Ellington, of course.'

SOON COME

The Guardian, October 1991

Steve Williamson is one of the most distinctive and commanding instrumentalists to have emerged from the Jazz Warriors stable that nurtured the black British jazz resurgence of the 1980s. Mostly indifferent to standards-playing and bebop revivalism, Williamson's inspirations lie in New Yorker Steve Coleman's line of jazz evolution based on the subtle and supercharged rhythms of contemporary funk and the rhythm-as-melody patterns of rap. Obsessed with the technical conundrums of the method, Williamson has sometimes been over-deliberate and mathematical in his saxophone playing, so who his partners are makes a lot of difference to the temperature of the show.

The new album (*Rhyme Time* on Verve) from which much of Monday's material was taken also features Cassandra Wilson among others, but the Jazz Café band did include a player not known for devotion to the impassive M-Base funk style in keyboardist Django Bates. Bates thus lent a vivid, splashy impressionism to a music otherwise built on the interweaving of rhythm motifs between horns, percussion and bass, which probably cheered up more orthodox jazz fans even if it was irrelevant to younger, rap-reared groovers whose idea of a tune is quite different.

Williamson began with two such fast, clattery pieces ('Soon Come', from his last album and 'Hip Revisited' from the new one), and in both revealed that his tone is now fuller and more resonant, particularly on sustained sounds. Bates cheerily hurled the attractive anachronism of what sounded like an accordion solo into the middle of the second piece, and Williamson revealed a sharpness about shaping the performance by using the closing notes of 'Hip Revisited' as the opening theme for his third feature, 'Running Man'.

Partly because of the indefatigable Mark Mondesir on drums, the sextet (occasionally augmented by a third bassist) now performs this unswerving collective soliloquy of rhythm with immense tautness, and the effect is compulsive listening, despite the absence of regular lyricism. In a conservative jazz age, Williamson is single-minded enough to make his lean, unsentimental, New York-driven music stick.

LOGICIAN
The Wire, October 1991

Ne Plus Ultra (Hat ART CD 6063, recorded 14 September, 25 October 1969.) This is one of the late West Coast tenorist Warne Marsh's best recordings, made at the point when his celebrated melodic inventiveness was beginning to mesh with more active rhythm sections than had happened under the iron rule of Lennie Tristano.

Much of the music is from the Tristano repertoire, including a scurrying, sliding 'Lennie's Pennies', in which Marsh exchanges his squawky-toned rumblings and bar-jumping legato runs with Foster's more amiable-sounding horn, the two circling around each other for several choruses, moving into a tussle, and winding up with a deliciously freewheeling high counterpoint. '317E 32nd' and 'Subconscious Lee' are similarly delivered with buzzy, unflamboyant relish, and the restraint (not to say downright censorship) that Marsh exercises over familiar diversions such as will-this-do volume changes, references to bolt-on licks from the jazz musician's traditional fallback position of blues, highlights his extraordinary linear inventiveness and freedom in riding over the regular architecture of a tune.

The style thus has a pristine quality that may have helped people to label it unemotional. But there's plenty of emotion in Marsh, just very little *emotionalism*. That's what makes him such a refreshing alternative in post-war jazz.

THE THRILL ISN'T GONE
The Guardian, October 1991

Nobody who likes jazz in its most spontaneous and unpredictable guises much enjoys big-venue gigs and 'all-star' orchestras – the sound systems usually homogenise soloists' timbre, the solos are too short, too loud and too melodramatic and the cheerleading atmosphere of organised fun gives

you a headache. Monday's show at the Albert Hall had all the apparent
symptoms but it delivered.

B.B. King, resplendent in cummerbund, dress shirt and patterned gold
jacket, was inevitably the main reason why the temperature shot up in the
second half, but the Gene Harris Superband (including genuinely super-
status soloists like James Moody, Ray Brown and Harry 'Sweets' Edison)
and singer Dianne Reeves left the crowd far from indifferent in the warm-
up. Reeves, extensively promoted as one of Blue Note's new stars in recent
times, is a fine orthodox jazz singer with good time, dramatic range and
agile jazz phrasing and if her classicist's respect for the tradition and her
occasionally perplexing weighting of lyrics allow her to evolve into more
distinctive personality, she may yet fill the yawning gap left by Sarah
Vaughan. But on King's arrival, everything went bananas.

He took the stage stony-faced, gave the band the double thumbs-up and
hurled himself into 'Let the Good Times Roll', just to break the ice. But
traditional blues shouting meets tough competition with a bristling band
like this one and it was on slower pieces, with minimal backing, that
King's operatic, incantatory style and ever-enticing guitar mix of violin-
like delicacy and hammering emphasis really bloomed. Ray Brown's bass,
a rock-like underpinning of the band all night, added particular tautness
to the quieter music, and by the time they got to 'The Thrill is Gone',
Brown's bass and Gary Smulyan's pumping baritone sax drove King to
that particular pitch of manic dignity which is uniquely his.

BODY AND SOUL

Q Magazine, November 1991

Coleman Hawkins's contemporaries were horrified by the physical
decline in such a charismatic artist towards the end of his life, but were just
as often amazed by his ability to produce impressive performances when
he seemed uninterested in anything that didn't arrive in a cognac bottle.
The contrast is pretty sharp here (*Coleman Hawkins in Jam Session and
Concert*, VidJazz 4) because the material comes from a stage-managed jam
session recorded for TV in New York in 1961 with Hawkins dapper,
vibrant and ferociously inventive, and a concert appearance several years
later in which he looks lost, scrawny and uninvolved, though his playing
still slams home.

Though there's a lot of fake jam-session bonhomie (a voice-over called
William Williams signs off with 'What say we make the scene again next
week?' and a woman informally attired in what appears to be a sequined
bathing suit dances occasionally), the playing on the early takes is dynamic, particularly from Hawkins himself, who launches into a sensational

version of 'Lover Man', attacking this usually wistful tune as if attempting to bite its leg. By 1966 his sound is more blurred and has lost most of its assertiveness, but still has its melodic freshness. The set of four tunes, including 'Body and Soul' also has the immense benefit of a scintillating Benny Carter, contrasting with Hawk in his feathery sound and sleek lyricism, but with an intelligence of construction that almost rivals him. Hawk rushes at 'Body and Soul' as if wearily anxious to get it done.

1992

*Symbolic occurrence of the year in the British jazz world was the accelerating
collapse of the national network of Regional Jazz Associations that had been set up
in the 1970s as subsidiaries of the Arts Council's local offices. Recession and
bums-on-seats values were tightening on the arts, and simultaneously a growing
cross-culturalism was leading to questions about why jazz was more entitled to
its own local arts agents than other forms were. But this national network of
advisory and seed-money bureaux had proved invaluable to practitioners of an art
form so disproportionately starved of funds, and it had helped many enthusiastic
but inexperienced promoters to get started.*

*This change went hand in hand with an increasingly hard-nosed commerciality
that seemed inclined to define 'good music' in terms of how many people pay for a
ticket.*

If Time *Magazine had run its 'New Jazz Age' cover in 1990, the press reports
were turning their backs on the idea by 1992. In London, the expensive and
ambitious Jazz Café project had gone bust, the Jazz FM radio station was in crisis,
and the generous contracts major record companies had offered to young jazz stars
a year or two before were being withdrawn. But just the same, there were qualities
about the new British jazz scene that the wider world was waking up to. The
revitalised American-run Blue Note label signed Stan Tracey (the most creative
elder statesman of British jazz) and Andy Sheppard too, while the jazz-funk label
GRP took young inventors Phil Bent (flute) and Tony Remy (guitar).*

*But if one of the symptoms of Jazz FM's insecurity about unconventional music
during 1992 showed up when the management fired a jazz-loving DJ on
air, unconventional music nevertheless surfaced on many fine live shows, like
the multi-national Dedication Orchestra's rekindling of the memory of the
prematurely departed South African emigrés Chris McGregor, Dudu Pukwana,
Mongezi Feza and Johnny Dyani; like the new-generation Cape emigré Bheki
Mseleku's work with the cream of younger New York sidemen; like West Country*

pianist Keith Tippett's tirelessly impressionistic and vivid free-improvising.

Once again, ex-Miles men and an ex-Miles woman also convincingly delivered – Jack DeJohnette with a muscular mix of postbop and world-fusion, percussionist Marilyn Mazur by galvanising one of the best-ever Jan Garbarek bands, and Tony Williams, Wayne Shorter, Herbie Hancock, Dave Holland and Wallace Roney with a Miles Davis tribute band that was movingly true to both Miles's spirit and theirs. Hermeto Pascoal and Tuck and Patti were vastly entertaining (savagely distorted Chick Coreaism in Pascoal's case, jaw-dropping gospel-jazz virtuosity in Tuck and Patti's) and tenorist Joe Henderson was the best bop-based improviser to visit Britain all year, displaying a tumbling improviser's imagination and effortless avoidance of cliché that rivals Sonny Rollins. Keith Jarrett's Standards Band played a delicious first half at the Festival Hall in the autumn, before Jarrett's relentless paranoia that he was being unlawfully recorded wrecked the second – and Betty Carter sounded more balefully, broodingly compelling than ever.

FROM THE TOP

The Guardian, January 1992

New Year's Day's Dedication Orchestra concerts represented a different form of reclamation of jazz history to the usual postmodernist bebop reruns. They brought back the spirits and skills of the prematurely-departed South Africans who so vividly helped refashion the London jazz scene with a mixture of townships dance and jazz in the Sixties and Seventies. Dudu Pukwana, Chris McGregor, Harry Miller, Mongezi Feza and Johnny Dyani may have gone in physical form, but their musical presence made Wednesday's shows at the 100 Club with a twenty-four-piece orchestra one of the inevitable high-points of 1992, whatever exotica and expertise the year otherwise brings.

Much of the material was originally written for Chris McGregor's Brotherhood of Breath, but it returned like a Brotherhood sometimes dreamed of in the old days, when you wished they'd have practised stopping and starting in the same place. This was such a lissome blend of tight discipline and freewheeling improvisation as to be an entirely different story, enhancing the qualities of these joyous pieces and the spontaneous poetry of the soloists equally. Among the players, the mingling of younger stars like Django Bates, Claude Deppa and Guy Barker with more grizzled ones like Evan Parker, Alan Skidmore, Keith Tippett and Harry Beckett led to a fascinating kaleidoscope of orthodox and free techniques, the two persuasions not only creatively mixed between the musicians but within individuals too.

On one characteristic confection of stomping trombone riffs and searing trumpet figures, Evan Parker inserted a delectable slow solo with Tippett's darting piano for company, passing through almost-conventional lyricism, abstract split-notes and harmonics and ending on a Ben Webster-like vibrato; Elton Dean was as rambunctiously atonal as Harry Beckett's trumpet was amiably jaunty; Django Bates's tenor horn sounded, as it usually does, like a bebop flugelhorn solo. The three vocalists (Julie Tippetts, Maggie Nichols and Phil Minton) were mixed too low but oscillated between choral stateliness and crackling instrument-like effects with just as much relish.

But as was appropriate for the last surviving member of the South African Blue Notes, the night belonged to Louis Moholo on drums. Closely shadowed by Tippett and Paul Rogers's bass, he was everywhere in the music, with a torrential display of hissing cymbal figures, military tattoos sliding into free eruptions, climactic snare-drum gunfire. The music will be available on CD from March, and it'll feel like a long wait.

TIMBRES FROM TIMBERLAND

The Guardian, February 1992

If you found yourself described by the hard-nosed American musical visionary George Russell as 'just about the most uniquely talented jazz musician Europe has produced since Django Reinhardt' you could be sure – Russell having worked with Charlie Parker and Dizzy Gillespie and influenced Miles Davis and John Coltrane – you were doing something right. Russell heard in Garbarek's poignant and desolate timbre, with its startling evocations of wind-blown snowscapes, alternations of quivering cries and sudden trumpet-like crispness and occasional folk-dance playfulness, a contemplative intelligence that stood out from endless photocopies of jazz landmarks. Now Jan Garbarek is a musical celebrity in his native Norway, recognised as one of European jazz music's all-time originals, has worked with leading figures in jazz including the pianist Keith Jarrett. He begins a short British tour this week with an excellent quartet including German virtuosi Rainer Bruninghaus and Eberhard Weber, and ex-Miles Davis percussionist Marilyn Mazur.

Garbarek's music, with its intense focus on tone colour rather than rhythmic momentum or tobogganing chord-changes owes at least as much to the landscape of the northern lights and its folk-forms as it does to jazz. By following his instincts and listening to his surroundings, he also unintentionally found an international audience outside the jazz cognoscenti. By audibly retaining some of the mechanics of orthodox jazz but in a non-jazz context, echoing a minimalism influential through the arts in the Eighties, and even voice-in-a-landscape New Ageism (though sharpened and toughened by improvisation) Garbarek has been both an original and an artist who has suited his time.

'I begin to see jazz as a completed art-form now,' Garbarek says. 'You can go on a four year course in it now, and come out playing any jazz style well. I played my share of bebop in the early Sixties for instance, and I feel it's done now. When Miles died they showed TV clips of his early bands and it sounded so good, in a way that even the best of the young players can't repeat. Because it's not a matter of technical facility, but the fact that those chords and that phrasing were new then, they carried a whole new creative aura. Miles always created space around himself too, and that was very enlightening to me.'

Garbarek took up the saxophone because he heard Coltrane on the radio ('that *sound* seemed to convey the spirit of the man, and the fact that a sound could do that really turned me on'.) But as a fourteen-year-old he didn't even know that what Coltrane was playing was jazz. Thirty years later, Garbarek has not only extensively explored an intensely personal music but worked interpretively, writing scores for Norwegian productions of Ibsen's plays including *Brand* and *Pier Gynt*. His music has also echoed sounds from Bali, Amer-Indian music, even from India – Garbarek has performed with Ravi Shankar on an album called *Song for Everyone*.

'For a long time I've found myself interested in music trying to break free of the boundaries of jazz, and of other musics too,' Garbarek says. 'In Norway when I was starting there was a good jazz scene, but our folk music was always on the radio too, an influence you couldn't escape, like the sounds of the cattle calls, which affected me a lot. That isn't an interactive music like jazz, or an improvisational one, but it is a music of space, a backdrop I could move against, and a lot of jazz sounds very cluttered to me. I felt I needed to go back to folk roots in jazz, but not by going to African roots that aren't mine, but my roots as a Norwegian musician.'

YANKEE DOODLE DANDSKI

The Guardian, January 1994

'Yankee Doodle Dandy' may have been playing on the palace phonograph on the night Prince Yusupov was trying to persuade the Mad Monk to lie down, but the relationship between jazz and Rasputin's part of the world blew hot and cold for decades afterwards. During the Soviet-Allied pact of the war years, it was in. Later, the authorities hounded jazz as bourgeois self-indulgence, forcing saxophonists to re-register with the state music agency as bassoonists or oboists, consigning some to the Gulag, even compelling the Riga Conservatory to drop a Prokofiev piece with a saxophone part in it. As late as 1963 Kruschev boomed, 'When I hear jazz, it's as if I had gas on the stomach.'

The Gorbachev years though, saw as big a change, with major festivals of Russian jazz and new music, and visits to the Republics by Sun Ra, Chico Freeeman and the Leaders, Gunther Schuller with the Mingus Dynasty orchestra, the Willem Breuker Kollektief and many others. The opened doors made possible the ten-part series beginning on Channel 4 tonight, the most substantial examination of new music from the Republics ever broadcast in Britain, or anywhere else for that matter. It takes in surreal Pop Mechanics pianist Sergei Kuryokhin (this newspaper called his 1989 Liverpool show 'divine madness'), Russian new jazz guru Vyacheslav Ganelin, gypsy-improv queen Valentina Ponomareva and a score or so of other artists working in territory all the way from near-jazz to folk music and academic music, from home-made instrumentation to standard line-ups.

That the formerly Soviet jazz is understood at all in the West, and that this series should ever have been made, are successes principally down to the energies of one man. Leo Feigin, a 54-year-old Leningrad-born expatriate Russian Jew is a broadcaster with the BBC's World Service and the presenter of the C4 series. He's an explosively ebullient jazz enthusiast who formed his cottage-industry record label, Leo Records, in 1979 when he was smuggled a tape by the Vilnius-based Ganelin trio in the days when bootleg Russian underground music was remorselessly policed.

When Feigin and several other aficionados first listened to that Ganelin recording in 1979, they were astonished by the vitality, virtuosity and wit of a form of the music that could have come from nowhere else but a country incapable of taking jazz for granted. By 1984, when the Ganelin trio finally arrived in Britain for a widely acclaimed Arts Council tour, Leo Records was already well under way. Feigin supports the label with more commercial releases and non-Russian music too, and his Cecil Taylor session *Live in Bologna* was the pick of 1988 in this newspaper. Two years ago, Feigin's crowning achievement was the release of an eight-CD set – some sublime, some indigestible – of new Russian music. It was a long way from the discs he first knew.

'When I was living in Russia [he left for Israel in the early 1970s] you could get good records, but it was all black market. The price of a good album on the black market was the equivalent to almost a month of an average salary. But by Soviet standards I had a very good collection, maybe 80 records by 1970. In 1988 I had to go away and work for three years in the middle of nowhere, and I paid a guy a lot of money then, 80 roubles, to tape all his collection so I wouldn't be lonely. And I met a fan there. Let me tell you, to sit in a place 3,000 miles away from Moscow and listen to Miles Davis, that's really something.

'I was a regular visitor to Leningrad Jazz Club. There were people who imitated Charlie Parker beautifully, like Gennadi Golstein – his nickname was Charlie – who had it all, the flow, the tone, the fluency. It was all information he had painstakingly collected over years in bits and pieces.'

Virtually all Russian jazz musicians are conservatoire trained, some of them playing jazz an an adjunct to straight orchestral work or movie sound-tracks. Anatoly Vapirov, one of the most celebrated Russian jazz saxophonists until his arrest for black-market speculation and eventual emigration to Bulgaria, was a faculty head at the Leningrad Conservatoire.

'Before Russians discovered free jazz they had to imitate, and jazz for them was a symbol of someone else's freedom,' Feigin says. 'Jazz was ten years ahead of glasnost.' Feigin thinks there are still challenges, maybe tougher ones than ever. 'They still have to make their music accessible and available to listeners, and now in conditions of total chaos economically and politically. But the biggest change of recent times has been the influx of musicians from the outside. Everyone goes there to play now. I've recorded Valentina Ponomareva with John Zorn and Bill Laswell, and a lot of American and European musicians have toured. Russian music will now merge with other musics. It's inevitable. The door is open.'

IMPROVISATION

The Guardian, February 1992

'Perhaps the air of mystery that surrounds it is inevitable,' began Derek Bailey, presenting the first of Jeremy Marre's sweeping four-part study of the role of improvisation in the world's music. 'Improvisation is to do with change, adjustment, development, elusive ideas.'

The driving force of the Channel 4 series is that improvisation is the most widely practised of all musical activities yet the least understood, and the least encouraged by the music industry because the risks involved may damage the saleability of a package. *On the Edge* is the result of an ambitious, perceptive and expensive musical world tour, exploring the improvisational core of medieval and baroque art music, jazz, blues, African, Indian and Scottish traditions, in locations as far apart as the organ loft at Le Sacré Coeur to Hebridean churches and the banks of the Ganges. In the films, and in Derek Bailey's book *Improvisation* (which was the inspiration for the series), musicians constantly describe the liberating, unsettling, and sometimes triumphant impact improvised music making has on them.

'People are given power in my pieces, and it's interesting to see which

people like to run with that power, which people like to run away from it, who are very docile and do what they're told and who try very hard to get more power. It's a scary, frightening thing to see these people blossom when they're in that band and become the . . . the . . . assholes that they really are.'
John Zorn, American composer, improviser and multi instrumentalist.

'It's a great adventure and a learning process for me. I find things out about myself as well as the other musicians. It gives me a lot of strength. This is quite a difficult thing for a classically trained musician to be doing. You don't have the music to hide behind. After each night I feel a sense of achievement because I've gone through it and managed to express something.'
Alexander Balanescu, Romanian classical violinist.

'Mozart's diaries record how he wrote a passage that he knew the audience would like and sure enough they burst into applause, in the middle of the movement. Who would dream of applauding in the middle of a movement in today's performances? However if you hear a jazz player play a great lick the audience applauds immediately

'If the average concert goer pauses to think that he or she has probably heard every work of Mozart's not only twice as many times but arguably hundreds of times more than the composer himself it says something about our ability to be flexible. The most important thing is the willingness to take risks and the acknowledgement that doing so invests the artist statement with a level of integrity and personality and uniqueness that nothing else can do.'
Robert Levin, American classical pianist, who improvises extensively in performing Mozart.

'The tradition of improvised music has survived in the liturgy . . . because of its practical function during the service. My improvisation is of course an offering to the Lord and I always try to do the best I can and though it is not always wonderful, it is my offering.'
Nagie Hakim, organist at the Sacré Coeur, Paris.

'It was like being given a pair of wings, it was an incredibly liberating experience. The first night I used up all my general ideas, like doublestopping, lip trills and certain kinds of sound. By the third night I wished I'd been a bit more sparing with them. I was never sure whether to play with people or against them, or to react to them. I had to evolve, very quickly, a new way of listening.'
Philip Eastop, English classical horn player.

Skaters

The Guardian, May 1992

On two successive nights in the same room at the Bass Clef, two female singers – one American, one British, and with thirty-odd years between them – ran through the rule book on putting craft to the service of feelings.

For Sheila Jordan, the Detroit-born singer with first-hand inspirations from Charlie Parker and pianist Lennie Tristano, a meticulous musicality articulates a private waywardness that has made her utterly unique since the Fifties. A small, dark, humorous-looking woman who clutches the mike close to her face with both hands, like a squirrel with a nut, Jordan ice-skates through an improvising style of her own making in that un-wavering, implacable, melodically ingenious manner which Gary Giddins called her 'cantorial ardour'. She hands audiences no ready-made reactions, and shines remorseless light on classic lyrics and some strong originals, some written by her superb pianist Steve Kuhn.

Sue Shattock, the young British vocalist who in 1988 revealed she had skill, tantalising timing and heart, and then promptly buried it all in an overheated fusion band that could have featured more or less any singer, demonstrated the next night on a rare London appearance that in the right playing circumstances (another intimate piano duo, in her case with Terry Disley) none of her manic chemistry of boppish improvisional agility, wil-ful slews from a confiding whisper to a panicked yelp and bursts of raw-nerve disclosure had faded, and if anything it was delivered with a this-is-my-show panache that hadn't been there before. In a repertoire that includes Annie Ross, Van Morrison, Paul Simon and Pat Metheny, and both a more theatrical dynamic range and onstage presence, Shattock meets an audience halfway, more than Jordan, with her canny, laconic delivery and absence of sentiment. But they're both women who can improvise like instruments without their personalities disappearing and who express emotions the audience knows inside out, but in ways it doesn't see coming. If jazz singing means anything today, that's it.

Don't shoot the Pianist Any More

The Guardian, May 1992

A piano player in an Ornette Coleman band? To the man's fans it's a proposition as likely to be believed as announcing M. C. Hammer is using a harpist. Coleman's overriding drive in a visionary jazz career has been to banish the fixed pitch of the keyboard and unleash an urgent, seething form of collective improvisation in which key centres spontaneously shift, and soulful, bluesy, bent-pitch intonation gets the show to itself.

As well as the piano, Coleman has been adding an engagingly dated showpiece paraphernalia of synchronised lights, spangly suits and Las Vegas announcements to his still impulsive, ricocheting, teeth-rattling music. But it was still reverberatingly Prime Time, the electric band that Coleman formed in the Seventies after two decades of some of the most highly charged and moving ensemble jazz in the music's history. With that shift to a kind of collectively improvised funk, Coleman diminished as a breathtakingly resourceful solo artist, partly because you simply couldn't hear him. But it was the big picture he was interested in, and he's been filling in large areas of it ever since.

Coleman entered bemusedly, looking, as he usually does, as if he'd walked into his bathroom and found himself in the Festival Hall – an impression only modified by that shiny silver suit. Then the band was off like a hare, jangling and hammering its way through a long set of mostly short pieces, sometimes little more than theme statements, but delivered with the mixture of approximate rhythmic unison and free-fall improvised counterpoint that gives Coleman's music such discordant, dynamic life.

Early on, the impossible seemed possible – that he might be shifting to a more chromatically focused music – as a series of short bursts from Badal Roy's tablas, Denardo Coleman's drums, the spindly high-revving guitar duo of Chris Rothenberg and Kenny Wessell, and David Bryant's mixture of condensed Cecil Taylorish arpeggios and gospel riffs preceded the saxophonist's entry. But from then on, Coleman used Bryant principally as coloration between tunes and to impart sporadic harmonic anchoring to the music. These effects didn't weaken the resolve of the previous 30 years, but further developed timbral devices that have always been Coleman's trademark.

The stream of pieces took in fast, free-funk, almost conventional blues, slow, spacey themes arching around Coleman's exquisite sustained high tone, New Agey folk-classical acoustic guitar passages suddenly stomped over by churning funk, a calypso, R&B, and the joyful minimalist dance theme from the Prime Time Seventies début album *Dancing in Your Head*, given an even more festive air by Coleman's horn variations this time. A few minor concessions to orthodox music haven't normalised Ornette Coleman. If anything they've only served to emphasise how enduringly and wilfully fresh his music is, even if there isn't a playing partner of James Blood Ulmer's or Jamaladeen Tacuma's calibre these days.

PRESSURE

The Guardian, June 1992

Joe Henderson, **Lush Life** (Verve 511 779-2)

Almost as heartening as the recent Jazz Café gigs that showed Joe Henderson to be one of the undisputed world leaders in the saxophone business (his consistency of invention has been unwavering in recent years, after dodgy flings with fusion in the Seventies) were the packed and youthful houses that proved the word had got around. Henderson is the younger Sonny Rollins in his manoeuvrability, impulsiveness coupled with immense technique, inventiveness of phrase lengths and shapes, and avoidance of the obvious. This disc is dedicated to Ellington's inspirational partner Billy Strayhorn, and though Henderson plays tenor throughout, there are places where it is hard to believe – like the flute-like intonation on 'Isfahan', or the owl-like hoots sliding into sighs, langourous swirls, Getzian murmurings and bits of swing-tenor expansiveness on 'Blood Count'. If Henderson's seven-league imagination isn't enough, Wynton Marsalis – playing in his best glowing Fats Navarro bebop manner – guests on three tracks.

Keith Tippett, **The Dartington Concert** (EEG 2106-2)

British improvising pianist Tippett's unleashing of the potential of a conventional piano goes a long way beyond jazz, and a tireless determination to pursue a personal music has left him unfairly sidelined in the minds of some as a Sixties expressionist eccentric. But Tippett recently brought home to a South Bank crowd who had come to hear Bheki Mseleku that he's not only one of the most imaginative improvisers ever raised in Britain, but the variety and drama in his music steps over its unfamiliarity. This 1990 live set, dedicated to the late Dudu Pukwana, is better than that South Bank gig – floods of liquid runs over brooding, thunderous chords, hurtling uptempo figures that sound like the accompaniment to a silent-movie chase run at triple speed, high-register trills that change tone colour by being unwaveringly sustained, so they turn into sounds of zithers, penny-whistles and violins. Accessible, atmospheric, virtuosic free improvisation.

SCOURGE OF THE FLATLAND

The Guardian, July 1992

In the late Seventies, it used to be said you could always spot a Keith

Jarrett gig by the number of lime-green Citroën Deux Chevaux parked outside, displaying 'Save the Whale' stickers. By the Eighties, the audience joke had shifted to New Ageists, competitors on the same patch overdosed on inner-city stress, fantasising about whittling sticks in a log cabin.

But needling Keith Jarrett's cosy, romantic appeal doesn't undo his achievements. An exceptional piano virtuoso he undoubtedly is: an eclectic latter-day Liszt who can play the socks off the nineteenth-century romantic, classical tradition and most jazz piano styles alike. In the jazz-funk Seventies, when his solo career took off, he was just about the only jazz musician able to command high fees and a worldwide mass audience, without deviating from the ascetic raw materials of acoustic improvised music. His productivity is astounding, taking in solo piano and small-group jazz recordings, orchestral and chamber works, as well as an exhaustive examination of Bach on both piano and harpsichord.

Jarrett's appeal lies partly in what his playing symbolises – flight from city neuroses, the crazed purr of marketing departments, the techno-sounds of digital sampling and FM radio. He has publicly loathed virtually all electric music since the Seventies. and TV addiction too, calling video and the impact of visual culture on life the victory of 'flatland', a universe of surfaces and shallowness.

He was, until the early Eighties, a student of the anti-ego teachings of the American-Greek guru G.I. Gurdjieff. On the other hand, though he'd call it simply unselfconscious ecstasy at music making, he's a spectacular showman on stage, with a repertoire of grunts, leaps and ecstatic cries, which prompted *Village Voice* critic Chip Stern to call Jarrett the 'Elvis Presley of high art'. As they are jazz heroes as big as he is, Jarrett controversially takes on the Marsalis family, calling trumpeter Wynton his 'arch-enemy', in his opinion selling audiences a hip image of improvised music without improvising.

The band that Jarrett brings to London next week is the piano trio he has run since 1983, devoted to improvising on the great Tin Pan Alley songs, and featuring two incomparable virtuosi in bassist Gary Peacock and drummer Jack DeJohnette. It is his best, most focused band, its method recalling the great Bill Evans trios. With characteristic didacticism, Jarrett intended the trio's name – the Standards Band – as a double-take. It means the trio plays standard tunes. But Jarrett also saw it as a representation of high musical standards, and a measure of the quality of involvement of the three players.

'Everybody writes their own music these days, and that's one of the reasons why there's so much bad music around,' Jarrett says, in the manner of acerbic relaxation that has replaced a good deal of the frost and prickle of earlier years. 'When you're playing your own music, your ego takes you to the point where it's not the music you're working on any more. You're thinking, "I wrote this tune and now it doesn't sound how I wanted it to." Playing the standards frees you of the responsibility of making the music exactly the way you want it.'

In reducing the interventions of his ego, Jarrett has a lot of ground to uncover – like being an infant prodigy at three, a recitalist at seven, stints with Art Blakey, Miles Davis and the famous Charles Lloyd group that helped to pioneer jazz-rock fusion. Jarrett's 1975 solo disc, *The Koln Concert*, was the best-selling piano record ever, and it secured the future for the Munich-based independent ECM, for whom Jarrett has worked ever since. Deep roots in the harmonies of nineteenth-century romanticism, overlaid with country music, gospel and the blues, have made Jarrett perfectly placed to hook upscale audiences all over the world.

The guitarist and author of the penetrating study *Improvisation* Derek Bailey says, 'I think of Jarrett as being descended from Liszt; he's in a long line of piano virtuosi.' But in acknowledging Jarrett's status as an improviser, albeit within conservative forms, Bailey points to the pianist's most serious preoccupation, profoundly hooked to his perceptions of the current music business and the state of humanity in general – the art of improvisation.

'I remember being backstage waiting to go on for a classical performance once,' Jarrett recalls, 'and it was Beethoven, Shostakovich, a lot of the big guys. I thought to myself, what's missing here? I realised that it was that I wouldn't be surprised. I would play well, or I wouldn't play well, or not very well, but whatever I did it would still be that everything was known about this music beforehand. I need to know now that there's a greater potential in it that's different from what I already know.'

His biographer, British trumpeter and author Ian Carr, says: 'He gets things out of music at very fundamental levels. Rilke said – it's a quote Keith likes – that it's important to remain a novice all the time, and that's what separated him and Miles from so many musicians, the ability to go on learning.' For Jarrett, there's a holy grail in discovering what making music for its own sake really feels like – rather than demonstrating a technique, or aiming a product at a niche. Only his most implacable critics would deny that he's found that.

'I find it impossible to think of any music other than jazz where to be good depends so much on a player's full consciousness. It primarily depends on the people playing it. And once you've discovered that consciousness as a musician, rather than just playing all the notes, you can't then say, "Oh no, that didn't happen." It's like people who say, "I don't know what love is." Then they fall in love. Whether it works out or not, they never say they don't know what love is again.'

Still Miles Ahead

The Guardian, November 1992

One band couldn't pay tribute to the succession of revolutions Miles Davis was involved in, and a group that just milked applause with his greatest hits would have been a travesty of his restless improviser's spirit. So the quintet that played two nights at the Albert Hall last week triumphantly did the right thing by making reference to some famous material and then playing it the way they feel today.

Three of its members – Herbie Hancock, Wayne Shorter and Tony Williams – were members of Davis's free-est and most collectively creative band in his immediately pre-funk period in the mid-1960s (funk was conspicuous by its absence last week) and they worked as fruitfully together now as they ever had. Dave Holland, a late replacement for the ailing Ron Carter on bass, played a handful of thunderous solos but also drove the ensemble with an effervescence almost equal to Tony Williams's avalanche of percussion. These four virtuosi paid the most telling tribute possible, by demonstrating all the spontaneous audacity and listening powers Miles hired them for and which he encouraged them to take to the limits.

Wallace Roney, the young trumpeter, had the hardest job. He was supposed to be both himself and Miles as well, to recall that muted, whispering lyricism and the sudden eruptions of passion that all Davis fans know almost as intimately as the voices of their loved ones. It was an impossible combination for him, but he invokes both Miles Davis's sound and the unpredictable shaping of his solos better than anyone else, and his transformation of 'All Blues' as a fast, explosive, open-horn solo revealed it in an independent way.

Hancock, Shorter and Williams did as much to expand, accelerate and advance Davis's Sixties music, and the show confirmed how much further they've taken it. Williams's torrents of cymbal sound and endless changes of pattern without disrupting the flow – flicking rimshots, big cymbal splashes, explosive rolls – has become magic and fluid where it was once dazzling but jagged, and it gave a fast opening version of 'So What' an irresistible urgency.

Pieces from Miles's best freebop discs – notably *The Sorcerer* – drew beautiful solos from Shorter and Hancock. Shorter's soprano playing was more abstract and less conventionally jazzy than formerly – it nowadays suggests a nature-movie soundtrack of birdsong or sea-life as much as it does John Coltrane – but full of deft, silvery runs and secretive puffs of air, notably in an unaccompanied passage that was one of the triumphs of the night. They wound up with two famous finales 'Tune Up' and 'The Theme', and an audience of many generations went wild.

ABSOLUTE GAS

Bluecoat Gallery Programme, Liverpool, December 1992

Near the apex of a triangular block of flyblown Victorian offices bisecting three traffic jams at London's King's Cross stood the early Seventies home of *Time Out* magazine. A 1980s business, however young and hungry, wouldn't have been seen dead there, but in the Alternative Society it was a status symbol. Most of its visitors then were either civil liberties activists looking for the News department, or bands, publicists, chancers and aspiring writers heading for the Music Room at the top of the winding, uncarpeted Dickensian staircase. If you got that far, you first concussed yourself on the low-slung platform bearing the budget-priced Heath Robinsonian air-conditioning machine – the scrawled inscription 'Mind Your Head' came too late, and anyway it was too ambiguous a message for a largely hippie readership. But if you crossed that hurdle without an instant lobotomy or mental crisis, you were in the Music Room, a closet-sized grotto with soot-blackened windows revealing only the silhouettes of limping pigeons, impervious to the fiercest summer sunlight. That was where I met Mal Dean.

The room housed two junk-shop desks, an assortment of scattered album sleeves and trampled press releases, and a shifting population of freelances, liggers, refugees from elsewhere in the building and sometimes from the street. Sounds in there were mostly limited to the Hoover-like hiss of deep inhalations through spliffs. Grateful Dead on the record player, maybe the rustling sound of a music critic hard ar work settling deeper into a bean-bag. Mal appreciated the bohemianism of the surroundings, but he didn't care for the music, nor for the occasional solemnity of Alternative Culture social life.

This was a period in London life which has now become the subject of a mixture of myth-making and caricature – the *Oz* obscenity trial, the Arts Lab, Soft Machine, psychedelia, revolution through love – but which was nevertheless driven by an intense and inspirational impulse to read what was written on the reverse side of a piece of received wisdom. A lot of the mannerisms of that subculture were hilarious, but we mostly didn't notice. Mal Dean did. He inhabited that world too and shared many of its assumptions because he was an idiosyncratic artist who needed a sympathetic climate to function in, but he was a little older than most travellers on the underground press, he possessed an indefatigable sense of the absurd, and his inspirations were quirkier and indifferent to fashion. They mixed, for instance, the double-takes of Magritte with graphic habits engendered in the period when the centre spread of the *Eagle* comic was designed primarily to enthuse the next generation of Empire-spanning British engineers.

Mal Dean was too much of an original to blend into the rather hermetic environment of the alternative press. Even his demeanour mixed the codes. He had long hair, but a wispy goatee as well, and he was resolutely a jazz fan at a time when an increasingly impressionistic and semi-improvised rock music was sidelining jazz commercially and culturally. These were choices that brought him closer to the era of the Fifties Beats than Sixties flower children. He liked the descendants of the Beat poets, like the Liverpudlians and the distinctive Pete Brown, another disciple of unorthodox rock and left-field jazz who ran a celebrated band called the Battered Ornaments and later wrote songs for Cream. Mal's drawings adorned a good deal of Battered Ornaments publicity.

Mal Dean's visual language was thus rich in surrealism and jazz-hipster imagery. The record covers of David Stone-Martin, the smoky Herman Leonard photographs of Lester Young, elevated the portrayal of a musician at work to the iconography of the outsider. But Mal's gift as a jazz illustrator lay in celebrating a romance with the mercurial spontaneity of jazz – after all, he was as deeply captivated by it as any jazz fan and more than most – without endorsing the negative mythology of jazz musicians as tortured, junked-up victims. In Mal's jazz drawings, the bloodshot, road-weary nocturnal creatures of the jazz life often appear both worldly and startlingly cherubic, childlike in the absorption in a music that only has eloquence when the personality of the player is free to reshape both the idiom and the technique that goes with it.

The Magritte connection was often noticeable, as in the drawing of Sidney Bechet, the Francophile New Orleans soprano sax genius, playing a baguette, for instance. But Mal's impatience with the superficialities of style surfaced in these drawings too, and what he would have made of the Eighties preoccupation with style is an entertaining subject to ponder. When the saxophonist Gerry Mulligan exchanged his crop headed Cool Youth Fifties image for a buckskin-and-bouffant Sixties one, Mal drew a profile of the '54 Model' accompanied by a cut-out-and-paste wardrobe and haircut to turn him into the '72 version.

I was covering jazz for *Time Out* then, so I would often meet Mal on gigs after that, mostly other people's, sometimes his own. He wasn't a sectarian jazz lover, but alert to the improviser's spark that could ignite anything from a Dixieland band to the most abstract of free ensembles. He just liked the precarious ingenuity of the music, and its dependence on the spontaneous inventions of square pegs and oddballs who didn't fit either pop culture or posh culture. Mal liked Ornette Coleman's notion of a new music, which the saxophonist had broken away from the Tin Pan Alley sources of most jazz tunes but which was always hauntingly melodic, light in touch, sang like a voice, and swung like hell. He wasn't keen on the heated, incantatory, trance-like music of later John Coltrane, despite, or maybe because of, the fact that it was just about the only fashionable jazz of the Seventies, when *A Love Supreme* was a big seller. I discovered this when Mal found me with a Coltrane disc in that Music Room one day.

'What's it like?' he asked, rather testily. 'Bang, crash, thump, smash. . .' he went on, without waiting for a reply. Coltrane seemed solemn to him, to a manic degree, and he wouldn't use one note if a hundred would do either. Mal himself was an approximate trumpeter, but an expressive one. He played with a blustering energy, like an artist painting with a distemper brush, but it was full of vivid colour, and you always knew it was him.

When we met by chance in Greek Street one afternoon Mal told me he had the same cancer from which his sister had died. He made little of it, except insisting offhandedly that he wasn't going to lie down and wait for it, and maintained that determination to the end of his life. 'How're you doing?' I would ask him, leaning on the bars of various jazz venues. 'Bag of shit, bag of shit,' he would say without rancour, half his attention still on the music. 'Still, I saw a doctor this morning who said, "What are you worrying about, Mr Dean, you're still here, aren't you?"'

It doesn't take much imagination to figure out how much of a joke Mal really thought this was, but his laugh about it wasn't mirthless and he meant you to laugh too. As he continued to draw in his last months, he used to joke that the trouble with cancer was that the bones in your bum hurt if you liked working on a wooden chair.

When the Amazing Band played its valedictory gig for Mal, the musicians – none of them much more disposed towards hippie New Ageism than he was – swore they saw him on stage, playing with them. It was the kind of urgent affirmation you hesitate to doubt, though it was such an emotional occasion that the subconscious of just about everybody there who knew him must have been seething with thoughts of Mal. Only one thing makes me wonder if he was really there on stage. It was certainly an eerie, haunting music they made, different from the way they often played. But it was a music appropriate to the occasion, and that's what Mal Dean's mischievousness might have found hard to leave alone. Sure, he might have been up there. But I think he would have called for 'Royal Garden Blues' or maybe even 'Girl from Ipanema' – and if they couldn't quite get their fingers around it, that would have made it all the better.

1993

The year began with the death of a hero, Dizzy Gillespie. But so hot and animated were the recollections of his career that it cast a glow instead of a shadow over the jazz world, serving instead as a vivid reminder of exactly what the virtues of the music were, echoing the insights of Max Roach when he said to writer Kitty Grime years ago, 'Jazz allows you to sound fifty when you are fifty, and when you're nineteen you should sound like nineteen. Jazz allows you to tell the truth.'

In Britain, what followed Gillespie's tumultuous exit in January was a year of such remarkable live shows as to stretch memory for a comparison. And if Dizzy were listening they would certainly have let him rest easy in the belief that the personal conviction and improvisatory attitude that fuel jazz players still flourish, even if the lack of infrastructure and cash, the conservatism of the entertainment business, and the impact of the recession on audiences don't help.

Bob Berg, the fiery, muscular saxophonist, was one of the first to demonstrate this early in the year, with a fortnight at Ronnie Scott's that even had the club staff who have heard everything hypnotised night after night. After a succession of average albums, and pressure to restrict himself to crowd-baiting sax-funk blasts in other people's bands, Berg's mixture of virtuosity, strength and intelligence when permitted to work exactly as he chooses (with an empathetic small group, on music with a lot of open space in it), was a big surprise.

High on the list of other gigs whose music reverberated on long afterwards was veteran guitarist Jim Hall's show at Islington's Union Chapel, a notoriously tricky venue for hard-driving jazz, but perfectly suiting his famous pin-drop delicacy. Hall recalled his old associations with the late Bill Evans by performing the show as a duet with pianist Larry Golding. Also on that ten-day-long London Jazz Festival in May was an evening devoted to hybrids of jazz and other forms, and though the uneven but full-blooded young trumpeter Byron Wallen's rap band wasn't always firing, and Indian multi-instrumentalist Nitin Sawnhey drifted close to New Ageism, the continuing indications of how flexible and inspirational the jazz impulse is made up for some gropings and wanderings. Hearing the New Orleans Rebirth Brass Band play Herbie Hancock's 'Headhunters' like street-party music was another indelible memory of the festival.

Carla Bley paid glowing tributes to orchestral history with her Very Big Band in the summer; the Art Ensemble of Chicago came here for the first time in over a decade and spectacularly played the blues (though a bit too much of them, and too little of their magical impressionism), and McCoy Tyner and vibist Bobby Hutcherson made a thrilling partnership at the Jazz Café, with the finishing touches provided by the brilliant drumming of Aaron Scott.

But Joe Henderson's South Bank gig dominated the summer months, a two-hour, non-stop masterpiece of trio improvisation (Dave Holland was on bass and Al Foster on drums) that ranked as one of the all-time great jazz performances for circuitous invention, group understanding, virtuosity and utterly unpredictable phrasing. Almost as rich and thrumming with surprises, though further to the margins of the jazz galaxy, was Anthony Braxton's all-improvised duet with British saxophonist Evan Parker, and the softening of free-jazz abstractions with something close to a Fifties Cool School lyricism did nothing to detract from the sense of adventure. Older heroes Sonny Rollins and Ornette Coleman (the latter with an acoustic band for the first time in years) showed that their personal skills were still astonishingly sharp, though neither of their groups entirely gelled. Pharoah Sanders preached a gospel to the Dingwalls' audience that made a revivalist meeting of his shows, and Cassandra Wilson made a mostly beautiful acoustic blues and roots record, suggesting she's a much better interpretative than original artist and none the worse for that.

Jazz FM, the radio station that hid its jazz output, won a ten-year franchise renewal, proving that another slot for a more robust rival was still needed. The Arts Council of Great Britain embarked on a national jazz survey, and the jazz lobby pledged to fight to keep recognition of the music's unique history alive rather than see it hurled into a beleaguered and underfunded outpost marked 'Ethnic and non-European Musics' or some such.

REBIRTH

The Guardian, May 1993

They staged an opening night party for the London Jazz Festival on Friday night, and the way the Rebirth Brass Band went about it shifted the definition of A Hard Act To Follow up several notches. Not that this careering New Orleans outfit intended to upstage anybody by playing the first night of this multi-venue ten-day event as if it were the finale – it's just the way they always play.

Rebirth formed in the mid-Eighties in New Orleans to play jazz roots, funk, pop, even reggae. Now that most of the gleefully blowing New Orleans veterans who seemed to remain parked at about a hundred and five years old for decades have finally retired to the bar at the end of the universe, early jazz is being celebrated either by eclectic young musicians like these in reversed baseball caps, or at the opposite extreme by the Wynton Marsalis school of cool appraisal. Rebirth sounded superficially like a regular polyphonic pre-swing outfit at first, but they gradually expanded the message with such items as a euphoric version of Herbie Hancock's Seventies chart hit 'Headhunters' (it made all the electronic paraphernalia of the original redundant) and some luxurious reggae too. It's showbiz, all right, but as a party-band it's a hoot, literally.

All this hullabaloo didn't obliterate the memory of the British singer Carol Grimes, who had preceded them with a folk-jazz group strongly featuring guitars, percussion and the graceful lyricism of Annie Whitehead's trombone. As a spine-chillingly powerful singer rooted in blues and soul (her version of 'Nothin' but the Blues' confirmed she's lost none of her appetite for that) who can nevertheless embrace vocal ideas from outside the African-American tradition, Grimes is forthright, moving and imaginative, and only 'Freedom Marching' seemed stuck in a protest-song groove in need of some new references.

Jim Hall, who has profoundly influenced such contemporary guitarists as John Scofield and Bill Frisell, then hypnotised the audience with sounds barely louder than a falling pin, performing in a duo with a good, if unsurprising, pianist Larry Golding in the manner of his classic partnerships with the late Bill Evans. Hall treats every note as if he's in love with it, the sounds softly glittering on Hoagy Carmichael's 'Skylark', soft chord-strumming like somebody running barefoot on the Latin-flavoured 'Pancho', breezily and unexpectedly uptempo on 'My Funny Valentine', even a subtle exploration of dissonance in the chiming chords of 'Mr Blues'. They used to call him the 'thinking fan's guitarist' but this music didn't need thinking about to reduce its audience to awed silence.

GETTING SERIOUS

The Guardian, May 1993

Though it was 1990 before *Time* magazine acknowledged that jazz seemed back on the block, and put Wynton Marsalis on the cover of its 'New Jazz Age' edition, the young New Orleans trumpeter had for most of the previous decade been unofficial generalissimo to an eager volunteer army of young musicians around the world who were just discovering jazz. When barely into his twenties, Marsalis looked and sounded like someone in charge of his destiny, and willing to shoulder being in charge of a lot of other people's too.

A child in the Seventies, an era in which marketing departments had all but banned the word 'jazz' as making anything associated with it unsaleable, Marsalis (whose father Ellis is an eminent pianist and teacher, and whose brothers all play) grew up talking to anyone who would listen about the jazz tradition, and about learning and respect. When he emerged with Art Blakey's Jazz Messengers at twenty, he demonstrated a tone, technique and maturity that seemed to bring a musical golden age (Fifties and Sixties lyrical Miles Davis, the glowing sound of Clifford Brown) back to life. But his technique was so comprehensive that he was just as comfortable with the European classics too, and at one point in the Eighties Columbia was alternately releasing jazz and classical albums by him.

'Looking at the past is a big part of any musician's work,' Marsalis emphatically reaffirms. 'And before the last thirty years, that's something that never would have been an issue, it would have just been assumed. But jazz has often been separated from its own history because it is a combination of a fine art music and a popular music. It has a ritualistic side, and a temporary side, so the mechanisms for criticising it properly didn't exist.' So where are his investigations going with his current band, the one that often intriguingly echoes a Twenties Jelly Roll Morton band wrapped up inside a snorting Sixties Charles Mingus one? 'We're just getting our sound together,' Marsalis says, repeating a favourite message. 'We're learning how to play softer but with more intensity. And learning how to make more intelligent decisions when we're playing as a group.'

Marsalis arrived at a time when the jazz past was neglected and many great musicians either sick, or sick and tired. By resurrecting respect for it, and making it possible to hear styles now available only on disc rebuilt for live shows, he has not only helped revitalise respect for jazz, but encouraged new working opportunities that have even benefited some of the surviving jazz heroes he grew up listening to. He was always forthright too about the effects of racial intolerance on the generations preceding his, and about how destructive the press's 'Tortured Artist' sensationalism over drink, drugs and early death in jazz was, calling it just a part of the process by which audiences convince themselves that they're getting a folk art that is 'authentic'. But he believes there's still a long way to go. 'A lot of other musicians really should be playing in somebody's band before they go on their own, but since there's not a plethora of bands, it becomes very difficult for the younger musicians to learn how to play. There's more teaching of jazz in schools, a lot of stuff about scales and everything, but when I go to schools I always say, "If you don't know your scales you're just not serious about being a musician." You shouldn't be in a college learning scales, you should be in a college learning how to play.'

Marsalis has lost count of his future plans. He's working on a Broadway show, on a mixed media project at the National Aerospace Museum in which he's going to play while the painter Sam Francis paints, and on a commission about the Lincoln Center, where he's artistic director of the jazz programme. And with all this variety, does he have a single aim in his own music? 'To be able to play all of the musical styles that have existed,' he says, 'and still add that extra thing into it to make it modern music.'

FALLING STAR

The Guardian, June 1993

Bill Evans, **Turn Out the Stars** (Dreyfus Jazz Line)

When the pianist Bill Evans played Ronnie Scott's Club in 1980, many of the witnesses marvelled at the apparent rejuvenation of a performer who – while he could never be less than musical – had sometimes seemed so lost in his own musings as to risk drowning in the ripples of his own arpeggios. Evans, a crucial influence on the development of many of the jazz keyboard virtuosi of the past thirty years (including McCoy Tyner, Herbie Hancock and Keith Jarrett), seemed to have found fresh vigour and exuberance, partly attributable to the suitability of a new rhythm section in Marc Johnson (bass) and Joe LaBarbera (drums). But a month later Evans was dead at fifty-one, so memories of that London season acquired an eerie echo.

This disc features seven tunes recorded on the last night of that run, 2 August 1980. There are other good recordings by this group (the Timeless label's *The Brilliant*, and *Consecration*) and generally the sound quality is better than here, since the piano is muddily reproduced in the lower registers and sounds tinny in the high ones. This is about as big a drawback as it could be with Evans, who was one of the subtlest explorers of piano tonality in jazz history. But nevertheless, enough of the vitality of this final stage of his career comes through. The flurries of arpeggios in the last section of 'I Do It for Love' have an almost abstract urgency, and there's a bursting vivacity about the explosive downward runs on the title track that was exactly what made the 1980 audience think Evans was starting a new phase.

BACK FROM THE BUSH

The Guardian, July 1993

The 'jazz boom' wasn't even a distant rumble when the Art Ensemble of Chicago last played in Britain at the beginning of the Eighties. Yet since it rose out of the settling dust of the black American avant-garde of the 1960s, this talented and theatrical band has, a quarter-century later, maintained an allegiance to a sizeable slice of the values espoused as if they were original (openness to all idioms, jump-cut switches between styles, a renewal of acoustic music) with one very significant extra: innovation.

On Thursday, the band made the links between the Chicago free scene and the city's blues traditions more explicit than usual, by augmenting the band with Sonny Boy Williamson devotee Chicago Beau – a harmonica virtuoso built like the Pyrenees and with a hat to match, organist/vocalist Amina Claudine Myers, plus extra horns and a guitar.

If this is a sign that the more outgoing inclinations of trumpeter Lester Bowie (whose popular outfit, Brass Fantasy, gives raucous street-jazz interpretations of pop and soul songs) has finally prevailed in the Art Ensemble, it is not an unmixed blessing, because the ways in which the original group's abstract pieces would very slowly coalesce into familiar forms and then unravel again was unusual and an irresistible source of surprises. The old methods were audible in the meditative beginning to the set (banshee wails and hoots, swelling and fading tom-toms, bird calls, whistles, Bowie's gravelly trumpet drawing the band towards fast free improvisation, notably a hurtling solo of astonishingly pure high tones from Roscoe Mitchell's alto) and in the fanfare-like ending, and the rest was blues from Claudine Myers (wistful, oblique) and Chicago Beau (avalanche-like). Trombonist Frank Lacy deployed the Union Chapel echo in a mixture of fierce hollers and slithery, evaporating sounds, a fine saxophonist – James Carter – played rhythm and blues tenor as if he wasn't mesmerised by its history, and a blues jam then rolled on for three-quarters of an hour, with enough distinctive interpretation to keep it hot. Bowie is a blues trumpeter at heart anyway, and guitarist Herb Walker played a solo of whirling repeated chord-patterns on a spine-chilling 'Hoochie Coochie Man' that sounded astonishingly like Buddy Guy spliced with Steve Reich. I'd still rather have had more Art Ensemble impressionism, but once you've embarked on a blues bash, it is hard to retreat – and what they did instead was still their unique angle on black music.

GURU
The Guardian, July 1993

Joe Henderson is loquacious, shy, suddenly enthused, sometimes formal, sometimes effusive, almost always absorbing. His tenor saxophone playing is the same. Recognised for thirty years as one of the most inventive of all jazz improvisers, now a Grammy winner one of the few saxophonists to be plausibly discussed as an heir-apparent to Sonny Rollins, even a participant in the jam-with-Clinton pre-election sax sideshows, Henderson is an unspectacular colossus whose time has finally come.

Henderson and his band appear on the South Bank on Monday (26 July), and the audience is likely to be a lot bigger than the handful who used to show up at Ronnie Scott's in the Seventies when he was already a jaw-dropping executant of sharp curves and four-wheel skids as a melodic improviser – but mostly playing jazz rather than funk, and therefore in the outer darkness as far as commercial appeal went at that time. Sonny Rollins and Charlie Parker are among his influences, but his sound is unmistakable and has been from the beginning. He dislikes pyrotechnics, generating drama from nuance and the resourcefulness of his phrasing instead, most of it delivered as a hollow, resonant tenor monologue, like a penetrating murmur, but with a high-register sound as pure as a flute.

When Henderson was in London earlier in the year, it was to put the word around about his follow-up album to the Grammy-winning *Lush Life* (a lovingly-crafted project devoted to the compositions Billy Strayhorn wrote with Duke Ellington), the *So Near So Far: Musings for Miles* album which was his way of saying thanks to the departed Miles Davis. It was perfect for traditional Miles fans – older classics like 'Miles Ahead', 'Flamenco Sketches' and an early forerunner of 'Milestones' are on it. But so is guitarist John Scofield, a powerful and popular blues-bop guitar hero of the Nineties. The session isn't as focused as *Lush Life* was, but it's taut, subtle, ingenious music, and no Davis replica.

'Miles wouldn't have appreciated us going in there and being a clone of what he had been. I couldn't do that anyway, neither could any of the others. He was known as the enabler, and he would choose material that would enable musicians to launch into directions that develop them as individuals.

'When we made the record, his presence was so thick and so much there that you could reach out and touch it; it may sound a bit dreamy but it's true. I was at a tribute to Monk once that was like that, a lot of fantastic piano players on it, and sometimes you'd swear it was Monk you were listening to, and you could see him shuffling and dancing on the stage the way he used to. He had a big influence on me, just after I got out of the military in 1962. I was writing tunes like Monk then. Most piano players I know, including some classical piano players, have got something of Monk that they can do. I always heard Monk the way I heard Hindemith, and I'm not surprised there are classical players recording Monk pieces now.'

After his army service, Henderson joined the bands of trumpeter Kenny Dorham and pianist Horace Silver, eventually co-leading a hard-bop group called the Jazz Communicators with Freddie Hubbard, and then working with Herbie Hancock and with Blood, Sweat and Tears. He toyed with jazz-rock fusion, not especially memorably. Henderson's powers as an improviser have always been too great to do anything but burst the zips of tight idioms.

'When I started playing saxophone for dances around Detroit,' Henderson recalls, 'it was inevitably a bluesier kind of music. But when I saw Charlie Parker, when I was fourteen years old, this was at a dance too. He was playing tunes like "Indiana", "Cherokee", very fast tunes, and everybody was swinging. At that time, they would dance to anything that you played, they would find a way to dance to it. But I found that trying to get mastery of one of those fast Birdlines was more intesting than with rhythm and blues lines, which were more like riffs – very important riffs, but repetitive.

'Once you've been in the shed (practising) for a while at that stuff, you get very adaptable. John Scofield is like that, and I like to be around those kind of people. If in a musical situation you've got to do all that talking, and explaining . . . jeez, man, it can just go on and on. But you get a certain group of people, you just have to count the tune in, or call the tune, or sometimes not even that, just start playing . . . and everything that's supposed to fall in place does just that.

'I went to a rehearsal at Miles's house once, and I wasn't a kid, I'd made a few records, but I was still thinking, what are we going to do? And Miles walked around the rehearsal room with a can of beer in his hand, just talking in this barely audible voice of his, and I thought I wish somebody would give me some instructions here, or something. And that's what the rehearsal was about, and next thing we're on the gig. And I'm thinking, where are my parts? But then it dawned on you, same as it was with Monk. Miles was indicating that he was leaving it up to you to figure that out.

'This is a demanding music, and a demanding lifestyle – and a fun lifestyle as well. But it's an eventful life, compared to all the people who appear to have nothing happen to them, nothing to talk about, the sun comes up and it goes down. What do you write on the stone at the end? Something you can sum up in one or two words? A guy like Miles has a couple of books you could put on it.

'When I was travelling around Europe on my own in the Seventies, working with house bands I didn't know, it was very rewarding like that – and with some of the European players, like the drummer Tony Oxley or the bassist Dave Holland, it was as much fun as I've had anywhere. Whatever it is that you have to deal with out there, you find a way of getting to where the sun is shining, you know? I'm going to get to that patch of blue whatever the situation is, I'm going to find me a door or a window – in or out.'

FURIOSITY

The Guardian, July 1993

Two great jazz musicians, the volcanic pianist McCoy Tyner, and the melodically ingenious vibraharpist Bobby Hutcherson, made a sublimely thrilling partnership on two nights at the Jazz Café last week. It wasn't just the chemistry of that imaginative pairing alone, but of a group performance of remarkably sublime energies. Bassist Avery Sharpe and drummer Aaron Scott avoided careering alongside the runaway truck of Tyner's furious solo style (as has sometimes seemed the case on disc) but utterly enmeshed themselves in the ensemble.

Tyner began on Friday night with a typical fast trio piece of mingled Latin and straight-time metres. The familiar devices were all in place, needle-sharp downward runs and ringing trills, breaking out of thickets of dense chordwork and incantatory vamps. When Hutcherson arrived he was a shade unsure rhythmically at first, but soon began building gracefully structured solos with his bright, hard sound. Eventually he adopted the visually absorbing practice of rolling a vibraharp run on down to the bigger keyboard of the marimba (an overall range that spanned the width of the stage) which he delivered with curling, unexpected melodic turns and some impressive footwork on these journeys too, as if traversing the stage in a private tango.

The pieces included a slow, quiet funk shuffle which Hutcherson ended in a long improvised duet with the bass, modulating keys in hypnotic displacements of the melody, while Avery Sharpe sustained a dark ostinato, and a beautiful ballad exchange for the piano and vibes alone. The second set opening was more considered and melodically circuitous, but was eventually dominated by an astonishing drum solo from Aaron Scott, who began with domineering Blakeyesque tom-tom and cowbell patterns, and shifted into dense, surging and ebbing cymbal swirls creating the impression of stopping and unstopping the ears under a waterfall. Like many things that night, you didn't want it to stop – and for drum solos, that's a rarity.

MAGNIFICENCE

The Guardian, July 1993

When Dizzy Gillespie died at the beginning of this year, a good many commentators – including this one – described in the obituaries the famous ballooning cheeks and the upturned horn. Writing about Gillespie's effervescence, magnetism and commitment, the words just fell under the fingers. Later, after all the tributes had come out, other images came to mind that told different stories about Gillespie, his music, and his life. The most affecting one was of the trumpeter, lit by a single anglepoise, playing chess with the proprietor in the backstage 'office' at Ronnie Scott's Club, surrounded by ashtrays and coffee cups. It was British photographer and writer Val Wilmer's picture, and its spirit is revealingly represented by her exhibition *Jazz Roots and Branches*, which opened at the Special Photographers' Company this week.

Though this is loosely 'music photography', there is hardly a stage shot among them, ballooning cheeks or otherwise. There are musicians waiting for something or someone, practising, hanging out, talking, laughing, contemplating, phoning, elated or exhausted. Some are of stars, but stars off-duty – Count Basie playing cards in Bournemouth in 1977, Muddy Waters doing the same in Croydon, Cecil Taylor backstage at the Five Spot in a moment of hilarity, Ornette Coleman on the telephone, back to the camera. Blues guitarist Albert King is under the spotlight, but in an instant that so startlingly catches a critical moment that the Time-Life *Library of Photography* series highlighted it as a photojournalistic object-lesson in capturing a musician's communion with his art. Some portray the roots of jazz obliquely, like the family going to church in Bentonia, Mississippi. Some recognise fine unsung musicians, like the guitarist called Satan (he braided his hair into two horns) who made wonderful music with washtub bassist Professor Six Million around 125th Street in Harlem.

The perceptiveness of these pictures about the way jazz is made and remade has had a lot to do with Wilmer's love of the music, to many journeys to America and Africa, and to many years on the British jazz scene, originally working for *Melody Maker*. She dislikes being thought of exclusively as a music photographer or reporter however, and she conclusively isn't. Apart from reportage on a variety of social issues, Wilmer is co-founder with Maggie Murray of the photographic agency Format, which celebrates its tenth anniversary this year.

'All music photographers are influenced by Herman Leonard, and by Francis Wolff of Blue Note, just as all documentary photography is influenced by Cartier-Bresson,' Wilmer says. 'But my biggest influences have been Lawrence Shustak, who shot a lot of the early Riverside covers, Eugene Smith for reportage, and a wonderful photographer called Roy DeCarava who was born in Harlem, collaborated on a book with Langston

Hughes and put together a collection of music photographs called *The Sound I Saw*. It's so different from the idea that a picture of a person on a stage blowing a horn against a black background means anything, because it doesn't. An EMI staff photographer I used to know called Ken Palmer would say, "There's only five angles to photograph a trumpet player." At the time I thought, "This is a wonderful job, what's he talking about?" but I understand him now.'

What Wilmer has loved about her own photogenic heroes is a mixture of content, artistry and politics – but also what she calls the 'quality of daring', the courage not to hit the shutter when the obvious image fills the frame, to look for something else. She might as easily have linked this with the quality of wisdom, knowing how to recognise the value of that something else through its illuminating relevance to a subject intimately understood. 'The special qualities of those people are their heart and their eye,' Wilmer emphatically states. 'Roy DeCarava took a picture of Billie Holiday with the pianist Hazel Scott and it's just a beautiful image of a woman waiting to sing, next to a woman playing the piano, none of that tortured artist crap.

'Photography is about content, and about politics, but the meaning of it is drawing with light, and that's what it should be,' Wilmer says. 'A lot of people wouldn't like this photograph for instance [of the saxophonist Dewey Redman] because people would expect in this picture for the focus to be on the person in the background. It's not an accepted aesthetic procedure to focus this way round – so I bring out the palm of his hand in the printing, and the light down the profile of Dewey Redman – using a local reducer like ferrocyanide. It really makes it stand out, and the highlights on the saxophone.

'Then there's Ornette on the telephone in the light from the window at nine in the morning. I was staying at his place and he didn't like being photographed, so I did very little there. But with that one, I saw "Ornette on the telephone", but I also had a feeling about him doing that that could translate into a picture, framed by those windows. Now some people will say, so what, we can't see his face. But you have to put yourself in there as well.'

Val Wilmer admits to feeling more estranged from current incarnations of jazz, particularly neo-classicist 'reruns of bebop', endorsing Lester Bowie's reservation about some of the young traditionalists that since one of the most powerful traditions in jazz has been innovation, you can't claim you're respecting it and not do it. Yet the love of the music that helped create these telling pictures is never beyond recovery. 'I was in New York when Miles Davis was ill,' Wilmer recalls. 'I was washing my hair and I heard his trumpet on the radio, and it was like my heart stopped, I knew he'd gone. I sat down, my hair dripping, and I couldn't stop crying – and I never thought I'd cry for Miles, who'd told me to fuck off once or twice. His music came out of all the windows that day, it didn't matter what nationality the people were originally – Chinese, Italian, Korean, African-Americans, Jews. But that's the emotional pull of this music, its profundity and depth. Its magnificence.'

INFORMALITY

The Guardian, September 1993

As two of the most riveting composer-performers in contemporary music, Anthony Braxton and Marilyn Crispell's weekend performances were always going to be among the unmissable events of the London Jazz Festival's final days – but in participating in some unscheduled meetings involving British improvisers Evan Parker and Paul Rutherford before the official start-times, Braxton almost eclipsed his own show. On Sunday at the Bloomsbury Theatre, saxophone improvisation of an intensity, virtuosity, drama and balance to tax the memory for comparison not just in this year but over many years took place between Braxton and Parker. It made few explicit references to any orthodox idioms, but by its sheer drive and forcefulness it made its own logic an entirely trustworthy guide.

Braxton and Parker are two of the foremost saxophone virtuosi to have developed out of the Sixties avant-garde. Yet Parker, though his first inspiration was John Coltrane, has constantly developed a saxophone vocabulary that was already massive by the mid-Seventies and has latterly augmented the hoarse dissonances of his investigations of harmonics with a quiet, reflective tonality echoing – who would have thought it – the white Lester Youngians like Warne Marsh and Stan Getz. Braxton is a long-time Paul Desmond as well as Coltrane fan, so though his set with Parker was improvised from the off, there were several passages in which it uncannily resembled Fifties Cool Jazz horn counterpoint without the beat.

But the effect of such modulations of traditional free-jazz methods was not to wade in jazz history but to provide dynamic contrast the style has sometimes lacked. Elsewhere, the two set an astonishing variety of sound resources in motion – fingers slapping pads shut, wind-in-trees sounds, circular breathing exercises in which Braxton would set swooping, ricocheting lines against the unflinching repeated figures Parker can sustain for minutes on end, percussive blurts like corks being popped. Towards the end of the set it was Braxton who referred to tunes more, and seemed to be intentionally challenging Parker's more implacable tendencies to explore repeated motifs in detail, but it was the differences as much as the similarities in their work that made the event so remarkable.

IRONY

The Guardian, September 1993

The late great Dr David Widgery described Canary Wharf as standing in the East End 'like an uninvited guest at a party which is over', and he hadn't even heard a jazz concert there. Whether the Cabot Hall was half empty because local audiences were unenthused by the prospect of a joint Sam Rivers/James Blood Ulmer band, or because they already knew what a frigid atmosphere the venue has, or because last week's council election result in the locality [a candidate from the extreme right-wing, racist British National Party was elected] put them off, is hard to judge. In the event, all the musicians – a quartet of black Americans and a quartet led by a Jewish saxophonist, to reinforce the ironies – made the best of a tough job.

Ronnie Scott played the first half with his quartet, the exposed setting of the smaller group startlingly energising his own playing. The band mostly stuck to a familiar territory of Sixties late-bebop and modal music including Joe Henderson's Latin piece 'Recorda-Me' and Miles Davis's 'Solar', but on a flying account of 'East of the Sun', Scott played with such urgent relish – skidding off the turns of the chords, reshuffling his favourite phraseology so quickly It gained a new intensity – that drummer Martin Drew clapped his sticks together in tribute, in the absence of much reaction from the floor.

The Rivers/Ulmer band was a comprehensive and fascinating contrast. The line-up alone – abrasive, free-blues Hendrix-like guitar, powerful, sophisticated saxophone, unswerving jazz-rap percussion and virtuosic, classical-influenced cello – was intriguing enough in itself. But the improvising method, veering melodically towards tempestuous 'harmolodic' free jazz and often hovering around clamorous, minimalist guitar figures from Ulmer, was explored with a bracing energy by all four. The influences of both Albert Ayler and Ornette Coleman strongly flavoured the show, and the only downside of a fiery collective performance was that Rivers's tonal range and improvising skills were often inaudible. Not all the music was so feverish, though. Rivers's romantic, fluttery flute against Ulmer's loose, splintery chords, and a light, effortlessly sketched soprano improvisation against a slow, bluesy backing that turned into a curiously brooding funk, went as far as anything could to warm the place.

GOOD OLD BOY

The Guardian, October 1993

Django Bates is growing up. If his delinquent choirboy appearance still

288 SHOOTING FROM THE HIP

makes you wonder, even a week after his thirty-third birthday, if he might keep a cardboard box containing a gerbil and an old cheese sandwich under his piano stool, the unpredictable Beckenham-born composer and improviser of Loose Tubes fame is getting down to some serious business. He has become a fully fledged orchestra leader. He has signed with Polygram, which has bought him time and resources. And he has stitched together much of his most expressive work of the Eighties with new compositions on his latest and best album, *Summer Fruits (and Unrest)*. 'I left a respectable period of mourning after Loose Tubes broke up,' is how Bates laconically explains the long wait before his writing talents found their most expressive setting.

In under a decade, Django Bates's career has taken in the collection of jump-cut impressionism he dedicated to Flann O'Brien's surreal novel *The Third Policeman* (complete with spinning bicycle-wheel noises), commissions from the likes of the Bath Festival for groups of classical virtuosi, a film soundtrack, the beginnings of a piano concerto for Michael Tilson Thomas and the LSO for 1996, and countless inventive contributions to other people's bands, notably ex-Yes drummer Bill Bruford's Earthworks. A regular Bates outlet through those years was Human Chain – a cooperative band given to engaging lurches between funeral dirges ('Strangely horrible, isn't it?' Bates would amiably enquire of the customers at the end of some tunes), tangos, bebop and twisted versions of cocktail-lounge muzak. And with the balletic Snapdragon Circus troupe, Bates wrote a selection of circus music that kept the idiom's eager, approximate charm and his own circuitous logic upright on the same tightrope – one example of which is on the current disc and dedicated to the late Angela Carter, whose novels he loves.

Bates's father William, a record collector of awesome catholicity, exposed his son to a mixture of jazz, Romanian fiddle tunes, African music and much more, and Bates is happy to name his primary jazz influences as Charlie Parker, Charles Mingus, early Keith Jarrett and bits of the adventurous Don Ellis band of the 1960s. Leaps between idioms are a characteristic of Django Bates's compositional method, just the way he heard music as a child.

If Django Bates was struggling to climb out from under Loose Tubes as a leader and composer, he knew he had to keep its unruly spirit burning. 'Most big bands generate a hibernating mode in musicians,' he says. 'You feel, "What I play won't be noticed, so I won't really blow my head off." In Loose Tubes it wasn't like that, everybody went for it. I look back at it and maybe some of the stuff had its embarrassing side occasionally, but so did punk rock. You're only young once, and you must do what you feel then, not be afraid to try. If you're doing that, the audience notices it.'

Django Bates is also one of the most free-thinking artists to operate in the delicate territory of jazz/classical hybrids, pursuing a creative partnership with the adventurous young concert pianist Joanna McGregor, whose participation was crucial to getting his piano concerto commissioned.

'I don't want the classical scene and the jazz scene to turn into one scene,' Bates says. 'But I do want there to be a lot more mutual recognition. There are some changes now but it's a very slow process. Joanna is one of a few exceptions. She took a risk asking me to do a couple of arrangements for a record she was doing called *On Broadway*, and it allowed me to write things for her that I can't play myself, very dense, detailed stuff. But she recognises the quality of spontaneity you get from improvisation too, which is a jazz musician's special skill. I always leave some space for improvisation in compositions even for classical orchestras, even if it's only a space on bar 56 for the oboe, or two seconds of all the musicians screaming at each other. You could write it out, but it wouldn't have the same danger to it.

'People need to trust their own feelings. Classical critics don't usually know what to say about work containing jazz, and vice versa. You can't talk about spontaneous music in terms of organised form, you get a much more natural form which reflects the feel of the evening. It's better to say just how you really felt about the music without worrying about . . . whether you knew how it was meant to go, or something. I'd like to read that. After all, it's the way most people listen to music.'

In Off the Street
The Guardian, November 1993

Of all the manifestations of jazz that look into the mists of the future rather than over its shoulder at a golden glow in the past, the brittle, jolting New York music of saxophonist Steve Coleman is one of the most striking. Coleman was at Dingwall's on Monday with his Five Elements band, and all the features of this lean, terse, Nineties version of jazz-funk (more ambiguously stated backbeat, spare, exclamatory guitar and bass figures against fast, dense horn and keyboard lines) were rattled out in a suite-like sequence of grooves that abruptly gave way to each other as if someone were track-shifting a CD player, or sometimes stopping it dead.

Apart from the gloves-off momentum of the Coleman band's slightly baleful expertise and the unflinching resolve of its steely music, the other pointer to its growing authority is an audience reaction far more gleeful and uninhibited than the earnest concentration that sometimes greets new jazz. The reasons aren't hard to identify. Coleman uses the rhythmic devices of contemporary funk and hip-hop, expressed by percussion techniques altogether quicker and more complex, more unpredictable in accent, and several classes lighter than the lumbering punchbag-thumping incarnations of early jazz-rock drumming. He lays over this melodic improvising that recalls the speed of Charlie Parker and the passionate vocalised vibrato of Ornette Coleman. It may not yet be the marriage of dance music's immediacy and jazz improvisation's elusive subtleties of thought which has been pursued by innumerable performers for years, but it's close.

Though the young Coleman's playing constantly suggests bebop in its intensity and sound, its feel is not the triplet saunter of jazz swing but the percussive, even stutter of fast funk. The atmosphere is constantly one of spontaneous composition, with ensemble passages appearing and disappearing in as informal a manner as the old 'head' arrangements of swing bands, brief abrasive harmonies that nudge the music on and then evaporate. Only the ascetic avoidance of dynamic contrast in solos (fearing cliché, these musicians are purists about relentless melodic investigations without big crescendos or party-pieces) creates occasional longueurs.

The current Five Elements band includes the eloquent guitarist Dave Gilmore, a long-time partner of Coleman's, whose latticework of clipped, laconic phrases and brief, drumlike chords in ensemble is balanced by an improviser's imagination as loose and full-blooded as the leader's. Coleman's exquisite tone was unfurled in a first-set feature that bordered on a ballad but occasionally hinted at a Latin American feel without ever explicitly declaring it, and he wound up with a foray into slamming funk that rattled the bar. Powerful, fearless new jazz.

POWER TRIO

The Guardian, November 1993

The way they bellowed for more as John McLaughlin's new power trio wound up its Tuesday night encore at the Festival Hall with a twenty-minute drum solo by Dennis Chambers and a final avalanche of crunching chords, it seemed as if there were plenty of fans in the audience who fondly remembered the guitarist's last regular forays into electric music in the 1970s.

McLaughlin was appearing with the Hammond organist Joey de Francesco (a creditable Miles Davisian trumpeter as well) and the thunderous Chambers on drums, the latter a man who makes Billy Cobham sound like a castanet player. The first half, a restless mix of jumpy time changes between bop grooves and bludgeoning funk, with rather amorphous themes, suggested that the gig was going to be swamped by the drummer, who was considerably louder than even his substantially amplified colleagues, and whose domineering playing was only occasionally offset by the silky flow of his cymbal beat delivering regular jazz time.

These contradictions made the most attractive feature of the first half a ballad for the guitar and de Francesco's muted trumpet alone, in which McLaughlin's inventive chordal promptings elicited phrasing from his partner a long way removed from simple Davis-cloning.

After the break, the band meshed far better, with McLaughlin's mixture of clipped, fragmented, horn-like figures and speed-of-light runs acquiring a relaxed fluency, and Chambers being able to sink his teeth into more straight-ahead bluesy grooves, at which his playing became a polyrhythmic blur. Joey de Francesco demonstrated why he's the young Hammond king on the mid-tempo section framed by a chunky rhythm and blues riff, avoiding traditional Hammond melodrama in favour of a crystal-clear precision and swing.

CRAZY SAINT
The Guardian, November 1993

A week after his former employer John McLaughlin's hot-licks organ trio performance on the South Bank, dominated by the carpet-bombing funk drumming of Dennis Chambers, Trilok Gurtu appeared in the same location at the end of his national tour with his own trio. The music could hardly have been more different, though the Indian can certainly be a sufficiently emphatic fusion drummer to invite speculation as to whether McLaughlin's new Free Spirits band with the brilliant organist Joey de Francesco might have been more musical if he had stayed in it.

As it was, the percussionist's trio with pianist Daniel Goyone and bassist Christian Minh Doky was an altogether more layered, complex, delicate and detailed experience, even if the stars of his new *Crazy Saints* disc – notably Pat Metheny and Joe Zawinul – weren't available. Goyone writes thoughtful, shapely and often poignant compositions (though his improvising exhibits a rather pale, inhibited quality) and Doky delivers engagingly reticent echoes of Steve Swallow's sound on bass guitar, and Charlie Haden's on the upright.

But it is inevitably Gurtu's show, even though his attentiveness to the music overall, and his sensitivity to the nuances of sounds, always maintain a sense of absorption in the ensemble's progress. Goyone's pieces often develop riff-based grooves out of ethereal, drifting Paul Bley-like themes, and Gurtu was devastating on these – crouching on one knee and delivering a crackling tapestry of abrupt cymbal smacks, low bass-drum rumbling (since he squats at a mixture of Western and Indian drums, he uses a conventional bass drum laid flat and hit like a tom-tom) and scurrying hi-hat patterns. Gurtu's driving time-playing ignited a neatly integrated blend of traditional Carnatic song and bebop chord changes, and mixed tabla and maraccas on a Latin feature, but the richness of his resources in abstract, tone-poetry pieces resulted in a miniature masterpiece of gurgling water sounds, swelling gongs, birdsong and ghostly rustlings and hootings on 'Blessing in Disguise'. Beautiful, conversational, all-embracing music.

ARRANGED MARRIAGE

The Guardian, November 1993

Ornette Coleman's inspiration has touched jazz in many fundamental ways, but one of the most enlightening has been through the rediscovery of spontaneous ensemble playing, an activity sidelined by the bebop era. The interweaving of improvised lines around free-floating tonal centres can approach an ideal balance of stability and spontaneity in the right hands, though the risks are high.

The British alto saxophonist Martin Speake, a founder-member of the prizewinning all-sax quartet Itchy Fingers, has been touring with the great American drummer Paul Motian (one-time regular partner to the late Bill Evans, Paul Bley and Keith Jarrett, among many), plus John Parricelli on guitar and Mick Hutton on bass. This has been a hastily arranged marriage, Motian having heard Speake's work on record and recognised a kindred spirit. The band's second-set performance at the Jazz Café on Tuesday showed how close in outlook they are.

Speake's saxophone sound is a haunting mixture of fragile, silvery high-register playing and a plush, buttery, flugelhorn-like mid-range, and his momentum (as befits a man who spent so long in a contrapuntal all-horn group) has an unassuming but unswerving resolution of tempo. In these respects he resembles a Fifties Cool School improviser, but his phrasing represents a far more contemporary chemistry of long zig-zagging lines, sudden octave jumps to sustained hoots, and unexpected resolutions. This mixture perfectly suited his and Motian's material, such as the glancing, whimsical Carla Bley-like 'Twisted Tango', the brooding overlays of slowly churning semi-abstract guitar chords, fluttery alto, flamenco-like bass figures and scurrying cymbal patterns on 'Gang of Five', lurching, Ornetteish dirges like 'Conception Vessel' and the country-tinged ballad 'Lullaby'. Motian's light, impulsive touch lent buoyancy to everything, but the London musicians sounded as if they'd worked with him for years. This writer has never heard John Parricelli, in particular, sound looser, or more freely inventive.

HALF-CENTURY

The Guardian, November 1993

Stan Tracey, the great English musician who looks from the rear like a man feverishly playing a football machine while seated at the piano, and who has delivered over several decades some of the freshest and most bombastically eager jazz music ever hewed in this country, was celebrating fifty years in the business on the South Bank on Tuesday. He put virtually all the incarnations of his prodigious music-making on stage through the evening, which involved a procession in and out of the dressing room of some of the most gifted defenders of the faith in Britain and at both ends of the age scale too.

Tracey himself is nearly sixty-seven, but in his music and his demeanour has lost little of his old gleam. One of his partnerships on Tuesday involved the young trumpet virtuoso Gerard Presencer, who played at least one of the most startling solos of the night, a set of blistering variations on an impromptu rendition of 'Misty'.

The show began with Tracey's quartet, opening with a truculent account of Monk's 'I Mean You' – and though it was a racy event, Tracey's splashy percussive sounds and lollopping runs can become a shade ritualised in this context, even if tenorist Art Themen's engagingly skidding runs and hollow, dolorous sound certainly aren't. Then came Tracey with young Presencer, and after a nervous start in which he sounded gifted but rigid, the trumpeter eased into a remarkable repertoire of slurs, deft runs and manipulations of the beat, all couched in an attractively flarey tone, particularly on Coltrane's 'Some Other Blues'.

Before a big-band finale however, and inauspiciously preceded by the star prowling the stage looking anxiously at his watch during Digby Fairweather's introductions, came the brief exposure of the most magical moment of the night. Tracey played 'Sophisticated Lady' unaccompanied, as a tapestry of walking bass lines, camouflaged melody, sly trills and poignantly shifted harmonies that must have made Ellington, somewhere, stand up and tip his hat.

GIVE US THOSE POSTMODERNIST BLUES

The Guardian, December 1993

They looked like the cast of *Reservoir Dogs* and played a repertoire that rarely strayed past the opening date of the Second World War. A.J. Croce himself, a young white singer/pianist who looks as if he's walked off the set of a Calvin Klein shoot, but sounds like a sixty-five-year-old bluesman from Chicago who drinks cognac and ground glass for breakfast, completes the usual postmodernist slideshow. From the off, I was prepared to dislike it very much.

Croce is touted as a rootsier Harry Connick, a personable young man who knows his way around a keyboard, is steeped in black American musical history, and doesn't get sidetracked by self-expression. But he isn't urbane and laid-back like Connick, and attacks everything as if his life depends on it. This vivacious application, and the truth which dawns as the show goes on, that Croce is a buff from his tousled curls to the tips of his socks, is what evaporates the grouchiest of seen-it-all-before moods. By the last twenty minutes of full-tilt Forties-style jump music it was impossible to dislike Croce, and very easy to join the chorus demanding more.

As well as a good deal of song material drawn from the Twenties and Thirties, and boilingly virtuosic episodes of ragtime, boogie and stride piano, Croce demonstrated in a string of originals echoing the manner of Randy Newman and Tom Waits that his shrewdness in devising laconically revealing morning-after lyrics matches his ear for telling material trawled from all over American songwriting history. Close to the end, he delivered 'Nobody Wants You When You're Down and Out' as a charging, frantic wail that may not have been the most spinechillingly truthful account this song has ever had, but which reconstituted it as classy nightclub entertainment in a manner that sounded neither maudlin, smartass or a clone of somebody else's version. A.J. Croce is going to do good business at the Jazz Café, and if it doesn't buy off the buff in him, nobody's going to object.

REAL TIME

The Guardian, December 1993

When pianist Julian Joseph's quartet played on the Outside In festival in September, it did everything except ignite. Joseph was promoting material from his second disc (*Reality*), a rather proper arts-centre concert hall setting seemed to diminish him, and the band's ensemble unity and ostensibly effortless rhythmic sophistication wasn't quite enough to turn on the heat.

But at the Jazz Café on Tuesday, to a packed house crouching around his elbows, Joseph's band positively sizzled. Peter King, the unnervingly swift and audacious altoist, took the horn parts – but such was the mischievous electricity at work between Joseph and drummer Mark Mondesir particularly, that even King occasionally resembled a man feverishly paddling a raft on a swollen river.

Joseph had already demonstrated his respect for his piano heroes in a solo recital at the Purcell Room over the weekend, so maybe the altogether more informal atmosphere on Tuesday triggered an impulse to cut loose. The most animated musical ensemble conversations occurred on a selection of up-tempo postbop themes, with nervy, zig-zagging melody lines resembling very fast Eric Dolphy solos running over emphatic bass-guitar vamps (Mark Mondesir's brother Michael was on bass), suddenly switching tempo into flowing swing. They would open with characteristically volatile King solos, giving way to variations by the leader that turned increasingly into reflexive duets with the drums as the show proceeded. Joseph would deliver wry, laid-back piano figures against the push of the beat, Mondesir would echo their shape but intensify them with a snare-and-tom-tom flurry. Joseph would dart into double-time, Mondesir would shower him with a blizzard of cymbal sounds. Joseph would try lolloping, Monkish out-of-tempo figures, fixing his drummer with a devilish, get-this grin, Mondesir would gleefully sidestep him and erupt into a blur of blows all around his kit, as if trying to scoop it all up in both arms. And although Joseph's slower ruminations were not the rhythm of the night, a collage-like blend of ballad lines in the first set demonstrated how far this pianist has come, and hinted at how far he'll yet go.

Playing by Ear

The Guardian, December 1993

The kind of jazz encounter in which the musicians go into huddles at the end of every tune to figure out the next one, a mysterious offhand intimacy of muttered shorthand song-titles, tempos and keys punctuated by explosions of laughter and phlegmatic shrugs, isn't so common as it was. It's as if younger musicians have come to distrust the practice as giving the audience the idea it won't get its money's worth unless the show comes gift-wrapped. But at the Bull's Head on Monday three superb and massively experienced saxophonists of quite different persuasions – Art Themen, Don Weller, and Bobby Wellins – built a riot of a performance out of such freewheeling methods.

The three were the front line of a Bull's Head house rhythm section (Tony Lee on piano, Tony Archer on bass, Ken Hall on drums), and as usually occurs in such jam-session set-ups they kept pretty close to standards and the blues. But their styles are so different that every sequence of solos even on the most routinely recycling chords offered something unexpected. Bobby Wellins, one of the great British saxophone improvisers of the 1960s and still a unique voice, built his reflections with figures that sounded like edited fragments of longer passages, constantly working off the rhythm section with long pauses and sudden coaxing phrases. Don Weller, a barn-door of a man who makes his tenor look like a penny whistle and who mingles modernisms with the imperious drive of the great swing saxists, who more effectively than anyone in Britain deceptively plays in a soft, smudgy tone much of the time, which maximises the shock value of his sudden eruptions into cantankerous whirrs and loud, grumpy trills. Themen shows the most explicit Coltrane and Rollins influences, but demonstrated a graceful lyrical ingenuity on this down-the-line material that he rarely exercises elsewhere. The inevitable 'Green Dolphin Street' and a good deal of chugging mid-tempo blues brought the best out of all of them, and the Basie-like riffs that the non-soloing hornmen busked behind each soloist established an atmosphere of exuberance that had the audience baying. It showed that juggling, not polishing, old materials is the way to keep them young.

1994

At either end of jazz-funk in 1994 – the 'cutting edge', where boppish virtuosity and James Brown soul merged, and the 'classic' version from the soul-jazz 1960s played by greying veterans – the quality was a lot higher and the music more relaxed and spontaneous than in the over-processed and market-conscious 'fusion' that was coming to sound increasingly dated. The young British guitarist Tony Remy, like John McLaughlin in the late Sixties, promised a mixture of tough improvisation, jazzy swing and contemporary pop on the basis of his debut GRP disc, Boof!. *The classic style was represented in 1994 by a memorable visit to Britain by Maceo Parker's band. Parker, the godfather of funk saxophone, James Brown and Parliament sideman and inspiration to David Sanborn, revealed just how much exuberance was still to be liberated from this unashamedly stylised genre.*

Another Parker, but a very different one, celebrated his fiftieth birthday with a major concert, having achieved legendary status around the admittedly small world of international free-improvisation fans. Briton Evan Parker, a formidable revolutionary of saxophone technique, rightly had his substantial influence on contemporary music acknowledged. So did another British reedman, John Surman, who was also fifty. Surman had done as much as any British jazz musician to wake the world up to the original music being made in the UK, and to play a vital part in liberating European jazz-influenced music from the dominant influence of the States.

Britain's South African émigré musicians watched Nelson Mandela's inauguration and celebrated a sensational week with a trilogy of African-angled gigs at the London Jazz Festival in May. On the same festival, the young American saxophonist Joshua Redman (son of Dewey Redman) played Ronnie Scott's all week, and let it be known that a massive improvising talent (though mostly rooted in orthodox postbop) was not just in the making but all but mature.

The Norwegian saxophonist Jan Garbarek came to Britain to perform ECM's latest arcane hit, Officium. *The material was jazz saxophone with Gregorian chants, a format ideally suited to Garbarek's ghostly sound and minimal need for external rhythmic propulsion – and the public adored it, inside and outside the jazz world. Joe Henderson, the other risen saxophone star of the era, after a long career in which his improvisational genius was overlooked by all but the cognoscenti, began to find his old recordings being rushed out in luxurious boxed sets. Having won a Grammy for his Ellington/Strayhorn dedication* Lush Life, *his career was belatedly on a roll.*

The saddest news on the British jazz scene was the premature death of the drummer John Stevens, one of the most passionate and dedicated of all defenders of unconventional music. And one of the most spectacular London jazz shows in years occurred with the return of the Brazilian multi-instrumentalist and composer Hermeto Pascoal, who drew a performance out of a mixed British and Brazilian band that was in its way a testament to precisely the sort of consciousness-raising and rhythmic confidence in UK players that John Stevens's career had been all about.

A Lot of Moonlight

The Guardian, March 1994

Dee Dee Bridgewater, the powerful, personable and experienced American vocalist, makes no secret of her work being a series of homages. Echoes of the great female singers in jazz infuse her performances, from the percussive, careering scat technique of Ella Fitzgerald, to the widescreen sumptuousness of Sarah Vaughan and the smokey intimacy of Billie Holiday.

Though jazz vocalists all over the world have rediscovered the standard song, Bridgewater's mixture of power and precision gives her a special edge. Only a rather edgy eagerness to charm (probably intensified by anxieties about her current throat trouble) and a tendency to shoulder-charge everything with fast scat and gospel-flavoured volume in the first half-hour blasted the enigmatic or oblique out of some of the material, and for a while it seemed as if the Queen Elizabeth Hall show was going to resemble the gallery-playing that happens on festival gigs. Miles Davis's 'All Blues', with Jon Hendricks's lyrics, suffered like this, but a ballad medley of 'I'm a Fool to Want You' and 'I Fall in Love Too Easily' were burnished in every nuance. A racing version of 'What a Little Moonlight Can Do' began with a crackling drum intro from the Mephistophelean André Ceccarelli, stopped dead, turned into a hustling walking bass line (Hein

Van Der Gein displayed as much of the chemistry of Mingus-like clout and lyricism as Britain's Danny Thompson) and ushered Bridgewater in in a smooth, gliding whisper that signalled the show starting to click.

By the second half Bridgewater had most of the contents of a soft-drinks cabinet standing beside the piano, but the condition they were countering hardly showed, and the young French pianist Thierry Euez played a series of solos that so startlingly displayed the arts of unclichéd spontaneous composition at breathless tempos as to suggest he's an international nouveau-bop giant on the way. 'Just Friends', 'Autumn Leaves' and 'Just One of Those Things' were all rich interpretations (though the last was best when Bridgewater hung on to the lyrics but twisted them deftly around stretched phrasing and before she resorted to wordless incantatory whoops), but her Sarah Vaughan dedication on 'Polka Dots' and 'Moonbeams' was exquisite, with a resonating stillness that the show could have done with a little more of. Very high-class jazz vocals, for all that.

TWENTY-ONE-GUN SALUTE

The Guardian, March 1994

The Hammond organ is such a twenty-one-gun salute of an instrument that supplementary sound effects in the shape of playing partners seem almost superfluous. Munich organist Barbara Dennerlein's gigs, in which the young virtuoso is often accompanied by expert but rather conventional drummers and saxophonists, usually occasion these thoughts. Playing unaccompanied, Dennerlein is devastating, her improvisations maelstroms of yelping trills against hissing, burst-main sustained chords, long, sweeping bop lines, light, ping-pong-ball runs and dancing foot-operated bass lines in which the familiarity of her raw materials seems to melt in the heat. But in a trio the repertoire she favours – blues, relaxed Latin dance and funk, bop standards – stays closer to its well-worn tramlines, and the leader's considerable capacity to surprise is revealed at longer intervals.

In her second set at Dingwall's on Tuesday, Dennerlein opened with a jazz classic, 'Out of Nowhere', delivered as a mid-tempo swinger and played pretty much on the nose by all concerned. As her own solo developed, the organist began to whip up some churning double-time and dark, lowering chordwork and then delivered a graceful, weaving bass solo with her feet (Dennerlein's footwork on the pedals is worth watching as a variation of tapdancing) that dropped some jaws around the room. The leader's faintly art-rockish salsa composition was complex though colourless, but the unaccompanied blues blast that followed stole the set with its slashing application of musical colours and exploration of her bugged Hammond's capabilities from swamping pier-organ sounds to skittish electric pianos.

This piece ('Stormy Weather Blues' – great titles aren't Dennerlein's forte) brought home how adventurously this devoted and engaging performer can transform the familiar licks of the blues-organ rulebook without obliterating them. But by so convincingly demonstrating the art of turning clichés upside down and shaking them until some colour returns to their cheeks, Dennerlein also unwittingly fingers the near misses she so often has with her bands. With the ENJA CD *Wow!* she had Andy Sheppard and Mark Mondesir to scrape their fingernails down the idiom and stop it from settling into lounge-jazz relaxation. On the road, she lets partners recycle the very licks her own imagination is so good at scaring the daylights out of, though the band did unite to take some lateral swipes at the vigorous bebop standby, Sonny Rollins's 'Pent-up House'. But Barbara Dennerlein's shows are truly worth the trip for the moments when the stage is hers alone. Only the deaf or the dead would then be in any doubt that lounge-jazz it definitely ain't.

KILLER
Q Magazine, March 1994

Sidney Bechet, **Jazz Classics Vol. 2** (Blue Note)

For drama and single-minded drive, Sidney Bechet between 1920 and the late Thirties couldn't be touched by anybody but Louis Armstrong, a performer who by a wilful mixture of a killing technique and unstoppable conviction and confidence redefined almost every piece of music he played as a tapestry of his own extraordinary mannerisms and firepower. These Blue Note sessions date from the New Orleans revival period between 1939 and 1951, and though you hear modern intonations in Frankie Newton's trumpet that wouldn't have been there a decade earlier, this is generally an engaging roll through a collection of raunchy blues and classic Dixieland workhorses like 'High Society'. Bechet's clarinet vibrato flaps like birds-wings.

Tony Remy, **Boof!** (GRP)

Tony Remy, like John McLaughlin in the late Sixties, is the new British guitar export capable of blasting improvisation and jazzy swing but also pop-angled ideas that broaden his audience. That's why GRP have signed him up, though in some ways *Boof!* says rather more about GRP than about a guitarist whose mixture of feline rhythmic touch and sudden eruptions of spontaneous energy make him such a hypnotic performer in clubs. Remy has angled his repertoire to a fusion and soul audience, so the material is dominated by a gracefully hushed contrapuntal funk, from the Stevie Wonder-through-a-vocoder vocal of the opening track ('Glide') to chattering hip-hop and a Metheny-like gentle lyricism. But though Remy and GRP have deliberately avoided a guitar-hero album full of long solos and featured instead the leader's inventive fascination with electronic textures and layering of many instrumental voices, there's still a tightness and rigour in the bigger group pieces, and the elbowing drive and percussive sounds of Remy's duet with drummer Pete Lewinson on 'Fewtcha Funk' packs a punch. It is beautifully produced, tiny finger-cymbal sounds fluttering around you like butterflies. But it is soft, compared to Remy's bite on stage.

BELOW THE WAIST
The Guardian, March 1994

Uh! Uh? Uh, uh, uh!! Get those deep-below-the-waistline grunts coming, it's the urban jazz funk dance party! Maceo Parker's heavy set, mafia suits' front line of himself on alto, Fred Wesley on trombone and Pee Wee Ellis on bar-walking funk tenor were almost charismatic enough as visual stimuli to set Thursday's packed Astoria dance floor jumping as much as there was elbow-room to, and on top of that they're hip and experienced enough to play an audience's reactions as unerringly as they play their horns, and attack everything as if sculpting granite. Parker, the godfather of funk saxophone, ex-MD for James Brown and sideman for Parliament, P-Funk and George Clinton, announced before this tour that his show was going to be two per cent jazz and the rest hip-swivelling music, and he stuck to it.

The Root Revisited Band, Parker's first solo project for twenty years, and launched in 1991, is the kind of funk ensemble that acts as a sharp reminder of how mechanical most soul-jazz groups are by comparison – the choppy, conversational cross-rhythms put out simply by the drummer, bass, keys and guitar laying down a groove would almost have held the show without the heavyweights, and such a vivid backup allowed the main soloists to embroider the music with their own particular brand of muscular understatement. The only drawback is that the idiom induces Parker to keep the story of how good a saxophone player he is to himself most of the time, except in some delectable flutters and flourishes on slow tunes. Fans of David Sanborn (a dutiful student of the legacy of Parker and other soul-sax legends) would recognise those urgent, interrogatory phrases, and Parker injects into it all a heightened sense of drama and a shrewder ability both to edit himself and extend a single repeated idea to breaking point before resolving it, sometimes gleefully running on the spot as his partners charge back with the beat.

Some of the slower music sagged a little, Parker talked a lot, and some more faith in extending the improvising wouldn't have blunted the momentum or bored the audience. But the abrasive, no-frills directness of this music, the blaring, effusive trombone of Fred Wesley, and one particular Pee Wee Ellis tenor solo – a mixture of light, dancing phrases and explosive bell-notes – against an ensemble sounding like a gospel choir confirmed that Roots Revisited delivers what it says and then some.

EXPANSIONIST

The Guardian, April 1994

Until Evan Parker's generation of European improvisers got rolling in the late Sixties, there was 'free jazz' (offshoots of the insights of Ornette Coleman, Cecil Taylor and the other iconoclastic African-Americans), and there was improvised 'new music' (as likely as not to be using materials associated with composers such as Stockhausen and Xenakis, and the random-association notions of John Cage). Parker, one of the world's towering saxophone virtuosi, who threw his fiftieth birthday party as a concert at Dingwall's on Sunday, has been crucial to the dissolution of these distinctions. His expansions of the sax vocabulary and approach to group improvising over twenty-five years sound, if anything, more adventurous than ever.

Sunday's show featured Parker with three quite different bands – the closest to orthodox materials being represented by the fine singer Francine Luce's collaboration with Parker, pianist Alex Maguire, bassist Roberto Bellatalla and drummer Tony Marsh, the most organic and intense being a trio with Barry Guy and Paul Lytton, and sometimes the most soloistically engaging being a memorable reunion with German free-jazz stars Alex von Schlippenbach and Paul Lovens. The last trio represented a restless succession of powerful individual contributions shifting in and out of stormy ensemble passages, with the musicians often seeming so diverted by a partner's decisions as to all but swap identities – pianist Schlippenbach (who sometimes mirrors a synthesis of Cecil Taylor and Bill Evans) resembling Parker's horn in a train-like sequence of churning bass figures and abstract, clapping treble chords, or Parker's tenor, suggesting hammers on damped strings in a series of percussive, spurting sounds. The set was full of such subversions of instrumental identity.

The trio that followed, with Barry Guy on bass and Paul Lytton on drums, was more of a display of group energy, generated in the kind of tidal waves that tend to follow Barry Guy everywhere. Parker began with a figure close to blues phrasing on tenor, while Guy and Lovens operated virtually as two percussionists. In a manner closest to his early Coltrane inspirations, Parker roared into a typically guttural, episodically explosive solo, while Guy sustained an astonishing alternation of high, lyrical bowed chords and scuttling runs, damping some notes by lightning shifts of the position of what looked like a drumstick jammed between the strings. Paul Lytton, who at times in the past has been something of a bludgeoning free drummer, has developed an illuminating precision and control of dynamics, making him a cornerstone of this band's astonishing richness of texture. It all ascended to a fluttering, aviary-like delicacy with Parker on soprano in the finale. Great free music, great free musicians, and a colossus celebrating a career of fearless, devoted, and inspirational independence. Happy Birthday.

Two-Tone
The Guardian, April 1994

Like a traveller negotiating a land he doesn't often visit, but who sporadically runs into compatriots, tenorist Dewey Redman sounds careful and deliberate when he plays standards and bop, and then rockets off into torrential loquacity when he improvises in the fluid and intuitive manner of the Ornette Coleman school, of which he is such a significant member.

Redman appeared on Sunday at Dingwall's with a versatile quartet featuring a superb young pianist in Rita Marcotulli, crisply supported by Cameron Brown on bass and Leon Parker on drums. In the early stages of his first set, Redman – who on conventional material exhibits something of the bulky, rugged, unhurrying quality and sinister trills of the late Dexter Gordon – played orthodox bebop and a version of 'The Very Thought of You' dawdling so far behind the beat as to make the sudden intensifying of the solo a genuine shock when the throttle of Parker's cymbal beat snapped open.

But it was on an Ornette Coleman piece featuring a Redman solo of crackling, seesawing phrases, hopping runs, squirmy, liquid sounds and bluesy squawks, that was the most arresting reminder of what a vivid, scintillating angle of jazz improvising this style is (avoiding chord changes, spontaneously shifting tonal centres for the others to pick up, like footballers receiving one-touch passes) and how little exploited it has been in its thirty-five-year life. Rita Marcotulli (a rising piano star if ever there was), who had played with a mixture of Bud Powell's percussive energy and Paul Bley's oblique ruminativeness on the standards, sat out Redman's solos on the looser structures to avoid harmonic clashes, then embarked on her own variations as restless endeavours to start each new episode of the solo with a fresh governing idea and syntax. In the second set, Redman went in for some engaging North African-flavoured rap (he sounded like a Moroccan Tommy Cooper) over an imaginative blend of mallet and stick playing by Leon Parker, and they all wound up with a funky blues (Marcotulli revealing a drumlike Horace Silver aspect) and a breezy 'Take the A Train'.

LIBERATION DAY
The Guardian, May 1994

Some of the freshest and most thrilling jazz made on these shores in the past twenty years has involved the black South African *émigrés* who settled here to take refuge from the political system finally consigned to the trash this week. From the fizzing cauldron of unruly hard bop and townships jive of the Blue Notes, who joined the British circuit in 1966, to the sumptuous, vocalised horn textures of the Ellingtonesque Brotherhood of Breath, to effervescent small bands led by prematurely deceased performers like Dudu Pukwana and Harry Miller and enduring ones led by the great drummer Louis Moholo, the story has gone on in all its impulsive, cliffhanging urgency. They always seemed to play as if it was their last gig. The spontaneous collectivity of African village life partly accounts for it, but so does being raised on the business end of a gun. The London Jazz Festival, starting 12 May, includes a trilogy of South African shows.

Sharing a sunny room in Brixton with four of the survivors as Tuesday lunchtime's news was confirming De Klerk's departure speech and Mandela's formal arrival was like being at their gigs – abrupt detonations of hilarity and flares of fleeting indignation, speech and songs combined if spoken language turns out to be inadequate to the message, bearhugs, handshakes, body language bulging the walls. Louis Moholo, whose short greying beard is about the only indication of his journey towards his mid-fifties, has just returned from his homeland, attending the elections and the unveiling of the first decent memorials to fellow musicians who died here and were flown home – like Dudu Pukwana, Mongezi Fezi, Chris McGregor and Johnny Dyani. Moholo is ecstatic, and his commentary on the pages now turning in his homeland's history cracks like his own snare drum. 'They interviewed the South African ambassador on TV the other day,' Moholo reports, rolling a cigarette. 'And the interviewer said, "It'll be a black South African doing your job now." "You shouldn't just think in terms of black and white," the ambassador says.' Round the table, all four are convulsed with incredulous laughter.

They have also – with the exception of the trumpeter Claude Deppa, who left the Cape with his parents twenty years ago – known most of the available absurdities and indignities of working the system's music business in their earlier years, with virtually all significant management, promotion and recording opportunities out of their control. Pinise Saul, the dramatic gospel-like singer who came here with the *Ipi Tombi* musical troupe in the Seventies and stayed, remembers how bored policemen would lift her off the street just to ask her if she knew the country's international vocal star Miriam Makeba. Louis Moholo remembers playing drums behind a curtain when working with white musicians, or taking white pianist Chris McGregor for a drink in the townships with boot-polish on his face and his collar turned up.

'Musicians are always a community, that's true everywhere, they share something that isn't spoken,' observes Mervyn Afrika, this country's adopted equivalent of Abdullah Ibrahim in his eloquent keyboard playing and arresting, raplike vocals. 'But apartheid tried to kill that, like it did every other way the people would get together. How can you have music if it's illegal for more than five black citizens to be in the same place? You couldn't travel to gigs without the right passes, everywhere you went you'd be hassled. Yet still the music was beautiful, they couldn't kill it. Beautiful music went too deep in South Africa.'

Claude Deppa points out that the role of music in everyday African working life made it a form of practical communication and constant accompaniment to work and play, which accounted both for its resilience and the paranoia it engendered in the administration. 'It'll never leave me, that background,' Deppa says. 'Wherever I work, I'm always a South African musician. I heard a gospel choir in London the other day, and they were singing in unison [he expels the word with incredulity]. That would never happen where we were raised. Group of singers get together, they all try to find a way of making it thicker, richer, get different lines going.' ('The Welsh do it too,' adds Moholo.) 'Then when we play instruments, it's the same thing.'

We watch the lunchtime news to the end, butter bread on Tuesday's front page bearing the headline, 'South Africa free at last'. 'Now the world will see,' Moholo says, 'what a wonderful place it is, how much it has to offer. Fantastic music there, every kind of music. We had to get out because it was mad, and then work for the country from the outside, giving people pleasure, showing them how fantastic we were, how much apartheid was poisoning our lives and our history but we still had so much to give.' They all acknowledge how much of a struggle remains, but they have already returned to play there, and will be going back whenever they're needed to work and teach. All four have roots here now they won't pull up, which is good news for the local jazz scene. 'People think it must have been hard for us to break into the music scene here,' Claude Deppa says. 'But it was easy. When you're raised in a situation like that, it makes you very hardworking, very determined to be good.' There are sounds of agreement.

'And there's another thing about all this . . .'

Expectant pause.

'No more benefits!' Deppa declares triumphantly.

'No more benefits!' chortle all four. In close harmony, of course.

METROPOLIS

The Guardian, May 1994

The three-borough London Jazz Festival, even more precipitously ambitious this year than last in its balancing of down-the-line jazz and world-music and its equal billing of local, European and American artists, has written itself up to the top of the jazz calendar in a big way. Chick Corea brought his Elektrik Band 2 to the Festival Hall on Tuesday, and though the gig was often breathtaking in its turn-on-a-dime ensemble precision and breakneck contrapuntal playing, and Corea's own solos remain models of fluent invention, it all had a rather heartless, muscle-flexing quality that communicated very little except dexterity in the end. On the same night, Django Bates's orchestra Delightful Precipice played the Bloomsbury Theatre, and although the band was far more ragged (in a wilful, exuberant, Loose Tubesian manner) it exuded joyous, humane, witty and quite uncategorisable music, mingling oompah circus rhythms with heavy-rock bludgeoning, football chants, fast bop and some of the most original composing currently in process.

A local artist for whom the absence of a solo album is a crime, the singer/pianist and composer Errolyn Wallen (she figured on the Young Musicians of the Year show a few months back) opened proceedings at the Union Chapel on Wednesday, with poor vocal/piano sound balance her only obstacle. Ms Wallen's broad musical origins make her solo work an attractive mixture of unjazzy yet forthright and swinging vocal performance, and stately classical-sounding keyboard accompaniment nonetheless delivered with a percussive and jazzlike drive. She veered into Thelonious Monk once or twice, and in her finale, 'Hurricane of Love', exultantly mingled atonalisms, stomping left-hand figures and a gracefully unpredictable vocal line. Her trumpeter brother Byron then took over with a ten-piece band (including flute and sax virtuosi Roland Sutherland and David-Jean Baptiste) and a new composition, the 'Tarot Suite'.

In its broth of Lat-Am shuffling, hip-hop clatter and fitfully spacey, impressionistic lyricism, it frequently suggested a 1990s *Bitches Brew*, and in his muted trumpet and soft flugelhorn textures against a boiling rhythm section Wallen often sounded what he is, the most interesting new European explorer of the legacy of Miles Davis. He also suggested audacious use of instrumental contrast, particularly for Sutherland's silky flute and Baptiste's grainy bass clarinet – but when he ominously announced the piece was 'a work in progress' he wasn't kidding, and it needs some tightening.

The young American saxophonist Joshua Redman played Ronnie Scott's all week, and though his repertoire is mostly unsurprising post-bop, his timing, development of a solo narrative, blending of atonal slides and chromatic phrasing and avoidance of cliché not only confirmed his overnight international status but suggested that a young-generation Sonny Rollins was here.

The veteran American saxophonist Pharoah Sanders played Dingwall's for three nights, and on Wednesday kidded his audience that he was walking through a leisurely Tributes-to-Trane routine before flowering around midnight with some delectable pad-fluttering noises and high harmonics on ballads, a lyrical exchange with the unexpectedly arrived soul-jazz diva Jean Carn on 'The Creator Has a Master Plan', and a raucous and funky vocal finale that set the audience leaping.

UPTOWN, DOWNTOWN

Unpublished, May 1994

Since McCoy Tyner, the fifty-five-year-old Philadelphia-born pianist and composer, is a performer of considerable charisma and independence as well as having been the late John Coltrane's most famous partner in the Sixties, it might be a source of some irritation to him to find Coltrane's name showing up in conversation as often as it still does twenty-seven years after he died. But Tyner isn't an easily irritated man, and he knows the spirit of the long-gone saxophonist still hovers benevolently over much contemporary jazz, as well as being a fundamental force in his own work.

Tyner is appearing in Britain with the excellent big band that got into its stride in the 1980s, but he had been a skilful composer and arranger from pre-Coltrane days, providing much of the material for the Jazztet he co-led with trumpeter Art Farmer, and on the innumerable Blue Note sessions he collaborated in in the Sixties. 'What I really always wanted,' Tyner says, 'was a band which had that Ellington quality of being a small band with a lot of members, that intimate but loose feeling. Then around the mid-Eighties, people were starting to ask me if I'd considered it. The great bandleaders were passing on, and though there were a few big bands around, they mostly seemed to me like a lot of guys sitting down playing notes, if you know what I mean.' (Tyner is a big, serene-looking man, and his chuckle has a lot of layers to it – in this case the creative jazz musician's dislike of routine music without improvisational danger.)

Tyner is still always happy to talk about Coltrane, and about an extraordinary decade in his musical life. In an era in which rock music blotted out everything, Coltrane's band exerted immense spiritual as well as musical influence, affected rock stars like Zappa and Hendrix, even had commercial success with the big-selling *A Love Supreme.* 'Coltrane and I grew up in a period when you were supposed to try to be different, not copy someone else. I met him at seventeen, used to sit on his porch with his mother – she had an old upright piano – and talk and play. He was amazing, and absorbed music so quickly that by this time the saxophone book was no challenge to him so he learned from a harp book instead – all those long runs. That was what affected those "sheets of sound" everybody talked about.' (An eyebrow rises at this.) 'It's true, believe me,' Tyner insists with another private chuckle. 'You're getting it from the horse's mouth.' Tyner is involved in a book about that period, and promises a lot more Coltrane insights like that one.

McCoy Tyner recognises that the inexorable journey towards dissolution of structures Coltrane was pursuing – and which eventually drove him from the band – didn't lead to a lasting jazz revolution, but though he dislikes the duplication of the past in some current versions of the music, he doesn't feel that free music was ever likely to dominate the scene. 'All art changes in different periods, you see it in painting too. I've come to feel that an artist has to be responsive to the public. You have an obligation to both challenge the public's imagination and make it feel good.' But he does regret the passing of the fertile jazz world of his childhood in which young musicians could find challenging players to learn from without even leaving their neighbourhood. 'That was so important, there were so many bands they were like schools. They taught the things schools can't teach, the things that are about feelings and not techniques. It's like anything else in life. The unwritten information.'

LONG GONE
The Guardian, June 1994

Mike Osborne, **Outback** (Future Music)

When Mike Westbrook, Chris McGregor, John Surman, Dudu Pukwana, Alan Skidmore and the other major figures of the British jazz generation which emerged in the late Sixties dominated the universe here, Mike Osborne was the saxophonist they all raised an eyebrow to, which is a big accolade in the jazz business. Illness took Osborne out of regular public performance in 1982, but his searing tone, distraught-sounding whirls into the upper register and sudden crunching descents into the alto's basement sounds, and his ability to negotiate the most intense free music without repetition or bluster made him the English Eric Dolphy, and his early retirement was an irreplaceable loss.

This fine, unruly Osborne session from the Seventies (replicating the original artwork, even down to the misspelling of his name) is as good an evocation as any of what Osborne's tense vitality was like. The other members of this quintet are Harry Beckett on trumpet, the late Chris McGregor and Harry Miller on piano and bass, and Louis Moholo on drums – the last two the rhythm section of Osborne's regular trio at the time. For anyone raised on Eighties postbop, in which soloists step respectfully out of each other's way and the groove is written on a hoarding, this is a teeming, tumbling, sometimes ferocious session, full of jolting, breathless disruptions of the pulse from Moholo and McGregor's typically jangling dissonances. Miller's arco does a convincing didgeridoo impression on the wailing title track, and though it sometimes seems to be functioning in a room of its own, Beckett's trumpet adds lightness and wit. A long way from background music, but a fascinating example of some of the stations British jazz has passed through.

WATERMELON MAN

The Guardian, June 1994

Considering the queues for Dr Yusef Lateef in London a few weeks back, it was surprising the Jazz Café was quiet for the opening night by Chico Hamilton – a performer, it could have been surmised, of equal retro-status who made a key appearance in the cult jazz movie *Jazz on a Summer's Day* with the late Eric Dolphy, featured posthumously-fêted dance-jazz guitar star Grant Green in the Sixties, and made as visionary a use of Latin tempos in bop form as anyone in the music's history.

Hamilton is in his seventies now, and looks like a mere fifty-year-old who has enjoyed a few protracted meals. He remains as irrepressibly dynamic a drummer as Art Blakey was at the age when dynamism might be expected to give way to eloquent circumspection. Though his early reputation was founded on expressive use of Latin-American hybrids, which typecast him, Hamilton really earned his dues as a percussion pioneer. On this show his drum sound was the restless sea on which the eager craft of the other three tacked and pitched. In accompaniment of soloists Hamilton often sustains fizzing cymbal patterns in both hands, and in the extended solos he plays on most tunes, two-thirds of his variations might stray hardly at all from the cymbals and abrupt, explosive snare rolls. The repertoire mixed originals and standards, the latter including a delectable version of 'Topsy', which Arnie Lawrence began in a casual Lester Youngian murmur over Hamilton's grinning cymbal pulse and offhandedly scattered snare accents, and which ended up as a flat-out tenor blast and a guitar solo remarkably blending breakneck speed and melodic invention from the gifted Cary DeNegris. Hamilton, who kept reawakening jaded sensibilities about the textural variety of drumming all night, signed off the tune with a whispering brushes sequence that was as warm and affable as drumming can get.

The Birthday Party

The Guardian, June 1994

The principally classical Bath Festival's fiftieth birthday special for John Surman was a lot of tribute, but no more than Surman deserved. He showed a ferocious reluctance to take the easy way out thirty years ago, playing sky-diving Coltranesque sax marathons on the huge baritone (the jazz equivalent of trying to give mouth-to-mouth resuscitation to an elephant) and though he divided the extremes of his baritone playing between the soprano sax and the bass clarinet later, and turned to more solitary, ethereal and often folksy music, his work continues to represent a truly personal reappraisal of jazz.

Surman has helped European jazz evolve in ways now taken for granted – into a lyrical but structurally broader idiom that mixes jazz tonality and phrasing with other forms, into scores for ballets, marriages of acoustic horns and electronics, relationships between jazz and European folk forms, even English church music in Surman's case. He tightly rations what's usually thought of as swing, but he's a highly rhythmic player with his own ideas about what swinging is. Much of this variety was available on Friday night.

Surman began the show at the Pavilion unaccompanied and in a favourite high-stepping jaunty manner, shadowing a jig-like soprano theme splashed with jazz ('Now's the Time' flitted briefly through it) with a synthesiser counterpoint. Karin Krog's cool, precise vocal lines then danced diaphanously with his smokiest baritone sound (Surman's exquisite slow playing on the heavy horn goes all the way back to an early influence, Ellington's Harry Carney), though the rapturous, swooping abstractions of Terje Rypdal's electric guitar swelled a spacey mood piece, 'In Candlelight', into the most intense and integrated episode by the Norwegians, whose contribution had occasionally suffered from the treading-water passivity characteristic of North European jazz.

They were followed by what Surman called his 'favourite rhythm section' – Chris Laurence on bass, John Taylor on piano, John Marshall on drums. This group, particularly through the tidal intelligence of Taylor's piano variations, performed with a dramatic ebb and surge of intuitive tempo-shifting around complex themes bristling with modulations – on the second of which Surman unfurled all his considerable improvising powers with a spine-tingling bass clarinet intro over Laurence's arco bass, and a soprano improvisation midway through that brushed aside the structural complexities of the music as if they weren't there.

The orchestral Brass Project, augmented by Taylor's piano, was the finale. Though the band is packed with fine soloists, the music (which often texturally recalls Carla Bley and Gil Evans) is very tightly drawn, so the players sometimes resembled fast cars picking their way through narrow roads. But Surman and his skilled arranger John Warren create a world of compellingly sonorous, sliding, rippling chords, the leader and John Taylor delivered an object lesson in inseparable duo improvising on Radio 3's new (as yet untitled) commission, and on a fast, stomping feature with the sort of thumping repeated theme an all-sax band uses, trombonist Pete Beachill and trumpeter Steve Waterman unleashed solos that came close to the contributions of Surman and Taylor for resourceful cliché-avoidance. Everybody reassembled for a blues that turned into 'Creole Love Call', and then a blast of amiable funk and an even more amiable calypso

BRASSWORK
The Guardian, July 1994

The sixty-five-year-old Iowa trumpeter Art Farmer has been narrowing the elbow-room at the Dean Street Pizza Express all week, and continues there until Sunday night. A dapper, mustachioed, faintly lugubrious-looking man, Farmer has sustained his deceptively casual talents into his senior years – and since the late Eighties, both on disc and in person, has often seemed to be playing better than at any time in his life.

Farmer's playing, rooted in Fifties hard bop, resembles the Miles Davis of the period in texture, and a confection of such other hard bop brass stars as Clifford Brown and Kenny Dorham (though with a deft, throwaway quality of his own) in phrasing, and his solos still take shapes that constantly surprise the ear.

On Thursday, Farmer delicately polished his inimitable brassware and turned it languorously this way and that in the light. He usually works with standards, whose familiarity enhances his variations. He played much of 'Have You Met Miss Jones' in a soft, withdrawn monotone from which he would periodically vault into a glimpsed upper register, altered the dynamics of the solo in the middle with a plush, Miles-like repeated note hit like someone gently punching a beanbag, then sprang himself into a sequence of silvery high phrases before pianist Colin Purbrook's cryptic-ally swinging solo. Mal Waldron's ballad 'Soul Eyes' drew out Farmer's distilled, gracefully pitched slow style, and his holding back from the underlying beat constantly informed a brisk account of 'Falling in Love with Love', in which the leader's physiognomy occasionally betrayed its only flicker of explicit emotion, with a raised eyebrow on the tighter bends in his improvisation over Clark Tracey's quietly hustling cymbals. Farmer wrapped up the set with a mid-tempo 'The Man I Love', bouncing odd phrase-lengths, velvety runs and occasional upper-register squirts off the sibilant whisper of the rhythm section.

GARAGE BANDS

The Guardian, July 1994

The Garage, an upstairs sweatbox over the old Forum 2 on London's insalubrious Holloway Road, recently hosted an odd phenomenon. Charles Gayle, the fifty-five-year-old American tenor saxophonist (a man who has lived the life of a Manhattan street musician for decades, often played for two drunks and a dog, struggled to survive, shown no inclina-tion to lead a band, declare an attitude or find a niche, or veered far from a ferociously personal account reinterpretation of the wilful free jazz of the 1960s) packed the place with a predominantly young club audience, most of whom wouldn't have been born when he first began delivering his uncompromising message. Gayle hasn't been the only venerable maverick at this venue. Peter Brotzmann, the equally fierce and abrasive German saxophonist, has recently had the same effect there.

But this isn't a plink-and-squeak avant-garde jazz club. Organised by the left-field independent operation Blast First and its enterprising pro-grammer Paul Smith, the menu might be just as likely to include contemporary folk 'New Troubadours' (or as *The Face* dubbed them, 'grit-tier nouveau-folk performers'), shimmery ambience-artists, lo-fi samplers and turntable-players, maybe reciters of poetry and even arty pornogra-phy. Even George Melly – reciting, not singing – is scheduled there for 1 September. The audience, which might mingle earnest jazz types, stray members of famous bands (part of Sonic Youth's lineup was recently spot-ted there), punky art-student kids with hardware through their lips, takes it all without a blink.

Last week Wynton Marsalis, the virtuoso American trumpeter and classicist, made his statutory pre-Festival Hall concert appearances in the British press, with such utterances as: 'They [critics] want the music played by people who don't know what they're doing but are on the cutting edge of something . . . they like the idea of jazz being outsider's music.' Marsalis hates the avant-garde, and reiterates the position whenever he can. Yet notions of new sounds, drawn from sharp-end classical music, free jazz, reconstituted punk-rock, New Age ambiances, electronics, sampling, scratch and any other available materials, continue to attract audiences unmoved by the music of experts honing expertise.

Running throughout this week until Saturday at the Place Theatre in Euston is Company Week – at which spur-of-the-moment combinations of the world's most unruly and uncategorisable performers form and dissolve in the unrehearsed search for what the event's founder and improv-guru Derek Bailey describes as 'the bridges that cross the spaces between them'.

The phenomena of both Company Week and the Garage are barometers of the small-scale, but persistent popularity of music that wouldn't get past the foyer of a concert hall or a mainstream record company. Wyndham Wallace, who works for the Disobey Club which staged Gayle and Brotzmann's shows at the Garage, says, 'There's been a reaction against lush over-produced pop. That's why some of the new stuff is a modern take on folk, with its protest element restored, some free jazz, some of it jokes about fashions in sampling or rap. We've had sell-out shows at the Garage where people came with the idea of having their ears opened to something new, and that's what happened.'

'Around 1972,' Derek Bailey says, 'you could have got most of the significant London free players into my kitchen, and that's where we used to meet, actually. I'd come from dance bands and jazz, but younger guys like Evan Parker and Barry Guy showed me people I'd never thought of listening to, like Cage, Stockhausen, ethnic music, Indian music. The same thing was happening in a few countries at the same time. But it was all related to jazz then. The gigs were still on the jazz circuit, even if you were really there either because somebody had made a mistake, or was curious, or you were there on sufferance.

'Now there's a new soup. The London Musicians' Collective which puts on festivals and disseminates information, represents it very well. Not all of it is to do with free music, it might include contemporary composition, musical/theatrical activity, pure novelty, and freely improvised music. It doesn't appear on jazz festivals now, but in this new area, at new clubs and venues, fringe rock groups alongside free jazz, *musique concrete* composers who hate improvisers, Charles Gayle at the Garage is part of the same thing. The audience now will listen to anything. This is what the audience was supposed to be like in the Sixties but it wasn't. People thought they were going to want what we did because it was new art, but it wasn't that the audience's expectations weren't met, they were spectacularly exceeded, and they didn't like it.'

The London Musicians' Collective, founded in the mid-Seventies, is a lobbying and promoting organisation which now stages festivals, produces a new-music magazine called *Resonance*, and spreads the word. The LMC's Ed Baxter says: 'Somebody who studies classical music at Goldsmith's, say, is now as likely to be as open to grunge, or Derek Bailey, as to Mahler or the opera. John Zorn's been very influential in this. There's an openness to different types of new music now, we see it on events we put on, and you can find it everywhere. It would be going too far to call it a golden age, but there's a lot of really good stuff happening.'

ANGELS
The Guardian, July 1994

Airplays for Jan Garbarek and the Hilliard Ensemble's *Officium* jammed radio station switchboards with queries last week, and ECM Records look like having a runaway success with it, if anything so contemplative can be associated with such an animated notion. A thumbnail sketch of it would be jazz saxophone with Gregorian chants, a formula so clearly suited to ECM's ethereal eclecticism it seems an obvious avenue once it has been done. But since Garbarek has for years been an improviser who doesn't need rhythm sections but harmony sections – the slower and more transcendental the better, and often associated with church music – as settings for the haunting poignancy of his sound, such a marriage is more likely to work with him involved than just about any other jazz-based musician on the planet. The Hilliards, an inspired and enterprising group whose work embraces Tallis and Perotin and Arvo Part and Gavin Bryars as well, have been developing this project with Garbarek over three years, and delivered it with him for an unbroken hour and a quarter in King's College Chapel last Friday.

The pieces took in the ancient chants of the monasteries, early polyphonic music by Perotin (the mysterious genius of this distant music) and on into the fifteenth and sixteenth centuries with more complex multi-voiced works, some of which used harmonic underpinnings on which Garbarek could form his lines in a manner close to chord-based jazz improvisation. These were also the pieces that allowed the saxophonist to intertwine with the other melodies rather than occupy his own lonely spaces, and they were the most integrated and successful episodes of the collaboration. For all Garbarek is rightly acclaimed as a musician who eschews convenient jazz phrasing and licks in favour of texture and sound, he does, inevitably, have licks of his own making – the shy, brief, downward-wriggling soprano phrase to start a solo, the gathering multiphonic trill to build intensity – and in occasional passages where his contribution was a solo commentary on a preceding vocal ensemble, Garbarek fell back on some cramped-sounding set-pieces.

But the solemnity of the music and the setting may have inhibited even an improviser so familiar with such an atmosphere, and in the group's most abstract-sounding piece over halfway in, Garbarek began to put together more varied phrasing – a compelling alternation of three and two-note figures varied in intonation and fitful sighs and warbles. David James's soaring counter-tenor then delivered an astonishing solo flight from the back of the church over a distant drone, and a hypnotic coda to the penultimate piece finished with the voices and saxophone emitting little more than hushed outbreaths. Garbarek, as if relieved by the response, played his firmest and most exultant tenor feature on the encore.

REOPENING THE GATE

The Guardian, July 1994

The ECM record label, in amongst a certain amount of somnambulant minimalism and whistling-in-the-dark, has caught the work of some of the most expressive and independent jazz musicians over the past quarter-century, and the Gateway Trio (which recorded twice for ECM in the mid-Seventies) was always up there with the front-runners. Featuring guitarist John Abercrombie, bassist Dave Holland and drummer Jack DeJohnette, Gateway had good tunes, DeJohnette's dazzling rhythmic resources, Holland's thumping beat and melodic intuition, and Abercrombie's ability to combine a Bill Evans-like lyricism transferred to a Fender with sporadic bursts of Hendrixisms that arrived like somebody breaking down the door. It wasn't the kind of band which comes along every day.

Gateway has re-formed this year, and was in London on Monday and Tuesday after its Glasgow Festival appearance. Though Abercrombie began, as he sometimes does, by enveloping himself in a mist of spacey, inside-out chord sounds and muttered runs (he looks like a geologist rather than a guitar hero, and plays as if in a reverie, a discreetness that magnifies his remarkable technique) they picked up the old connections as if time and their own substantial separate careers had stood still.

The opener drifted with rather unfocused tone-poetry at first, but turned into mid-tempo swing on the solos, intensified in DeJohnette's first drum break (a typical mix of blowtorch eruptions and double-take pauses) and resolved in Abercrombie's tantalisingly arching slurs, a manipulation of the underlying beat he particularly favours and which does much to heighten the band's rhythmic ambiguity. There followed a kind of secretive Latin dance piece built around a three-chord vamp, in which the guitarist's lines grew increasingly plastic and unpredictable as he warmed up and Holland played a delectably fluid solo, then some fast bebop in which DeJohnette's mingling of seamless blurs of sound and sudden smacks and clatters made everybody lean a little further forward, musicians and audience alike.

Loudmouths in the front bar of the Jazz Café almost swamped the acoustic-guitar ballad 'Timelessness' (a piece of undulating lyricism that sometimes suggested a countryfied 'In a Silent Way', and on which DeJohnette played dewy piano) until a deputation from the audience discouraged them. A fast, twisty Dave Holland postbop piece followed, galvanising Abercrombie into spine-tingling electronic yelps and wails and featuring a memorable overture to the composer's bass solo by DeJohnette, who dragged the intensity dramatically down by increasingly delayed snare-drum blows, like someone crossing a stream on ever-more-separated stepping-stones, before Holland's soft power took the tune out in skittish flurries and streams of new melody.

JAMAICA BY NIGHT
The Guardian, September 1994

Max Roach, one of jazz music's subtlest rhythmic adventurers, and one of its shrewdest analysts, once said to the British writer Kitty Grime: 'Jazz allows you to sound fifty when you are fifty. When you are nineteen, you should sound nineteen. Jazz allows you to tell the truth.'

When the jazz giants of the swing era of the Thirties grew old, and their youthful mow-'em-down virtuosity waned, it blunted the appeal of very few of them and enhanced the expressiveness of many. By the Sixties, the great tenor saxophonist Ben Webster's performances had become uneven, but he adopted a technique of playing fast tunes as a series of laconic, minimalist doodlings, sporadically splashed with raucous colour, that acquired a grumpy animation as diverting as any of his work. What's often sentimentally regarded as Billie Holiday's 'broken' last years were frequently, for all their fractured pitching, tantalising, revealing and defiant performances. The sound of the magisterial Coleman Hawkins, clinging to life by a thread during his last relentless years on the road, changed to a gravelly, irascible-sounding distillation of everything he'd ever played.

Andy Hamilton, the seventy-six-year-old Jamaican-born tenorist who cut his debut disc in 1992, isn't as easy to romanticise as those jazz legends were. He takes care of himself, his favourite telly shows include *Songs of Praise*, he goes to church, hardly drinks, has ten children (and had long decided not to put a foot into the treacherous waters of the record business until the youngest of them had flown the nest) and has been embraced by a widening circle of family and friends in Birmingham since the mid-Forties. Though his band accompanied the crazed hedonism of Errol Flynn's yacht raves in the Caribbean before he emigrated, Hamilton took a longer view of life even as a young man, and merely says of his old employer, 'He liked to dance.'

Hamilton's music mingles ska, bop, soul and traces of early John Coltrane overlaying the sumptuous lyricism and fastidiousness about intonation that marked out Webster and Coleman Hawkins – and if, like Webster, he sounds now as if slow pieces are his natural habitat and faster ones a territory of inhospitable winds, he echoes the late American star's ability to convey a wealth of associations with a single smoke ring of sound.

Hamilton came to England after the war and settled in Handsworth. During the decades to come he played when he could, supported his family with factory jobs, and came to be regarded by many saxophone students as an inspirational teacher. He had also stubbornly weathered the bigotry of some local white musicians in the early years, and gloves-off violence from Mosleyite hoodlums, and wanted nothing more than to live quietly, raise his family, and spread the word about what he believed to be the healing power of music. 'Silvershine', the tune he wrote for Flynn's band as a youth and which became the title of his first CD, had come back to him in a diabetic coma in 1986, over a four-decade chasm, and he claims the song beckoned him back to life and triggered his late-flowering recording and touring career.

'I was often told I should leave Birmingham, that I'd get a better start somewhere else,' Hamilton reflects now. 'But I spent a lot of time trying to get people together, starting mixed bands, mixed clubs.' (He laughs, an affable, inviting sound.) 'I always believed in all kinds of intermarriage. Maybe that's why I don't have any money.'

In later years Hamilton made his playing home a rugged, cavernous Handsworth pub called The Bear, where many touring jazz stars were to drop by and raise an eyebrow at the old man's haunting, cello-like sound. Then in 1990, when Hamilton was making only his second appearance in London in a lifetime, he was signed by Nick Gold of World Circuit Records. Several celebrities who had heard Hamilton at The Bear – including American sax virtuoso David Murray and Simply Red singer Mick Hucknall – made guest appearances on the album. Graeme Hamilton, then playing with Fine Young Cannibals, had to tell his father who Hucknall was. But Hamilton Senior was on his way to making one of the most belated career moves in jazz history.

He went back home in 1993, for the first time in forty years, to play on the St Lucia Jazz Festival, and much of the material for the new *Jamaica by Night* disc was put together then. 'Otrum', an exquisite ballad named after a

Jamaican river, takes its swelling and ebbing momentum from childhood memories of the leaps and submersions of the fish, flashing in the sun.

Andy Hamilton had been into hospital again in the month before the record's release date, and the chances of him making the launch show at the Birmingham's branch of Ronnie Scott's looked slim. But on the night there he was, white suit, straw hat, as dapper as on Flynn's yacht decades ago, and says that from that moment on he 'got stronger by the day'.

DEPARTURE TIME

Q Magazine, September 1994

David Sanchez, **The Departure** (Columbia)

Casual listening makes this virtuosic postbop disc sound like a lot of others at first, with its pervasive time-chopping influences from the mid-Sixties Miles band, strong flavour of Latin music, and its impassive atmosphere of being in a hurry to get somewhere it isn't telling you about. But twenty-five-year-old David Sanchez, though he isn't as strong and spontaneous as Joshua Redman among heavily promoted new sax stars, brings more musicality to his affection for the tradition than most and so do his sidemen. Much of the music is played with an attractive reserve and containment, despite the upfront materials it draws on, to which the highly selective and delicate trumpeter Tom Harrell is a significant contributor. Pianist Danilo Perez adds an engagingly Monkish angularity in both his compositions (like 'You Got It Diz') and his playing, and Sanchez has a querulous tenderness on ballads unusual in a young virtuoso. The title track is a sharp mixture of bleak, punctuation-like hip-hoppish melody and open swing. 'Cara de Payaso' is a slightly stiff nod to Rollins. The ensemble flexibility, particularly Sanchez's line running against Perez's piano, show a boldness that promises a lot.

GREYHOUND

The Guardian, September 1994

John Stevens, the great English jazz drummer, was the kind of musician who banished intimations of mortality. He always seemed too intensely, nervously, garrulously alive for that, too greyhound-like and streamlined in the drum-chair to be troubled by frailties, too ecstatic about his passions for music – and not just jazz, but many of the world's musics, which influenced his technique, his outlook, and his graceful, liquid style. He died suddenly at his home on Tuesday morning, and European contemporary music is deprived of an irreplaceably dedicated, imaginative and catalytic artist.

Stevens was almost never in the mainstream, either idiomatically or in terms of the British jazz world's social life, because he singlemindedly followed musical leads that intrigued him no matter into what thicket they led, he could be combative and demanding, and his choices of partners followed no fashions. Avoidance of the more accessible jazz fundamentals of song or dance-based forms prevented Stevens's achievements from putting him on the kind of pedestal in British jazz that Ronnie Scott or John Dankworth (and latterly Courtney Pine or Julian Joseph) have ascended to. But if they have been achievements of a different kind, they have been massive in their own ways. Individuals, institutions and broadcasting and arts-funding policies have been influenced by his vision and energy.

John Stevens leaves a legacy on three counts, any of which would have guaranteed him a significant place in this country's casually marginalised jazz history. First, he was a wonderful player, both to listen to and watch, his cymbal beat loose and fizzy, his movements seeming to be in an ethereal slow motion against the torrent of polyrhythms, sudden swerves and diversions, explosive accents and surges of straight-ahead swing they were producing. In some more austere improvising situations he would pare his kit down to a flat snare drum and a cymbal, and speak volumes with both.

Second, he was one of a very small coterie on the British jazz scene of the early Sixties who were listening perceptively to the American avant-garde artists such as Ornette Coleman and John Coltrane and looking for opportunities to develop their structurally adventurous ideas here, and the enthusiasm led both to a succession of remarkable improvising bands all bearing the name Spontaneous Music Ensemble, and to the use of London's Little Theatre Club as an oasis for sharp-end players in a world of big-band music and bebop pyrotechnicians.

Third, Stevens's growing conviction that improvisation in music could be a source of emotional and spiritual sustenance not just among professional players but between people of all ages and abilities, led to an influential and often inspired contribution as an informal, intuitive educationalist. Stevens's bigger projects frequently involved amateurs or untrained players as well as professionals over the years, and he had a genius for talent-spotting. Some of the first opportunities Londoners had to experience saxophonist Courtney Pine in a jazz context were with Stevens's powerful twelve-piece Freebop in the mid-Eighties, and the drummer was bending the ears of anyone who would listen about the promise of the young singer Claire Martin at least two years before she became a celebrity on the British circuit.

Stevens took up drums at seventeen. His father could tap-dance and he considered it too, but eventually he went to art school and then into a design studio, which he hated. Already listening to jazz records, and practising drum licks on a biscuit tin, he joined the RAF a year later, in 1958, principally to use the services of the air force's music college at Uxbridge. Several young jazz musicians were in the RAF's orchestra, including the exciting saxophonist Trevor Watts, with whom Stevens developed a long and exploratory musical partnership that lasted into the Eighties. Posted to Germany, Stevens and Watts heard the kind of avant-garde American jazz played on local radio stations that was never broadcast in Britain. Back home, though he worked on and off in good bands that included Tubby Hayes, Ronnie Scott and John McLaughlin, Stevens felt uneasy with the oblique and laconic approaches to playing that sometimes constituted hipness on the jazz scene, and wanted an environment and a style in which he could devote himself to musical conversations wherever they led him, even if it was away from conventional tonality and rhythm, or the necessity for a harmonic structure or tune.

In January 1966, Stevens was given the use of the Little Theatre Club six nights a week, and threw it open to all improvisers who couldn't be heard elsewhere. A nucleus of the most inventive upcoming players became regulars, and Stevens even persuaded a hitherto recalcitrant BBC to give airtime to a band including himself, trumpeter Kenny Wheeler and saxophonists Alan Skidmore and Ray Warleigh, a precedent that finally opened the doors to at least a little new jazz on the network.

Throughout the next two decades, accepting a life that might have been a little easier were he not swimming so hard against the tide of received musical wisdom, Stevens worked with a remarkable range of unconventional performers, from pianist Stan Tracey at the jazz end, to saxophonists Dudu Pukwana and John Tchicai from avant-garde jazz, Derek Bailey and Evan Parker from free-improvised music, even John Lennon and Yoko Ono. As a percussionist, Stevens, like the rock drummer Ginger Baker, carried on a torch for the British drum genius Phil Seamen (oddly, all three men superficially resembled each other in their stripped-to-the-bone physiques, and shared the same obsessiveness), Seaman having obliterated by example the common convictions of the Fifties and Sixties that British drummers couldn't catch the elusive American rhythmic feel that so subtly mingled intensity and relaxation. Seamen and Stevens co-led a band called Splinters in 1971, which signalled the younger man's resumption of interest in more predetermined music.

Stevens's balance of guileless exuberance, technical sophistication and encyclopaedic knowledge of all kinds of drummers and drum-styles was at the core of the communicativeness of his playing, but his love of musical communication in general led him to a second career founded on the conviction that music could be force for social good. He won a Thames TV Award for his community-music work in 1972, and directed the former Jazz Centre Society's Outreach Community Music Project from 1983. The project's home was intended to be the planned National Jazz Centre in Covent Garden, but when that foundered Stevens became the driving force behind Community Music Limited, an independent charity. He threw himself into teaching, working in summer schools, community projects, with schizophrenic patients, with children – and what he called his 'search and reflect' method, an improvisation course he devised for music teachers and intended to bridge wide differences of culture and training, has just been adopted by the Open University.

Shortly before his death John Stevens had completed a major work, *Celebration with Voices*, for a sixty-strong choir, string quartet and jazz octet. Moves are already afoot to stage it in the coming months.

He leaves a wife, Ann, and two children, Richie and Louise.

> *John William Stevens, born London, 10 June 1940, died London,*
> *13 September 1994*

Spontaneous Combustion

The Guardian, October 1994

One of the most electrifying jazz concerts on the South Bank in years – a decade wouldn't be overstretching it – roared off the stage of the Queen Elizabeth Hall on Thursday. It wasn't simply an astonishing display of group empathy and vivacity by a band that lives together, debates, creates, investigates and rehearses seven hours a day together and is led by the most inventive jazz-angled Latin-American musician currently working, but a revelation of commitment, technique and enthusiasm by a specially assembled British big band that defied comparisons. Brazilian jazz genius Hermeto Pascoal's multinational big band is on tour in England and Wales until 15 October.

Pascoal, a square-set, bespectacled fifty-eight-year-old whose silver ponytail is marginally ahead of his beard in the race to reach his waist, and who periodically brandishes a capacious felt hat at both the audience and his musicians as a sign of satisfaction, has written many of the most memorably convoluted themes to have emerged from the liaisons between jazz and Brazilian folk music, struck Miles Davis as one of the world's great contemporary musicians, and has acted as mentor to many younger Latin jazz stars. His music often sounds as if bands led by Chick Corea, Miles Davis and the late Frank Zappa are all hanging on by their fingertips to the same roller-coaster car in a typhoon, with a nature-in-the-raw soundtrack from a David Attenborough show. Pascoal vibrates with music (his own keyboard solos, if he feels he's connecting with his partners, are often augmented by his manic, chattering scat, whistling and tea-kettle blowing, and his body starts to quiver as if he's close to spontaneous combustion) and the catalytic effect on other musicians, even unfamiliar ones, was confirmed by Thursday's gig.

The set-up was built around Pascoal's own dynamic octet, dominated by the leader's headlong keyboard flights, some fleet and fluid postbop saxophone from Vinicius Dorim and a breathlessly intense three-man percussion section. This and the British big band alternated accounts of Pascoal's jubilantly intricate work, periodically coming together. The music included compositions simply for shakers, children's bathtoys, wooden clogs, whistles and chanting, dark, swirling Ellingtonesque reed/brass conversations and Mingus-like trombone-and-sax dirges, and typical Pascoal splicings of fast repeated figures spinning like freewheeling bicycles, bursts of percussive exclamation-mark chords and episodes of relaxed jazz swing. Everybody played above themselves, but Mark Mondesir's drumming responded to Pascoal's every move, Claud Deppa played a high-note trumpet solo that endangered the glassware in the second half, Julian Arguelles and Iain Ballamy played a couple of tenor solos of delectably lyrical swing amid the turmoil, Guy Barker played as crisply as ever and conducted as well, and nobody flinched at the hairpin bends in the ensemble writing. A triumphant collaboration.

EXPERTS

The Guardian, November 1994

For all that the Brecker Brothers consistently deliver a tight and fast-moving jazz-funk on the big festival gigs they usually turn up on, they haven't always sounded as relaxed a band as the idiom invites since their comeback as an item in the early Nineties after a decade of separate ways. They lock the arrangements up very tight, run a sometimes predictable string of push-button diminuendos and crescendos, and the soloists have often sounded as if they were queuing up to show how flash they were, guest drummers particularly.

The Breckers are now at Ronnie Scott's until Saturday, with material extensively drawn from their current *Out of the Loop* CD. Two factors may have contributed to a generally looser, more open and convivial feel to their music. One is the venue, which doesn't oblige them to make an impact on somebody eating an ice cream two hundred yards away. The other is a superb young drummer, Rodney Holmes. Like Mark Mondesir in this country, Holmes sounds as if he's grown up with fusion playing and jazz time living in happy cohabitation, plays with great intensity at subtly controlled volume, and he listens to his partners.

The result is that the brothers' immense technical assurance and improvising skills – tenorist Mike remains one of the finest saxophonists on the planet, and in an open situation can play jaw-dropping streams of spontaneous melody without repetition – currently has a setting that makes musical sense. On their opening night on Monday, they began with three tracks off the current record, starting with a characteristically complex mid-tempo funk piece that emphasised their effortless closeness in ensemble and split-second direction changes, followed by a Miles Davis-like brooding electric ballad sporadically peppered with explosive uptempo solos and a seamless shift to 'Nightwalker', another brisk groove but with a boppish melody line. Randy Brecker's devotion to the muted sound and curt, episodic manner of mid-Sixties Miles Davis coloured all his solos, though the grandstand finale of his improvisation in the Thelonious Monk tribute 'Spiracle', reaching dramatically for ever-higher notes, was his own particular trademark, and unexpectedly affecting. So was guitarist Dean Brown, who for all his Spinal Tap onstage antics delivered a manic high-register solo on the same tune that had a cool and clear logic under the fire and brimstone.

On the final piece of the opening set, a Latin theme with straight-ahead jazz blowing sections called 'Little Miss P', Randy Brecker played a fast, flaring solo, but Mike the best improvisation of the set, spinning separate episodes out of spontaneous sub-themes like Sonny Rollins, confirming the beauty of his tone in the upper register, never lowering the beat. This is certainly the Breckers at their best. Booked seats are all but gone though, so queue early, or after midnight.

CAT WALK

The Guardian, November 1994

Johnny Griffin, the short, dapper, restless tenor saxophonist who always looks as if he's late for an appointment somewhere else, and has been blowing the daylights out of bebop music since 1945, isn't a man whose history automatically brings to mind the marbled elegance of the Wigmore Hall, or for that matter working with a drummerless band in which there is no fizzy cymbal beat to surf on. But on Sunday night's final show in pianist Julian Joseph's excellent October series at the Wigmore, Griffin not only found both the mellow acoustics and Joseph's and bassist Alec Dankworth's inventiveness quite inspiration enough, but reaffirmed that despite some ballad-angled albums recently, he hasn't lost his laconically exultant inclination to play chord changes at the speed of light.

Over two sets largely devoted to standards, Griffin, Joseph and Dankworth sounded like a full-time trio after about three choruses of the first tune, a bumpy Monkish mid-tempo piece with a lyrical release. Then the saxophonist opened 'If I Should Lose You' in a delicate, tremulous high register, accelerating through a passage of sleek, rounded phrasing streaked with quivering long notes, moving into racing double time, Joseph dropping out to leave him unrolling indignant flurries, pattering runs and raw, blurty sounds over the muscular murmur of Dankworth's bass.

Julian Joseph played beautifully all night, his playing in recent times having moved from gracefully respectful acknowledgement of influences to an improvisational dynamism of skidding mid-flow direction changes (sometimes his fingers halt suddenly in mid-descent at breakneck tempos, then charge off somewhere else), driving rhythmic impetus and an atmosphere of on-the-fly reworkings of his materials that have now put him in the big league with the masters he has learned from, notably Herbie Hancock. On Griffin's funky, Ray Charlesian 'The Way It Is' he built a superb solo narrative that ran from unexpected romantic balladeering to gospel. He followed Griffin's sly, Ben Websterish sighs on 'All the Things You Are' with at least three highly competitive alternatives to the tune, and he hardly took his eyes off Griffin at any point in the show, as if reading his mind from his raised eyebrows. When they started swapping closing choruses in the final numbers, they split them up smaller than four-bar breaks to the point where they were exchanging pithy epithets that seemed to emanate from one artist playing two instruments. Griffin accompanied Joseph's and Dankworth's prowling bass lines on 'The Cat' with loud miaowing noises. It was that kind of gig.

That's Entertainment
The Guardian, November 1994

'The Cat Is Back!' wailed the posters outside the Hammersmith Palais. The queue down the Shepherd's Bush Road showed the message had got through to an audience whose listening habits probably ran all the way from Kiss FM to Radio 2. Greying, heavy-set men in checked shirts with denim jackets tied around their waists like jumpers, middle-aged women in sensible coats, pencil-thin teenagers in black, comfortable Caribbean couples dressed for church, even a mod at the bar who looked like Pete Townshend's *doppelgänger*, circa 1965.

The Palais reflects these ambiguities. The mirror balls that reflected the last-dance clinches which began thousands of affairs are long gone, but the decor isn't quite contemporary, more like the Seventies edition of the *Starship Enterprise*. And the star of the show was Jimmy Smith, the dazzling Hammond organ virtuoso who helped launch the enthusiasms of a generation of jazz fans thirty years ago and who is now embraced again by the jazz-dance generation for whom his pumping riffs, earthquake bass lines, simple, bluesy themes and all-round sideshow glee are reinvented Paradise.

JFM DJ Peter Young played discs for longer than he expected to, but the ones he did play – Hank Mobley, Art Blakey, early Herbie Hancock among others – testified both to their own popular virtues, and to Jimmy Smith's. It was all percussive, riff-dominated music in which simple, chant-like tunes, bass lines and drum-fills bulged the walls, and the improvised solos were secondary or sometimes inaudible. 'I think we can say we're laying down some pretty decent grooves here,' said P.Y. somewhat incongruously as the start time passed into history. Then, with audible relief: 'And now, here he is – the original Hammond organ groovemaster.'

Smith is sixty-eight now, but looks taut, wiry, and youthful. He came on with a towel around his neck like a fighter, and used it extensively as a prop – whipping it across the keys to produce a sharp, exclamatory dissonance, playing a short fast phrase and then mopping his hand as if the sweat of the sudden inspiration was profuse. Smith's gestures were as active as his playing – admonishing glares to his saxophonist Herman Riley, imperious waves to drummer Jimmy Johnson to back off, sometimes playing with his forehead flat on the keyboard as if in supplication to it.

Fundamentally a rhythm and blues player with a bebop melodic technique – most of his solos have lengthy episodes of headlong double time – Smith wrings every snarl, sob, cuss and sigh from the familiar vocabulary of the idiom with big, ballooning chord crescendos, stabbing runs like guitar breaks that suddenly skid to a halt, then unexpected stealthy passages which have audiences craning their necks. The direct and funky blues 'Back in the Chicken Shack' was greeted with a roar, but the procession of blues solos had a routine offhandedness until guitarist Terry Evans broke a string, slewed into unexpectedly colourful slurred and off-pitch sounds, and the other three performers abruptly turned up the heat to compensate, Riley's tenor lurching into some gripping bar-room honking and grimacing. Riley won himself the credit to keep the crowd quiet even with a slow ballad after that.

RAP WITHOUT ATTITUDE
The Guardian, December 1994

Astrud Gilberto's success in the 1960s with bossa nova jazz makes curious connections with rap – though rap without attitude, a shy, wistful version of it. There's the same subordination of lyricism to rhythm, the same avoidance of dynamic extremes, the same engaging liberation from Tin Pan Alley song shapes which dominated the mainstream of popular song for most of the century and still do.

When 'Girl from Ipanema' was a hit thirty years ago, the ingredients were completely fresh and an almost perfect combination. Astrud Gilberto sang, not like a vocalist but like a drummer playing brushes, and though her technique was limited and her delivery all but expressionless, the effect made a good deal of pop singing sound stagey, overblown and old-fashioned. Stan Getz's graceful tenor sax completed the picture.

Gilberto still sings 'Girl from Ipanema' – it was greeted ecstatically on Thursday night by at least fifty per cent of an audience that couldn't have been born when she first recorded it – and now delivers it with a punchier, jazzier instrumental section, probably to stop herself going to sleep with the repetition of a song that will never leave her alone. Virtually all the rest of her material in the current season at the Jazz Café (she's there until Sunday night) is self-penned, and though a few of the departures from the trademark Latin shuffle veer into bland funk ('You Got Me Turning Around' could have been anybody's song) most of the music on her familiar ground still has fresh melody and considerable charm.

Gilberto's band is a percussion-dominated group that featured some fluid interjections from trombonist Jay Ashby, and on a fast, stuttery song the leader delivered in an effortless stream of quietly exclamatory sounds, the percussion players' break exhibited a good deal of the blasting momentum of the Airto Moreira band. More of that, and a greater willingness to experiment with the skills of her sidemen might have given a little extra edge and fizz to the gig, as occurred when drummer Duduku Da Fonseca embarked on a remarkably expressive berimbau solo taken out by the ensemble as the opening chorus of 'Milestones'. But Astrud Gilberto sounds hardly changed at all, so that the audience undoubtedly gets what it came for.

1995

Midway through the last decade before a new millennium that might see the status of jazz transformed for good, the Arts Council of England (a body that in earlier incarnations has perceived jazz music as worth public money only since the late Sixties) issued the draft of a comprehensive survey of the state of jazz in the land. It included the following proposition: 'Jazz . . . has completed the journey from rough-hewn folk art to a sophisticated creative vehicle in barely ninety years, paralleling the progression of European classical music across five centuries . . . in many ways, it can claim the title of "the art music of the twentieth century".'

The fact that the Arts Council should have come to this conclusion in 1995, whilst not necessarily an indication that it was about to extend its fairly parsimonious funding for jazz, was evidence of just how far the music's journey had gone towards its due respect. That this kind of acceptance can be a poisoned chalice to a spirited and revolutionary music is a reservation which has to be steadily maintained on the back burner as the twenty-first century approaches – certainly previous attempts to evolve a 'respectable' jazz for the delectation of the dinner-jacket audience have not been crowned with musical virtue. But the enormous influence of jazz and jazz musicians on the sound, rhythm, song and even speech of the present century is now being generally acknowledged all over the world.

In Britain, 1995 was a year in which some of the best effects of the post-modernist resampling of jazz history began to surface. A burgeoning new jazz scene in the North of England focused on the Creative Jazz Orchestra, a band of flexible membership and size, which appeared to be taking on the overdue responsibility of becoming a repertory band for the best British orchestral composers. Three more superb orchestras played British tours in 1995. One was led by an American who should have had the opportunity years ago, but he being one of the most in-demand session orchestrators in New York never found the time. Don Grolnick proved in person to be just as succinct and witty a Thelonious

Monkish pianist as he had sounded on his rare recorded outings in that persona, and his band was wonderful, recalling Monk and Mingus in its ensembles, and drawing some spectacular tenor saxophone playing from Mike Brecker.

The second memorable big band was led by another jazz recluse (and for the same reason) in Colin Towns, a TV-score and studio musician who unleashed the full force of his wide experience and enthusiasms in the Mask Orchestra, with its explicit and implicit references to Stravinsky, West Side Story, Ellington, Mingus and South African townships jazz.

The third was the New York Composers' Orchestra, led by writer/players Wayne Horvitz and Robin Holcomb. This was the band that probably explored the potential crossovers and hybrids of late-twentieth-century music to the most adventurous degree, though it was more tautly organised and proscribed in its movements than the others.

At the very sharp end, Leo Records (an independent that began as a samizdat operation, helping avant-garde musicians of the former Soviet Union to get their work heard in the West) celebrated its twentieth birthday. At the cosy and amiable – but consummately musical – end, the veteran pianist Jimmy Rowles (a favourite accompanist of vocalists including Billie Holiday, Sarah Vaughan and Peggy Lee) made a classy record with the British singer Norma Winstone.

The ripples from the British 'jazz boom' of the Eighties continued to wash up some imaginative travellers. The effect of the long-disbanded but immensely influential ensemble Loose Tubes, was audible in the 1995 work of the band's one-time drummer Steve Arguelles, by now living in Paris. Arguelles evolved an attractive confection of bop, tangos, Piaf-like torchiness and Ornette Coleman in his kaleidoscopic and humorous band. Another fashionable young Eighties sax-star, Scotsman Tommy Smith, finally proved his real class with his most thoughtful and thought-provoking work, a dedication to the Scottish poet Norman McCaig that exhibited melodic variety, strong soloing from a powerful lineup, and some of Smith's most eloquent playing.

On London's South Bank, rock star Elvis Costello was given the job of programming an ambitious mixed-idiom festival called Meltdown, one of the most high-profile concerts of which featured pop singer Debbie Harry as an avant-jazzy vocalist with the semi-free New York band The Jazz Passengers. Other successful cross-border collaborations included classical saxophonist John Harle's unexpectedly freewheeling and fruitful performance with Andy Sheppard.

Joe Henderson, by now firmly ensconced as The Boss of postbop tenor-sax *improvising in the hearts and minds of jazz musicians of all generations the world over, played a brilliant concert with the Brazilian band that had sounded rather subdued and hesitant on this year's CD,* Double Rainbow. *And American Carmen Lundy, a cult singer in the British clubs but seriously underrated in the wider world, showed in a fine Jazz Café performance that not only was the tradition of Ella Fitzgerald and Sarah Vaughan in safe hands, it was also clay being caressed into beautiful new shapes by a mistress of the art.*

MR FIXIT

The Guardian, January 1995

You can trawl a lot of jazz reference books without finding Don Grolnick's name which – considering he's in his late forties now and has been respected for a couple of decades by some of the leading figures in the music – is an interesting omission at the least. Grolnick isn't in the books because he has spent much of his life as a studio arranger for the likes of Bonnie Raitt, James Brown and Steely Dan's Fagin and Becker, and has hardly recorded on his own account. But treating jazz – for which he appears to have a starting natural facility since his teens – as a hobby hasn't cramped either his improvising flair as a pianist, or his ingenuity as a composer. There was two-and-a-half hours worth of evidence to that effect on Wednesday night at the Queen Elizabeth Hall, on the London leg of the Grolnick band's Contemporary Music Network tour.

Thelonious Monk and Charles Mingus are names that come to mind when Grolnick gets to work. The mid-tempo opener, 'Heart of Darkness,' was a typical confection of lurching, criss-crossing horn lines (the harmonic movement between the instruments in his arrangements affect a kind of lazy intensity that's a particular trademark) and sudden flurrying figures, as if the notes have unexpectedly struck a solid object and run into each other like railway trucks.

The long first half of the show showed Grolnick's considerable hand – a cool chamber-jazz contrapuntal pirouette that opened out into the solo feel of the Fifties Miles Davis group, a country-tinged piece occasionally echoing early Keith Jarrett, a Latin version of 'What Is this Thing Called Love' that brought on the exultant conga sound of percussionist Don Alias, one of the most musical hand-drummers in jazz. ('We've tried holding him back until the second half,' Grolnick announced. 'But when we get to the dressing room at the interval most of the food and drink has gone.') Grolnick introduced the tune unaccompanied with a beautifully succinct, rhythmically ingenious piano solo that shuffled abrupt, exclamatory arpeggios, hopping Monkish runs, fragments of quotes. The leader's piano playing was constantly varied, and a principal solo attraction all night, even in a band of stars like this.

But if the first-half improvising was up to the pedigree of the players, the second half was less stately in ensemble (Grolnick's pieces make the players peer pretty intently at the charts) and its strong Latin emphasis seemed to let the musicians off the leash. Michael Brecker delivered his most trenchant and tantalising journey from throaty warbles, whirring trills and skidding elisions to explosive wailing on the Latin blues 'Rainsville', Robin Eubanks's trombone was so astonishingly delicate on Wayne Shorter's 'Water Babies' as to sound like a moth fluttering in lamplight, and the langourous, Carla Bley-like 'Cost of Living' found the whole band hitting the leader's intricate sketches with glee as well as accuracy. Don Alias and drummer Peter Erskine uncorked the obligatory percussion barrage on the penultimate 'One Bird, One Stone', but drumming as melody rather than aerobics is a byword with both of them.

UNDERCOVER OPERATION

The Guardian, January 1995

Ned Rothenberg, the American virtuoso saxophone improviser, didn't go in for long preambles before his intricate and ingenious solo flights on Tuesday, but the little he did say went a long way. 'Support Leo Feigin,' Rothenberg offhandedly told the audience. 'He's one of the real Don Quixotes.' Feigin is the founder of Leo Records, the cottage-industry independent label whose fifteenth anniversary was being celebrated by the presence of Rothenberg and other new-music and improvisation luminaries from the States, Russia, Greece and Britain. The Quixote image was as clear and pointed as Rothenberg's remarkable playing.

Norwegian sax star Jan Garbarek's recording with a group of Gregorian chanters may have been 1994's headline-making example of how widely welcomed jazz now is in all kinds of musical contexts, but Tuesday's opening show at the Purcell Room merged Rothenberg's post-Coltrane multiphonics with the extraordinary Tuvan singer Sainkho Namchylak's elemental Mongolian mountain chants and Vyacheslav Ganelin's characteristic mixture of Cecil Taylor-like free piano, spy-movie synth chords, bebop drums and electronically generated brass and bass sections (he does all this on his own, and simultaneously).

Rothenberg played a varied and imaginative opening set, sometimes functioning like this country's Evan Parker in his seamless minglings of two or even three horn lines at once, but with closer allegiances to orthodox tonality, often reminiscent of Anthony Braxton in his exclamatory reed sounds, and always retaining a remarkably pure tonality. When he adopted bass clarinet instead of the alto, he grew jazzier in the fluency of his melodies, sometimes dropping to a hushed monotone in which the rhythmic accents were banged on the head by sudden popping sounds at the mouthpiece. Vyacheslav Ganelin then delivered a startling display of multi-instrumentalism which, while it sometimes resembled a routine by an impressionist and had its moments of melodrama, used jazz effects (fragments of Dave Holland-like bass lines, Milesian trumpet, Bill Evans-like arpeggio romantics) not as linear narratives but as splashes of colour within a poised compositional framework that is uniquely his.

High point of the night was Sainkho Namchylak. 'How does he do that?' they always say on Ryan Giggs's *Soccer Skills*, and it was the same with her. A small, dark, impassive woman, she can sing with a Western diva's chromatic purity, or take on a steely cantorial insistence, drop to a deep, growly sound full of overtones like a jew's harp or a distant didgeridoo, defy human anatomy altogether to resemble a creaking millwheel or a chain straining on a winch, then become birds fluttering in and out of trees. Namchylak sometimes works in the States with Rothenberg, and this unlikely improvising combination was tightly and precisely demonstrated at the close of Tuesday's show. It was enthralling, Company-style improvising, but Namchylak on her own is one of the musical wonders of the world

REPERTORY BAND

The Guardian, February 1995

Creative Jazz Orchestra may be a little on-the-nose as a name (is there a jazz band that thinks it isn't?) but it is about the only obvious avenue this ambitious and enterprising outfit has so far pursued. Drawing a flexible, rep-company pool of performers from the increasingly fertile jazz scenes of the North of England, the band's composer/arrangers have been able to present both original material and the work of such prominent figures as Kenny Wheeler and Mike Gibbs. The nearest thing to a permanent contemporary jazz orchestra Britain currently possesses is the National Youth Jazz Orchestra, but the CJO increasingly looks like the rightful inheritor of this considerable responsibility for its originality, expertise, inventive celebration of British jazz talent, and complete absence of sectarianism about the many forms contemporary jazz now takes.

At the Purcell Room on Wednesday, an eight-piece version of the Orchestra played the penultimate gig of its tour of composer/pianist Nikki Iles's suite *The Printmakers*. Iles is one of the most refreshing and promising figures to have emerged in the UK in recent times, with a liquid sound and supple, obliquely resolved phrasing as an improviser which confirm her enthusiasm for Paul Bley and the late Bill Evans, and composing skills that embrace lustrous, semi-classical deployment of French horns and cellos, and the roaring reed ensembles of a swing band.

The band opened with two pieces by pianists – Bill Evans's reflective 'My Bells', strongly featuring cellist Andy Wardell, and John Taylor's 'Oh', which had a choppy, foxily lyrical theme but was played a little tentatively as if they were driving in bad weather. The plangent, sustained textures of the cello and French horn coloured most of the music on the show, and in the first half contrasted at their most effectively with the booming tenor of Andy Schofield on another set of Bill Evans echoes, Nikki Iles's 'Secret Place'. But the music displayed a reined-in, chamber-music decorum until the second half, with Charlie Haden's heated, splashy Latin piece 'Sandino', an Iles dedication to Carla Bley and Steve Swallow that neatly caught Ms Bley's sinister-tea-dance quality, and a jubilant, swaggering swing-orchestra dedication to Mary Lou Williams. The solo variety was good, but the glittering prizes went to Iles herself, and the magnificent guitarist Mike Walker, in whom the UK has about as scorching a concoction of John Scofield, Pat Metheny and an original improvising brain as local jazz guitar freaks could ever wish for.

LIGHTING-UP TIME
The Guardian, February 1995

Joe Lovano, **Rush Hour** (Blue Note)

Michael Brecker may continue to catch the bouquets in the world of post-bop tenor sax, but Joe Lovano – an American of Brecker's generation who worked in comparative obscurity for years until appearances with ex-Miles guitarist John Scofield put the lights on – has earned the right to the same treatment. On a succession of punchy discs with Scofield and in his own right, Lovano has cultivated a territory that draws on early players like Lester Young for narrative and atmosphere, and the free-associative improvising style of Ornette Coleman. Now comes a collaboration with the composer and jazz academic Gunther Schuller, which looks at first like an industry apparatchik's attempts to resituate Lovano in the marketplace – lush string sections, classical vocalists, complex orchestrations. But it works. Lovano's tumbling eloquence and hard, urgent sound get plenty of space, he doesn't have to tie himself in knots to accommodate the writing, and the repertoire includes Charles Mingus, Thelonious Monk, Ellington, Ornette Coleman and several originals by Lovano and Schuller. The writing for the strings is sometimes honeyed to the point that your feet stick in it, but Schuller's angle on jazz classics is often incisive and original (the slow drag of Monk's 'Crepuscule with Nellie' is delectably appropriate), Lovano plays superbly all through, there are some sharp interventions from other soloists, including a bristling Jack Walrath trumpet on the boppish 'Rush Hour on 23rd Street', and there's some savagely propulsive drumming from George Schuller.

LATECOMER

The Guardian, February 1995

It is the season for late debutantes on the jazz circuit. The American pianist/composer Don Grolnick was last week's proof that a bandleading career embarked on in middle life, after years as a pop-score studio mechanic, can be a triumphant revelation. This week it is Colin Towns's turn – a British pianist/composer this time, who surfaced briefly on the local jazz scene two decades ago, but devoted himself to TV and moviescore work until last year. Towns brought his own big band to the South Bank last Wednesday, and goes on a national tour in March.

Both Grolnick and Towns had sent eloquent messengers about how good their shows were likely to be in the form of excellent recent albums – Towns's Mask Orchestra went out on a double-CD last year for Danny Thompson's adventurous Jazz Label. But Wednesday's show, featuring several new pieces including a long suite, still bristled with surprises and was beautifully played. Should the year present many more unusual, impassioned and powerfully executed jazz events, it will be one to cherish for a while.

If as a composer Towns is more of a dramatist than a melodist (his faster pieces use a lot of seesawing, fire-siren brass riffs somewhere between modern straight music and George Russell, and his more reflective ones frequently draw on churchy, Abdullah Ibrahim-like chords) it only serves to intensify the strength of the relationship between his propulsive scores and the inspirations of the improvisers. The music made a brilliant crop of soloists hang their wheels over the bends even more exultantly than usual. It brought out all the throaty fluency of tenorist Alan Skidmore (rarely heard in London these days), displays of unerring bop phrasing and controlled multiphonics respectively from trombonists Mark Nightingale and Richard Edwards, and it made trumpeter Guy Barker let his hair down with an assortment of Don Cherry-like squeals and New Orleans gutbucket growls. Veteran altoist Peter King and young trumpeter Gerard Presencer, in a series of dazzling solos, demonstrated that elusive delicacy of timing which swings independently, rather than piggybacking the rhythm section.

The material included an opener that shuttled between townships music and a prancing, gavotte-like soprano sax figure; echoed *West Side Story*'s 'When You're a Jet' in its slashing brass effects on 'Music To Type By'; turned into a runaway steam engine on the heavy rocker 'Not Waving but Drowning' (not surprisingly, Towns's music often sounds as if it should accompany images). Towns alternated whoopy, wriggling abstract horn ensembles against dreamy Ellingtonesque bluesiness suddenly changing to flat-out uptempo jazz time in the early stages of the second-half suite, and took it through dewy romantic interludes (Peter King's alto glided evocatively past), more belting jazz grooves, wraith-like piano links where the dynamics dropped so sharply the audience strained to catch them. Towns's is a music of great dynamic variety, and if it sometimes seems as if he has more ideas that can be packed without hyperactivity into a single night's work, that's only a measure of how much he has to offer now his jazz career has resumed. The Mask Orchestra is on the road in March.

TIMELESS PLACES

The Guardian, February 1995

Jimmie Rowles, the shrewd and hilarious ('my singing voice sounds like a canoe being dragged across a road') miniaturist piano genius, can count among his past and present fans singers of the calibre of Billie Holiday, Peggy Lee, Sarah Vaughan and Ella Fitzgerald, and he accompanied all of them. He can also include, for what it's worth, the city of Los Angeles, which even went so far as to declare 14 September as 'Jimmie Rowles Day'. Rowles is that big which, for someone who devoted his jazz life to supporting other people and very little of it to more self-aggrandising ambitions, marks a display of gratitude on the part of much bigger names than his that is almost unique in the music business.

Rowles's name isn't usually on the lips of British jazz admirers, but the subtle and intelligent British singer Norma Winstone is doing her best to put it there every night this week at Ronnie Scott's, as well as easing through her own distinctive repertoire of deftly whimsical material. One of the most haunting of her songs is a remake of a Rowles original, 'The Peacocks', a delectable piece of lyricism full of eerie, sliding harmonies and slow-motion water-droplet sounds, which Ms Winstone put some atmospheric words of ambiguous love to and rechristened 'A Timeless Place'. She has always hunted out good songs that haven't been run into the ground by everybody else, and her independence recently led to recording an album of shrewdly chosen and atmospheric material with Rowles himself in California, thus joining the illustrious line of gifted vocalists he'll give the time of day to – which, considering the competition among his colourful memories, is no small reckoning.

Norma Winstone has been one of the few key vocalists on the European jazz scene since she won a *Melody Maker* poll that did the unthinkable and displaced Cleo Laine in 1971. Through most of the past quarter-century her direct, unembroidered style (her earliest influences were Frank Sinatra and Lena Horne and she still prefers to massage and burnish words rather than pretend to be an instrument) brought a casual, conversational lyricism to the bands of Mike Westbrook, Kenny Wheeler and the European radio orchestras, as well as the looser and more improvisational setting of the *a capella* group Vocal Summit (which also included Bobby McFerrin) and the great chamber group Azimuth with pianist John Taylor and trumpeter Kenny Wheeler. Without straining for drama or dynamic extremes, Winstone has always probed inside the meanings and contours of songs. Now with an excellent band including the Pat Metheny-like guitarist John Parricelli, a suitably artful drummer in Steve Arguelles and a fine young vibraharpist in Anthony Kerr, Winstone's career might be on a roll.

SOUNDS OF SURPRISE

The Guardian, March 1995

Some shows are getting more than they deserve when the hall's half empty, but Tuesday's performance at the Queen Elizabeth Hall by two percussion-led improvisers' bands – American Gerry Hemingway's and Briton Steve Arguelles – deserved a lot better. Both groups play as if they're not only expecting to surprise the audience but still surprise each other, and considering the care both leaders put into pretty intricate compositions, it is a tribute to the intuitions of the interpreters. The Hemingway and Arguelles bands are now on a Contemporary Network Tour running until Sunday, and though the subtleties of neither ensemble are especially suited to large halls and the repertoires stretch the definitions of eclecticism, they're well worth a trip to replenish optimism about how original reappraisals of traditions can be.

Arguelles's quintet played first, displaying some of its eccentric wares from its current *Busy Listening* album, an attractive mixed bag of intense Parisian accordion music, flared-nostril tangos, wacky genre hybrids and regular jazz. Anyone who ever liked Loose Tubes will know what Arguelles is getting at, and his current residency in Paris is clearly influencing compositional and arranging skills that make almost everything the band plays attractive. The delivery was something of a mumble for a while on Tuesday, and some of the playing seemed diffident (though the opening Ornette Coleman-like horn lines over what sounded like the rhythm and blues riff from 'Can I Get a Witness' established the flavour of the set), but the tumultuous hand drums and strummed bass intro to 'Nice Work if You Can Get It', Julian Arguelles's drifting, saxophone lyricism on the reflective 'Wild Blueberries' and Stuart Hall's hoedown violin opening to John Scofield's 'Big Fun' were all memorable.

Gerry Hemingway's quintet played harder and more crisply, though with less amiability. Hemingway has visited the UK as Anthony Braxton's drummer, but this wasn't Braxton's taxingly algebraic music but in parts a surprisingly sassy and freewheeling roll past the jazz landmarks, including an account of 'A Night in Tunisia' that began in the abstract (slithery soprano sax over arco cello, banshee sounds and squalls) and which gradually accumulated the famous seesawing riff out of Ernst Reijseger's whirring, baroque cello figures. Hemingway plays jazz time with a stinging, whip-like venom, reed player Michael Moore shifts between chorister's purity and abrasive pungency, and trombonist Wolter Wierbos is clear and strong anywhere between free improvisation and an expansive, big-band bravura. The long suite that occupies much of the set reveals Hemingway's genius for textural variety, deft brushwork against whooping clarinet, dark, splashy trombone with cello, lashing backbeats as the band canters through episodes of bop. Hemingway believes in getting ensemble music out of this assembly of virtuosi, and it shows.

Horn Culture

Jazz UK, May 1995

More than most improvising geniuses, Sonny Rollins alternately inspires and frustrates his public – his work lurches with opposites. Rollins has long been the self-contained performer from whom creative generosity often rolls off the stage in waves; the effusive calypso fan who nevertheless dances to a private step; the improvising adventurer whose materials are often perplexingly humdrum; the sometime partner of Miles, Monk, Roach and Clifford who for years appears to have felt no need for heavyweight partners; the spontaneous reinventor of his own rulebook who wishes he'd had lessons.

Rollins has been called the 'greatest living improviser' and it is not an idle contention. When he's at his best in performance, careering impetuously across the bar-lines and chord-shifts, whacking resolving notes into the box-seats as if despatching them with a baseball bat, catapulting himself abruptly from casual, even desultory strolls through his materials to explosive bursts of speed and power, it's a view even strengthened by contrast with the unassuming personalities of many of the songs he elects to blow on, and the unassuming personalities of some of the accompanying musicians he chooses to hire as well.

'Well, basically, there'll be nothing obviously new . . .' Rollins utters these words as if the thought that there might be has caught him unawares, and of course even the most cursory survey of his career and the type of wilful and idiosyncratic improvising he does reveals that compositional or formal preoccupations have never tied him down that much. Eventually, almost reluctantly, he states what he and every one of his admirers around the world knows to be the obvious.

'It's . . . basically . . . me,' Rollins concludes. 'That's how it is in this type of a group, it isn't a collective group like the MJQ were, for instance. And as for the repertoire, there'll be, you know, something old, something new, something Caribbean [his parents came from the Virgin Islands] some ballads. I'm always covering every possibility among the things I like, but really it relies on the hope that me and the band will be inspired on the night.'

Sonny Rollins's recent performances in Britain have borne out all the extremes of his playing, and the occasional frustrations that he doesn't accompany himself with the kind of powerful partners that Joe Henderson, for instance, regularly does. But Rollins's spectacular contribution to jazz has certainly earned him the right to run his own show if anybody's has – and, more than most improvisers, he has consistently demonstrated that some of the most catalytic sidemen in his life have been the clamorous voices inside his own head.

'Well since I'm an improviser,' Rollins says, 'improvisation is obviously my main concern. There's lot of beautiful music I can listen to and get inspired by, some of it jazz and some not, but it might not lend itself to improvisation – my kind of improvisation. When I choose a piece of contemporary material, it might be something I've heard on the radio, but it has to be something that would suit my specifications for what I can improvise on. Something that offers freedom, but that's structured enough to carry some kind of message.'

Theodore Walter Rollins grew up in New York at a turning point in jazz, one of several musical siblings (all the others played classical music, but a saxophone-playing uncle showed him the blues), and he learned fast enough to be able to keep up with the sharpest operators in the music by the end of the 1940s. He rehearsed with his neighbour, Thelonious Monk, while still at school, and the connection made a lasting impression on him, both technically and in attitude.

'I played with Monk when I was fairly young,' Rollins recalls. 'I've heard it said that Monk influenced the way I space things, and maybe that's true – but I didn't personally set out to play like Monk, and I'd prefer to leave it up to the students of the music to judge that. But I rehearsed with Monk when I was in high school. And I'd certainly say his lifestyle had a big personal influence on me. By that I mean that he felt that music was the most worthwhile thing in life – everything else had to be subordinated to it. Even though there have been times when I've grown frustrated with the business side of things, or taken time out from playing publicly, that dedicated attitude those kind of people had has always stayed with me. I've always had my horn with me, wherever I've gone and whatever I've done.'

As a saxophone student, Sonny Rollins absorbed the transformations that had hit the instrument across little more than a decade and a half, from Coleman Hawkins's rescuing of the tenor from its novelty role and hitching to it a piano-like approach to improvising, through Lester Young's poetic variations on a bulging scrapbook of memorable melody, to Charlie Parker's splicing of the two approaches.

Rollins shared with Parker an apparently encyclopaedic memory for fragmentary phrases that could be endlessly shuffled and reprofiled, and his best solos have been based on a motivic juggling that constantly seems to anchor the listener in the familiar, only to turn it inside out and tie a knot in its tail at the next bar. He also liked the gregariousness of pre-rock jump-band music, an attitude that still provides the extrovert opposite to his wilfully introspective flights. The mixture led to Rollins being hired by two of the most creative leaders in 1950s jazz, Miles Davis and Max Roach, and an astonishing period of creative fluency which resulted in some of his finest records, like *Saxophone Colossus* and *Way Out West*. 'People will naturally say that they like one creative period of mine more than another one,' Rollins observes. 'But it doesn't feel like that to me, its all one big *mélange*.'

So what makes Sonny Rollins go on running, continue to pursue this private wrestling match with his own creativity, yet combine it with a modesty about the scale of the projects he sets himself and the partners he seems to feel are right for him?

'I came from a background where some of my family had had a musical education but I hadn't, so I always felt a little bit uneducated, and still do. I felt I had a long way to go to catch up with my peers, and when I started to get noticed in the Fifties I felt like the youngest guy on the scene and the least trained. I've always had that feeling. Even though I've learned a lot, I wish I'd had that formal training too. I might have been able to write scores, extend myself more. But there are some things I haven't done before that I'd like to do. One thing I've wanted to do for a long time as well as my usual work with the band, is make what you might call a nature recording.'

Nature recording?

'Well, like, against the ocean. I used to do this a lot when I was in California. There were places where you could walk along the beach alone and just blow. I did that with Ornette Coleman in 1957, too. I really want to try that again. Because your reactions to what's around you, responding to the natural sounds of the tide coming in and out, are completely different to what's happening in a band of course. I'll have to convince the record company, and I don't know how my playing would fit into the situation. I know there's a fashion for "ambient music" now, but a lot of that sounds bland to me, and I know whatever I do with the horn it won't sound like that.'

And if this is Sonny Rollins's project for a still unfolding future, he is as devoted to the ongoing project of trawling his own cultural past in search of old jewellery he can burnish in his inimitable way. 'There are so many songs that I heard when I was younger or that go back earlier, to the Twenties for instance, that I haven't done yet. Something like "When Day Is Done". I hate to use this word – you can call it the N-word – you know, nostalgia. I guess that has something to do with it. But it's not just looking back on the past. There has to be something about it, maybe in the progression of the harmony, the kind of feel it has, that evokes something soulful or spiritual. It's got to be something that has a deeper meaning for me. "Embraceable You", for example, might not have any effect at all on some people. But I might hear a chord in it that says something special to me.'

If he hears it, you can bet it is likely to end up meaning something to a lot of other people as well. Sonny Rollins is a contradictory giant, but a giant he resoundingly remains.

HARD MAN
The Guardian, May 1995

Since he argued himself into Charlie Parker's company, and later chose glowering talents like John Coltrane and Wayne Shorter to be his front-line partners, the late Miles Davis's endorsements in the saxophone department always made the jazz world take a lively interest in whoever the latest addition was. During what has been dubbed his 'avant-disco' phase in the mid-Eighties, Davis hired Bob Berg, the bony, sombre-looking saxophonist from New York.

Since the radio-playlist inclinations of that band required subjugating the improvisations to the groove, Berg's talents (which had been plain in Horace Silver's and Cedar Walton's groups) weren't always easy to discern beyond stamina, volume and Coltrane-inspired melodic intensity. But in a club, with a sympathetic small band, Berg reminds audiences that he's a superb sax improviser, even in territory also occupied by Joe Henderson, Joshua Redman and the senior guru, Sonny Rollins.

On his opener on Tuesday at Ronnie Scott's, Berg ripped through the theme statement of an uptempo piece of Coltranesque hard bop with his supple, singing tone (he is far less bleak in sound than many exponents of this idiom), then promptly left the spotlight to pianist Dave Kikowski, an indicator of just how much of an ensemble performance this is. Kikowski and drummer Gary Novak interact like a pair of killer table tennis players (some of their early dialogue was highly reminiscent of the best Herbie Hancock/Tony Williams exchanges) and the same intuitive empathy goes on between the pianist and the leader.

One fleeting episode found Berg winding up a chorus with a bap-bap-de-bap percussive phrase that Kikowski instantly fed back to him (shaping the saxophonist's construction through the next headlong bars), then Berg reversed the process by handing the pianist a ferocious high warble that he picked up and echoed in a solo of ringing keyboard trills. The second tune was a rather colourless Kikowski composition for Berg's soprano, but a Sonny Rollins blues got the full bull-charging tenor treatment.

HEARTS AND MINDS
The Guardian, May 1995

Hold everything, a superb contemporary orchestra is on the road. The past six months have seen an unfamiliar bonanza in creative jazz and semi-jazz big bands travelling the UK (Hermeto Pascoal's musical avalanche last autumn, Don Grolnick's and Colin Towns's ensembles this year), but the New York Composers' Orchestra edges ahead of all but Pascoal's for ingenuity, variety, excitement and surprise. Formed in 1986 by composers Wayne Horvitz and Robin Holcomb to explore new music freely mingling jazz and contemporary notated forms, it has commissioned work from writers from all areas of late twentieth-century music. The current version augments a quintet of visiting Americans with a premier-league team of locals, including saxophonist Iain Ballamy, trumpeter Kenny Wheeler, and trombonist Pete Beachill.

The band played ten pieces at the Queen Elizabeth Hall in London on Wednesday, and the scurry of ideas in the majority of them confirmed that the traditional notion of classical/jazz hybrids as dry or distractingly pre-occupied with form is finally laid to rest, in Ms Holcomb's work particularly. Her 'First Program in Standard Time', opening like a more mellow and pastoral Charles Mingus and winding up in stuttery, percussive sax soloing over incisively punchy brass, established the mood of the night, saxophonist Marty Erlich's tenor shared a swirling contrapuntal dance with Wheeler's flugelhorn on the 'American After All', and Wayne Horvitz's 'Prodigal Son Revisited' (a fast post-boppish piece which the composer conducted as if he were slicing cucumbers with a meat cleaver) crackled with fragmentary, tumbling bop-lines all slightly out of phase with each other, like a cross between Charlie Parker, Anthony Braxton and Steve Reich.

Episodes of evocative tone-poetry like twittering birds turning into taut, nervy swing (Bobby Previte's drumming was masterly all night), echoes of Celtic pipe music, street-marches, systems music, and a concentration on carefully wrought dynamic changes explicitly closer to classical music than big-band jazz kept the pot boiling for a two-hour show that shot through the hall like a comet. The band also reasserts the confidence, technique and attack of British musicians these days. Hermeto Pascoal apparently asserted that his Brazil/UK band last year was the best he'd ever led. Something big has happened on the British scene in the past decade. Maybe the famous 'jazz renaissance' did leave something behind.

COMING OF AGE

The Guardian, May 1995

Of all the young British jazz stars hurled on stage when the curtain suddenly went up on the UK 'jazz renaissance' of the Eighties – the list includes Courtney Pine, Steve Williamson, Andy Sheppard and Jason Rebello – the Scottish saxophonist Tommy Smith started his career earliest, and resolved it last. He's currently on a national tour with the best music he has ever made.

Tommy Smith still looks studiedly dapper, as if he's wearing the suit he keeps for Saturday nights, he's formally informal in his dealings with audiences, he always recalls the teenage sax prodigy he once was. But if he broke on the jazz world before he was ready in the mid-Eighties, there was both a sombre romanticism and a quickwitted bop-derived melodic imagination struggling around the edges of the spotlight in which Smith demonstrated his cop-this technical execution and elegant tone, and with the arrival of the album *Misty Morning and No Time* (Smith's current show runs down the entire content of that disc), it has all finally fallen into place.

Misty Morning and No Time, dedicated to the Scottish poet Norman McCaig, has fourteen themes oscillating between tricksy, rhythm-hopping, melodically crowded uptempo pieces and spacious, meditative exercises for Smith's remarkable subtlety of intonation and pitch. The saxophonist has augmented his regular ensemble with the young Aberdeen pianist Steve Hamilton (a sensitive devotee of Chick Corea), the whimsically eloquent ex-Loose Tubes saxophonist Julian Arguelles and the sophisticated and technically flawless trumpeter Guy Barker.

The fast pieces, which echo the sassy American postbop of the late Art Blakey and the insatiable, tumbling soliloquies of John Coltrane, are packed with stuttery, machine-gun melody lines, sudden crash-stops, multi-theme switchovers and elisions from one time signature into another. But they have a tautness and focused momentum that testifies to the leader's growing compositional subtlety, and they're balanced by delicate, lament-like slow episodes. After a late start a mixture of spacious, meditative sustained sounds that enabled Smith to unwrap his Jan Garbarek-like tearful warble, and a bossy, percussive funky counter-theme bristling with sharp, exclamatory chords, began to suggest that the show would be as out of the ordinary as the new album is.

Guy Barker, recently a pioneering British signing to the legendary American Verve jazz label, was maybe influenced by this pole-vault in his career to play just about everything he knows on trumpet, which is a lot. But Smith's compositions represent a sufficiently pragmatic balance of sportive, sharp-shooting jazz virtuosity and evocative subjugation of jazz reflexes to overall design to contain the highly varied persuasions and enthusiasms of his band. Julian Arguelles, as he often does, delivered some of the most memorable improvising of the night – playing alto saxophone throughout, and resembling a more skittish Ornette Coleman on it in his blend of slurred sounds, plaintive cries and jolting downward runs like somebody descending a staircase on a tray.

Smith was at his best on the slowest and most open pieces, his breathy sound, exquisite pitching and gliding ascents into a chorister's upper register on the tenor sax sometimes seeming to suspend the temporal altogether. There are a few compositional misjudgements – one Scottish horn lament turns into swing when it might have been best left where it was – but generally this is Tommy Smith's long-delayed triumph. He must find it a consolation that despite an already long career, his twenty-ninth birthday is still nearly a year away.

WHERE WE GOING?

The Guardian, June 1995

Jazz was invented around the beginning of this century, ignored, misunderstood or patronised by the dinner-jacket arts establishment for most of it, and approaches the millennium with a better than even chance of being perceived as building a gigantic buttress of the classical music of the twenty-first. Whether this will be a good thing for music or human sensibilities is a matter for suspicious speculation only, but at the Barbican on Saturday, concluding their highly successful tour, three skilful, imaginative and open-minded performers – classical saxophonist John Harle, jazz saxophonist Andy Sheppard, and jazz/classical pianist Steve Lodder – explored some of the boldest and most invigorating possibilities of a widening global musical consensus.

Working independently in the first half, the two saxophonists present their more orthodox selves – Harle on a repertoire of Debussy, Dowland, Michael Nyman and others, Sheppard with Carla Bley material and his own increasingly identifiable stamp on quirky postbop originals and sly funk. Harle's tone control, which sounds like a chorister in a cathedral in the top register of the legendarily temperamental soprano saxophone, is one of the most remarkable phenomena on the contemporary music scene – he applied it exquisitely to Debussy's delicate 'Syrinx', Ravel's Spanish-flavoured 'Habanera' (full of glowing trills and seamless slides across the extremes of the register), and then to Russian composer Edison Denisov's fierce, squally 'Sonata'. The piece suggests both free jazz and the blurted, episodic rhythms of contemporary notated music, and it demonstrated Harle's grip of the technical demands of both.

Sheppard opened his account with about as drastic an affirmation of African-American rootsiness as he could – a raucous piece of gospel shouting on tenor sax, Carla Bley's 'The Lord is Listenin' to Ya, Hallelujah'. Most of it was in scalding double-time runs capped with helicopter-rotor vibrato – but, as if giving a nod to Harle's delicacy at low volumes (which often makes the sound of the flapping pads a mellow textural addition to the notes), he resolved part of it with a foxy run of pad-sounds alone.

The second half opened with one of Sheppard's best compositions, the sunny, Caribbean-sounding 'Where We Going?', from the upcoming *Inclassificable* disc, and music from his score for the recent Peter Sellers TV documentaries. But the highest-profile episodes of their collaboration were two pieces that each saxophonist had written for the trio to play together. Sheppard's 'Trapeze' was a technical cliffhanger of fast, downward-spinning scales for the two sopranos, followed by solos (Sheppard cooler and jazzier, Harle straying powerfully into soprano territory also mapped out by Evan Parker), shifting into a soft, padding jazz groove and then the chordal helter-skelter of Coltrane's 'Giant Steps'. Harle's 'Terror and Magnificence', based on a fourteenth-century poem by the writer, composer and cleric Guillaume de Machaut, mixed frail soprano mantras with baleful taped recitation in French, bursts of open, swirling lyricism like a Nyman piece, then explosive passages of pre-recorded percussion leading into funk. Some of the tonal contrasts – Harle blowing piercing, violin-like alto against Sheppard's hot and soulful tenor sound – were dazzling, though the idiomatic jumps should perhaps have stopped short of splicing disco pulses with medieval French poetry. But the piece was born out of a genuine, even-handed collaboration. There haven't been many successful blends of the rhythmic and intonational differences between European art music and the powerful legacy of African-American music this century, but on this evidence the odds are improving.

MELTDOWN

The Guardian, June 1995

When Debbie Harry glided on stage on Friday night to the kind of reception only those who have touched plenty of hearts and minds ever receive, in an ensemble that made her startlingly resemble an affluent blue mermaid, and with an ensemble that batted back the lyrics of her torchy opener with free-jazz blurts and squalls, the sentiments that Elvis Costello had in mind in programming this year's Meltdown Festival were confirmed pretty fast.

It wasn't that Debbie Harry, one of the most intelligent and enduring pop icons of the Seventies and Eighties, surpassed the performances that had made her famous. It wasn't that the Jazz Passengers, the witty and resourceful New York freebop band (whose co-leaders, saxophonist Roy Nathanson and trombonist Curtis Fowlkes bear the kind of engaging resemblance to Groucho Marx and Bill Cosby that suitably reinforces their devotion to a mixture of sardonic vaudeville, anarchic improvisation, affection for human foibles and eclectic expertise) never made music so audacious or surprising before. It wasn't that Elvis Costello, who made a guest appearance too, sounded either in his element or particularly compatible with the spiky improvisational unpredictability and one-touch rhythmic alertness of a band like this. But put them all together, and a show that inspiringly suggests a musical future in which the quick reactions and encyclopaedic references of contemporary improvisers plays a major part, comes right out of the hat.

Friday's Meltdown show at the Festival Hall was kicked off by the New Orleans Rebirth Brass Band and the London percussion ensemble Afro Blok. But if the Rebirth Brass Band shifts idioms briskly, the Jazz Passengers make the art into a flicker-book. They splice brash Thirties swing, squawky Sixties free jazz, elegant cool-school softness like the Modern Jazz Quartet (the addition of vibes and violin to a sax ensemble gives them immense textural range for a quintet, which sharp techniques exploit to the maximum), atmospheric ensemble textures as quirkily evocative as Carla Bley's.

It took Debbie Harry, who weaved and gesticulated like someone trying to coax a cobra out of a basket, and who sounded a little coarse at first, until her second appearance to settle down, but when she did the show began to unfurl some of the evocative possibilities of bravura and eccentricity the billing implied. Ms Harry doesn't borrow from the jazz vocals tradition but from an ironic version of the confessional Broadway manner, coupled with a jagged, percussive phrasing suggestive of avant-garde straight music. With growing relaxation her timing showed an empathy with the rhythmic unpredictability of the Passengers' music that was genuinely sympathetic and expressive. Elvis Costello also tellingly delivered

'A Man Out of Time' against a blend of soft swing and wriggling free jazz. It was a new one on his fans, but the development has time on its side.

SUBTERFUGE
The Guardian, July 1995

Despite Grammy awards, Presidential inauguration saxophone sessions, elder statesman status and all the incidentals of recent years, Joe Henderson still inhabits a concert stage as if he had no business to be there, and occupies his time when his partners are playing like a preoccupied man at a bus stop.

Hitherto this diffidence only ended when he blew through the tenor saxophone, but on Thursday stardom finally went to Henderson's head, and he arrived on stage at the Queen Elizabeth Hall in a suit that made him startlingly resemble an orange lollipop. Everything else, though, exhibited his now celebrated devious reserve. Henderson is one of the greatest saxophone improvisers alive, and the fact that he hardly ever resorts to a grandstand effect, a hot lick, or even much dynamic deviation from a steady, methodical mid-range volume only goes to make his remarkable harmonic and melodic imagination all the more audible.

Henderson was performing with the basis of the Brazilian band that worked on his recent Jobim-dedicated *Double Rainbow* disc – including the elegantly propulsive Oscar Castro Neves, one of the most creative guitarists ever to avoid soloing. But where the samba music was taken care of by the Brazilians on that record, and the bebop by a group that featured Herbie Hancock and Jack DeJohnette, on the concert all of Henderson's broad musical interests were supported by the same players, and they were a revelation that the album hardly hints at.

The players respectfully shadowed Henderson at first, and the gig initially threatened the rather metronomic quality the first half of the *Double Rainbow* disc exhibits. But when the engagingly named Hello Alves began a piano solo with the silvery fluency of Michel Petrucianni, drummer Paulo Braga set to elbowing and nudging him with an eager buoyancy that transformed the band, and as the show developed they set about applying this pressure to the leader as well. Henderson immediately responded to the raised stakes, and his playing shifted from its early manipulations of tonal contrasts and phrase-density to subtler and faster juggling with fragmentary phrases and motifs. 'Lush Life' and 'Take the A Train' were both approached with typical Henderson subterfuge, the first unaccompanied and via abstract phrases spinning into the deep space beyond the chords, the second prefigured by unrecognisably disjointed figures in a raucous overture that eventually kicked into a driving straight-ahead pulse.

CHAMELEON

The Guardian, July 1995

Since the 1960s, there must have been a lot of would-be guitarists weaving around their bedrooms with tennis rackets who fancied being Kenny Burrell alongside Jimmy Smith in a Hammond organ hot-bop trio. Charlie Hunter, the young San Francisco guitarist, has found the perfect solution. He has decided to be both Kenny Burrell and Jimmy Smith at the same time, and throw some exclamatory Nineties funk into the deal for good measure.

Hunter is a bass guitarist and regular guitarist at once – he plays finger-style on an eight-string guitar with slanted frets and two sets of pickups, which gives him a softly thumping bass line with his thumb and a slashing, treble-packed chordal attack with his fingers. The sound of a Hammond organ, in other words. But this is no sterile display of a single bright idea. He is also a fertile and imaginative improviser with a singing, eager sound, and his partners Dace Ellis (tenor) and Mike Clark (drums) are easily his equals. The repertoire covered stuttery street-beat sounds, postbop (over baleful, ticking jazz time), straight-ahead blues and a first-half finale of raucous funk that bizarrely dipped in and out of Brubeck's 'Unsquare Dance'. It doesn't exactly reinvent Nineties music, but it sure as hell reinvents electric guitar playing, and it raised a lot of smiles at the Jazz Café on Tuesday.

HOW COULD YOU DO THAT?

The Guardian, July 1995

Carmen Lundy has had a cult following in London since the days in the Eighties when the 'British jazz revival' could be discussed without a raised eyebrow. Like Dee Dee Bridgewater, Ms Lundy has put nature and self-nurture to the service of carrying the torch for the great American female vocalists like Ella Fitzgerald and Sarah Vaughan – but unlike Bridgewater, whose angle is gospel, blues and classic jazz, Ms Lundy is a contemporary singer remoulding history, and a less flouncy and more charismatic artist in general. If she is anybody's natural heir, she's Betty Carter's.

At the Jazz Café on Saturday, Lundy's popularity with a new cognoscenti was supported by the fact that you couldn't reach for a pen without examining one neighbour's credit cards and forearm-smashing the other, and the singer acknowledged her fans here by descending the stairs with an almost Shirley Bassey-like magnanimous regality. These were, however, the only elements in Carmen Lundy's performance that hit

a hollow note. She paces her repertoire with subtle intelligence, her originals are very striking and her approach to standards almost recklessly
bold, and her telling use of lyrics for their sound as well as their meaning
intensifies all her work.

Ms Lundy was dynamically accompanied by her pianist Billy Childs (a
consummate musician with his own astute take on Herbie Hancock's
chiming funkiness) and powerful locals Wayne Batchelor (bass) and
Winston Clifford (drums). The singer often stays in the middle and lower
registers (she sometimes resembles Cassandra Wilson in her reverberating
deeper tones, and the broad, plush tenor tones of Nat King Cole as well)
and though this unusual tonality sounded uneven and wobbly on her
opening song, a ballad soon settled it. Lundy's sense of contrast in texture
was thumped home in the exquisite rejection song 'Firefly', which began
with majestic deep sounds and suddenly took off into a demanding, im-
patient mid-range cry.

Carmen Lundy baits a group into vigorous life the way Betty Carter
does, and they all locked on to her vibrant wavelength on a percussive,
hustling 'My Favourite Things' over a crisp funk pulse. She has a new disc
out (*Self Portrait*), from which much of Friday and Saturday's material was
drawn, and the most heartening aspect of her work is that there's probably
a lot more of it still to come before you start hearing the same things again.

RECLAMATION

The Guardian (with Ronald Atkins, unpublished), October 1995

A decade or so ago, it used to be a frustrating business representing jazz
interests on the Arts Council's Music Panel. The opportunity to raise a
squeak about the subject came so rarely in a long meeting mostly devoted
to classical music that you could miss it if you cleared your throat. When
the chance did come, the jazz representative could be forgiven for feeling
like somebody trying to flog booze to a temperance meeting. Last Monday
morning [October 2, 1995], however, the first ripples of a sea-change may
have occurred, with the publication of the Arts Council's long-awaited
Green Paper on the state of jazz in England.

It's taken an eleven-member investigative body of musicians, promoters, and arts administrators nearly two years to figure it out. . . But. . .
the report starts by unequivocally acknowledging the music's high status
and influence with the words: 'jazz . . . has completed the journey from
rough-hewn folk art to a sophisticated creative vehicle in barely ninety
years, paralleling the progression of European classical music across five
centuries . . . in many ways, it can claim the title of "the art music of the
twentieth century".'

INDEX